Me and Ted
Against the World

Me and Ted

Against the World

Reese Schonfeld

The Unauthorized Story of the Founding of CNN

Cliff Street

An Imprint of HarperCollins*Publishers*

HarperCollins books may be purchased for educational, business, or sales promotional use. For information please write: Special Markets Department, HarperCollins Publishers, Inc., 10 East 53rd Street, New York, NY 10022.

FIRST EDITION

Designed by Fritz Metsch

Library of Congress Cataloging-in-Publication Data available.

ISBN 0060197463

01 02 03 04 05 RRD 10 9 8 7 6 5 4 3 2 1

On the night of June 10, 1958, I sat at the editor's desk in the United Press Movietone office on New York's West Side. Algerian-French paratroopers were about to descend on Paris to overthrow the Fourth Republic. I was alone except for the wire puncher. We were waiting for a revolution.

Bells were ringing on the UPI wire as bulletin after bulletin advanced the story. Between 9 p.m. and midnight, I wrote and rewrote a half dozen leads. Would there be a revolution, would Charles de Gaulle return to power, were mobs taking to the streets? Whatever UPI Paris bulletined, I rewrote for television. The wire puncher sent it out on the wire, but it was only words; we could not send video.

Television anchormen in every time zone read the leads as they went on the air, but they did not have the pictures to go with them. At that moment I realized that television needed a twenty-four-hour news service that flowed with the news, just like UPI. In my head I'd created the first fluid medium, only UPI had been doing it for half a century.

Author's Note

There are two kinds of media: fluid and static. United Press was fluid, and so was CNN, at least when it started. The Internet is the most fluid of all.

Books are the most static of all. That's the trouble with writing a book. As I was writing this one, I discovered that Ted was talking about buying NBC. The story got in the papers and on television. I went on Neil Cavuto's show on Fox News in May. Neil called the idea wacko. In August, I go back on Cavuto's show, and now he thinks maybe Ted can do it, everything's changed. I'm finishing *Me and Ted Against the World* three months before it gets into the bookstores. A lot of things are going to happen between now and then, and that's why I'm starting MeandTed.com. It's the only way I know to answer a lot of questions that are still hanging.

- Will the AOL/Time Warner merger go through?
- Will Ted buy NBC?
- Will AOL's vice chairman, Bot Pittman, run TBS?
- Will Terry McGuirk keep his job?
- Will Steve Heyer get Steve Case's job?
- Will Tom Johnson keep his job?
- Will Burt Reinhardt ever retire from CNN?
- Will CNN's ratings go up?
- Will Reese Schonfeld ever get back in the news business?

MeandTed.com will answer the above questions and report on other CNN happenings as they occur. In the spirit of UPI, we'll keep you up on all the breaking news. Stay in touch. *It won't cost you anything.*

Thanks

Patricia O'Gorman, the mother of CNN and the godmother of *Me and Ted.*

My children, Alex, Ellen, Orrin, William, Ida, and Juliette, for accepting ten months of broken dates and "regret my presence precluded" with understanding and good humor.

Karim Kamal for helping with this and running everything else as I wrote.

Jake Larkin for researching the hard way, in libraries, not just on the Internet.

Maggie Ruggerio, muse-in-chief; Jennilie Brewster, Melanie Greenberg, and Randi Rosenblum, for musing along with her.

Chris Chase for grabbing the title out of thin air. She suggested *Ted and Me;* I insisted on *Me and Ted.* It's my only chance to get first billing.

Carolyn Fireside, the finest editor a writer could find—she adds no words, but takes away plenty.

Members of the class of 1980 who recalled the events that make this book live: Roz Abrams, George Babick, Cissy Baker, Frank Beatty, Paul Beckham, Mike Boettcher, Dan Brewster, Rick Brown, Jay Bushinsky, Jane Caper, Jean Carper, Chris Chase, Tench Coxe, Ron Dean, Lou

Dobbs, Phil Griffin, Lois Hart, Doug Herzog, John Hillis, Gerry Hogan, Françoise Husson, Derwin Johnson, John Kalish, Mike Kandel, Sandy Kenyon, David Koff, Don Lachowsky, Nory LeBrun, Denise LeClair, Jeff Levine, Bob Lilly, Stuart Loory, Eddie Madison, Jane Maxwell, Jim Miklaszewski, Tom Mintier, Reynelda Muse, Janet Northrup, Bill Papa, Guy Pepper, Burt Reinhardt, Richard Roth, Jim Rutledge, Will Sanders, Bernie Shaw, Dan Schorr, Kandy Stroud, John Towriss, Dave Walker, Wendy Walker, George Watson, Tami Weine, Liz Wickersham, Mary Alice Williams, Sam Zelman, and Bill Zimmerman.

Contents

Prologue: **Panicsville**

June 1, 2000, and it's Panicsville in Turnertown. Seems the public is losing its taste for the CNN product, and the media are exposing weak ratings as never before. They may not have discovered that the emperor has no clothes, but they clearly see that he's down to his jockstrap. On the twentieth anniversary of "Ted Turner's invention," nobody's watching it.

Nevertheless, the world is coming to Atlanta, thousands strong, to celebrate. Most of the folks who worked for the network twenty years ago have been invited, along with the current advertisers, and the pioneer advertisers, and all the affiliated TV stations in the United States, and all the affiliated TV networks around the globe, and kings and queens, and presidents, and ex-presidents, and wannabe presidents.

CNN doesn't even have to foot the bill for the party. Technology companies and major advertisers and anyone else who will pay are getting sponsor recognition for what is supposed to turn into a great television spectacular.

But the glory is cloaked in gloom, Ted's gloom. He has just realized that he has been outfoxed in the AOL/Time Warner merger. He has not assured himself of a role in the company he created. He's been raising hell, complaining about "marginalization," and threatening to upset the merger or to abandon CNN entirely and buy a network of his own, maybe NBC.

There is reason for panic in Atlanta on June 1. Business is down, the chairman is off his leash, the press is getting hostile, and a new owner is on the horizon. People are afraid for their jobs; anxiety is everywhere. It's a great time to be writing a book about CNN.

I have been invited to the gala. I *am* writing a book about CNN. The celebrations will be my last chapter. I plan to play the "bastard at the wedding." I will be a reporter for my own venture, I will be cynical, I will be tough. For the moment at least, I have the last word.

I have come fully armed to Atlanta. I have done my interviews, I know numbers, and I know the facts. Up front, CNN is my invention. I did not invent twenty-four-hour news; a dozen guys thought of that, but I did create "fluid news," the style that differentiated CNN. I have followed CNN for eighteen years and watched it grow sluggish and constipated. It was better in 1982 than it is now. It had promise then that has never been fulfilled. On June 1, when others come to applaud its triumphs, I come to mourn its shortcomings.

Forty years ago, Ted Fetter, a vice president at ABC, taught me the most important lesson I ever learned about broadcasting. Ted was not a creature of television; he'd acted on Broadway, and written lyrics for hit songs, including "Takin' a Chance on Love." In the forties, he took a wrong turn and wound up in TV. Ted was so naïve about the medium, he thought it might be an instrument of cultural improvement. Worthington Minor, the producer of many of the best dramas in the Golden Age of television, wised him up. "Teddy," said Minor, "television people are not like us. We sell tickets, they sell their audience. The advertisers buy it and that's how they make their money."

Television is the great democracy where people vote with their eyes. When they don't watch a program, advertisers don't buy the program, and the program is dead. The size of the audience is measured in ratings. No ratings, no program. It's the way television keeps score.

In the first quarter of 2000, CNN's New York City audience shriveled. The city has 1.6 million cable homes. Of them, only five thousand are watching CNN. Fox and MSNBC get fifteen hundred each, and Headline News has no discernible audience. These are the four national and international news channels. Between them in a typical quarter hour, in all of New York City, according to Time Warner's New York 1, they have only eight thousand viewers.

Where are the other New York news viewers? Twenty-two thousand are watching NY1, the local all-news channel. Ten thousand are watching CNBC, the all-financial news channel. New Yorkers are expressing their interests. They're interested in their neighborhoods and their wallets. Twenty years ago when Ted and I started CNN, CNN's ratings were three times as high as they are now. In 1980 CNN found an audience eager to follow world news. CNN can't find that audience anymore.

In 1980 Ronald Reagan was elected president, and he changed the rules. He announced to the world that he was going to downsize Washington. He was going to deregulate everything, and he was going to return power and money to city and state governments. Economic power was going to Wall Street. Capitalism would reign unfettered.

Journalism didn't pay much attention. The big media companies grew their Washington bureaus bigger and bigger. Small companies that didn't have bureaus opened them.

Regardless, Ronald Reagan made good on his word. Power was shifted to local governments. Wall Street was given control of the national economy, excepting only Alan Greenspan on interest rates. Despite the power shift, the media stayed in Washington.

People watch news that has relevance to their lives. The audience wants to know what's happening in hometowns and state capitals. More than half the audience now owns equities in New York City. Almost four times as many viewers care about Main Street and Wall Street as care about Pennsylvania Avenue and the whole rest of the goddamn world.

Moreover, CNN has become worldwide and skin-deep. It spends more time in Fiji and Sierra Leone than it does in Omaha, Nebraska, or Salem, Oregon. Its coverage splashes over everything and saturates nothing.

CNN rarely originates news. Twice, when it tried, it disgraced itself and all of journalism. In *The Noriega Case,* CNN violated a court order, ran confidential jailhouse tapes, was found in contempt, went all the way to the Supreme Court, and wound up apologizing on the air for twenty hours. Along the way, it wounded two constitutional rights. In the Operation Tailwind documentary, *Valley of Death,* CNN promoted and ran a story about U.S. use of poison gas in Vietnam. When challenged by the Pentagon, it retracted, fired the people who produced it, and paid off almost everyone involved in the segment, including both the people who said it wasn't true and those who said it was true.

Ignoring its failings, CNN has created its own mythology. At the anniversary bash, I hear time and time again how much CNN has grown, how much it has improved. This is a dangerous myth because it reverses the truth. CNN's ratings have declined by 70 percent from May 1982 to May 2000. In the great democracy of the eyeballs, it is worse now than it was then. This correction is meaningful to my ego, but more importantly, it gives whoever tries to build another twenty-four-hour news network a valid idea of what works and what doesn't.

The *New York Times* went down to the twentieth anniversary gala and came away with the impression that, in its earliest days, CNN had "absolutely negligible ratings." Not so. From January to June 1982, the last five months that I ran it, CNN averaged one full rating point. After I left, over the next seven months, it suffered a 20 percent decline, but still wound up at the end of the year with a .91. These ratings were surpassed only in 1991, the year of the Gulf War with its great Baghdad coverage; 1982 was the second best year that CNN ever had. There is a reason for all this early success, and that's part of what this book's about.

When CNN started, the idea was that we'd show viewers a skeleton, the framework on which everything would hang, and they could watch us do the hanging. We wanted to expose the entire news making process. Everything was open, we had one enormous room in the basement of an old country club, and the studio was in the middle of the floor, the anchor desk was on the floor, the control room was on the floor, the editing rooms were along one side, everything out in one unenclosed area, everybody yelling back and forth. You could see it all and hear it all. It was like the newsroom of a newspaper but with lights and cameras. I wanted it that way. The audience was meant to see what we were doing and how we were doing it.

The three networks ran a closed shop. They made their news seem like magic; nobody could see the tricks of the trade. Correspondents reported from front lines all over the world. Somehow, by some secret process, their words and pictures arrived in your home. Television news was romantic and mystical. CNN was going to show the nuts and bolts.

RATING POINTS

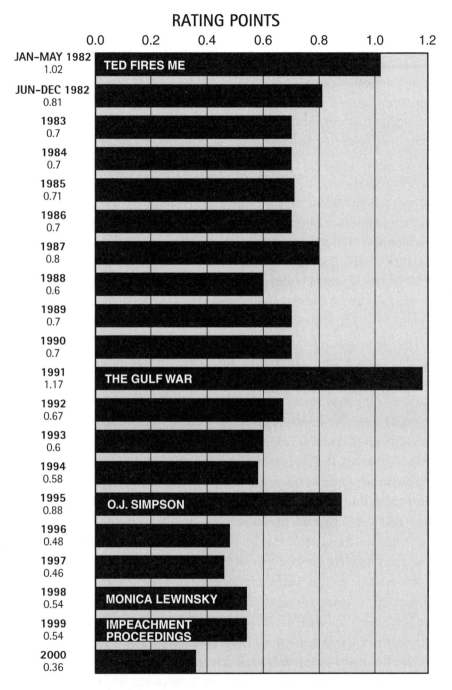

CNN ratings history: 1982 through September 2000.

I was a deconstructionist before "deconstructionism" was part of the vernacular.

My first year at CNN was spent building a structure that would support a bottom-up news philosophy. We had twenty-four hours to fill. We wanted people in all our bureaus to send us stories, preferably original stories that our producers would fit into their programs. Sure there were the big stories, the automatic stories that everyone had to cover, but we trusted our bureau chiefs to know about them. We wanted some added attractions, and they gave them to us. CNN had some of the most outrageous news stories ever on air in its first two years. That's what made it "randomonium," which is what Frank Zappa called it when he fell in love with CNN in 1980. Randomonium is what I wanted CNN to be, only I didn't know a name for it.

What I did know is I wanted it to be fluid, to be spontaneous, to reach Frank Zappa and the other dopesters, even while it appealed to their seventy-five-year-old grandparents retired and living in Miami Beach.

The big problem was that most of the people who came to work for me didn't know from randomonium. They still wanted to turn out perfect little half-hour gems. Over the course of the next two years some of them learned and some of them didn't. Some of them adjusted, and some of them never would. Before I could fire the guys who never would adjust—Ted fired me.

I want *Me And Ted Against the World* to be open. I want to tell you who I am and why I'm writing this book. First, this is being published by HarperCollins, which is owned by Rupert Murdoch. Both Rupert Murdoch and Ted Turner are media barons. There is a certain baronial courtesy, and the contract of this book was not signed until the publisher made sure that News Corp. executives felt comfortable with the project.

Rupert Murdoch is not perceived as a friend of Ted Turner. They see each other as rivals. Murdoch is lord of newspapers and satellites and the Fox television network and a book publishing company that would be major for anyone else but is only two blips on his radar screen. Ted was, as I started writing this book, the god of CNN and chief of the rest of the Time Warner Cable programming empire. He is no longer, and that's part of this book too.

Murdoch and Turner are the largest individual shareholders in two of the top three media companies in the United States. Despite their rivalry,

I intend to be evenhanded. To prove that, I'll give you my honest opinion of Fox News. Two years ago, on Jim Lehrer's PBS show, I said that CNN gets the CEO audience, CNBC gets the CFO audience, and Fox gets the UFO audience. Fox is gaining on CNN, its ratings are going up, but that's because there are more UFO watchers than there are CEOs.

Ten months ago, Peter Arnett, an excellent war correspondent whom I'd hired for CNN, said to me, "Reese, Ed Turner and I are going to do a book about the beginnings of CNN." (Ed Turner—no relation to Ted, as everybody who writes about him points out—was hired to run the CNN domestic bureaus a few months before we launched.) Both Peter and Ed had left CNN under difficult circumstances during the last few years. Originally their book was to have been about media in general, but when they shopped that idea around, the response was discouraging. "We're up to here with media books," one agent told them. "What about a book on CNN?"

So they decided to switch their focus. Good time to sell a CNN book, twentieth anniversary excitement, whole lot of noise. Now Peter's on the phone saying he'd like to talk to me because I was CNN's first CEO.

I ask him if it's going to be an authorized book. He says Ted Turner has agreed to be interviewed and so has Tom Johnson, now chairman of CNN. I say I haven't come off well previously in authorized books. Peter brushes aside my protests. "You're very important to the start of CNN, and we're going to write about you whether you talk to us or whether you don't talk to us."

I tell him to call back when he has a publisher, and after he hangs up, I think about it. I realize what he is saying is, "Look, if you talk to us, we're going to screw you, and if you don't talk to us, we're going to screw you," and I figure now is the time to write my own version of the CNN story.

I didn't really have time to write a book now. I'm embarked on the biggest news project that I've tried since CNN. I'm inventing the CNN of the twenty-first century. It's my project, I'm paying for it, and if it works, I'm going to be the owner/operator. And if it works, I'm going to want Peter Arnett to work with me, because he's the kind of journalist that my new journalism requires.

Another reason that I don't want to write the book is I believe that he who can does, and he who can't writes about it. I've labored in the news business for more than forty years, and I'm not going to give it up, so this isn't a good time for me to write a book. But there never will be a "good time."

The last time I thought about doing a book, the *Providence Journal* came to visit me, and I spent the next four years turning the Food Network from an idea into a network that now gets better ratings than CNN does, at least with people under fifty-five. I never know what's coming next, what the next opportunity will be, and as some people say, "I've never met an idea I didn't like."

Therefore, for me, this book is an interruption, a detour, but my ego demands an act of antirevisionism, and I want to tell my story of CNN. I'm also writing it because I remember my plans for CNN and I would like to put on the record the difference between what CNN is now and what I dreamed it was going to be.

At this point I'm thanking Peter Arnett. Let him do his book, and I'll do mine. I know one thing, twenty years is a good time to look back and see what I did.

Round 1: **Bear Witness**

In this world things happen that most of us would rather not see. In seeking bliss, many embrace ignorance. It's a damn fool thing to do.

During 1997, I spent a month in Beirut and a month in Sarajevo. Both cities were devastated. God-fearing peasants from the hills had dumped thousands of shells on secular cosmopolites living in the central city. In Beirut, it was Muslims shelling Christians. In Sarajevo, it was Christians shelling Muslims. The press saw these events as isolated incidents, not a trend, presenting a "look at what these damn fools are doing to each other, but it can't happen here" approach that made the conflicts seem irrelevant to most people living in the Western world, which meant, in turn, there was nobody concerned enough to bear witness.

The Cable News Network, which I cofounded with Ted Turner in 1979, was created to bear witness, to ensure that no sorrow go unmourned, no joy uncelebrated. Of course CNN was also created to make money. It was created to offer information and understanding of current events, to place them in historical context, and to illustrate them with arresting images. It was created to permit its viewers to talk back to CNN. It was created to provide, for the first time, timely financial news, sports news, entertainment news. It was created to offer news from 6 a.m. to 6 p.m. to 6 a.m. again. It was created to build the largest audience possible so that it could sell commercial time and make money. I believed then, and still believe, that the best way to build an audience and sell commercials and make money is to do the best news in the world. To do that news live as often as possible. To seek out stories of which others knew nothing. To demonstrate the significance of stories that others dismissed. In short, to be original from 6 a.m. to 6 p.m. to 6 a.m. again. In originality would lie our strength.

Let me say at the outset that there is plenty of news to fill a twenty-four-hour news channel. It matters not what apologists say about CNN's low ratings, or MSNBC's lagging performance. There's plenty of news to go around, they just don't know where to look for it. I admit it's harder now than it used to be. We had the Cold War, we had race, easy subjects, good guys/bad guys, plenty of developments, long-running stories. Those were the themes on which we riffed throughout the fifties, sixties, seventies, and part of the eighties.

William Randolph Hearst used to say, "There are no bad news stories, only bad reporters." I say, "There are no slow news periods, only slow editors, slow producers."

For twenty-three years, from 1956 to 1979, when I worked in the news business, there were always more stories than I had the money to cover. I dreamed of having enough money, enough airtime, access to enough homes, so that stories that should be told would be told, would be seen by a worldwide audience. It was a case of "the truth shall set you free." I thought the task was simple: If we delivered the facts about everything we saw as important in the world, people would act righteously, and the world would be a better place. What newsman could have a better dream than that?

It took twenty-three years for technology, mostly satellite and cable, to catch up with my dream. During those years, I grew smarter. I learned that governments were not necessarily to be trusted, that corporations and labor leaders practiced deception to further their causes. I came to believe that everybody had an angle, and before you could understand their story, you had to understand their angle. I grew angry at the three networks whose promise to bear the torch of truth masked a sound commercial motive—they used news as an alibi for the mindlessness of the rest of their schedules. I was gambling that I could make it better.

To backtrack a little, I went to work for United Press Movietone News in 1956. We had two products, a newsreel that was distributed to theaters and news film that was distributed to television stations. One of the big stories was school integration in the South. We covered it, cut it, wrote it, and our television stations used it, but that story never appeared in the newsreel. One day I asked why. Ben Lowree, the newsreel boss, looked at me as if I were the dumbest man on Earth. "You think this'll play in Mississippi?" Lowree said. "They'll slash their seats, they'll throw stink bombs in the bathrooms, they'll blow up the whole theater." I was the dumbest man on Earth. It had never occurred to me. Movietone made only one newsreel for the whole country. If southerners wouldn't permit pictures of racial violence in their theaters, no one else would see it, either.

Television was different. Network pictures beamed nationwide. Local television stations carried the pictures right into the living room. Nobody, no man, no group of men, no community, could keep reality from getting through. Nobody, no man, no group of men, no community, could say, "I didn't know." Television compelled Americans to bear witness to the significant events of the day, no matter how painful they were. "Significance" was determined by the networks, a task that combined enormous power and enormous responsibility.

The networks had other responsibilities. They had to make money, and they could make more money entertaining than bearing witness. For the next twenty-five years, the networks restricted news to thirty minutes a night. "You will watch the news when we tell you to watch the news, or you will not watch news at all," they told the audience. I knew that news happens "round the clock," "deadlines every minute." Wire services fed updated news twenty-four hours a day, seven days a week, over several wires. Even newspapers, stuck with the technology of printing presses and delivery trucks, published four or five editions a day.

None of this mattered to television networks. They made more money with their entertainment programs. As for news, it was a loss leader, an obligation; cover it, put it on the air, bite the bullet, and get it over with. They weren't in the news business, they were in the entertainment business.

In 1980, all three networks did news pretty much the same way. They'd have a morning meeting for executives, producers, and anchors. They'd sit around and discuss the AP daybook and the front pages of the *New York Times* and the *Washington Post*. Since they had way too many stories to fit into the thirty minutes, every correspondent, every producer was fighting for air. Everybody said his story had to be on the air that night.

Most of the stories came off the Associated Press wires or the morning's *New York Times*. The executive producer and the Washington bureau chief would fight for control of the half hour. Even then, Washington thought it was the center of the universe and nothing important happened west of the Potomac, unless of course the president was traveling. New York, on the other hand, paid attention to other worldwide capitals and would occasionally tolerate stories from the provinces. The executive producer would then tell the bureaus what stories he wanted for "his show." The anchor would nod his approval, but if he said no, the story died.

The battles between Walter Cronkite and Bill Small, CBS Washington bureau chief, were legendary. Both were great newsmen with their hearts in the right place. Bill's heart came from Chicago, and Walter's from Kansas City. Bill spoke for the Eastern news establishment, and Walter spoke for the hinterland. Between the two of them, they licked the platter clean, which was one of the reasons CBS was always first in the news ratings.

CBS ran from the top down. Everybody did what he was told, and "the tellers" were the Cronkites, the Smalls, the Ernie Leisers, and the Les Midgleys, the guys who produced the CBS *Evening News.* God help the man who didn't follow their orders.

The Independent Television News Association, aka ITNA, which I helped found in 1975, did news a different way. At ITNA, I assigned stories in Washington. I asked Visnews or WTN in London what they were covering overseas (sometimes I would dare make a suggestion), and then I would call my local stations and ask them what they were covering, and they would offer me better stories than I could find on the AP daybook or the front page of the *Times* or the *Washington Post.* Good newsmen know more about what happens in their hometown than the AP does. Marty Haag, at WFAA, Dallas, was months ahead on Texas death row stories. Ron Golobin, WCVB, Boston, owned the New Bedford poolroom rape story. Both of them sent their stories to ITNA before they sent them to their own network.

I had learned all of this and a lot more in the twenty-three years I'd spent in the news business before Ted Turner called. In 1979, Ted asked me if a twenty-four-hour news service would work and if I would run it. I told him yes. I flew down to Atlanta, he said he had the money to finance the network, and I jumped at the chance to be part of it.

I was the news professional; Ted was the amateur. First, he told me his plan for CNN, which was very different from mine. His plan was static: a two-hour rotating block containing four half-hour segments updated as necessary. The first half hour was to be news, then sports, then finance, then women's features, then back to news. I told him, "That's not for me." I let him know what I wanted to do and what I thought CNN could become. He heard the plan. Nobody ever said Ted was dumb. He bought it, and we were off to the races.

I do not intend to use the V word. I have heard too many amateurs whine, "Oh, that's not my vision," as they flush their projects down the drain. In regards to CNN, I didn't have a vision, I had a plan, a plan designed with a lot of holes in it. Holes through which CNN would grow and shape itself in any way it chose. I believe that institutions, works of art, are in themselves a life form. They will tell the maker in which direction they will grow. If the maker pays attention, if he does not force a pattern on his creation, it may become better than whatever he conceived. CNN would form itself as it found itself.

Live news had never been the raison d'être for a network. Who knew how it would work? "Twenty-four-hour," "live," "call-in," "satellites," "studio," "digital graphics"—all these concepts were developed and then redefined by CNN. Only a maniac would say that he could determine how they would evolve. The creator had to watch and listen as these little revolutions brushed one against another and became a system. What I saw was opportunity, and opportunity coupled with experience leads to success.

That said, I did have specific ideas about what CNN should be. For one thing, television newsmen all over the world, not just in America, knew more about their cities than AP did. They also knew it sooner. If CNN tapped into them, if we took advantage of their knowledge and speed, we could create a world news that differed from the conventional layouts of AP or Reuters or the *New York Times* or the London *Times*.

Live was our métier. If we knew where to put the camera, if we guessed right, then the whole world would watch us. If we guessed right, wire services, newspapers, and television networks would be reporting about what we had shown well after we'd shown it. We would help to set the news agenda for the world.

I expected CNN's bureaus to tell its producers what to carry in their programs and not to have the producers tell them what to cover. I expected stories to bubble up to us. San Francisco knows more about San Francisco than Atlanta does. If the bureau chief can't find better stories than the Atlanta assignment editor, he doesn't belong there. I wanted reporters who would tell a bureau chief stories that the bureau chief did not know. I wanted the Atlanta assignment desk to tell the producers about stories that the producers did not know. Then, I wanted the producers to run the stories that nobody knew about. If the story surprised the executive producer, it would certainly surprise the viewer.

If a tree falls in the forest, and there is no one there to *see* it, did the tree fall? If a child starves, if a missile tips over, if a mob slaughters hundreds, and no one sees it, did it really happen? CNN needs to have a camera there when the tree falls. We see it, we hear it, and we feel its repercussions. If we choose to turn a blind eye, we put ourselves at risk; the tree may fall on us next time. CNN should scream "attention must be paid."

As I've said, I was the news professional and Ted was the amateur, but I was playing with the amateur's money, and ultimately he controlled the game. Between 1979 and 1982, I ran the game with Ted's money, and we flourished to the tune of 15 million viewers and one full rating point. I'd gambled, I'd staked my life, and I'd thought I'd won my bet.

In 1982, Ted wanted to play his own cards and for me, that was that. Our wild ride together had ended. It wasn't quite the end of my world. In 1984 on Long Island, I started News 12, America's first twenty-four-hour local news channel. In 1992, Ted offered me my old job, but by then I was working with the *Providence Journal* to start the Food Network. They were good jobs, and both networks have succeeded, but they were carpentry. At CNN, I was an architect.

Back to CNN. When an amateur gambler plays the game, sooner or later he loses. If CNN bites the dust, Ted Turner's got to take the heat. A lot of people will say, "We told you so. Twenty-four-hour news will never work." I think all it proves is that twenty-four-hour news will never work in the hands of an amateur.

Round 2: **Who Is Ted?**

I met Ted Turner in 1974. He was sitting behind his desk at Channel 17, wearing a filthy white yachting cap. His desk was a mess, and his carpet stained. I'd come down to Atlanta to learn about satellite dishes from a man named Sid Topol, who was chairman of Scientific Atlanta, a company that made satellite dishes. Before Sid took me to his plant, we dropped in on Ted. Ted wanted to find out if satellites could help him and what they would cost. Help him do what, I did not know. But in 1974, I knew as much about satellite applications as anyone, and I knew what Western Union planned to charge for satellite time. I told Ted it would cost him a million dollars a year. He said, "Is that all?" I said, "Yes." He nodded, we left. I do not recall his saying thank you.

Later, I saw him at a convention of the Independent Television Station Owners (INTV). He had just bought the Atlanta Braves and the other independent station owners were in awe. He was on an INTV luncheon panel, and someone in the audience asked him how he felt about his triumph. His then wife, Janie (the former Jane Smith), was sitting next to him. Ted said, "Buying the team was kind of like getting married. Before you do it, you want it more than anything else in the world. Then you wake up in bed the next morning, and you say, what did I do this for." The audience laughed, but no one wanted to look at Janie.

The next time I heard about Ted was 1977, and he was winning the America's Cup. ITNA was covering the event, and there was Ted at the victors' press conference with a bottle of booze in front of him, gloating in his cups. Every once in a while, Sid Pike, Ted's Atlanta station manager, took the bottle of booze and hid it under the table. Every once in a while Ted bobbed down and brought the bottle back up. Winning the Cup made Ted famous in yachting circles. Drinking the cup made him nationally notorious.

He'd won the race on his own terms, he would treat the press on his own terms. Ted's winning boat was named *Courageous.* After the press conference, he would forever be known as "Captain Outrageous."

At the annual INTV conventions, Ted's behavior was treated as a standing, wobbling joke. I had been trying to sell Ted on doing news since 1976. ITNA was a consortium of independent television stations that did news. We thought that it was time for Ted to start a news show in Atlanta. Ted said he never would. He had enough entertainment product to last him forever, and besides that, he didn't watch news, he hated news.

At the conventions, my owners, the ITNA board, would set up a moment where I would pitch Ted the news show idea, and then they'd stand back and watch. Ordinarily, Ted would have a blonde on each arm, a couple of drinks in him, and he would deliver a wonderful rant on why he detested news. His reasons were all over the place: He could make more money with entertainment, nobody watched news, it was all about rapes and murders, and he'd wind up shouting, "I hate news." We'd all laugh, and move on. In those days nobody took Ted seriously.

Though I'd been running into Ted for five years, I didn't know any more about him than I had when I first met him in 1974. It wasn't until August 1979, when I relocated to Atlanta, that Ted's life story was dumped on me. I got a half-dozen versions from a half-dozen different people even before my furniture arrived.

There was the pop psychology version: Ted was a driven man because his father, Ed Turner, had been a driven man. Moreover, his father had driven Ted. Down in Savannah, Ed Turner had built a prosperous billboard business out of nothing but his wife's money and his own skills. He did not believe that Ted could do as well. Ted's life was dedicated to proving his father wrong.

There was the Peck's Bad Boy version: Ted was just that kind of guy. When he was a kid, he'd always been in trouble. As he progressed from childhood to young manhood, he'd gone from naughty to mischievous to just plain bad. He was kicked out of Brown for having a girl in his room. That's bad, but he had become notorious on campus for his open admiration of Adolf Hitler. That's worse. He just had too much damn fun being bad, and he was gonna go on being bad for the rest of his life.

Then there was Ted the competitor: One of Ted's crew on the *Courageous* said that Ted was just an average sailor, but the best racer that yachting had ever seen. He would not be beaten. He was fueled by competition, and bent on spending the rest of his life winning everything he could.

Then there was Ted the businessman: Within a couple of weeks of my arrival, Tench Coxe (Ted's lawyer), Will Sanders (Ted's CFO), and Irwin Mazo (Ted's previous CFO) all told me how Ted had fought to prevent the sale of his father's billboard operation. The senior Turner, apparently in contemplation of death, had contracted to sell the business, which consisted of several different companies, to four old friends, in order to keep it out of Ted's hands. He'd intended to take the money and invest it so that it might support the entire Turner family. Then he shot himself.

Ted's business friends say that Ted bought the billboard business back because he thought it was worth a lot more money than his father had gotten. He regained control by claiming that Ed Turner was of unsound mind when he sold out. Irwin Mazo, who had been Ted's father's financial advisor, told Ted not to fight the deal. He said, "Ted, you ought to go through with the sale. You don't have the experience, and you don't have the confidence of the bankers. Take the five million dollars and go sailing." Ted said, "No way. My father didn't leave me this money to go sailing."

In the end, Ed Turner's cronies didn't want to fight his son at the expense of Ed's reputation. They sold the business to Ted and, what's more, they gave him five years to pay them off. Ted used the billboard business to build his fortune, which now amounts to about $8 billion. (It would be $10 billion, but he's given a lot away.) Ted has always said he didn't really care about the money itself, but in capitalism, money is the way you keep score, and Ted has always wanted to be a winner.

Getting back to the pop psychologists, most Turner biographers write that Ted modeled himself on, even idolized, his father. Conversely, Mazo claims, "I never knew Ted to worship his father. They had a very difficult relationship." Ed Turner was supposedly a cold, difficult, ruthless man. Ted Turner is manic-depressive, although he was not diagnosed until the mid-eighties. Whatever his father was or wasn't would've had little effect on the ailment.

Admittedly, Ted's life was full of tragedy. When he was nineteen, his father divorced his mother. When he was twenty-two, his much-loved younger sister died. When he was twenty-four, his father shot himself. Combine the tragedies with the bipolar disorder, courage, and tenacity, and somehow Ted Turner emerges. Maybe I'm too hard on the pop psychologists, maybe Ed Turner did instill courage and tenacity in his son. But anyone who's ever been around a manic-depressive knows that in his manic phase he has more courage and tenacity than is good for him.

In CNN's most perilous days, when Ted was desperately raising money to keep us on the air, he would routinely pull a gun out of his desk drawer, hold it to his head and say to the potential lender, "I might as well pull this trigger. If you don't give me the money, I'm dead anyway." I left CNN in 1982. In the mid-eighties, Ted's pilot girlfriend, J. J. Ebaugh, convinced him to see a doctor and to take lithium. I don't know if he's held a gun to his head since, but I wish he'd gone on lithium while I was still there.

Ted's personal life has never been as important to him as his businesses. By the late sixties, Ted had turned the billboard operation around, it was making a lot of money, and he chose to bet that money on television. In 1970, he bought Channel 17, then called WTCG, in Atlanta. (He wanted to rename it WTBS, but a small radio station in Boston had those call letters. Ted bought the call letters eight years later.) Irwin Mazo and some of the other stockholders did not approve. "It was within a month of going off the air," says Mazo. "It had lost $900,000 the year before. A lot of Ted's friends—including me—fought tooth and nail to keep him from buying it. That was when I quit. I'd gone through the trauma of helping put the billboard company back on its feet, and I didn't want to have to start all over again. I thought Ted was going bankrupt, and enough was enough. I just didn't want to be around to see it." For a short time Mazo and the other shareholders won their battle. They raised a bare majority and briefly killed the deal, but Ted and Will Sanders, who became the CFO of Turner Broadcasting, managed to convince some of the dissenters to vote their shares for Ted, and Ted got what he wanted.

Another reason Mazo wasn't around was because he was one of the dissenting shareholders who had fought Ted. Ted is not one to forgive those who question his judgment. Ted bought out Mazo and some of the other dissenters, and once again, many of them, including Mazo, were generous enough to give Ted time to pay off the money he owed them. Mazo now admits, "Ted went against every piece of advice I gave him, and he was always right. Everything he touched turned into a success."

In an unbelievable bit of irony, Irwin Mazo came back into Ted's life in 1995 when Time Warner bought TBS. A Savannah doctor who had been one of Ted's father's partners in his billboard business claimed that his shares in the operation had become stock in TBS and were worth tens of millions of dollars. (The doctor was the husband of a woman who was reportedly the last mistress of Ted's father. After Ed Turner's death, she drove her car on the railroad tracks and waited for the train.) Mazo represented the Savannah doctor in his claim against Ted.

Ted's father had had many billboard partnerships; some of them did well, some of them went bankrupt. The question was, which partnerships had the Savannah doctor invested in? The billboard companies had been sold years before, and sixty years of records languished helter-skelter in a vast warehouse. They would be difficult, almost impossible, to find, and who knew what they were going to prove? Many of Ted's advisors urged him to settle with Mazo, pay the doctor a few million dollars, and be done with him. Ted said, "If I owe him the money, I'll pay him all of it; if I don't owe him, I'll pay him nothing." Ted sent lawyers in, and just days before the case was going to court, the lawyers located the right records. All the doctor's billboard companies had gone bust. End of story.

When it came to buying WTCG in 1970, Mazo's advice not to buy was 100 percent right. Ted's purchase defied all logic. The station was in competition with another Atlanta UHF independent station, and the competition was outperforming WTCG. Moreover, Ted's opposition seemed to have better funding; it was part of a five-station independent TV group, Commonwealth Southern. Then came the 1973 downturn, and both Atlanta independent stations were hurting. Commonwealth Southern was losing a lot of money in its other markets. Its owners decided to shut down one station. They chose Atlanta because it was the only city where they faced competition from another independent. Now Ted had a monopoly.

In 1973 or 1974, WTCG acquired TV rights to the Atlanta Braves. Ted outbid WSB, then the NBC affiliate. WTCG was the first UHF station to carry a major league baseball team, and Ted paid a lot of money to get them, but for him they were worth it. He put together a Braves network throughout the Southeast.

The Braves were a lousy ball club, and they lost a lot of money. In 1974, the owners put the team up for sale, asking $11 million. Ted paid it, a million dollars down and a million dollars a year for the next ten years. It was less money than he would have had to pay for the broadcast rights. Thanks to the Braves, Channel 17 became a national network, a Superstation.

Cable systems throughout the country wanted live baseball. Most American cities saw baseball games only once a week on NBC's *Game of the Week.* Ted gave his cable systems 162 Braves games a year. The Braves may have been lousy, but they were the only team in town, so the Braves became "America's Team."

Ted needed new worlds to conquer. In 1978, for better or worse, he found one. News. And that's where I come in.

Round 3: Ted Was Cable Before Cable Was Cool

The idea for the Superstation first came to him from Don Anderson, vice president of the National Cable Television Association. Anderson had been in Wilkes-Barre, Pennsylvania, when the cable system there was failing. The owners decided to bring in the Yankees games by microwave, and the next morning there were lines of people two blocks long waiting to subscribe to cable. Anderson told Turner that the Braves could do the same for cable in the South.

Ted planned on using microwave to send his TV signal to cable systems all over the country. But microwave is expensive. Microwave pictures travel thirty, forty miles a hop, so every thirty miles or so you had to put in another transmitter. With a satellite you got the whole country on one hop.

Ted hired Anderson, and he, Ted, and Terry McGuirk journeyed from town to town, selling cable operators on the Braves games and signing them up for Ted's network. Anderson said it seemed they ate in every greasy spoon in Dixie, learning about cable, telling cable operators about Channel 17, and offering them Braves baseball. It was at these meetings that Ted earned his stripes with the cable industry. He was going to provide fresh programming, different from the three networks, and he was providing it for just pennies a month. Ted agreed to dismantle his Braves broadcast network, and give the Braves games exclusively to cable. He was giving up broadcast revenue to help cable operators. Ted bet on cable when it was not a sure thing. Ted was cable before cable was cool.

Round 4: **Whose Idea Was It?**

When I first met Ted, he was running this dinky little independent television station in Atlanta. The Superstation was just a dream. I thought, who would ever want to put Ted's station on their cable system? I was just like all the other wise guys, but I should've known better. In 1974, only 35 percent of the country was able to watch any independent television station. Sixty-five percent of the country had nothing to watch but the networks. Ted reached out to the 65 percent, middle America, and freed them from network triopoly.

By the time I saw him in 1976 at the INTV convention in Vegas, I'd started ITNA. We were struggling, but we knew we had a winner. Ted was in the same place. My ITNA independent station owners were a pretty colorful bunch. There was a former used car dealer from Sacramento, an ex–fruit and vegetable peddler who had turned his company into the largest independent of them all, and a family whose most important member was a major Las Vegas casino figure. There were also more conventional owners like the Chicago Tribune Company and Cox Enterprises. They were the guys who got their kicks out of Ted's antinews rants. I believed Ted's rants, but I had never taken him seriously about anything else.

Therefore, I was doubly surprised when in September 1978 I got a phone call from Ted Turner. "Reese," he says, "I want to do a twenty-four-hour news network. Can it be done, and will you do it with me?" I say, "Sure." It's what I've been waiting for, for twenty years.

People still ask: "Whose idea was CNN? Yours or Ted's?" So far as I know, it was Gerry Levin's. He conceived of it as an opportunity for HBO, the Time-Life division that he ran. The year was 1977.

In 1975, I had wanted to bring HBO into the ITNA fold. We were just starting ITNA; we had a budget of $1 million a year. I had nine member stations each putting in $100,000. HBO would've been the tenth. We needed their money.

I told Stu Chismar, who worked for Levin, that HBO could join for $100,000. Chismar wanted to know why HBO would want to join ITNA; they didn't do news. I said to him, "Someday you'll want to, and this will get you into the club. It will give you access to news whenever you decide to bring out your news service." But back then, HBO was $20 million in the red, and they bowed out. ITNA's nine members raised their dues to $110,000 a year, and we rolled out.

In 1977, Levin decided the time had come for an HBO twenty-four-hour news network. He approached me at ITNA through Bob Weisberg. Weisberg and I talked seriously for several months and then met with Levin. He gave us the go-ahead and asked me to take it to the ITNA board.

The ITNA board consisted of the general managers of the ITNA member stations. They'd heard just enough about cable to be afraid of it. They didn't want to give it "their" news. I argued that the HBO contribution would make us a much better news service, they'd all have better news shows, they'd get better ratings. They still refused to give "their" news to their rivals. In desperation, I suggested that we might take an ownership position in the HBO project. They still didn't want it. Jim Coppersmith, the GM of WNEW New York, spoke for the Metromedia stations. They had four votes out of nine members, and Coppersmith picked up a fifth. "Cable is the enemy," he said. "I will not let them kill me with my news and then piss on my grave."

After ITNA said no, Levin continued to ponder the idea of a twenty-four-hour news service. Weisberg kept calling, and I referred him to other people who might help him. HBO spent a few dollars doing schedules, business plans, sample reels. Weisberg, who had fallen in love with the idea, was waiting for the go-ahead from Gerry. Early one morning, he got a call. Levin said, "I've just gotten out of the shower, and I get my best ideas in the shower. I've decided we're not going to do news." When Doris Weisberg, Bob's wife, told me the story, she said, "If I were Gerry Levin, I'd never take a shower again."

That was well before 1996, when Time Warner bought CNN along with the rest of TBS. In the end, Gerry got what he wanted—it just cost him a lot more money. Regardless of whose idea CNN was, and who wound up owning it, it was Ted Turner who had the balls to start it.

After Levin's pondering, after the ITNA meeting, the cat was out of the bag. Lots of people were talking about a twenty-four-hour news network, but Ted called me first. He knew me from ITNA, knew what ITNA was doing, and knew it was successful. So he called.

I flew down to Atlanta, paying my own expenses—I would not be beholden to Ted. He met me at the airport in his little Toyota. It was one of his affectations. No limos. No big cars for Ted. He saved money on everything, he even flew coach.

We drove back to the same building where I had visited Ted four years before. The building looked as decrepit as ever, but the office was spruced up. It seemed bigger, more organized. Ted introduced me to Bob Sieber, the head of TBS research and the house intellectual. At the time, I didn't know what Sieber did. He was just sitting there quietly on the couch, taking notes.

Ted opens by saying he is going to call the news company the "Cable News Network." He says, "It will be the only thing I ever own that doesn't have 'Turner' on it." He is making sure that everyone in cable identifies with CNN and that CNN belongs to the cable industry. It will be their thing.

Ted is frank. He still doesn't want to do news, but he says it is the only form of programming left open to him. He would rather do sports, but ESPN has preempted that. He would rather do movies, but HBO has preempted that. He would rather do entertainment programming, sitcoms, dramas, and quiz shows, but the networks own all that. He will settle for news because that's where the opportunity lies. To quote George Washington Plunkett, Ted "seen his opportunities, and he took 'em."

Ted tells me his ideas for CNN, the two-hour rotating-block idea. I tell Ted I think CNN's a terrific idea, but he's going about it the wrong way. I can include all four elements: news, sports, finance, and women's in a program schedule that actually works; twenty-four hours that will flow, that aren't chopped into little news blocks like "you give me twenty-two minutes and I'll give you the world" radio. Ted buys my plan.

He turns his attention elsewhere. "Do you believe in stars?" Ted asks. He's not talking about astrology, he's talking about "name talent." "Yeah," I say. "Who do you think we can get?" he asks. "Dan Rather," I reply. Ted asks, "Who's Dan Rather?" "The CBS anchorman-in-waiting," I tell him. "One of the five top names in TV news."

I knew that in 1978, Rather had lost about 50 percent of his CBS income. He had been anchoring *Who's Who?*, a soft news prime-time hour. CBS had been paying Rather about $250,000 a year to do the show, and when the show was cancelled, so was half of Dan's salary. He was still CBS's White House correspondent, but his stature had been diminished and his salary had been cut. I thought we had a shot.

"How much would he cost?"

"A million dollars a year."

"A million dollars a year just to have a guy read the news?"

"A million dollars a year to get a guy away from CBS network."

Ted thinks about it for a minute, or maybe less. Suddenly, he says, "Well, I just offered Pete Rose a million dollars to play baseball, and he only works half a year." (Just a month before, Pete Rose had come into Atlanta with a forty-three-game hitting streak. It was broken on his second night in town. But the hitting streak games had brought in 76,000 people instead of the expected less than 20,000. After the game, according to the *Washington Post*, Turner grabbed Pete's hand and said, "Pete, you've made more money for my club than any of my players. . . . What about a bonus?" Rose said, "Shhh . . . You're in enough trouble with the commissioner already.")

Having settled on personnel, Ted moves on to location. "Can we do it in Atlanta?"

Now it's my turn to think for a minute. Traditionally, television news comes out of New York and Washington. Atlanta is just a four-man bureau. I tell Ted that anchoring from Atlanta would add a couple of million dollars a year in costs and require a lot of satellite dishes. Ted ignores the costs.

"How many satellite dishes?"

"Seven."

"Is that all?" Ted's already envisioning the row of satellite dishes outside our headquarters that will immediately grab the attention of the media world. No one, least of all me, would ever undervalue Ted's ability to sense PR possibilities.

Machinery comes next. "What do we need in the way of equipment?" he asks. I tell him eight 1-inch tape machines and twelve ¾-inch machines, but there's waiting time. "Get Gene Wright up here," Ted calls to Dee Woods, his secretary. Gene is Ted's chief engineer. "Gene," says Ted, "Reese says we need eight 1-inch tape machines and twelve ¾-inch tape machines. Order them NOW—they're backed up." Gene turns to leave. Ted stops him. "We can cancel them, can't we Gene?" Gene says, "Yes, Ted. We can cancel them."

The most difficult part of forming a cable network is finding a way to reach an audience. That means getting cable systems to agree to put your network on one of their channels. In fifteen minutes, we've settled personnel, location, and equipment. Now Ted turns to the really important stuff. Ted shouts to Dee, "Get me Gerry Levin and Russ Karp." Levin is the power at Time-Life Cable, Karp the head of Teleprompter. Time-Life and Teleprompter are the two biggest cable companies in the country. He tells me, "I'm going to offer each one of them one-third of CNN, but CNN will be based in Atlanta, we'll control it, and you'll run it."

I know little about obtaining affiliates—that's Ted's business—but I trust him to make the best deals he can. Ted gets through to Karp. Karp's not interested. Gerry's secretary says he'll call back. I ask Ted if CNN is a definite go. He replies he'll be going to the Western Cable Show in December. He'll run it past the cable industry, and then get back to me.

On the plane back, I review the meeting in my mind. Despite the exhilaration, all of Ted's talk, all of Ted's actions, nothing's been settled. Ted has made sure he can cancel the tape machines. Ted has not yet committed to CNN. Beneath the wacky razzle-dazzle, Ted is a cautious man.

Round 5: **Who Is Me?**

I am not a cautious man. Often, I've leaped before I looked, and mostly it's paid off. I have, however, been more modest than Ted. Ted wanted to be rich, powerful, and famous. I wanted to be comfortable, important, and well-known. Ted has gotten everything he wanted, except real power. Since the TBS/Time Warner merger, he calls himself "the richest man in the world who works for somebody else." I've gotten most of what I wanted, I do work for myself, but I am far from the richest self-employed man in the world.

As I write this, I sit in an office on the thirty-first floor of 630 Fifth Avenue and look down on the Rockefeller Center skating rink and NBC. I've looked down on NBC for forty years. I look down on all the networks. It may have been the envy of the boy with his nose pressed against the glass, but I thought the networks were lazy, inefficient, and, sometimes, corrupt. I fought them every day for twenty-five years, and I think I won more than my share of the battles. That's another difference between Ted and me: Ted fought with the networks to buy one. I fought with the networks to beat them.

Beating the networks was a big deal for a kid from Newark, New Jersey. Newark was a city of second stringers, guys who couldn't make it in New York. We were born underdogs. Longie Zwillman was the boss of Newark. He'd been Joe Kennedy's partner in bootlegging days and Jean Harlow's lover in Hollywood, but he was only vice chairman of the syndicate. Lucky Luciano was chairman. Lucky came from New York. Zwillman is sadly neglected in the annals of crime, but that's what happens when you come from Newark, New Jersey.

One of Zwillman's associates, Al Borok, lived across the street from us. His son Bert was a friend of mine. He showed me his father's gun collection, but he never explained why Al didn't keep his car in the garage like everybody else on the block. Instead, his Cadillac was delivered to him every morning by a black man who turned on the ignition at a neighborhood garage and then picked up Mr. Borok.

Next door to Mr. Borok lived the chief of police. No one believed this was entirely coincidental. Next door to me lived Newark's leading rabbi, who had only recently fled Berlin and Adolf Hitler. He'd also fled a messy divorce, which had alienated his Berlin congregation but probably saved his life. Decades later, he was one of the two clergymen who marched with Martin Luther King across the bridge in Selma, Alabama. I was a friend of his daughter.

Until I was ten, we lived in a different part of Newark, outside the ghetto. Our neighbors were mostly German, with some Scots and some English. All the kids, including me, went to Madison Avenue School. There were maybe one or two Jews to a class.

My parents supported FDR in the 1936 election, they practically worshiped him. They were probably the only two people in the entire neighborhood who did. I remember, when I was turning five, the other kids on our block running up and down the street chanting, "Landon's in the White House, rah, rah, rah; Roosevelt's in the outhouse, ha, ha, ha." On election day, Alf Landon carried only two states. It didn't make my neighbors like Roosevelt any more.

On weekends some of the neighbors wore brown uniforms and jackboots. They marched off to attend meetings of the German-American Bund, where people booed the Jews and cheered Hitler.

At home we worried about Hitler. We read the *New York Times* everyday and *Time* magazine every week, and we listened to H. V. Kaltenborn on the radio every night to find out what was happening to the Jews. That's how I picked up the news habit.

It wasn't till I was about ten, and he didn't have to support his entire family, that my father had enough money to move us into a neighborhood of rabbis, police chiefs, and Al Borok, which is where I learned the ins and outs of local politics.

Longie Zwillman had gathered a coalition of Jews, Italians, Poles, and blacks, who together had enough votes to defeat the Irish-German political bloc that had run Newark since the turn of the century. Then, in the early forties, when Zwillman finally lost an election, we heard rumors about the "Treaty of the Cathedral." It seemed that an Irish bishop had brought together the Irish and Italians, who until then despised each other. (The Irish thought the Italians were untrustworthy and called them wops; the Italians said the Irish were dumb and called them donkeys.) But the bishop said they were both Catholics and the time had come for the Irish and Italians to take Newark back from the Jews. The Irish would run the city; the Italians would run the rackets. They won the election.

We got the *Newark Evening News* every night, but I didn't read about the Treaty of the Cathedral in the *Evening News*. I learned that in the street. The street is the eyes and the ears of the action. I have always loved action. I have always listened to the street.

My father never listened to the street. He believed what he read in the newspapers. He had always been a "good boy," and had done the "right thing." The oldest son of Jewish immigrants, he left school at fourteen to support his family, abandoning his dream of becoming a lawyer and instead starting out as an office boy for a glass manufacturer. Twenty-five years later, he was a partner. He supported two and a half families. He bought a house for his parents, sent his brothers and sisters to college, and paid off his brother-in-law's gambling debts. During the Depression, he helped my mother's family with the rent, bought a grocery store for my mother's sister, and of course took good care of my mother, my brother, my sister, and me. And of course, he tried to run our lives.

I was not a very good boy. By high school, I was running the football pool and booking bets for people who, at some level or other, were working for Longie Zwillman. I would go to Al Borok's house and play cards in his "rec room." In those days, everybody had a "rec room": pine paneling halfway up the wall, loud wallpaper above it, a bar in the corner and a stuffed swordfish mounted over it. I played poker with Bert and friends at one end of the room, while Al Borok played gin at the other end, sometimes with Gerardo Catena, an underboss in the Genovese family.

I was a good poker player, and I won regularly from Bert's friends. Mr. Borok was a very good gin player, but I do not think he won regularly from Mr. Catena. Catena subsequently did time for contempt when he refused to answer mob-related questions before a judge. He served more time for contempt than any other mobster, but he never talked. I do not think it would've been good business for Mr. Borok to win too often from Mr. Catena.

At school I was thought to be smart, promising, but I was constantly in trouble. I cut classes in public school and Hebrew school, I put down my teachers, I even stole the rabbi's daughter's diary. When the rabbi passed my father in the streets, he would say (or so my father told me), "Philip, how is that rebellious son of yours?" My father, the soul of respectability, was mortified.

Despite his many good deeds and his almost proverbial honesty, my father was not my hero. When he finished grammar school, he had been accepted to Townsend Harris High, a school that was known as the first step toward greatness for the children of immigrants. Felix Frankfurter had gone from Townsend Harris to City College to Harvard Law School to the Supreme Court. My father couldn't go to Townsend Harris; he had to support his family. He went to work in a glass factory. Since he had always wanted to be a lawyer and never had the chance, he wanted me to follow his dream.

I didn't know what my dream was, but it was not to be a lawyer. I knew there were other things besides the law. Since I was ten, I'd been reading *Time* magazine and the *New Yorker*. I saw the pictures in *Life*. I knew there was a world beyond Newark, I just didn't know how to get there.

From all this, I emerged the classic underachiever; great board scores and mediocre grades. Still, I got into Dartmouth and Harvard Law. At Dartmouth, I played cards. I won big at poker, bigger at bridge. In my senior year, my partner and I were National Collegiate Bridge champions. My allowance from home was seven dollars a week; I lived off gambling.

I tried to do the same thing at Harvard, but it caught up with me. My adventure there lasted seven months, until a teaching fellow, who was also my drinking buddy, turned me in to the dean, Erwin Griswold. Griswold was a man of courage. He had refused to fire law school personnel after Senator Joe McCarthy branded them communists or communist sympathizers. He was also famously puritanical. There was no drinking at his house; when he held faculty dinners, the faculty got drunk beforehand. Above all, Dean Griswold detested gambling. Figuring I was running a gambling den, he sent the vice dean (not the dean of vice) to head a raiding party on my old apartment. By that time, I'd moved out and was living in a dorm. The vice dean found nothing, but Griswold expelled me anyway.

I'd been doing okay in my class work, and I suggested to him that he let me finish that year, take exams, and transfer to another law school.

He was intractable. "When you apply to be a member of the Bar, the examiner will ask if you were in attendance at Harvard Law School this year. And you haven't been!" I was history. Funny, Ted was thrown out of Brown for having a girl in his room, and I was thrown out of Harvard for having a card game in mine. Neither of us has changed much. Ted still takes girls to his room, and I still gamble.

After Harvard, I took one more shot at law. This time, Columbia let me in. The summer before I started, the Columbia employment office told me there was a summer job as a copy boy at United Press Movietone News. It paid thirty-five dollars a week, but it got me into the news business.

United Press Movietone News stood on the southeast corner of Fifty-fourth Street and Tenth Avenue. In 1956, the building must've been forty years old. It housed the biggest soundstage in New York City. Frederick March, "the Jewish bank teller," as my Irish film crews used to call him, had made movies there. The crews used to reminisce about watching the action in March's open-ceiling dressing room from the scaffolding while his wife, Florence Eldridge, searched for him on the studio floor.

The building was a movie factory. It was not air-conditioned above the first floor except for the screening room. The windows were security glass with chicken wire running through them, typical 1910 factory windows. Iron chains wrapped around iron hooks tilted the windows to keep them open. Even in the fifties, in the hot summer some of the writers wore shorts, T-shirts, and sandals to work.

My first job as copy boy was to run off mimeograph copies of the writers' scripts. Every story was numbered and titled. Before I mimeographed the scripts, I read them, and saw how experienced writers wrote to film. I was also required to monitor two of the three network newscasts and list their rundowns so we could wire them to London. The third news show was watched by the immediate past copy boy, who had graduated to the grand title of "foreign editor."

UP Movietone (UPMT) also offered a library service. Clients were permitted to store UPMT film and use and reuse it so long as they remained clients. I had to type on an index card every picture in every film shot by shot. As I made out the index cards, I learned how film was edited: CU, MCU, MLS, Pan, Tilt—close-up, medium close-up, medium long-shot, pan, tilt.

When I recorded the running order of a television news show, I learned how news producers organized their programs. I also had to pack rolls of film in small green boxes, insert scripts, and hand the boxes to our motorcycle guys, knowing that before our guys got to the airport, somebody at CBS had pushed a button, and CBS's version of the story was already all over America. I knew our system was obsolete, but I knew no better way to learn the news business.

I joined UPMT in June 1956. The *Andrea Doria* went down in July. All our crews rushed down to the docks. Later in July, half the office went to the Republican convention in Los Angeles. In August, the other half went to the Democratic convention in Chicago. It was a rerun of Ike versus Adlai. I was part of the world I used to read about, and I didn't want to leave it.

I was going to law school that fall, but my boss, Bill Higginbotham, made me an offer. If I could arrange my schedule at Columbia, he would meet me halfway and give me a work schedule that would dovetail with my law classes. So I worked from 2 p.m. to 10 p.m. and took classes in the morning. Later, I worked from 6 a.m. to 2 p.m. and took the afternoon classes that I had missed.

Even in 1956, UPMT was in deep trouble. Our U.S. clients were dropping us: they could get their film from the networks via coaxial cable; we were shipping by air. It took UPMT seven years to die, and I had the privilege of watching while it withered, a great education in learning what not to do and what had to be done.

Round 6: **Movietone**

There are some things I learned the right way at UP Movietone: how to write, how to edit, how to produce, how to choose a story, how to do an interview. And I learned the power of television.

Writing was easy, almost mechanical. Two and a half words a second, making sure to identify each face, each action, as it pops on the screen.

It's carpentry, but it's also great discipline. I learned from the best, hard-core UPI wire writers how to create a cohesive, readable news story, fast. If you couldn't write—if you couldn't write fast—you couldn't survive.

Then I learned editing from Movietone editors, who called themselves "cutters." Some of them had been "cutting" since the twenties. They were used to 35 mm film. They hated 16 mm, which was a television standard. They called it "spaghetti."

I made mistakes. I learned from them, too. When Nikita Khrushchev went to Hollywood, he spoke to the Hollywood elite, praising the values of communism. Spyros Skouras, the chairman of Fox, the owner of Movietone, spoke in reply. He praised the virtues of capitalism: "Only in America could a poor shepherd boy from Greece. . . ."

It was a Sunday, so there was no projectionist. We cut the film on the tiny lens of a "bullseye" hand viewer. For a cutaway, we used a shot of the people on the dais applauding after Skouras's speech, but on the tiny lens, we couldn't see who the applauders were. The next day, we looked at the footage on the big screen. There was Mr. Skouras, applauding himself. We had sent the film to our seventy-five television clients worldwide. Luckily, the newsreel editors caught our mistake. They recut the film so Mr. Skouras did not undergo the pain of seeing himself applaud himself in his own movie theaters.

I became a good editor. I learned how to "save a story." One morning when I was on the 6 a.m. shift, I found a minute and a half of 16 mm film from Tennessee on the editing bench. Klansmen had been harassing blacks demonstrating against school segregation. Violence was in the air and our local stringer was hiding his camera under his arm, beneath his jacket. When nobody was looking, he opened his jacket and sneaked a shot. Some of his film was fogged, some of it shot out of frame. All of it was shot out of context. From this mess we culled forty seconds and turned it into a cohesive television story.

When the stringer saw it on his local station, he could not believe that he had actually shot it. Of course, he *didn't* shoot it. He shot a bunch of three-second bursts, and we made order out of the disorder, altering the details, but capturing the essence. NBC bought the film from the UPMT library and featured it in its first *White Paper,* on segregation.

Even before I was on the assignment desk, I recognized a good story. Working for Burt Reinhardt, I learned not only what story to assign but how to assign it. Burt was the Movietone managing editor. Technically, I did not work for him; I worked for UPI. But Burt was the man who decided what stories would be shot on film, because Movietone supplied the film while UPI provided the words. Burt was a wannabe cameraman. In the war he'd been in the camera corps. When General MacArthur strode through the Pacific onto Leyte Island and did his "I shall return" to the Philippines, it was Burt Reinhardt who was waiting on the beach to take his picture. Burt never got into the cameraman's union, which was a real father-and-son shop in those days. Instead of being a cameraman, he became the cameraman's boss.

One afternoon in 1958, an air force bomber dropped an A-bomb on South Carolina. By the time the UPI wire carried the story, I was alone at the desk, and I called Burt at home to get his okay to cover the story. Burt said, "Go for it, but don't make it definite." I found a cameraman in our freelance book. The cameraman wanted $350. I called Burt. He said, "Offer him $250." I was embarrassed, but the cameraman accepted immediately.

The bomb's explosive material blew up on impact. The nuclear device did not explode, but one house was destroyed, six people were injured, and bomb fragments were spread all over the neighborhood.

None of the networks carried the story the next day. In the days of fifteen-minute news shows at 7 p.m., they didn't have room to carry yesterday's news. WPIX, the UPI station in New York, ran the story at length. The pictures were good, and WPIX, which was owned by the *Daily News*, liked good pictures. Reinhardt told my boss, Bill Higginbotham, that I showed promise. For Burt Reinhardt, promise meant getting the right story cheap.

Bill Higginbotham taught me about reporting. In 1958, George Lincoln Rockwell, the American Nazi, was in New York demanding a permit to speak in a public park. Mayor Wagner refused to grant it. Rockwell went to court, and he had the ACLU on his side. Everyone knew he was going to win.

At that time, there were only three companies covering television news in New York City: CBS, NBC, and us. For the hearings, CBS had reporter Tom Costigan, NBC had Gabe Pressman, and for that day, I was UPI.

Mr. Rockwell emerged from the courtroom into the rotunda of the New York State Supreme Court building. We three reporters had agreed to do one-on-one interviews. We flipped a coin, and Costigan went first. I was to go second, and Pressman last. Costigan did his thing, the standard "freedom-of-speech-for-even-the-most-hateful-ideas" interview.

I went next. Since Rockwell wanted to be president, I asked him how he would handle the Jewish question if elected. He said he'd treat all Jews justly. "Those that are loyal Americans will prosper, and those that are traitors will be executed, just as the Rosenbergs were executed, not because they were Jews but because they were traitors."

"Oh," said I, "what percentage of Jews do you think are traitors?"

"Ninety percent," said Mr. Rockwell.

It was a rainy day. The Jewish War Veterans who were there to protest started smacking their umbrellas down on my head and on Rockwell's. With one hand, I tried to fend off the umbrellas, with the other I kept the mike in Rockwell's face. Gabe Pressman charged in.

"He's blocking our lens!" shouts my cameraman.

I push Gabe out of the way. "You're blocking our lens, and it's my interview—"

"When you start a riot, it's anybody's interview," yells Pressman.

"He's back in the picture," yells my cameraman.

Pressman and I wind up on the floor. The cops break it up. Then the cops and I link arms around Rockwell and walk him out of the courthouse. Gabe got no interview. (The *New York Post* got the picture of the four of us—three cops and me walking him off the floor—and ran it the next day with the caption "Cops and bodyguard escort Rockwell to safety.")

I remember rushing back to the office, thinking I had a great story. Before I even got there, Gabe had called Burt Reinhardt and asked to buy our film. Burt thought twice, but said no. When we started cutting the story, the "90 percent of Jews are traitors" quote was in. Higginbotham took it out. "Why?" I wanted to know. "Because," said Higginbotham—who had grown up in Missouri—"too many people agree with that S.O.B."

I learned that a free press has a right not to print a story. It's probably just as well we lost the "90 percent are traitors" sound bite. Thirty years later, the Rockwell interview is preserved for posterity in a PBS documentary, and who knows how our great-great-grandchildren will react to Rockwell?

A couple of years later, I followed Higginbotham's advice, and I didn't cover a story that would've made scandalous headlines. The official residence of an important local politician with national aspirations burned to the ground. I was tipped that there was a big story behind the fire and that the cops wanted to talk about it. According to the guy who tipped me, the politician's wife had been out of town, and he had invited a musical comedy star to share his bed. It was a candlelit romantic evening, complete with wine and roses. The wife arrived home early. There they were behind drawn curtains in a four-poster bed. She grabbed a candelabra and threw it at the bed, the curtains turned to flame. The politician, his girlfriend, and his wife escaped, but the house burnt to the ground.

Another thing I'd learned in the news business was to know my place in the food chain. If the cops were looking to talk, they must've offered this story to a lot of other people, like the nets or the wire services, before they got down to me. None of the big fish had bitten, and neither would I. Later, I read that the politician, whose family was rich, put up the money to restore the official residence despite the fact that it was covered by insurance. I guess the politician had reason not to make an insurance claim. But even with all that evidence, we didn't print stories like that in those days. Back then, politicians' bed companions were not public business.

I also learned that sometimes the free press has the right to be a pain in the ass. In one day, July 11, 1961, I confronted two great screen goddesses, both of them in unfortunate condition. None of this could happen now, when the news services are owned by movie companies, and movie companies would never risk offending a star whom they might need for their next picture. Back then movie stars were still fair game.

Movietone sent me to Idlewild (now JFK) Airport to get a statement from Elizabeth Taylor. Taylor, Eddie Fisher, her then husband, and Rex Kennamer, her then doctor, were going to Moscow on a mission for the USIA. Taylor had just recovered from a serious illness. The three of them walked through the pleading press corps into the VIP lounge and locked the door. No reporters allowed. I dug out my Fox Movietone News card. On the back, I wrote "Spyros Skouras requests you to do an interview." Since Mr. Skouras ran 20th Century Fox, I was already working for him, and Miss Taylor was soon to be working for him in *Cleopatra*, which is why they wanted her picture in the newsreel.

Liz, Eddie, and the doctor head for the plane, but Fisher diverts her and leads her over to our camera. Liz looks awful. She's been on serious medication, and her throat is scarred by her recent tracheotomy. Her eyes are still a lustrous purple. I can't remember what I ask, or what statement she gives me. It is short and not sweet. She is very angry.

Ignoring Eddie, the proximate cause of her unhappiness, she walks the rest of the way to the plane on the arm of Dr. Kennamer. Fisher turns, grins, and shakes his fist at me. I do not care, I have an exclusive.

No sooner did I get back to the office than Burt said, "Take the crew down to Fiftieth Street. Marilyn Monroe's getting out of the hospital." When Marilyn was wheeled on a gurney out of French Polyclinic, a mob of people, press, and fans was there waiting. There had been rumors of a suicide attempt.

Even though Monroe's PR people have said "no interviews," I bull my way through the crowd, kneel down, and press my microphone to her lips. "Are you feeling better?" "Yes," she whispers. "Was it serious? Were you very sick?" "I'll be well as soon as I get home." Here again, I can't remember everything I said, but what she said was touching and tragic, the way Marilyn always was, and she was marvelous. I was asking gentle questions, but she was the wan, fragile blonde who America loved, and I was the villain. I asked if she'd seen Arthur Miller. I asked if Joe D. had sent roses. She smiled and said she'd heard from everybody.

Apparently, the smile was pure acting. She later claimed she had been terrorized by the huge turnout in the street. So there I was, at the birth of the paparazzi, and I was leading the charge.

Anyway, as she was being wheeled toward the waiting ambulance with me following along, I suddenly realized there was no strain on my mike cord. I turned around. The cord had been cut, and a policeman stood over it with his knife in hand. He claimed the cord got caught around his neck.

The press corps hooted and called the cop a liar to his face. The cord never touched him. One reporter went even further. He said he saw the PR man slipping the cops some money. Later, a guy named O'Brien, head of the New York TV and Radio Reporters Association, phoned Burt Reinhardt. The association wanted to lodge a formal complaint to the police commissioner. Burt told O'Brien to forget it. Burt does not make waves.

I am of two minds about the interview. I've always objected to PR rules. If the PR man didn't want the press there, the story shouldn't have been on the wires. The "swarm" would've been just as great had I not been talking to Marilyn. I knew that if the interview had been recorded, it would now be part of television history. Twenty-five years later, these were the kind of stories I wanted for CNN's *People Tonight*. Unfortunately, we never had the resources.

UP Movietone often covered stories on assignment for client stations. The client would pay for the crew, and the film would be shipped directly to the station. Burt Reinhardt handled that end of the business, and he was always looking for two-for-one. That is, shoot the story twice, ship one roll to the client, bring the other back and use it for the service. There was a problem. Television stations shoot their stories on positive film. Since we had to make prints, we shot ours on negative. A couple of times I got stuck with a two-for, and at least twice, the stories turned out better because of it.

At some point during his playing years, Ted Williams, baseball's last four hundred hitter, met a boy named Jimmy who was suffering from cancer in Boston's Children's Hospital. Williams visited Jimmy often. While Jimmy recovered, Ted established the "Jimmy Fund" to help other young cancer patients. After that, the Boston Red Sox annually played the Boston Braves in a charity game for the fund. WBZ, the strongest station in Boston, televised the games.

Then the Braves moved to Milwaukee. In 1957, they are coming back east to meet the Red Sox, again for the "Jimmy Fund," and Hank Aaron, who has emerged as a major Braves star, has never before played in Boston. But first the Braves have a twi-night doubleheader against the Giants in New York.

WBZ is making a promo for the Jimmy Fund, and they want Burt Reinhardt to send a crew to the Polo Grounds to interview Aaron. On the appointed day, my crew and I go uptown, and as it's a twi-night game, we arrive at dusk. Burt, in his penury, has not sent an electrician. We have to work fast while there is still light. But of course, I have to do two interviews. One for WBZ, and one for the *Harry Wismer Show*, which is a sports show we are then producing.

Nineteen fifty-seven is Hank Aaron's second year in the majors, and he is not the most sophisticated of men. His manager, Fred Haney, has told him about the interview, and Hank is ready to do it but very shy. We have set up behind third baseline, and as Hank comes to the camera, Willie Mays comes trotting in from center field. He kneels just out of camera range. We tell Hank to look at the camera, I hold one of those big old-fashioned mikes up to his face, and Willie asks, "You getting paid for this, Hank?" Aaron is startled. I say no, this is news. Willie Mays says, "Boy, Henry, you dumb. You some dumb nigger you don't get paid for this." Aaron is confused. Haney trots out and says, "It's okay Hank, this is for charity." I do the WBZ interview; it's fine.

When we're ready, I do my questions for the Wismer show. Then I ask Aaron to swing the bat for me a couple of times. We want to get shots of his wrists. Aaron's wrists are supposed to be the fastest in baseball. The cameraman moves the tripod to get a better angle. Mays gets mouthier and mouthier. "Henry, we get three, four hundred dollars for something like this." Hank shakes his head. Finally, we're done. I thank Aaron. I turn and walk away. Hank stands there looking at me, half angry, half bewildered. He spits at my feet. I deserve it. We had copped a free one. Willie Mays did his job too. He had gotten into Hank's head. Hank did not start in either game of the doubleheader. In the second game, he pinch-hit and walked. He did not get a hit all night.

Much later, when Aaron and I were working for Ted Turner, I came to know Hank, but I never reminded him of the incident. I never told him that Willie Mays was right.

The other client story was assigned by WGN Chicago. It's 1958, and Cardinal Stritch, the archbishop of Chicago, is sailing on the *Independence* to Rome. He is going to be named head of the Congregation for the Propagation of the Faith, the first American to be so honored. Two hundred church dignitaries and priests, including three other cardinals and the Pope's Apostolic delegate to the United States, are assembled on the deck, awaiting the cardinal.

Before the ceremony, the cardinal sits in the ship's salon, behind a coffee table. I interview him on negative film for United Press Movietone. New York's Cardinal Spellman is sitting next to him. Before Stritch can rise, I blurt, "Do it once more, Father, for WGN and the people of Chicago." Spellman glowers. He starts to rise. Stritch puts his hand on Spellman's arm, and says serenely, "For WGN, of course."

Now the drill begins again. The cameraman changes magazines, five more minutes, Spellman glowers, Stritch remains serene. When we are ready, Cardinal Stritch waves my questions away. He wants to say good-bye to the people of Chicago his own way. He looks directly into the camera and says: "I shall take my country with me. . . . I want to assure the people of Chicago that I will carry them in my heart with me to Rome. I will always remember them, pray for them, and I hope they will pray for me."

Even as he says this, Stritch knows he is not well. There are tears in the eyes of the photographers. The film plays in Chicago that night. Forty days later, Cardinal Stritch dies in Rome. WGN, always classy, makes the film available to all of its competitors, and it plays on all three networks. We produced the perfect epitaph, all because Burt wouldn't send a second crew.

At UP Movietone, not having the networks' bottomless pockets was an advantage. We had to make money from our news product. Before the 1960 election, I produce six- or seven-minute biographies of JFK and Richard Nixon so our stations will be ready no matter who wins. Higginbotham likes the films. He asks me if there is enough material to do a half hour on JFK. There is. A week before the election, Higginbotham says, "Do it and make a Spanish version." He is betting that JFK will win and that since JFK is Catholic, every Spanish-language country in the world will want a half hour about him, and we'll make a lot of money.

I do the film, JFK wins, and we make money. Hig is much smarter than the USIA. The USIA is so sure that Nixon will win that they do not have a JFK biography in the can. They're a bunch of bureaucrats whose jobs depend on Kennedy's goodwill, and they don't have a film to distribute overseas. Worse than that, they don't have an English-language version to show the president that they were thinking good thoughts about him. The USIA asked Mr. Higginbotham if they can buy our film. We make a lot more money. The next year we get the contract to produce *JFK, the First Year*. I loved it.

I loved it in part because it was a gamble, a gamble that paid off. And then I began to think that all news was a gamble. With limited resources, you have to place your bets and take your chances. Every day there are winners and losers, and ratings are the way you keep score. It was a business made for me, and it had one added attraction, the power to do good.

Doing good has always got to be defined. Good for who? is the question. In the late fifties, the answer was easy. Doing good was defending integration and fighting communism. In 1956 Movietone's Herman Blumenfeld shot the only film of Russian tanks going into Budapest. The State Department called Mr. Skouras and asked him to make the film available worldwide to show the evil in the Evil Empire. Mr. Skouras cooperated. Movietone lost its exclusive, but Fox was helping to make the world a better place.

That's what I learned at United Press Movietone News.

Round 7: **UPITN: Failure After Failure**

In 1963, UPI and Movietone divorced. More than that, they exchanged bosses. Bill Higginbotham, my boss at UPI, became editor-in-chief of Movietone, and Burt Reinhardt, my boss at Movietone, became general manager of UPITN. I went with Reinhardt. It was a wise decision. Fox shut down Movietone within the year. It was also a wise decision because I learned from Burt Reinhardt.

Burt had started out as a cameraman, but he moved on. He has great news sense, and his heart is in news. He also has a sly, tough sense of humor. When I worked for him at UPITN, it was Burt and me against the networks. They never gave us credit, but we did all right, and they'd come to us when they missed a story. Sometimes we gave it to them, most of the time, not. If anything prepared me for the hard times at CNN, it was that job. Trying to cover the news with no money and to keep the company solvent . . . well, that's what I did for two years at CNN.

With Burt, I started out on the assignment desk, but there wasn't much executive talent around, and pretty soon I became Burt's number two. Burt made a "suit" out of me. And we made our name, but slowly.

It's early fall, a gale is blowing, and a German freighter is sinking off the coast of Newfoundland. The Coast Guard is attempting a rescue. They assure us that they will have a cameraman on board and provide us with pool footage that will be shared among all news companies. Burt Reinhardt does not accept their assurance, but there is no film cameraman available in Newfoundland. Burt Reinhardt does not regard that as an excuse. He just orders me to get a cameraman on the story.

There are no planes from New York, where we have cameramen. There are no planes from Boston, where we have a cameraman. Burt Reinhardt says find a way. There are no planes from Toronto, but there is a midnight flight from Montreal. I find the cameraman, he makes the plane, he arrives just after the Coast Guard plane takes off. He wants to go home; Burt Reinhardt says no. The Coast Guard does not find the freighter. The plane returns. When it takes off again, our cameraman is on it. The other networks are still relying on "the pool."

The plane is big enough for a platoon of cameramen, but there are no others. Our cameraman is on the right plane at the right moment. A Coast Guard cutter has found the freighter. It has lashed a line from the cutter to the sinking ship. The freighter's crew is climbing hand over hand across the line. They are saved. It is a dramatic one-of-a-kind rescue picture, and UPITN is the only one who's got it.

The Coast Guard is flying the film to McGuire Airport in Fort Dix, New Jersey. By now, the other networks have discovered the story, they have learned there is film of it, and they have learned that the Coast Guard did not shoot any pictures. Burt Reinhardt bet on that from the beginning and he has won. But the Coast Guard invents a rule. They say that any film shot from a government vehicle is automatically pool because the government provided the transportation. What they really mean is that the Coast Guard has performed heroically and successfully and they want the pictures on the networks so that everybody can see how good they are.

Their plane is due to land at 6 a.m. Now the networks want to lend a hand. CBS says they will send a courier down to pick up the film. Burt Reinhardt is not dumb. We tell them that we have a courier who lives ten miles from McGuire, he will pick up the film. He brings us the film, we develop it, cut it, strike prints, and ship the film. Meanwhile, CBS is writhing and waiting. Finally, they file for an injunction. Late that afternoon the judge rules that if the Coast Guard says it's pool, it's pool. We must give the story to the nets. Burt does not fight the ruling. We surrender the prints, and the story makes the three network evening news programs.

The networks are the big guys. They make the rules, they tried to push us around. When you come from Newark, you can't let that happen. You don't get mad, you get even. During the next twenty years, I learned every trick of the pool trade, and finally, in 1982 after I sued the networks and President Reagan, they made CNN a full pool member.

In the fall of 1963, there was a news explosion. On November 1, Ngo Dinh Diem, the president of South Vietnam, was killed. On November 23, President Kennedy was assassinated.

Diem died in a coup that was backed by the U.S. I had my own take on the story immediately. I thought that it was JFK's declaration of war against North Vietnam. Diem could not have been deposed without Kennedy's consent. Why would Kennedy want to overthrow Diem? Well, there were lots of reasons: Diem was a Catholic in a Buddhist country, and the Buddhists were marching against him. Diem was corrupt. Diem was losing the war. But I saw a different motivation.

Diem was Catholic, and Kennedy was Catholic. In the 1960 campaign, JFK was questioned about "divided loyalty." He assured the nation that he would always defend America's interests, not the Vatican's. If he was going to send U.S. troops to Vietnam, he better make damn sure that nobody was going to be able to say he was sending "American boys" to die for the pope. I saw it as ethnic politics, Newark style but on the grand scale. I also saw that it meant that U.S. participation in South Vietnam was inevitable and that UPITN had better build its own bureau there.

In 1963, UPITN depended on the UPI bureau in Saigon. Neil Sheehan ran the bureau and UPITN was represented by Tran Dai Minh, a cameraman who was so good a newsman that he regularly tipped the news side and the photo side to big stories. He had contacts with the government and the Vietcong. He always seemed to be in the right place at the right time, and he did very well for us when Diem was overthrown. But Minh was fired because "Asia Ernie Hobrecht," the UPI vice president in charge of Asia, thought he was too close to the Vietcong. We were naked on the eve of a great war.

Then JFK was killed in Dallas, and all bets were off. Burt and I never worked better together. For four days, he became Mr. Outside while I worked as Mr. Inside.

None of the cameramen traveling with the president got any film of the president's being shot. We all heard that a Dallas garment manufacturer named Abraham Zapruder had 8 mm film taken at the moment of assassination. Burt got on the first plane to Dallas. I stayed in New York.

In New York, UPITN salesmen sat working the phones, drinking booze from the bottle, and selling the two Kennedy documentaries I had made at Movietone to television stations all over the world. They were the video equivalent of an instant obit. ABC must have run each one of them three times, treading water while they tried to find material to fill their airtime.

In the midst of all this, we learn that Harry Truman is in New York. Our reporters are out, so I grab a crew and rush over to the Carlyle, where he's facing the press. He says, "I'm going to bed." He is brusque, no platitudes. I can't believe it. I ask him if he is going to Washington. "I'm going upstairs, I'm going to bed," as curt as before.

Thirty years later, I heard the interview again on the CBS network. Perry Wolfe, the great documentary maker, had put together a film on the day JFK died. Truman's words must have surprised him as much as they'd surprised me thirty years before. Truman sounded as if he didn't like JFK. Truman had supported Lyndon Johnson for president, and he always thought JFK had pushed too far too fast. Maybe Truman hadn't forgiven him or maybe he was just showing his deep grief in another way. Maybe what he was really saying was, "I just want to go to bed and pull the covers over my head."

Burt Reinhardt gets to Dallas. He's prepared to pay any price for the Zapruder film, and Bill Higginbotham at Movietone has agreed to go halfies with him. It was not, it turned out, a question of money. Zapruder was very aware of being a Jew in Dallas, and he didn't want to be seen as profiting from the assassination of the president. Dick Stolley of Time Inc., was bidding for the film. Time was the most respectable, the most waspy of the news companies, and Zapruder elected to sell the film to them for $50,000, even though we offered more.

Burt, who is a very smart man, went around and talked to the guys at all the 8 mm film labs in Dallas. He gave them his card, wrote the UPI Dallas phone number on the back, and said, "If any film of the JFK shooting shows up, let me know, and I'll give you a hundred dollars." Next day, at his hotel, he gets a call from the Dallas bureau chief for UPI. "Burt, we got a lady here, Marie Muchmore, she says she's got a piece of film showing the Kennedy assassination. What should we do?"

"Lock the door," says Burt.

When Burt gets to the bureau, he asks Miss Muchmore if she had ever shot the camera before. Not often. How much of the event had she filmed? No idea. Burt said, there are two ways we can do this, I could go down to the lab, pay the overtime, we could develop the film and see what it looks like. It may be underexposed, or overexposed, it may be out of focus, it may be scratched. Maybe you missed the event. We'll know that after it's developed and then we'll make you an offer. On the other hand, I'll give you a check for $5,000 right now, sight unseen, and we'll assume the risk no matter what it looks like. Miss Muchmore took the check.

A couple of months later a Mr. Nix showed up at our office. He was a Dallas postman who had also shot film of the assassination, but he'd turned his film over to the government, and it had been months before he'd gotten it back. Now, nobody seemed to want to buy it. We got it for $5,000 and a Stetson hat. That's the film you read about in all the "Kennedy conspiracy" books. It's the one that shows the "man on the grassy knoll." There's nobody on the knoll in his film. I spent ten years of my life working that film over and over, and I know there's nothing there, but the conspiracy theorists will never believe it.

That was the fun part of the business, but 1963 was also the year that Burt taught me the business end of the business. I began to do budgets with him. I tried to sell the service to potential clients. I tried to find ways to deliver our film faster. But mostly, I learned how precarious was the state of UPITN's existence. Burt and I knew that sooner or later there was a good business here. Our problem was how to get from sooner to later. We picked up a new partner, England's Independent Television News (ITN). We agreed to become the news arm of two start-up networks, the Overmeyer Network and the Eaton Network. Both expired in days or months, and we ourselves teetered on the brink of extinction.

The sixties were also "the sixties." We sent a cameraman named Reggie Smith into the South, and he covered integration for us. We did a half hour film on Haight Ashbury. We were at Kent State. Our film of the Columbia University riots is the stuff of which a dozen documentaries have been made. And of course, there were the conventions. We were there in 1964, and 1968, and 1972. While everybody else went live, we shipped film. The conventions deserve a chapter of their own, and they get one later in the book.

In 1972, I attempted an alliance with PBS. They had just completed their national video hookup. I proposed that they give us a half hour to transmit our news over their lines. Our local subscribers would pay them a fee, equivalent to the print and shipping costs that they had been paying us. PBS stations and the PBS network would also have the right to use the material in their broadcasts. Jim Lehrer, who was then coordinator for news and public affairs at PBS, bought into the plan.

He proposed the arrangement to the PBS stations at their convention in Atlanta in September. They accepted enthusiastically, probably more for the money than for the news. However, after his reelection, Richard Nixon had made changes at the Corporation for Public Broadcasting (CPB), the parent organization of PBS. He replaced John K. Macy, a liberal Republican who was a Lyndon Johnson appointee, with Henry Loomis, a former *Life* editor and USIA boss with unquestionable conservative credentials. Republicans had little faith in PBS's "objectivity." Of course, they were right. In the seventies, many PBS local stations were doing off-the-wall news, most of it making fun of Republicans. Nixon did not want to give them another weapon, same-day news from around the world. Loomis agreed with Nixon.

Some Republicans wanted to kill PBS altogether. Some thought it could be tamed and was worth saving. A Texas Republican backer brought in Jim Lehrer to try to save the network. Lehrer wanted to accept our offer. Henry Loomis did not. He killed the deal, and once again UPITN was dead in the water.

When Burt started UPITN, he signed contracts with the various film unions. In 1973, we couldn't afford the high union salaries. We couldn't afford the huge "occasional rates" of AT&T land lines. We asked for relief from the unions. They gave us none. We joined in an industry lawsuit to lower AT&T's occasional rates. They raised the rates. Burt Reinhardt searched for partners. Every time he got close, they took another look at the books, and they passed. Finally, he found Bob Pauley, an ex-ABC Radio executive who had a strongly conservative bent. Pauley was not impressed with us, but he liked our business. He liked it so much that he went out and tried to raise the money to start a conservative version of UPITN.

We were faced with the possibility of competition. Burt tried to find a partner for us. It was a race, Pauley versus Reinhardt. Pauley got there first. He found the Coors brothers, Joe and Bill, hard-line conservatives, who wanted to start a right-wing news company to offset "network liberal bias." Burt found Paramount Pictures, and Paramount put its money into UPITN as a business proposition. For one year, competition raged: Coors looked at the business as propaganda. Paramount looked at the bottom line. Paramount surrendered. Coors bought UPITN and three people from it; one of them was me.

Round 8: Coors Lite News

Joe Coors was so conservative, he made Bob Pauley sound like Leon Trotsky. He was enormously rich and liberal only in his support of right-wing causes. He and his brother, Bill, had inherited Coors beer. For the most part, Bill ran the brewery while Joe attended to political causes. He created and funded the Heritage Foundation. When Pauley presented his news plan to Joe, Joe bought in. He wanted to believe it. It was a sucker play, but Coors was willing to put up the cash if he believed in the cause.

Joe had little business sense; Pauley had lots. After Coors had committed to TVN (TeleVision News), but before the network launched, Pauley brokered the sale of a Fort Worth, Texas, television station. He made so much money that he abandoned TVN, the company he and Joe had founded, to become a full-time station broker. Coors hired an ABC advertising sales executive to replace Pauley. A year later, they fired him. The company was left with no professional leadership.

From its inception, TVN had made every amateur mistake. Despite their antilabor attitude at the brewery, they signed a contract with the New York television unions that provided for a union shop. They leased AT&T coaxial cable at a cost that was greater than their total revenue. They were in the red before they had hired a person or produced a story. They gave Reuters a 5 percent stake in the business to provide foreign coverage, and they paid them a large fee. After I joined them, I could not come up with a business plan that showed them making money in the foreseeable future.

When it came to content, they hired a dozen professional newsmen, some from networks, some from local news, expecting them to follow the Coors party line. Their expectations were in vain; a newsman did not produce propaganda. By the time I arrived, they had started on a second generation of newsmen with no better results.

Joe Coors told me that he hoped TVN would act "like a tugboat, pushing ships that were veering to the left back to the right, just a little bit day by day." I decided to avoid the mission, to stay out of the news side and to concentrate on operations. I reopened negotiations with the labor unions, who proved to be as dumb as they were obstinate: They engaged in a secondary boycott and put it in writing. Our negotiations ended in their total surrender.

Then I turned to distribution. I convinced Joe Coors, who was an engineer, that satellite transmission was the future of news gathering. He told me he'd back me. I contacted Western Union, who was planning to launch their first communications satellite in 1975. I told them what we wanted to do, I told them that Coors beer was backing us, and I asked them what it would cost to buy a video channel (transponder) on their satellite. Western Union asked what TVN could afford to pay. I said our budget was a million dollars a year. They said how about $90,000 a month. I said I could live with that.

The next week Western Union and TVN held a press conference. I told the press what we were going to do. The *New York Times* carried the story, and Sid Topol, chairman of Scientific Atlanta, read it. Scientific

Atlanta manufactures large satellite dishes and Sid needed customers. He was impressed, not because we were in the news business, but because we were in the beer business. He said we bring "beer money" to the table. He invited me to visit his factory in Atlanta. On the way, he took me to meet Ted Turner, the man in the yachting cap.

Afterwards, Topol and I got down to business. He told me that the FCC required that satellite dishes be ten meters in diameter. They cost more than $100,000 each. TVN could afford the satellite time, but our stations could not afford $100,000 receive dishes. The plan would not work.

I go out on the road and I talk to television station operators. Most of them tell me they don't have room for a ten-meter dish. When I suggest the parking lot, one general manager says, "I'd lose twelve parking places. I don't have enough parking places now." We will have to get FCC permission to use smaller dishes.

Joe Coors tells me that FCC chairman Dick Wiley is a friend of his. Wiley will help us. I meet Wiley in Washington, and though he may be Coors's friend, he is not his yes-man. Wiley tells me to take the question up with his engineers. His engineers have been brainwashed by the networks. When I suggest that receive dishes are passive and cannot interfere with other signals, the FCC engineer tells me about "bounce lobes." He explains that the satellite signals will hit the antenna and bounce out unless you have a ten-meter dish to catch them in.

It was preposterous, but the FCC stuck to its ruling until late in 1975, when the small cable operators challenged it. They wanted to get HBO, and they couldn't afford big dishes. So they said they were going to use small dishes and let the FCC sue *them*. The FCC never sued. Years later, when I asked Dick Wiley why he backed down, he said he hadn't backed down. His engineering department could decide on the size of the dishes. But Dick Wiley would decide who the FCC sued. He wanted to make satellite transmission work.

By now I was having trouble at TVN. They still think of news as propaganda; I think news is business. They hire people on the basis of political attitude; I hire on the basis of competence. Senior executives at TVN believed that Joe Coors would continue to fund TVN so long as they got "the message" out. I didn't think so. At a TVN board meeting, I had heard Max Goodwin, the Coors CFO, say that for the $20 million TVN had lost, he could have built a brewery on the East Coast. I believed that sooner or later, "beer money" would triumph over "news money." I thought of myself as the lone professional in the midst of politically motivated amateurs. I was disenchanted.

For the record, TVN was as disenchanted with me as I was with it. TVN decided I was leaking to the press. I believed they were wiretapping my phones. I knew my days were numbered. I served out my contract and departed.

It was August 1975, and I left TVN knowing more about satellites than anyone in television news. I also knew that financial reality would sooner or later hit TVN. It was sooner.

In September, Coors announces that TVN will shut down on October 31. A dozen independent television stations will be left without news. I decide it's time to take my shot. I draw up a plan for a cooperative independent television news agency modeled on the Associated Press. I call it ITNA.

Round 9: **I Get It Right**

Before you take a shot, you have to figure the odds. That's a risk/reward proposition. When I thought about ITNA, my consideration was something like this:

Define the proposition: To create a TV version of Associated Press for independent stations in the United States; a not-for-profit television news cooperative that will gather news from around the world and the U.S. on behalf of its member stations and clients. Deliver that material nightly on a timely basis to its members and clients. Members and clients must agree to provide the association with coverage in their own areas. Founding members must agree to provide first-year funding of $1 million a year. The association would be governed by a membership board and run on a day-to-day basis by its managing director, Reese Schonfeld.

Examine the proposition, starting with the cons: First, everyone who had tried to do an independent news service had failed. They'd all lost money, gone out of business. Maybe that proved it couldn't be done. Second, even if it could be done, membership organizations are notoriously difficult. It's bad when your customers make the decisions about your business. Third, cooperatives rarely work, especially when the members compete with each other in the same markets. Fourth, it was not for profit. Nobody was ever going to make any money out of it. Fifth, even if I overcame all the other obstacles, would the members choose me as managing director?

Now the pros: First, market conditions had changed. There were more independent stations doing news, they were getting better ratings, they had to buy their national and international news from somebody. A million dollars—$100,000 dollars a station—was about what they'd been paying to TVN. Second, satellite technology cut distribution costs by 90 percent. Third, it was clear to me that the new association would not have to hire union labor. Fourth, good local coverage was available from the independent stations who covered their own markets. Fifth, we could buy foreign television news and a wire service at low cost. I could count on competition in those areas to keep the prices down. Sixth, there were plenty of bright, competent, somewhat experienced kids who could handle the editorial side of the business. Seventh, $1 million a year would cover our costs. Even in year one we were a break-even business. Eighth, I thought I would get the managing director job because I knew more about the news business than anyone else. I had spent twenty years learning from other people's mistakes.

What I would get out of it: Well, I had a wife, an ex-wife, and six kids. Worst case, I'd get a job out of it. Middle case, I'd grow the business and it would become a better job. Best case, I'd do so well that somebody would come along and offer me a better job doing it for them. Best, best case, I'd do it so well, I'd get an investor to back me, and I'd start a news business of my own. That's what I wanted, and I put my money on it, even if it was a long shot.

What was the down side? I'd waste sixty days trying to do the right thing, and if it didn't work, I'd have to go out and find a job.

For me, there was an additional, nonmonetary, maybe ego-driven up side. I was laying the groundwork for a news revolution. I was going to overthrow the network news monopoly. For thirty years, Americans had been taking whatever the networks offered in the way of news. What time do you want to watch? Well you've got three choices: 7 p.m., 7 p.m., and 7 p.m., NBC, CBS, ABC. What are you going to see on the network news? The same follow-the-daybook AP, *New York Times, Washington Post* lineup. Who's gonna tell you the news? Even now, you've got your choice of Tom Brokaw, Peter Jennings, Dan Rather. Tell me the difference, and you win a dollar. The same kind of people made the news decisions at all the networks. By and large, they were graduates of journalism schools or good Eastern colleges. They'd worked in print, they were all first-rate, but they saw things through the same set of eyes. It was as if you were running the same raw material through the same strainer and expecting different results. No matter how many times you ran it through, the product was always pretty much the same.

ITNA would be different. We would produce some different stories, present them differently, and offer them at different times. The network way, a lot of important news never got on the air. If I won my gamble, ITNA would offer an alternative. We would prove that you didn't have to do twenty hours of entertainment programming every day to support one half hour of news. If our proposition worked, a more open, less rigid news structure would emerge, and that's what ITNA did. Its success proved that a news company could survive on television without an entertainment subsidy. In other words, ITNA was the laboratory in which we proved that news could be a business unto itself. It was the blueprint for CNN.

We started with nine members, most of them in major cities, most of them carrying their news at 10 p.m., most of them tabloid style. Ten o'clock tabloid news had been invented by Metromedia's Larry Fraiberg, first in Washington, then in New York. To run his New York news, Fraiberg hired John Corporon from WDSU, the NBC affiliate in New Orleans. He sent Corporon copies of the *Daily News* and told him to turn "The News" into television. Corporon did. His program carried all the news concisely and colorfully. It had attitude. It was street-smart and consistently skeptical. From the night it went on the air, it was a hit.

Originally a half hour, it quickly expanded to an hour. Once Metromedia made it work, other independent stations followed. These were my prospective customers, the future members of ITNA.

By 1975, Corporon had shifted from Channel 5 New York to Channel 11 New York: from a Metromedia station to a Tribune station. Metromedia and Tribune were the Montagues and Capulets of independent broadcasting. I had just one month to bring them together if I were going to make ITNA work.

First, I tried the Montagues: Larry Fraiberg of Metromedia's WNEW. He hedged. One of his guys wanted Metromedia to start a news service of its own. Unbeknownst to any of us, Al Krivin, who ran the Metromedia empire, had sent a letter to all three networks demanding that the networks make their national and international news feeds available to the independent stations. Krivin believed, probably rightly, that his ratings depended on good local coverage. In 1975, he had good local coverage, and his ratings were great. National and international news were an afterthought. He wanted the networks to supply it to him at a fixed price and be done with it.

If Krivin had had his way and we had not launched ITNA in 1975, if we had left the battlefield to the networks, it would have cemented the network news monopoly. The networks would have had another million dollars to cover the news the way they saw it, and the fourth voice would have been preempted.

With Metromedia hemming and hawing, I went to the Capulets, the Tribune Company. John Corporon adopted the idea and me immediately. There was one proviso: If Metromedia decided to start a news service of its own, he would join them and drop me. John was being realistic.

I called my former UPITN clients. I used the old Ben Franklin line: "We must all hang together, or we shall all hang separately." Six of the clients sign up, but Metromedia hangs back. On Friday, October 31, I sit in a cramped office at WPIX, eating a grilled cheese sandwich, waiting to find out if I still have a future in news, waiting for word from Bill Carpenter, general manager of WTTG Washington, a Metromedia station. Carpenter wants to join ITNA, but he needs an okay from Kriven. Kriven won't call him back. Finally, Carpenter calls Kriven's secretary. "If I do not hear from Al by three o'clock, I'm joining ITNA." Back at WPIX, John Corporon pokes his head in every hour. "Any word?" he asks. "Not yet," say I.

At three o'clock Carpenter calls. He hasn't heard from Kriven. He's going to join ITNA. I thank him. Corporon says, "The rest will follow."

Two weeks later, they do. Meanwhile, I have three days to build a news service.

For me, it was my last shot. I had convinced nine television stations to invest their money in me personally. If I didn't make it work, I was washed up.

Even before I'd gotten the go-ahead I'd signed a contingent contract on behalf of ITNA for a daily half hour's time on the Western Union satellite. I'd reached an agreement with UPITN for foreign news coverage. (In 1974, Paramount had sold its 50 percent interest in UPITN to John McGoff, a Michigan newspaper publisher with pronounced conservative views. McGoff was secretly funded by South African money, but none of us were aware of that yet.) UPITN also agreed to supply us with Washington coverage: two crews, one to cover the White House, the other to cover everything else that moved in Washington. Member stations would cover the news in their own area. ITNA would hire freelancers or buy station coverage for the rest of the United States.

We approached the big networks about pool access. Originally, pools were created because the president or another official said, "I don't want to be overwhelmed by the press. Send one guy in, he can take notes on behalf of everybody." These days the guy sent in is usually the AP. He comes out and reads his notes to other reporters. The same thing holds true for photographers.

When television came in, with all its equipment, pools were even more necessary. All presidential press conferences were covered by pool cameras. When the president traveled, a travel pool was assigned to accompany him. The networks rotate the travel pool on a monthly basis. That pool accompanies the president in his car, on Air Force One, and it tapes him coming in and out of buildings.

When the president goes overseas, many events are limited to pool coverage. One network might cover the president shaking hands with the chief of state, another network will cover the luncheon speech. If the coverage is live, any network may carry the event as it occurs, no matter whose camera is shooting it. If the event is not carried live, the pool tape is dubbed, and copies are immediately sent to all pool members. No pool member may use the tape until all pool members have it.

Pooling is far more common than it should be. Sometimes, "pools of convenience" are created. If a building has three exits, three networks may decide to cover one exit each so the subject can't slip away, but sometimes, pools of convenience are created just to save money.

For twenty-five years, pooling had been the private preserve of the three networks. Now, ITNA is busting in. We say, "A pool to one is a pool to all. You must make pool material available to us." The network lawyers agree that a pool to one is a pool to all, but they do not want to use ITNA tape; they'll take money instead. We haggle, they postpone pricing, but meanwhile they do make the material available.

In a matter of days, we had arranged a worldwide coverage system, an affordable distribution system, and we were not burdened by union contracts. ITNA was no longer a blueprint. It had structure, coverage, distribution, and network pool access, if only pro tem.

For the next four years I sat in an office in the *Daily News* building, making it work. Gradually, the service got better and better, new members came in, more money was available, and we became more and more of a pain in the networks' ass. They thought we were working magic. Somehow, we were tricking them. We drove them crazy.

On Monday, November 3, 1975, I was the only ITNA employee. I flew down to Washington to organize our coverage there. Corporon volunteered to cover the New York end. Our first feed was scheduled for 7 p.m.

By the time I arrived at UPITN Washington, ITNA had one foot in the grave. Vice President Nelson Rockefeller had called a press conference to announce that he would not stand for election in 1976. Paul Sisco, the UPITN bureau chief, had missed the story. He'd pulled a Burt Reinhardt and sold the crew ITNA was paying for to the USIA.

There we were in the first hour of our first day, and we had already missed one of the biggest stories of the year. We had disgraced ourselves. Then Sisco pulled a miracle. He called his friends at ABC, and they gave him a tape of the story. I couldn't understand it. "Why would ABC give it to you?" I asked. "It's Washington courtesy," said Paul. When he had arrived in Washington, the other bureau chiefs took him to lunch. They explained Washington rules. In Washington, bureau chiefs helped each other, unless the story was exclusive.

Paul said when he worked at UPI, he would no more have given the AP a story than kill his mother. The Washington bureau chiefs said, "We protect each other's ass. We may be rivals, but we can't fire each other. If we miss a story, New York can fire us. New York is our enemy. You save our ass, we'll save yours."

On November 3, Paul's "Washington Rule" saved ITNA. I thought it was a lousy practice, but six years later, I remembered Washington's fear of New York and saved CNN on a story even bigger than Rockefeller's withdrawal.

Within weeks, we had hired three news people for our New York office. The staff worked eleven hours a day: four days one week, three days the next. Within months we'd hired a bookkeeper and established relationships with television stations in cities where we did not have ITNA members. And we found another provider of foreign news: the European Broadcasting Union (EBU).

The EBU was in some ways the foreign equivalent of ITNA. The European television networks had arranged for a twice-daily news exchange among all their members. The three American networks were associate members. They exchanged their news stories with EBU, and they were entitled to EBU material. The American networks treated the EBU with the same arrogance with which they treated ITNA. We were the best, perhaps the only, alternative to the networks' arrogance.

Vittorio Boni of RAI was chairman of the EBU's news group. He learned of ITNA and contacted me. Could ITNA help the EBU obtain material from the United States? I said, "Sure." I meant, "Sure, I hope." But Vittorio knew what I meant. He and I had some things in common. He had been a teenager in Rome when American troops marched into the city. He had made himself useful as a messenger, translator, and all-around fixer. He was a master of making things possible. He was charming, he was gracious, he ran a meeting better than anyone I ever worked with. He could phrase a motion so that the vote always came out the way he wanted it. I found it impossible not to like him. He offered ITNA an associate membership in the EBU news group. I accepted.

We now had direct access to all the news material that European networks provided each other. We had leverage over UPITN. In return, EBU could call on ITNA for U.S. coverage and particularly for help with U.S. facilities. If EBU needed a floor pass for the political conventions, ITNA supplied it. When EBU wanted access to a network pool feed, the networks wanted thousands of dollars. ITNA gave them access for nothing. ITNA became the EBU fixer in New York. Mostly, it was a game. Boni would make a request of the network pool. The pool would say they couldn't do it. Boni would call ITNA. ITNA would find a way. Boni would inform the networks that ITNA would do it. Then the networks would find a way.

I still had to get access to the network news pool. I wanted in. They stalled. I offered to pay one hundred dollars per story. The network newsmen said: "Pay one quarter of our pool costs." I called the network lawyers and shouted "antitrust." Their news departments said, "Fuck Schonfeld." My lawyer called their lawyers; he mentioned "antitrust." Their lawyers were concerned, and in the end the lawyers always win. The lawyers told the newsmen to take our hundred dollar offer, and they did.

In 1976, we sent our own crews and a satellite truck to the Republican convention in Kansas City. It was a first. We shared our floor passes with our local affiliate member stations, meaning they could finally report live from the floor. KSD, the NBC affiliate in St. Louis, frequently worked with us. When they saw what we were doing, they asked if we would put their political reporter on the floor and let him report live into their news shows. We fed three live inserts back to KSD. It was a revolution.

The next day, a dozen NBC affiliates demanded that their network do the same for them. By the time we got to the Democratic convention in New York, ours was no longer the only satellite truck. The networks were giving their affiliates floor access. Affiliate news shows now looked more like network news shows. ITNA had begun to change the network affiliate landscape.

Our contract with UPITN was running out. I had attended the White House press dinner with Paul Sisco and John McGoff, UPITN's owner. A marginally integrated chorus entertained us with patriotic songs. McGoff heard nothing, saw only the few black faces, could not ignore them, and "niggered" at me across the table throughout the whole performance. This ultra-conservative racist was even worse than Coors. The South Africans were getting their money's worth. Paul Sisco, in Washington, avoided the politics. In London, Ken Coyte fought them to a standstill, but ITNA could not be an instrument in the politics of McGoff and company.

Given the political biases of the UPITN ownership, ITNA dropped them in 1977 and signed up with Visnews, a Reuters subsidiary. ITNA and Reuters together created the first daily regularly scheduled news feed from Europe to the U.S. We bargained for an American in London to voice-over two or three Reuters stories a day. Now, ITNA was becoming more like the AP. An ITNA client could lift a Visnews story off the news feed, insert it directly into its news show, and have a distinct voice reporting and signing off in London.

Previously, American networks had satellited stories on an ad hoc basis. If the story was big enough, they'd buy the time to bring it in. I have a business credo: If you want your employees to do something, pay for it in advance. I wanted to use more foreign material in our feed. If an editor had to spend money whenever he bought satellite time, he would judge the value of the story against the state of his budget. If the time has been paid for in advance, he takes the best stories of the day, everyday.

In 1977, ITNA expanded to an hour. Our foreign service was so successful that NBC and PBS joined with us to help pay for the costs of the Reuters feed. But there was one disadvantage of our Reuters deal. Reuters did not have a Washington television bureau. ITNA found a small production company to supply us with two camera crews, editing facilities, and two reporters who would identify themselves as reporting for ITNA. They were nonunion of course, and they did better work than UPITN ever did. They began to establish the principles that would in time make CNN succeed.

ITNA had other triumphs. I managed to snare former CBS newsman Daniel Schorr, who, down on his luck, was making his living as an after-dinner speaker. He needed a news credential. I offered him a hundred dollars a day, three days a week; his agent said, "You got him." From there on in, Dan tagged himself on his speaking tours as "White House Correspondent, ITNA." By 1972 ITNA is seen in New York, Chicago, L.A., and fifteen other cities. Schorr's dinner guests think he's a big deal.

Occasionally we beat the networks on big stories because our news judgment was better than theirs. When Elvis Presley died in 1977, our coverage was coming from the CBS station in Memphis. The station had agreed to feed the Presley story to ITNA live off its newscast at 6 p.m. Six p.m. central time is 7 p.m. eastern time, when the CBS network news show was broadcast. CBS was working at the Memphis station, getting its own story ready. There was only one loop from the Memphis station to New York. If CBS chose to lead the Cronkite show with Presley, the station would not be able to feed their Presley story to ITNA.

Bud Benjamin, the Cronkite producer, decided there were more important stories than Presley that day. He led with them. We were able to take ten minutes of Presley directly from the station's air and put it live onto our news feed. Our clients loved it. The Memphis station fed CBS later. Bud Benjamin lamented that his gravestone will read: "Here lies Bud Benjamin. He did not lead with Elvis Presley."

Initially ITNA covered sports the way everybody else did. Our members offered us stories from their news shows, and we aired the best of them. Then we found a better way. Since we were satellite savvy, we knew that baseball teams were using satellites to bring their away games back to hometown television. ITNA got permission to record games right off the satellite. We edited them and transmitted them to our stations. When Pete Rose's National League–record forty-four-game batting streak ended in Atlanta on August 2, 1998, we pushed a button, made a dozen edits, and transmitted the story nationally. Major League teams gave permission readily. They wanted the national exposure. It presaged a fundamental change in sports coverage.

ITNA also began to expand internationally. We opened a Jerusalem bureau with Jay Bushinsky as our correspondent. After all, in much of America, Israel is a local story. On our own we sent a crew to Jonestown, Guyana, to cover the Jim Jones massacre. By the last day of the story, NBC was pleading for our coverage.

Still, all through my tenure at ITNA, we battled with the network poolsters. We could not agree on what material was pool. They would not let us provide pool cameras. They denied creating pools of convenience, but we caught them at it and demanded the material. We cited chapter and verse. The network lawyers believed us. We made a deal. We would get access to everything we asked for, but we would be limited to ninety-second use.

The last piece of the puzzle, the time factor, fell into place in 1979. ITNA began to feed additional news stories after 7 p.m. for our West Coast stations since their deadline was 1 a.m. New York time. I demonstrated to myself the fluidity of time, and I established to my satisfaction the special advantages of, even the necessity for, a twenty-four-hour news network.

In 1979, I proved my principle, even though I lost my biggest ITNA bet. I believed that the CIA (never bet on the CIA) would not permit Ayatollah Ruholla Khomeini to return to Iran. The ayatollah's plane was scheduled to land in Tehran at midnight New York time, 9 p.m. on the West Coast. We had five West Coast stations with ten o'clock news shows.

The shah's people still controlled Iranian TV. They were broadcasting the ayatollah's return live. Tens of thousands of Iranians were at the airport to welcome him. We arranged for a feed of the live broadcast from Tehran to Switzerland, to New York, and on to our West Coast stations.

Then the CIA did nothing about the ayatollah. His plane landed safely. Nobody shot him. It cost $10,000, and all we saw were pictures of an old man in a turban and robe walking down the ramp into the cheering crowd. We did hear the ayatollah's revolutionary guards take over the control room of the national television station and then our screen went black.

The event demonstrated the flexibility of time. It was midnight in New York when the ayatollah landed; there were no more news shows scheduled, but it was 9 p.m. in California, and half the population would be watching news during the next two hours. We brought our stations the story "tonight," everybody else had to wait until "tomorrow."

Properly promoted, the ayatollah's return could have become the biggest story of the month. The stations could have promoted the event as "What will happen? Will he live or will he die? Will the army fight or will it run? Will the revolution succeed or will it fail? See the news live at nine and find out." When you don't have the steak, you can sell the sizzle.

The Ayatollah Khomeini story showed that ITNA could advance the news one full cycle by covering a story live. ITNA proved that you could run a successful news business without unions and without AT&T. We had proved that ITNA could establish news alliances with local television stations, even network affiliates. We had fought our way into the network pools. We could pull our sports coverage right out of thin air. And we were now able to make news available anytime anywhere in America.

Ted Turner had called in September 1978. We'd had our meeting. I was ready to go, but Ted had put CNN on hold. Then he called again.

Round 10: "The Two Most Powerful Men in the World"

Between September 1978 and April 1979, I checked in with Ted a couple of times to see what was happening. He hadn't picked up enough support from the cable owners, he couldn't make up his mind. Suddenly, in April, out of nowhere, he called me.

Bill Lucas, the general manager of the Atlanta Braves, was dying. He was the first black general manager in baseball. He was in his forties, tough and strong. Ted told me Bill had had a cerebral hemorrhage and was in the hospital near death. "None of us are going to live forever," Ted said. "Let's do this fucking thing." The "fucking thing" was CNN.

I went down to Atlanta again. It was the day Lucas was buried. Ted came right from the funeral, I came right from the airport. We met at the ballpark. We made a deal. Back at his office, we talked some more, and signed a letter of agreement. I'd always known I'd take the offer, but before I signed I asked, "Who's gonna run it?"

"You," he said. "It'll be all yours." I was CEO and president of CNN.

There was a problem. Between September and April, I'd grown tired of waiting for Ted and signed a contract with ITNA. The contract had only seven more months, but Ted wanted me in Atlanta immediately.

In Atlanta, I told Ted that I might not be free until November, but I'd do my best to get down sooner. He said he'd live with that. As we signed the letter of agreement, he said, "This is going to make me the most powerful man—" then stopped and amended his statement. "This is going to make us the two most powerful men in the world."

Back in New York, I asked the ITNA board to release me. They did their best to change my mind. Lev Pope and John Corporon, general manager and news director of WPIX New York, told me a story. Lev had to deal with George Steinbrenner. WPIX carried the Yankees games. The story was one I never forgot. It was on my mind every day I worked for Ted Turner.

When Steinbrenner first bought the Yankees, Gabe Paul brought him over to meet with Lev Pope, his broadcast partner. Paul was the general manager of the Yankees, an experienced baseball man. He had previously run the Cincinnati Reds, and several of the World Series–winning Yankee teams were his creation. He was the guy who talked Steinbrenner out of trading Ron Guidry, and he was the guy who made the deals that brought Chris Chambliss and Willie Randolph to the Yankees.

At their first meeting, Steinbrenner told Pope, "I'm just the owner. I don't know baseball. Gabe Paul is the guy who's gotta run the team. I'm just gonna sit here and listen. That's the way it's gonna be from now on." Then Lev looks me right in the eye. "Three years later," Lev says, "Steinbrenner was sending Gabe out for coffee. Turner needs you now, he says you'll be the boss, you've got all the titles, but three years later, he'll send you out for coffee."

I listened, and when I eventually got down to Atlanta, I made myself a promise: The first day he sends me out for coffee, I'm gone.

Now, ITNA was saying I couldn't leave until I found a successor. I suggested Ted Kavanau, one of ITNA chairman Corporon's original henchmen at Channel 5. But Kavanau had made too many enemies, seemed too far off the wall, and the ITNA partners told me to keep looking. Meanwhile, they forbade me any contact with Turner.

Then Ted changed the rules. He said he needed me to appear with him at the National Cable Show in Las Vegas in early May. I talked to my board. I said, "It's on a weekend, I'll take vacation time, it won't interfere with ITNA." Corporon called for a board vote.

Ted was unwilling to accept "delay" as an answer. There were just two big cable conventions a year, and Ted said he needed me for this one. I had to wait for the board vote. Ted called screaming, "You're gonna let those ITNA guys run your life? You're afraid . . ." I yelled at Ted, "I have a contract with those ITNA guys, but I don't have any money. If I go to Vegas, they're not going to sue *me*. They're going to sue *you*. Then you'll really scream, and I don't want to start out that way." But we had already started that way.

Finally the board voted. My friends voted no. They wanted me to stay at ITNA. My enemies, the Metromedia stations, voted yes; they wanted me out. Mark Monsky of WNEW cast the deciding vote. It was to let me go. He wanted to run ITNA himself. He didn't get the chance, because I was finally able to replace myself at ITNA. The board accepted Chuck Novitz, who had been in charge of the ABC newsfeed to its local stations. I agreed to stay until August 1.

When I met Ted in Vegas, it was a real pissing match. Ted was furious. I'd gotten there late. At first I was apologetic. Then I got angry. Thank

God for Liz Wickersham. Liz was Ted's main girlfriend at the time. She was a strikingly beautiful blonde with a Mae West quality about her. She was a strong woman. She had boyfriends other than Ted, and Ted wanted her to give them up. She asked Ted if he was ready to give up his other girlfriends. When Ted said no, she said no, and they lived happily for a while after. Liz stepped in between Ted and me. She treated us both like little boys spoiling for a fight. She soothed us with kind words, particularly to Ted. In our final exchange, Ted asked, "What makes you so fucking smart?" "You picked me," I replied. Liz beamed, and we managed to live through the night.

The cable convention opened Sunday, May 20, 1979, and Ted was looking to announce a "name" anchor during it. Rather was out of the question. I had tried Howard K. Smith, who was gone from ABC. His wife was his agent, and she wouldn't take my calls. Then there was Dan Schorr, who was still at ITNA. I knew what I paid him. I knew what CNN would pay him. I was sure I could get him, maybe. Dan wasn't sure about working for Ted. He was liberal, Ted was conservative; he was ponderous, Ted was flamboyant. But the job at CNN had a hell of a lot better future than ITNA. Schorr might wind up back in the big leagues.

Beforehand I worked out a deal with Dan's agent, Richard Liebner. I told Liebner I couldn't sign it, I wasn't even a CNN employee. He would have to conclude the agreement with Ted Turner. I called Ted, gave him Liebner's office and home numbers, and told him he would have to call Liebner to say yes. On Schorr's part, he wouldn't sign the deal before he met Ted Turner.

At 2 a.m. Sunday morning, the weekend before the Las Vegas convention, the phone rang at Liebner's house. He got out of bed, naked except for a T-shirt, and went downstairs to the kitchen. It was a boisterous Ted Turner, calling from somewhere down south. He told Liebner the deal was fine, and they would meet in Las Vegas to sign.

Schorr, a "CBS" newsman of the grand tradition, would not work for just anyone. He must approve his boss. He must have the right to resign if Ted Turner said anything publicly that would embarrass Dan Schorr. He must have the right to resign if Ted interfered with what Schorr wanted to say and what Schorr wanted to say was reasonable. Finally, Ted must agree that he would not ask Dan to do any commercials. It was an ego dance, which for once, Ted did not choose to join.

Schorr and I flew out to Vegas. Ted handled Schorr. He was modest. He would agree to Schorr's conditions. He told Schorr that in a few minutes, we would announce to the convention, that in one year—on June 1, 1980—Cable News Network will go on the air. "And I'd like you to be there with me." Properly flattered, Schorr agreed. Liebner wrote the "Schorr clause" into the contract. Dan and Ted signed the deal. It was the only contract I've ever seen where a guy could leave the company for something his boss said. Burt Reinhardt (my first CNN hire, and he's still there) always held the Schorr clause against Dan. After my departure, Schorr was not renewed.

At the convention, we walked up to the podium. Dan was there, I was there, and Ted was there. The press conference was packed. I had political balance. On the right, I had Ted Turner; on the left, I had Dan Schorr. I was in the crossfire. I talked about how we were going to cover the news, what "live" meant, where we were going to have our bureaus, and how many people we'd employ, and got ready to take the questions about how we could ever run a network with so few people.

Ted talked about the future, the satellite, and how he had signed Dan Schorr. He told the audience about our columnists: Joyce Brothers, Bella Abzug, Phyllis Schlafly, and Jean Dixon (the nationally known seer). He said that Dixon had predicted great success for CNN. Then he talked business.

He told the cable operators CNN's price would be fifteen cents per subscriber per month for any company carrying his Superstation. He'd said the same thing at the Western cable show, six months earlier; few had bought. This time, it was different; we were real. The room was electric. Potential customers swarmed around us. They believed something big was coming, and they wanted to be part of it.

Finally, Dan Schorr made his comments, his faith in us, his faith in the future of CNN. He said he was betting his reputation on Ted Turner and CNN. Ted said he was betting his fortune on CNN. I said I was betting my life on CNN. And I meant it.

Round 11: **Last One to Leave, Please Turn Out the Lights**

Ted is not famous for his patience. I couldn't get down to Atlanta until August 1, and Ted didn't want to wait. Neither did I. Who knew what that crazy bastard would do before I got there? Ted thought fast. He became an ITNA client. Now he could call me whenever he wanted, because he had ITNA business to talk about. He called a lot.

Burt Reinhardt, my old boss at UPITN, bailed me out. I'd talked to him about replacing me as head of ITNA. He was more interested in CNN. I hired him as executive vice president.

Burt joined CNN on July 1, to hold Ted's hand. Burt could be trusted. We'd worked together for eighteen years. I explained to him how CNN was going to operate—live, nonunion, a training ground for kids—and he got it right away. I hoped that he could keep Ted under control. Looking back, I see that figuring out how to keep your boss under control is a recipe for disaster.

Before I got to Atlanta, Ted had already put together an affiliate relations team and an advertising sales team. He'd even picked a logo. Somebody in Atlanta had the idea that twisting a piece of cable into the letters "CNN" would be the perfect symbol of our new business. Some folks thought it looked like snakes fucking, but I was stuck with it.

When we got our own art director, we put the snake in big block type background and it became the CNN icon. We did have a complaint from the Canadian National Railroad, who said we'd stolen their trademark. We told them that trademark infringement arises only in cases where there is a possibility for product confusion. It was unlikely that passengers on the Canadian National Railroad would book tickets on CNN.

Ted was still chafing, so I agreed to fly down to Atlanta to look for a place to live. While there, I'd see Burt and Ted. Ted walked me through the Progressive Club, an old red brick mock-mansion on Techwood Drive. White columns across the front porch reflected its pretensions: The newspapers called it "Turner's Tara." Ninety thousand square feet on twenty-one acres. The club was the former Russian-Jewish country club, located right in the middle of Atlanta, which had gone belly up after a Georgia attorney general banned slot machines from private clubs.

By 1979, it was a derelict building that had become a hangout for the homeless. The odor of stale sweat, stale butts, urine, pot, and whiskey hung over the basement. The basement, said Ted, will be for CNN. "Can you make it work?" Yes, I told him. The first floor, with its "ballroom studio," would go to the Superstation. The second floor would be occupied by Ted, me, and the other TBS executives.

We walked around the building, through the weeds; one side of the basement was above ground. I could break out the wall, install floor-to-ceiling glass windows, and get some light into the dungeon. I told Ted that the field we were walking in would be our satellite farm. Behind the window would be the CNN newsroom. We would shoot out of the newsroom at the satellite farm. It would be our signature shot. Ted nodded. In those days, there was almost nothing that Ted and I, together, couldn't make work.

Back in New York, I was scouting for talent. I tried to recruit my neighbor Tom Wolzien from NBC as head of operations. I talked to Ted Kavanau. Kavanau had been John Corporon's assistant when Corporon had started the ten o'clock news at Channel 5. After Corporon left, Kavanau took over. Kavanau was legendary. He carried a gun on his ankle. He fought with everybody in sight. He couldn't get along with his anchorman, and in the end he always quit his job or was fired on a "matter of principle." By 1979, he'd gone through four jobs and four bosses. He was out of work, living on a friend's couch and on whatever work I could give him at ITNA. I asked Kavanau about coming down to Atlanta, but he was working on the pilot of a Hollywood gossip show.

I met with Sam Zelman at CBS—he was someone I really wanted. I talked to Lou Young, the editor of *Business Week,* about using his magazine for our financial coverage. He was encouraging. Looking for inexpensive on-air talent, I met with Richard Liebner, the major news agent who represented Dan Rather and Dan Schorr. I talked to Fran Haney of WPIX about graphics. And I talked to Irv Rosner about equipment and engineering.

Rosner had been a CBS engineer in the great days of the Tiffany Network. Then he broke the network mold and designed and engineered PBS. I'd had a problem at ITNA. Client engineers complained about picture quality and sound levels. I brought in Rosner. He talked engineering talk to the engineers. He tweaked and he twisted. The quality improved, the other engineers shut up. Now I hired Rosner for CNN. He and I were equipping the studio even before Ted bought the Progressive Club.

When I was in Atlanta, Ted filled me in on what he was doing. I had dinner with Bill Gantley, the TBS advertising sales chief. I had meetings with Terry McGuirk, who was heading up the affiliate relations team. Ted had hired two guys who had been UPI salesmen, Roy Mehlman and Frank Beatty. They were not people I would have hired, but Ted couldn't wait, and they were now on Terry's staff.

August 1 finally came. I was free at last.

My wife, Pat O'Gorman, left CBS to accompany me. She would be in charge of our taping operation, one hundred people. At CBS she had edited four Peabody-winning documentaries. Her last job was editing Walter Cronkite's *Letters to CBS*.

Before she left, she had done CNN recruiting on CBS premises. She found the producer of our financial show, the executive producer of special projects, and a half dozen young kids who wanted in on CNN. The line was, "Will the last one leaving for CNN turn out the lights."

Round 12: **Dial-a-Prayer**

I'd been conned. Ted didn't have the money to do CNN.

Recruiting me, he'd boasted of his assets. He had the billboard company coining money. He had the Superstation already in the black and making more money every month. He had a television station in Charlotte that he'd just sold to Westinghouse for $23 or $24 million. He'd doubled his money in gold. He had $10 million in peat bogs in the ground on his plantation (Ted believed that oil prices were so high that peat would replace it for home heating). And he had a $30 million line of credit from First Chicago Bank. What he didn't tell me was he had no money.

When I first arrived at CNN, Will Sanders was the CFO of TBS. He'd had the job since 1970. Every time Ted needed money, Will found it for him. Bill Beckham, Will's assistant, says that when he got there in 1970, they had no money and no financial records to help raise money. Ted spent everything as soon as Will got it. Ted bought the Braves, bought the Hawks, the Atlanta NBA basketball franchise, bought the Charlotte television station; now he wanted to start CNN, and he still had no money. Beckham says, "Ted spent it all we got as soon as we got it."

Sanders thinks that the best thing he did for Ted was not to raise the money but to help Ted regain control of his company. While Will was there, Ted's ownership of TBS was reduced to less than 50 percent. When Ted wanted to buy WTBS, the board, then controlled by the majority stockholders, tried to block him. With Will's help, Ted acquired enough stock to turn the board around. Then Will slowly, over a period of time, managed to reacquire enough stock to get Ted back to an 80 percent ownership. He put the company back in Ted's hands, and that gave Ted the authority to run the company his way, even to start up CNN.

Will says that he gave away nothing of substance in exchange for the stock. Irwin Mazo confirms that in spades. Mazo sold his stock back to Ted for a $4,000 note. On the day Time Warner merged with AOL, Mazo computed the value of the stock that he had traded for $4,000. According to his calculations, it was $36 million.

Just as I was arriving at CNN, when Sanders was still CFO, First Chicago called in its loan to TBS. Ted had made a typical Ted speech in Chicago attended by some First Chicago executives. A combination of charm and attack, sometimes brilliant, sometimes incoherent. Afterwards, I learned that a senior First Chicago executive asked his loan officer, "Why are we backing this guy? He is a very peculiar person. Let us end this relationship." But the bank was very nice about it. The loan officer gave TBS a year to pay off the loan. By the time it came due, it was no longer Sanders's problem; Bill Bevins had come on board.

Bevins seemed very young and very serious. He had come from a Big Six accounting company. He wore black suits, white shirts, dark ties; his face seemed very white, and he wore big glasses. He might have been taken for a bean counter, but his intelligence demanded that he be taken very seriously. He was creative in funding, hardworking, and enormously disciplined at work. His private life was not disciplined. He drank too much, he smoked too much, but he was capable of performing magic. Keeping CNN alive required magic.

The $30 million owed to First Chicago was partially secured by Turner's contract of sale on the Charlotte station. It had been Sanders's idea to sell the station to Westinghouse. He had negotiated the deal, and the $23 million price was regarded as a very good price for Ted. It's one of the few deals in which Ted, through Will Sanders, outnegotiated the other side. Sanders calls Ted a "lazy negotiator." He'll pay whatever you ask if he thinks he needs it. If he thinks he doesn't need it, he won't even return your phone calls. Charlotte was Will's deal. The money he got Ted for the station was the money that was supposed to start CNN.

In 1979, the sale of television stations was regulated by the FCC. The seller had to get community approval. Ted's management in Charlotte had offended the black community. The NAACP fought the sale. Ted had to factor the contract just to bring some money to hand for CNN's start-up costs. Finally, he reached out to the opposing groups and agreed to donate several million dollars of the money received from Westinghouse to local community groups. We got the rest of the money ten months late and 10 percent short. In 1979, I was not wise enough to know that this was a problem. I thought Ted had all those other assets to cover us. I still believed in the gold and peat bogs.

I didn't realize how bad things really were until we were purchasing the electronic cameras for our news crews. Ikegami was the industry standard. Sony was bringing out a new lighter product. RCA was playing catch-up. It offered the "Hawkeye." The Hawkeye was cumbersome and awkward. Bevins said, "Please buy the Hawkeye." "Why?" I asked. "Because they'll give us a lease-purchase deal." So, we got to pay $500,000 over five years and our crews got to carry five extra pounds for five years.

Even without urging, I was frugal. We bought used furniture. We bought used tape stock from NBC for our tape library. When we covered the 1980 convention, I forced our Atlanta people to fly to Washington "hopscotch." Piedmont Airlines offered a considerable discount if we would fly to New York on one- or two-stop flights; the talent was unhappy.

By the time we got on air, almost all the cash was gone. Beckham recalls going into Bevins's office one day and telling him, "We got no money in the bank and I don't know what to do." Bevins said he knew what to do, and, without looking up the number, he punched in "Dial-a-Prayer." After a minute, Bevins hung up and said, "The line is busy." Later that week, Turner got a refund for taxes he never paid in the first place. It got the company through the next couple of weeks. Later—much later—Ted paid the money back.

Just before we launched, we got another gift from God. Bill Daniels, one of the great pioneers of the cable industry and owner of many cable systems, offered to lend Ted more than $10 million with a promise of more if needed. But the loan was convertible into stock, and Ted had learned the hard way what happens when you give up stock. He turned the offer down, and we remained impoverished.

To skip ahead of myself, in August, Ted called me in Washington. He was in Newport, Rhode Island, for the boat races, and his friends must've been telling him how good CNN was. He asked me what I was planning to do about money. I told him I planned to cut back. At that point, we'd already been on the air for ninety days, we'd made our first impression, and now was the time to save money. Ted said, "Don't do it. That's not your job. I'll find the money."

Round 13: **Getting the News**

On August 1, 1979, as I began work at CNN, its organization was composed entirely of two senior news executives, Reinhardt and me; one on-air reporter, Daniel Schorr; and a half dozen freelance columnists that Stan Berk, our Washington talent scout, had signed up. We had no anchors, no reporters, no studios, no bureaus, no technical equipment, no technicians, no system of coverage, no video lines, no wire services, and, most pressingly, no program schedule. It was all there in my head, but nothing was on paper.

The *Washington Post* was considering doing a twenty-four-hour cable news service. Joel Chaseman, the boss of the *Washington Post* television group, had created WINS New York, the first successful all-news radio station. He had called me at ITNA in March, after my first meeting with Ted but before Ted had committed to launch. He had talked to me about doing all-news television and asked me not to sign with anyone else until I heard from him. When Ted asked me to come to Atlanta, I called Chaseman. He was on vacation. I told his assistant to let him know that I had called and in his absence I was going to sign with Turner.

Obviously, the *Washington Post* did not regard me as irreplaceable. They had continued to study the twenty-four-hour news project, and Ted feared we might face competition even before we launched. But the *Post* had not yet decided. They had only a limited amount of money to invest in new ventures. Chaseman and the television division pushed for the twenty-four-hour news channel. The magazine division wanted to do a sports magazine. There was a major cable convention coming up, and Ted was at his competitive best. He wanted to influence Katharine Graham's decision. He would show her that CNN was well underway.

I designed a schedule, pretty much like the one with which we went on the air. We listed the bios and connections of the few people we had hired. We designed pretty color illustrations of studios that existed only in our minds. As I recall it, we did a map showing all our prospective bureaus, our land lines, our satellite links, and put the package into a handsome cover. We printed it on slick paper, took it to the cable show, and shoved it under the doors of the attendees. We shoved two or three copies under the door of Mrs. Graham's representative, Len Giarapputo.

When Giarapputo returned to Washington, he passed our package around. Mrs. Graham and the board were unduly impressed. They decided to go ahead with a sports magazine and forget the cable project. Ted had faked them out.

Next, I turned to news gathering. At ITNA, I had built a coverage system using Reuters or Worldwide Television News (WTN), the two competing video news agencies, for foreign coverage. I had also established a relationship with the European Broadcasting Union, which gave ITNA access to all video news shot by European broadcasters. For domestic news, I followed the Associated Press model, creating an ITNA Washington bureau and relying on coverage from the member stations. In cities where we didn't have members, ITNA would buy stories from network affiliated stations. Stories from Asia, funneled through WTN or Reuters, usually arrived a day late.

As I had used AP as a model for ITNA, I was going to use ITNA as the model for CNN.

In September, there was a meeting of the EBU in Berlin. Thanks to my friendship with Vittorio Boni, the EBU chairman, I'd retained my status as an associate member and was invited to the meeting. At a formal session, Vittorio and I explained what CNN was going to be and why it was worthy of associate membership in their organization. The consummate politician, Vittorio pushed our cause through the EBU board despite the objections of the American networks (who were also associate members and therefore, like ITNA, would have no vote) and the hard-line opposition of the BBC (who seemed to object to anything new as a matter of principle). CNN was in.

The meeting was also attended by Reuters television and WTN. I knew I would make a deal with one of them before I left Berlin, and it was going to depend on price. EBU had arranged a boat ride, and as we sailed around Berlin, I talked to Ken Coyte, president of WTN. Coyte and I had known each other at UPITN. When he was head of the European division of the company, I was head of the American side, and we both reported to Burt Reinhardt. At ITNA, I had originally used WTN as our foreign news source, but, as I've mentioned, it had been contaminated by the racist views of John McGoff, who had bought half the company using South African government money.

By now the McGoff connection to the South African government was known. ITN, the British commercial broadcast network, bought McGoff out, and my old friend Coyte was now in charge of the entire company. He did not want me to go back to Reuters. As we walked along the deck, looking out over the blue waters, it was as if, after twenty-five years in the business, we were finally going to have a chance to do something first-rate together.

With Reuters, we had launched the first daily news satellite from Europe to the United States. Thanks to our EBU membership, CNN was going to be able to bring in material from all the European broadcasters as well as from Reuters. The overseas feed was rich, much of the material was never shown on broadcast stations, and ITNA stations were able to develop a different style of newscast: more news from more places around the world.

Now, I told Ken Coyte that's what CNN wanted to do, but I also told him that CNN had very little money. Coyte knew that. I told him that if he could help us over the first two years, we would help him over the long haul. We agreed at a contract price: $50,000 for the first year and $75,000 for the second, as I recall. It was easily affordable, and we shook hands on it.

I had intended to speak to Reuters as well. At that price, I thought that I could afford both services. Before I got the chance, Nick Hutton, the sales head of Visnews, talked to Coyte. NBC was a partner in Visnews. My old rival, Bill Small of CBS fame, had just become head of news at NBC. Hutton told Coyte that Small had forbidden Visnews to do business with CNN. Hutton said, "Reese's all yours now, Ken. Put it to him good."

Coyte looked at Hutton and said, "You're too late Nick, Reese and I shook hands on a deal half an hour ago." To say Coyte was a man of his word is insufficient. He had us over a barrel, and he walked away. He contributed more to the success of CNN than many of those who worked there.

In addition to WTN and the EBU, CNN would open bureaus in London, Rome, and Jerusalem. Through Sir David Nicholas, I arranged an exchange agreement with ITN, the British commercial news network of which he was chairman. With all that, we had the Continent, and most of the rest of world, pretty well covered.

ITNA had originated a unique method of covering the United States: At a time when the big three networks were establishing bureaus around the country, ITNA was forced to rely on its member stations to cover their own areas. We had set up a news cooperative for ITNA stations: You cover your area for us, we'll cover the rest of the world for you. By and large it worked, but there were many areas where there were no ITNA stations. Our desk would call affiliate stations in those areas, offer to buy stories we needed, and tell them we would help them out wherever we could. Some stations said no, some said yes.

By the time I got to CNN, I knew what stations were likely to say yes. Surprisingly, those stations were usually the strongest in their market. They wanted access to as many news stories as they could get, and they were proud of having their stories shown nationally. They were also pleased that they could use us as a stick to beat their own networks.

This was the golden age of network arrogance. The network news shows did not want to share. It was in the interest of the producers of the Cronkite show or the Chancellor show that no one see national news until their show came on the air. They wanted local news to be purely local. When ITNA got national stories into the hands of local affiliates and the affiliates, whose shows ran earlier, beat the network news to the story, the network producers went nuts, but the better news directors were immensely pleased.

Imagine you're publishing a newspaper, and you're not permitted to carry a national story, no matter how important it is to your local audience. It is mind-boggling, and it is frustrating when your own network will not allow you to do your best. In those days, the networks acted in contempt of audience. It did not matter that they had a big story completed at 5 p.m. It did not matter that there was local news at 6 p.m.

The networks deliberately withheld material to preserve the ratings of their 7 p.m. news programs, thereby frustrating the audience and local news producers. To some extent, ITNA capitalized on that frustration, but for CNN, that frustration was the foundation of the best domestic coverage system on television.

Once I got to CNN, I called John Corporon, Bob Bennett, and Marty Haag. Corporon was the news director at WPIX New York, Bennett the president of WCVB in Boston, and Haag the news director at WFAA Dallas. WPIX was the ITNA flagship station in New York. WCVB and WFAA were ABC affiliates, and dominated news in their markets. Both stations had worked closely with ITNA. Each of them was very news smart. They understood that CNN would be, among other things, a twenty-four-hour news service that they could tape or use live in their news programs. (We did not permit them to use live stories outside of their scheduled news shows.)

I offered them exclusive market rights to CNN. They accepted immediately. Corporon, as an independent, had no problem publicly acknowledging his role as CNN's corresponding station. Haag wanted to keep it quiet. He was only a news director, not a general manager. Bennett, who owned a piece of his station, could afford to be less discreet.

When *Advertising Age* called to ask how CNN was going to get national coverage, I told the reporter about our corresponding stations, independents, and network affiliates. She believed independents might help us, but not network affiliates. Not only was WCVB an ABC affiliate, but Bob Bennett was the president of the ABC Network Affiliate Association. I suggested she call Bob.

Bob told her that WCVB would indeed be a corresponding station. She asked, "How can you do that? You're president of the ABC Affiliates." Bob said, "Because ABC doesn't run my fucking station, I run my fucking station." The reporter printed the quote, minus the "fucking," and it was as if CNN had hung out a neon sign. Once Bob went public, other network affiliates were quick to follow. Even before we went on the air, there were few holes in our national lineup.

Later, Bennett came down to CNN and visited Ted Turner at his plantation. I wasn't present, but the story comes directly from Bob. On the night of a visitor's arrival, Turner had a habit of asking his visitor to watch a tape of *Gone With the Wind*. When he asked Bennett to watch it, Bennett agreed.

Bob was silent until about ten minutes into the film, then he said, "Ted, I know you must hear this all the time, but the resemblance is so amazing that I just can't help myself. Every time he walks across the screen, I think it's you. I wanna say, 'Ted! Ted!'" Bennett paused, Ted beamed, and then Bennett said, "Ted, you're . . . Ashley Wilkes!" All weekend long, Bob called Ted "Ashley." If Bennett wasn't afraid to confront ABC, he certainly wasn't afraid to rib Ted Turner.

Next on my agenda was video transportation. That's a catchword now, but in 1980, the networks thought there was only one way to transport video, and that was AT&T. First, they would call AT&T and buy expensive land lines. Then they would call the local phone companies in the transmitting city and order a "local loop" to take the video signal from the local station and connect it with the AT&T land line. Sometimes the video couldn't be delivered, because the land lines were blocked or the loops were tied up on another feed. It was like getting a busy signal. CNN could not tolerate busy signals.

At ITNA, we'd found an alternative to AT&T. It was the Western Union satellite system. In 1975, I signed the second satellite contract ever signed by a U.S. company. It was the contract between ITNA and Western Union. We delivered our news service to our member stations over Western Union satellites. Occasionally, we used Western Union to bring stories back into our headquarters.

CNN, with its great appetite for news, needed a permanent connection between Atlanta and all its bureaus. What we needed was a Western Union video channel twenty-four hours a day, 365 days a year. They were abundant, because Western Union had made an unfortunate business decision: Western Union had built satellites with twelve video channels, while their competitor, RCA, had put twenty-four channels on theirs. It took one receive dish to watch one satellite. A cable system operator could receive twenty-four different program networks with one dish on the RCA satellite. He could receive only twelve from Western Union. Since he had to pay for his own satellite receive dishes, he got twice as much for his money on RCA. RCA became the sole source of cable programming; Western Union had lots of capacity and few customers.

When I visited Western Union, their response was cold. They had been snubbed so often by cable networks, they no longer trusted them. They believed we were out to get a good price from them so we could knock down RCA's rates. I had to explain it three times, first to the chief of satellite operations, then to the president of the Western Union Satellite company, and finally, to a vice president at the corporate level. I told them I really wanted to use Western Union. I was not going to send CNN to cable systems on Western Union; I was going to bring news stories from our bureaus back to CNN on Western Union. Finally, I found a phrase they understood: Western Union was going to be our "backhaul network." They glowed with excitement. Somebody was finally going to buy a Western Union transponder for cable use. Backhauling was something they could do.

But I wanted something in return. I wanted to co-locate all the CNN bureaus with the Western Union satellite uplinks. We would be in the same building with the Western Union uplink. We would run cable right from our bureaus, from our tape machines, up to the uplink. All our bureau would have to do to feed a story was call the CNN Atlanta satellite desk, tell them to roll tape, and press a button. In Atlanta, the story would be either fed live or held for later use.

From our first week, we could feed live from seven different cities in the U.S. instantaneously to a universe of millions of people. No third parties, no phone calls, no bookings, no lines, no loops, no busy signals. CNN was in control of its own video network.

It enabled news producers to operate with unprecedented flexibility. They would be freed from rigid rundowns; if they had the guts, they could produce entire programs on the fly. They might not be sure of what was coming next, but if they weren't sure, the audience wouldn't know either. And what's wrong with a little suspense?

CNN had bought one AT&T video line to connect Atlanta with New York via Washington. Before the line was installed, CNN had to guarantee AT&T $1 million a year for the next ten years to pay for the installation. The line had a problem. New York and Washington couldn't feed video at the same time. When New York fed, Washington went dark. When Washington fed, New York went dark. We had to be able to switch feeds instantaneously. AT&T and the local phone companies had to coordinate on switches, and using standard procedures it took five to ten minutes to do it.

I asked our AT&T representative, Paul Desjardines, to install a video switch in our Washington office. He said he could make it happen, and he did. By May 1, 1980, we had our own switch, the first client-controlled switch in AT&T history. It gave us control of our own network. We could get pictures from where we wanted whenever we wanted. Client-controlled switching has now become a business. There are switches in major cities around the world, and I'm happy to say that Paul Desjardines owns two of them.

CNN created its bureaus in every city where Western Union had an uplink—Chicago, San Francisco, Los Angeles, Dallas—in addition to our major transmission centers, Atlanta, Washington, and New York. For a CNN bureau to go on the air live, all it had to do was push a button, Atlanta would push another button, and the story would go out to the world. From day one, CNN's transmission system was more flexible than any system hitherto created. What that means to a news company is that it has immediate access to all the stories it has gathered everywhere.

In Asia, we created a bureau in Tokyo, and otherwise decided to rely on WTN. Then we got a break. The Washington Bureau of NHK, Japan's government-owned network, had heard about CNN. They offered to exchange their world coverage for our world coverage. Burt Reinhardt flew up to Washington and signed the deal. That was a mistake; he should have flown to Tokyo. We later learned to our regret that nothing counts in Japan unless the deal has a Tokyo seal.

With news coverage in place, I still had to bring in the wire services. UPI was easy. They asked for a fee, and we paid it. In those days UPI was a world-class news service, fully competitive with AP. AP was not easy. They demanded a fee per subscriber. They did not charge their newspapers a fee per subscriber. They did not charge their television or radio clients a fee per viewer or listener. I would not pay per subscriber.

The AP board held a meeting in Hawaii. Sam Zelman and I flew out there to make our case to the board. Katharine Graham was on the board, so was a Sulzberger and a Newhouse. The newspapers were demanding CNN pay a fee per subscriber. I was adamant. Finally, I rose pointing my finger at Mrs. Graham, and said in a polite voice, "CNN will pay per subscriber the day after Mrs. Graham pays per subscriber." I walked out of the room and subscribed to Reuters.

A year later, Brown Brothers Harriman sent me the offering book on UPI. Scripps Howard was putting the wire service up for sale, and they wanted to sell it to me. I didn't consider buying it. After all, I thought CNN was the future, UPI the past. What I didn't take into account was that Ted Turner owned the future. If I'd bought UPI, I'd have owned something, and it's always better being an owner.

The AP salesman in Atlanta had been wooing CNN ever since we went on the air. Every story we got first, every time we matched the other networks in our coverage, every time other news organizations had to quote us, it was proof that a first-class news organization could survive without AP. We were embarrassing them. The Atlanta salesman was so embarrassed that his price kept coming down, but he still insisted that we pay per subscriber. After seeing the UPI investment book, I decided I'd better take the deal with AP before UPI went out of business. I did. Getting the news was golden. But now I had to think about getting the people.

Round 14: **Getting the People**

I pride myself on making Burt Reinhardt my first CNN hire. When I called him, he was a vice president of Paramount Pictures. I've said repeatedly that Burt is the best day-to-day news executive I've ever known, and that statement still holds true.

When UPITN died, a little bit of Burt died with it. He was out of the news business, a business he loved as much as I did. Paramount Pictures, a co-owner of UPITN, brought him out to Hollywood, made him a vice president, and put him in charge of home video. When I called him initially about taking the ITNA job, he'd been away from news for four years, and he wanted back in. He came to Atlanta for less money than he'd been making at Paramount. He was a retread, but he had a lot of rubber left on him. As I mentioned, twenty years later, he's still at CNN doing heavy lifting for Ted Turner.

Next I needed a television operations guy. I got Jim Kitchell from NBC, but he was a weak second choice. I had tried to hire Tom Wolzien, who is now the media analyst at Sanford Bernstein & Co. Wolzien was a bright young guy, ready and willing to introduce new technology. He was Kitchell's assistant at NBC. NBC refused to release Wolzien from his contract, but he told me that they were ready to release Kitchell. I offered Kitchell the job. He took our offer back to NBC and tried to better it. They said good-bye. Wolzien was twenty years younger than Kitchell and had worked at local stations before joining NBC. Kitchell was dyed-in-the-wool network. To him, bigger was always better. Expensive was the right way to go, no matter how little money we had.

While interviewing Wolzien, I'd learned that "electronic graphics" were in the works—that's graphics that are made in a machine, not on a drawing board. I understood nothing about electronic graphics, except that they could be instantaneous and therefore would help CNN. NBC was a beta tester for the new technology. They were working with test models to improve the product. If CNN couldn't get Wolzien to teach us about them, I thought I needed a Kitchell, so I hired him.

Sam Zelman was next, as vice president for news. Really, he was the executive producer of the whole network. He had been a CBS network producer, writer, and executive for twenty-five years. Then he made a bad decision. He became a local news director at Channel 7, WJLA, in Washington. The life of a local news director can be short, and Sam was out after a few years. He went back to CBS, and this time he worked in the Stations Division, where he reviewed the news performance of the CBS-owned and -operated television stations. Additionally, he was the chief talent scout for the O&Os.

Zelman's eye for talent was legendary. He may have been on the sidelines at CBS, but for CNN he was a starting player. He chose most of the network's on-air broadcasters; a half dozen of them are still anchoring there. He too was a retread, but that was CBS's mistake.

Ted Turner found us our financial vice president, whose name I will not reveal, in order to protect the guilty. He had been a TBS financial guy for some time, and Ted thought he would work well with Burt and me. We thought so too and brought him over. At about that time, somebody at TBS began to wonder how he was able to afford a Mercedes. Shortly afterwards, he was dismissed.

Then I discovered that CNN needed a vice president for sports, a position originally unbudgeted. ITNA had been able to pick sports stories live off the satellite. We asked to record ball games for news use. The teams thought it was good PR, and permission was readily granted. I counted on doing the same for CNN, but permission was tough to get. Despite owning the Braves and Hawks, Ted was not universally loved by his sports brethren.

I thought of Bill MacPhail. Bill had been head of sports at CBS for many years. He put the Olympic Games on television—CBS of course. He put the NFL on network television—CBS again. Under MacPhail, CBS had the rights to racing's Triple Crown, major golf tournaments, especially the Masters, the basketball championships, and just about everything except the World Series.

MacPhail was the scion of one of America's great sports families: His father had invented night baseball, and later owned the Yankees, his brother was president of the American League, his nephew is now CEO of the Chicago Cubs. Even more valuable was MacPhail's connection to NFL Commissioner Pete Rozelle. He'd been best man at Pete's wedding. Together, they had brought about the marriage of professional football and television.

Drinking was part of the culture of CBS sports. Finally, it got to Bill. He went through rehab, entering as the nicest man in sports and emerging sober and still the nicest man in sports. I had known him since the beginning of ITNA, when he had helped us in our negotiations for satellite time with Western Union. Now, I needed him desperately. He arrived, solved our sports rights problems with a half dozen phone calls, and went on to run the sports department at CNN for fifteen years. It was the happiest department at the network.

We hired Alec Nagle as senior news producer. When Ted Kavanau declined to come down to Atlanta, he recommended Nagle. Ted knew Nagle from San Francisco, where Alec had worked as an executive producer at KGO, the ABC station, while Ted was news director at KTVU. KGO was an ABC-owned station, and it did its share of tabloid journalism. Nagle had gone to Dartmouth, as had I. An Ivy Leaguer who had turned tabloid was perfect for CNN. At KGO, Nagle, not yet forty, had suffered a heart attack. He was a health rehab, but he was eager to come to CNN, even though he knew the stress would be much greater.

Then Kavanau came back needing a job. His syndication show had failed. He was in New York, down and out, jobless and homeless. He said I had promised him a job. I hadn't. Now the jobs I had wanted him for were filled. Sam Zelman had one, and Alec Nagle had the other. But Kavanau's drive and energy, his news instincts, although tabloid, were so valuable that I created a position for him and named him another senior news producer.

And then there was Dan Schorr. He was famously a CBS reject. After working there for more than twenty years, overseas and in Washington, he'd run afoul of his bosses and his fellow workers. Schorr had gotten hold of a classified report of a House of Representatives intelligence committee. He wanted CBS to produce a one-hour documentary based on it. CBS declined. The material then turned up in the *Village Voice* and Schorr was suspected of leaking it. When questioned about it, Schorr was at first evasive, suggesting that the material might have been leaked by Leslie Stahl, who was dating Aaron Latham (they are now married). Schorr finally admitted that it was he who had given the material to the *Voice*.

Schorr's actions offended his bosses and infuriated his co-workers. They thought he was a misleading snitch. Schorr settled his contract and went off on a career as a luncheon speaker, which is where I found him at ITNA. Despite all this, he was perfect for CNN. He was one of the most intelligent newsmen in America. He had great contacts and was a superb reporter. You can still hear him every weekend on NPR, where he has more listeners than CNN has viewers.

Earlier on, we had picked up Jim Rutledge. He was assistant news director at WSB Atlanta, one of the few guys with a job and a future who actually came over to CNN. We needed somebody local, and Jim was it. He was to run the assignment desk. Jim's instincts were pure CNN. As assignment desk chief, he coined the phrase, "Can't means won't, and we will." He still glories in the battle. He says, "We were outmanned, outgunned, outfinanced, and we put up with a lot of crap, but we won our share, and it was still my greatest time in journalism."

The last senior hire was Ed Turner (no relation). Ed had been news director at Channel 5 Washington, doing the ten o'clock news. He'd lost that job. He'd come to work for us at UPITN when we were battling TVN, the Coors news service. When we lost, Ed went to CBS for a year or two. Then he was a news director for an Oklahoma television station.

Ed's handicap was alcohol. From the Oklahoma television station, he'd gone into rehab, reemerging in the winter of 1979/80. He was a great writer, but we did not need great writers. He was smooth with PR, but Ted Turner was the best PR attraction in America. There was no slot for him at CNN. Ted Kavanau and Stan Berk, who had both worked with him, went to bat for him. They asked me to help him get back on his feet. They mentioned "mitzvah." They said I'd be doing a blessing that would help get me into heaven. I hired him at a middling salary and put him in charge of the bureaus, all the while hoping that he would shortly find work as a local news director. It did not work out that way.

Round 15: **Piece by Piece**

Orson Welles said that when he went to Hollywood to make *Citizen Kane,* there was a world of new technology awaiting him. For a generation, the best ideas of craftsmen and engineers were being ignored by the studios. Hollywood was not ready for change. The same was true of television when I went down to Atlanta to do CNN.

In 1979, the television networks were still doing their news shows from enormous studios, with big control rooms, lines of film chains, rows of tape machines, audio booths, huge lighting grids, and dozens of studio technicians, all for the sole purpose of sitting one man behind one desk for one half hour a day, on the air. I had been to Canada, and I had seen Global, Canada's maverick network, put three anchors on the air from within the newsroom. They were shooting against a flat wall. I planned to turn that around and show the anchors sitting in front of the newsroom. And I was going to take it one step further. I was going to put the control room on the studio floor.

Tape was replacing film in the broadcast industry by 1979, but half the local stations were still using celluloid. Hell, all the stations and the networks were still using typewriters. For the previous six months, I had been advising Arbitron, the broadcast rating service that competed with Nielsen, on how to build a computerized newsroom.

Almost all of television was doing graphics by hand, but NBC had begun testing electronic graphics, and we had Kitchell to teach us about that. When it came to video transportation, AT&T and the local Bell companies still controlled all but six hubs in the United States. Within a year, we would change that.

I had no concerns about finding people to work for CNN. In 1980, half the kids in America wanted to work in television. I had no worry about unions, either. Atlanta was an open-shop city, and Ted had been running TBS nonunion for ten years. ITNA had proved that CNN would be able to contract out its technical jobs in all the bureaus, including, especially, New York and Washington. We hired our own editorial people, but I did not fear AFTRA (the American Federation of Television and Radio Artists) or the Writers' Guild. There were too many potential anchors, reporters, and writers who would work nonunion, and AFTRA tolerated it so long as their members who worked for us paid their union dues. Nationwide we were a nonunion shop.

I arrived at CNN in August to discover that Gene Wright, the TBS chief engineer, had already ordered two film chains, which cost $500,000 each. I canceled the order.

"How will you put film on the air?" asked Gene.

"I'm only going to put tape on the air," I said. "We're going to have only tape cameras, and we'll edit on tape."

Gene asked, "What will happen if you get a story on film from a local station?" I asked Gene if WTBS had a film chain.

"Yes," said Gene.

"I'll borrow yours," said I.

I engaged Irv Rosner, who had helped me at ITNA. He had credentials that Gene Wright would respect, and I knew from ITNA that Irv would order only what was necessary, but he would not cut corners.

At first, Gene was uneasy with Irv; he didn't want to run his schematics past another engineer before I would approve them. As time went on, Gene became more comfortable with Irv, and I became more comfortable with Gene. I watched him take joy in doing things the most efficient way. We had only one more battle, over generators. Gene was concerned about a power failure. I came from New York, where, with the exception of the blackouts of 1965 and 1977, the power never failed.

I was willing to take my chances, but Gene told me I didn't know Southern Power and Light. I said we had a backup, since we could always run our network out of our bureaus in Washington or New York. Gene persisted, found a small generator that cost only $85,000, but would light only half the studio. I said, "What the hell," and bought it. Gene was right about Southern Power and Light. We had to use the generator three times in two years. Later, CNN's competitor, Satellite News Channel (SNC), bought two generators at a million dollars each, but then SNC was half-owned by Westinghouse, and Westinghouse made the generators.

When we turned to a computerized newsroom, I called my old friends at Arbitron. Burt Reinhardt and I met them at the RTNDA (Radio Television News Directors Association) meeting in Vegas in September. Since I had worked with them, and they were designing their system to my specs, it was an easy negotiation. Burt Reinhardt was with me. We told them we'd let them use our newsroom as a pilot plant, and we'd pay hardware costs. We shook hands. Burt was going to sign a deal with them the next day.

The next day, they didn't want the deal. Someone from CBS had blown smoke up their skirts and said, "You want to do this with CBS. You want Walter Cronkite up there using your computers." Sure they did. What the CBS guy forgot to tell him was that CBS was a bureaucracy and nobody in the room had the authority to sign off on the deal.

Burt went down to the convention floor and found a couple of young guys who had designed a computerized newsroom for the CBS radio station in San Francisco. He watched it work, called me over, and I did a deal on the spot. They spent ten months working in our newsroom and had the system almost finished on the day we went on the air. When it was ready, it worked. It was branded Basys, and became standard equipment for television newsrooms all over the world.

Kitchell handled graphics technology. Before the new machines were available, it would have taken dozens of artists drawing, cutting, and pasting onto black cardboards to provide an adequate illustration for a twenty-four-hour news network. Now, working with the same company that Kitchell had been using at NBC, all we had to do was press two buttons, and we had graphics on the air. In April of 1982, Les Midgley, who had been Walter Cronkite's producer at CBS, came to visit us. He was now retired and looking for part-time work. As I toured the newsroom with him, I heard the anchors say, "We'll be back in a moment with the latest 'cost of living' figures." We walked over to the graphics camera, I pulled my wallet out of my pocket and arranged the dollars within the wallet in a fan. I put the fan under the graphics camera.

We walked back to the control room switcher. The T.D. pressed a button. A wallet with five one dollar bills arranged in a fan was on his monitor. The commercial was ending. We came back to the anchor. He said, "And now for the 'cost of living.'" In a box, over his left shoulder, was my wallet and five dollars, with the words "cost of living" superimposed. Midgeley was impressed. He agreed to come down and work for CNN four days a week, but I was gone before the deal was finalized.

CNN also applied for a microwave frequency in Washington so we could feed our reporters live from the White House, Congress, or the State Department to our bureau. Each of the networks had one. A microwave frequency is a radio circuit in a special frequency that only the FCC can license. The FCC told us that frequencies were not granted to networks, only to local television stations. NBC had a local station in Washington, but CBS and ABC did not. I asked Bill Henry, CNN's lawyer and a former FCC chairman, "How did CBS and ABC get their frequencies?" It turned out that CBS held its frequency in the name of WCAU, its Philadelphia O&O (owned and operated station), and ABC held its frequency in the name of WABC New York. I said, "Why can't we get ours in the name of WTBS Atlanta?"

The FCC thought that Atlanta might be a little bit far away from Washington. Bill Henry said that when it came to microwave, New York wasn't any closer. If we didn't deserve a frequency, neither did ABC. We had a meeting in Washington. The three networks were present. NBC objected to our request. ABC and CBS supported us. They were afraid of losing their licenses. We won 3 to 1. At ITNA, I had always been outvoted. Now, we had forced two of the networks to come over to our side.

Round 16: **Grab 'Em by the Eyeballs**

At the networks, scheduling is a fine art. At CNN, it was a piece of cake. The method to our madness was "counterprogramming."

Counterprogramming is like painting by the numbers. What you do is study the network schedules and the independent station schedules. Whatever they're doing, you do something else. If they're going to start news at 7 a.m., CNN will start news at 6. If they're going to have their national news at 7 p.m. and local news at 10 or 11 p.m., we'll counter with business news at 7, news call-in at 10, and sports at 11 p.m. We'll do our main news program (*Prime News 120*) from 8 to 10 p.m., when nobody else is doing news at all. CNN will overcome a thirty-year habit by offering the audience a choice.

Counterprogramming is about zigging when they zag. When they do entertainment, you do news. When they do news, you do financial news, or sports news, or news talk. Metromedia proved it works.

In 1967, when Channel 5 New York introduced *News at Ten,* I didn't think it would work. I couldn't imagine Americans abandoning entertainment to watch news. But I was young. I didn't realize that there were viewers who'd want to go to bed at 10:30 instead of 11:30, and they might wanna watch today's news and tomorrow's weather before they went to sleep. *News at Ten* was a quick hit. It got great ratings: nines and tens. Independent stations in other major cities copied Metromedia. I learned there was always somebody out there who, for whatever reason, would watch news if it was available.

I was an early riser. I wanted to watch news at 6 a.m. There wasn't any. From day one, I knew CNN would begin its news day at 6 a.m. I also knew that CNN would do news overnight. Nobody did news overnight, but 4 a.m. New York time was only 1 a.m. on the West Coast. And a lot of people wanted to watch news after they saw the *Tonight Show.* When Ted, who was not a news watcher himself, saw the schedule, he said, "People are going to watch news at 6 a.m.? People are going to watch news overnight?"

"Yes," I said. Ted shook his head and left the room.

CNN offered four different kinds of news: hard news, financial news, sports news, and news talk. We tossed in a bit of soft news and hoped for a lot of live news, because our strategy called for unpredictability. News is very often dull. Particularly if people are telling you all day what's coming, hyping the hell out of it, and then disappointing you with the actuality. Every time I hear "coming up at eleven," I want to shout, "If you know what's coming up, and it's so damned important, tell me now."

The unpredictable is never dull. If CNN could become a network that seemed to be "advancing the news" every minute, telling or showing a story you had never known before, or adding a fact to a story that you had heard about, or providing insight into a story that you knew about but had never thought about that way, viewers wouldn't switch from

CNN. Even if CNN didn't do it all the time, even if CNN did it just often enough to make viewers afraid they might miss the event of a lifetime, we'd have 'em by the eyeballs.

News stories occur randomly. It was CNN's mission to present live, random news as it occurred, without attempting to force a relationship between one story and the next. *Prime News 120* represented our two-hour attempt to put some perspective on this randomness.

The recognition of "randomonium" (as Frank Zappa called it) makes CNN a better business. The best way to keep viewers interested is to keep them guessing about what's happening next. At a commercial break anchors say, "Coming up next." I think it's a hell of a lot more effective to say, "I don't know what's coming next. Let's all find out together." CNN was designed to bring in fresh news from all over the world, all the time. I wanted the producers to grab news on the fly, to build their news shows while they're on the air. I wasn't concerned about technical glitches or a temporarily confused anchor. I wanted constant flow. I never got it while I was there, and after I left nobody tried.

The basic framework was simple. In 1980 there were only three networks and a dozen or so independent stations doing news. Since the nets ran their flagship news at 7 p.m., I scheduled *Moneyline,* our financial news show, for 7 p.m. We went upscale as the networks went after a general audience.

The networks did soft morning talk shows with some news inserts at 7 a.m. CNN would do hard news at 6 a.m., financial at 6:30, and at 7 a.m. would begin an hourly rotation that lasted until noon, when Don Farmer and Chris Curle present *Take Two,* a soft news show targeting women at lunchtime. From 2 to 6 p.m., we'd resumed an hourly rotation, from 6 to 7 p.m. we ran *Early Prime,* a complete hard news roundup, trying to scoop the networks by showing, in depth, stories that they were going to report on an hour later. Then we went to *Moneyline,* where it was going to be Lou Dobbs and Dan Dorfman against Walter Cronkite, Peter Jennings, et al.

We did sports at 7:30 p.m., when most television stations ran soft magazine shows. Sports were important because although in 1979 fewer than 20 million U.S. homes had cable, all the bars did. Live professional games went on television at 8 p.m. so I wanted to feature the latest odds and other "inside" information on our 7:30 show. Gamblers gather in bars and want the latest information before they put their money down. I thought if we could give them that, every bar in America would be tuned to *CNN Sports* at 7:30.

In 1980, after I announced my schedule, some baseball teams announced they were going to start their ballgames at 7:30. I ran into my first fight with Ted Turner. I flipped *CNN Sports* and *Moneyline:* sports at 7, finance at 7:30.

Ted said, "You can't do that Reese, we've sold out our financial show at 7 p.m. The advertisers expect it at seven." I tried to explain to Ted about the change in the baseball schedule, but he wasn't interested. He'd made the schedule change a money issue, and since he was boss of the money, we would have to do things his way.

Eight months later, when we were about to go on the air, a *Washington Post* reporter was researching her opening-day story. Ted told her that we were going to give tips and odds on our sports show. I told her that we weren't going to, because bookies don't take bets after the game starts. Maybe Ted finally understood what I was talking about.

Eight to 10 p.m. was our flagship show, *Prime News 120.* We had no competition. But at 10 p.m. the local stations, my old ITNA group, carried local news; they averaged 6 or 7 rating points. Since I didn't want to go head-to-head with them, we invented the first national news/talk call-in show, which we later called *Freeman Reports.*

At 11 p.m. we would do sports, countering all the local news shows. By then we would have the scores in and tape of all the games. We would obsolete the sports sections in the next day's papers. At 11:30 we did a financial recap, mostly for the West Coast. Midnight to 1 a.m. was our final heavy-effort news hour, and then we went to *People Tonight.*

People Tonight was going to be the entertainment gossip hour. It was live from Hollywood at 1 a.m. We would have a reporter in New York and a reporter in Washington. In New York we'd also have a reviewer to report on Broadway and films, and in Washington we'd cover the social scene, which I'd always thought was vastly undercovered. It may be just as important to know which senators are out drinking with each other as to know what they're saying to each other on the floor of the Senate.

From 2 to 2:30 a.m. we did *Sports Final,* which included West Coast scores. At 2:30, we began a repeat cycle that included our last news hour, our news talk show, *People Tonight,* and *Sports Final.* We kept a live anchor at the desk for breaking news, and we called the bloc *Hawaii Prime Time.* I hated the repeat cycle, but we didn't have the money to go the full twenty-four live. At 6 a.m. it all started over.

Round 17: "Never Tell Me Anything You Don't Want the Whole World to Know"

"**T**alent," that's what we call people who put their face on the air. Talent is what they're supposed to have. Sam Zelman knew everybody who claimed to be talent in every city from Glendive, Montana, to New York. Once word got out about what CNN was doing, we got tapes from all of them. Sam judged talent on television appeal. I judged it on news intelligence. It was rare that we got both.

I originally planned on single anchors, mostly male, mostly from the networks, who knew a lot about the news and had worked in the field. Every reporter dreams of becoming an anchorman. I thought we'd have lots of candidates. We got a few, Bernie Shaw, Bill Zimmerman, and Don Farmer, all from ABC, which was not a happy place at that time. Roone Arledge had just taken over and everyone feared for his job.

Zelman suggested that an hour was an awfully long time for one face to be on the screen. His years in local news suggested to him that female anchors might work as well as men. He thought we ought to fish in local waters. There was a big difficulty. By and large, local anchors are not as smart as network reporters. If we hired them, we would sacrifice news intelligence for on-screen charisma. I compromised with Sam, and we hired some of each.

I accepted Sam's recommendations about dual anchors. The budget automatically went up. We had twice as many faces on screen as we'd budgeted for.

I wholeheartedly accepted Sam's recommendation about female anchors. It's easier to hire from a group that has been discriminated against. By and large, the tapes we got from female anchors were superior to those from the male candidates. Women were having a harder time making their way up the ladder.

At this point, I was really working for Sam Zelman. He would point me in a direction, I would try to sign the talent, and when I couldn't, Sam would point me somewhere else. For *Take Two,* the noon show, Sam wanted Natalie Jacobson and Chet Curtis, her husband. They were the dominant anchor team in Boston. Natalie is one of a kind. Her news intelligence is obvious, but she never flaunts it. She's superior without ever making her audience feel inferior. For once, it was the male who played the perfect sidekick, and Curtis was good at it. There was probably no better team to host a two-hour hard news/soft news noon program. Chet seemed interested; Natalie was not. The sidekick never wins.

Sam had known Chris Curle, a local anchorwoman in Washington, when he worked at WJLA. She, too, was smart, warm, and lovely. She was married to Don Farmer, a solid ABC reporter who covered the Senate for the network. Sam brought them down to Atlanta, and they signed up. Sam did the selling job. Sam thought Chris was a star; Don could be her sidekick. Unfortunately, Don didn't agree, and *Take Two,* although it did some of the most interesting things on the network, never really took off.

Sam also found and signed Dave Walker and Lois Hart out of Florida. They were easy to take. It was one of the few times when four men—Sam, Burt, Ted Kavanau, and I—needed only thirty seconds of tape before we knew we'd make them an offer. Sam did, and they accepted. Their style was laid-back, but when the occasion demanded, Lois could deliver a hard edge and Dave a sense of urgency. They knew news and they played well off each other. We could put them anywhere on the schedule, and they would keep their audience.

Then came the women. Kathleen Sullivan, Marcia Ladendorff, Reynelda Muse, and Denise LeClair. Sullivan was Sam's find. She was working at the third-ranking station in Salt Lake City, and she was being stalked. For one reason or the other, she had to get out of town. After she got on CNN, every man in America loved Sullivan, but I loved her from the beginning. She combined intelligence, sauciness, and vulnerability. She showed them all on the air. Although she was not yet a "newswoman," she wanted to be and was willing to work hard at it.

Ladendorff had been on Sam's wish list from day one. He wanted her or Sullivan to coanchor *Prime News 120.* He'd approached them both. Sullivan accepted; Ladendorff hesitated, but as CNN buzz grew, she decided she wanted to be part of it. We used her to fill the five to seven slot; tops on looks, okay-plus at news.

In television news, weekends are always a pain in the ass. Nobody wants to work them, news never happens, the producers are lightweights, and the talent is usually the bottom of the barrel. Except at CNN. Twenty-four-seven permits no down time. It's got to be ready to roll whenever. Try getting a number one anchorman to sign away fifty-two weekends a year. Once again CNN got lucky. We found Denise LeClair. Denise was a throw-in. We had hired Guy Pepper out of Providence as our senior director, and she was anchoring at his station. They'd been dating. She loved the idea of CNN, and she was a very good anchor. Also, she liked Guy so much that she took a weekend shift.

Sam knew that Reynelda Muse, a black woman and the best anchor in Denver, wanted to work weekends. She had two kids and was working Monday through Friday, the early and late news at the CBS affiliate. If she worked weekends, she'd have a chance to see her kids and still do television. We agreed to fly her from Denver to Atlanta every weekend. On the weekends, she ran her own programs, checking out every story the producers gave her. It was like having a weekend managing editor in the newsroom. "It was a personal challenge like no other," says Reynelda. "Anchoring and reporting combined. No slickly packaged thirty-minute news cast that the anchor simply reads. At CNN, you were all the way live, and if news happened on your watch, you had better be ready to fly with it. Better remember what you learned in Econ 101 or History 460, because there was no time to leave the set to do research. You had to suck it up from your gut, and come up with a question to ask the person on the phone or the interviewee on the satellite screen. It was exhilarating and terrifying at the same time. . . . And like Dorothy and Kansas, I knew I wasn't in Denver anymore."

Reynelda was the first black woman to anchor on CNN. During the next two years, we hired three more black women of enormous talent: Pat Harvey, Beverly Williams, and Roz Abrams. Each one of them went on to become a longtime anchor in a major market: Roz in New York, Pat in Chicago, and Bev in Philadelphia. Black female anchors were not standard procedure in 1980. Reynelda Muse writes, "I think research will bear out that no other network was offering that kind of opportunity and exposure at the time."

I hired three CNN regulars against Sam's advice: Bernie Shaw, Bill Zimmerman, and Mary Alice Williams. Sam thought Bernie was dull, Bill dour, and Mary Alice cold. He was probably right, but I signed them all anyway and have never regretted it. We weren't casting some eleven o'clock local news show. We were staffing 24-7. There was room for people who neither sparkled nor gushed. Shaw, Zimmerman, and Williams may not have sparkled, but they had news smarts, and dull, dour, or cold, they projected intelligence and confidence on air.

When CNN launched, I thought we had only five reporters able to go live from any event: Shaw, Zimmerman, Williams, Don Farmer, and Dan Schorr. I was scared every time I saw anybody else with a mike and no script. Within days of launch, I found out that two junior reporters, Mike Boettcher and Jim Miklaszewski, were born to do live. Within months, I learned Lou Dobbs could do anything and everybody else was a crapshoot, except Reynelda, and she worked only on weekends.

CNN needed reporter/anchors. In conventional television, that term applies to people who "report" three days a week and anchor on weekends. At CNN, reporter/anchors had to do both jobs at the same time. Traditionally, journalists reported only events at which they were present, but television had worked out a system in which anchors reported stories that occurred thousands of miles away from them. CNN was going to change that. If we didn't have a reporter at the event, the satellite would bring the event to us. Our anchor had to report the story on the fly, watching it live in the studio. That required general knowledge, quick wit, and a sure instinct.

Mary Alice Williams was good at it. After leaving CNN, she went to NBC. On occasion she would sit out of sight under the anchor desk when Jane Pauley was anchoring. Jane is a great anchor/reader so long as the news follows the script. If unexpected developments occurred, Jane was supposed to slip out of her seat and turn it over to Mary Alice. Mary Alice said that she would then "report" the breaking news.

I paired Bill Zimmerman with Kathleen Sullivan for *Prime News 120*. It was sweet and sour and it worked. She may have been the star, but he was no sidekick. She genuinely looked up to him. He genuinely liked her. On camera one-upping was done in good spirit. Instead of phony camaraderie, genuine friendship. He could scoff, she could sting; it was a joy to see them work together. It was also a bonus to discover how funny Kathleen could be.

Bernie Shaw became our Washington anchor, and for twenty years he's been the spine of CNN's Washington bureau. I thought Bernie could become Walter Cronkite if he were not so stiff. He had Cronkite's measured delivery and authority. What he did not have was Cronkite's folksiness. If I had stayed at CNN, I would have worked on that. I thought it was a fault of Bernie's blackness. I thought that Bernie was worried about being seen as "folksy" by the white world. I appreciate that concern. Even now that may be a risk, but still I think that Bernie could have managed it and become Cronkite, loved as well as respected.

While we trolled for anchors, we also searched for specialty reporters. Stan Berk found us a veterinarian, and we did a pets insert. Steve Kritsick was his name, and he was considered gorgeous. He became our first male sex symbol, and the pet show was a hit. In Dallas, we found an MD to do our Bristol-Myers's medical reports. Later, Chris Chase came to us through Jimmy Griffin at the William Morris Agency. She'd been doing essays on the CBS *Morning Show,* but nobody likes to get up at four o'clock every morning. Meanwhile, I was searching for a fashion reporter.

Ted Turner sent me a candidate. Ted rarely sent anybody to see me, but if it was a woman, I expected the worst. Generally, I had been right. In this case, I was wrong. Kay Delaney worked in the fashion industry. She was tall, elegant, handsome, and smart. She taped designer collections and distributed them to the media. She was a friend of the people who ran Rich's, Atlanta's most important department store. Rich was a major advertiser on WTBS, so Ted sent Kay over to see me.

I had scheduled a style show for weekends, and Kay had everything I wanted for the program except broadcast experience. I asked her about that, and she said, "I've got as much broadcast experience as anybody, except maybe Elsa Klensch." I asked her who Klensch was. She said that Klensch was the fashion correspondent for the *New York Post* and had done on-air work at WCBS during the New York newspaper strike. Elsa should've made Kay her agent.

As soon as Kay left my office, I called Mike Kandel, whom I had just hired away from the *New York Post* to be managing editor of CNN financial. Mike knew Elsa from the *Post;* I asked him to talk with her about CNN. We set up an interview in New York, I offered her the job, talked money briefly and successfully, and walked away with *Style with Elsa Klensch,* already staffed and titled. Elsa had only one stipulation. Her boss was away and would not be back until Monday. She asked me to hold off any announcement until she had a chance to tell him.

Ted was in New York doing PR, and I met him for lunch. He asked what I had done that morning. I told him that I'd hired Elsa Klench, who she was, and what the show would be. I told him that we couldn't announce it until the next week. Of course, as is seemingly inevitable, his afternoon interview was with *Women's Wear Daily,* the only paper in the world where Elsa Klensch was front-page news. And of course, Ted told all. It was headlines. Elsa was angry and embarrassed. I was just embarrassed. I reminded Ted that I had told him to keep it quiet. He said, "Never tell me anything you don't want the whole world to know."

Round 18: **Living in a Fish Bowl**

After my lunch with Ted, I set out to find a suitable address for what I hoped would become television's leading source of financial information, our New York bureau. New York was the financial capital of the world. We had to be there. We had to be there in the right building, and I discovered the "fish bowl."

The World Trade Center was one of New York's most prestigious buildings, and its mall was one of New York's most traveled thoroughfares. Within it, standing vacant, was the perfect Wall Street television studio. In the lobby, opposite the main bank of the World Trade Center elevators, there was a forty-foot-wide parabolic glass window. The space was about thirty feet deep, and in the center of its back wall was a map of the world, Mercator projection, formed in lights, against a black background.

The workspace included a small balcony for executive offices, first-floor storage space that we could turn into editing suites, a large area in the foreground that would be the newsroom, and room for a couple of cameras that would point at an anchor desk against the back wall with the lit map of the world for a backdrop. Of course, we could turn the cameras around and show crowds gathering outside the windows to watch what was going on inside. Thousands of people stopped and stared everyday. They quickly learned that when the lights went on, the bureau was live, and their faces might be on the air. But there was a risk. Sometimes we got more than faces. This was New York, and a lot of people gave us the finger or grabbed their crotches. We didn't worry; this was live television.

We might not have gotten the space were it not for John Tillman. Tillman had been an anchorman at WPIX for twenty years. Now he was head of public relations for the Port Authority, and the Port Authority owned the World Trade Center. Tillman understood the public relations value of hosting a live television network. He carried the ball through the Port Authority bureaucracy, and in New York, where everything is "location, location, location," CNN had a great "location."

Years later, CNN left the World Trade Center to move to Eighth Avenue in the thirties; from the heart of the financial district to the outskirts of the garment district. I thought of it as a metaphor: CNN was dropping in class. Mary Alice Williams, who made the decision to move to Thirty-fourth Street, thinks differently. She remembers water rats running around the floors of the World Trade Center. There were no rats uptown. Of course Mary Alice may be prejudiced—the move uptown saved her life. In 1993, when terrorists blew up part of the World Trade Center, half the building came crashing down right on the spot the CNN bureau used to stand. After the explosion, Ted Turner called Mary Alice and congratulated her on the smart move.

I found Mary Alice as a quid pro quo for Dan Rather. I thought I had been gypped, but it turned out I got the better end of the deal. In 1980, the papers were full of news about the "the anchor wars." Walter Cronkite was due to retire. Who would succeed him, Dan Rather or

Roger Mudd? Mudd seemed to be the favorite, but Rather had a standing offer from ABC, and his contract was coming up for renewal. My old friend Richard Liebner, Rather's agent, told CBS that Rather would not renew unless he was promised Cronkite's job. CBS was forced to make a decision before it was ready.

The controversy about television news dominated the news in general, and Ted Turner heard about it. Ted has a good memory. He recalled that in September of 1979, I had told him that Rather was the guy who could be CNN's star. He asked me to try and get him. "It's too late," I told him. "Dan can go other places and get more money now." "Do it anyway," Ted said. Ted has a credo that has served him well: Never give up no matter how slim your chances are.

I called Liebner and suggested to him the opportunities CNN provided. Rather would be the centerpiece of innovation. He would make new television. We'd give Rather lots of options. If we succeeded, our options would make Rather richer than any offer from any of the other networks. Richard laughed. He was thinking "a bird in the hand is worth an option in the bush," especially since he got a percentage of Rather's earnings. I asked Richard to present the offer to Rather. Richard said he would, on one condition: that I meet with Mary Alice Williams, his client who had just been axed by WNBC.

When I got to New York, Liebner told me that Rather was not interested. I was not surprised, but I kept my word and met with Mary Alice. I had known her from my ITNA days, when she was a producer at WPIX, the ITNA host station in New York. We had worked together, she knew news, and at WNBC she had gained on-air experience and recognition. She may not have been A-level, but she was B plus.

By the time I met with her, she had been offered a job as NYC deputy police commissioner/spokeswoman. She preferred journalism. In New York, I had planned to hire two people to do three jobs. One would be a bureau chief/assignment manager and the other a news anchor. When I saw Mary Alice, I realized that I could do my two-for-one a different way. She could be the bureau chief/anchor, and I'd only have to find an assignment editor. Williams was smart and well-organized and had strong New York connections from her years at WNBC, and I thought she was a good anchorwoman. I offered her the job, and she took it.

She started work in February 1980 and had to turn the empty space at the World Trade Center into a broadcast studio, complete with control rooms, editing rooms, and an anchor desk. New York has its own way of doing business, and Mary Alice remembers that in the midst of all the construction, she was visited by a couple of gentlemen from the union who explained to her that they could be of great help in getting everything up and running if she would give them $12,500 upfront and then another $4,000 the following week. They reminded her that an office right over our studio had had a bad accident. Somebody poured acid into two brand new Hewlett-Packard machines. They didn't want that to happen to her.

Mary Alice Williams was a genius at PR. She told me, "I handled it this way. First, I said, 'Gentlemen, would you come downstairs with me for a minute.' I led them down to the assignment desk where there was a whole crowd of people, and I got up on the desk and said, 'These men have told me that unless I pay them $12,500 today and another $4,000 next week, something bad may happen to our equipment. I think they're asking me for a bribe, and I think that bribery is illegal.'

"My brother Judd (who was working as a cameraman) came up and grabbed my arm, and muttered, between clenched teeth, 'Do you want to get dead?' But the two gentlemen disappeared very fast and were not heard from again." Maybe they realized you don't fool around with someone who has just been offered a job as deputy police commissioner.

Mary Alice's last challenge was finding a way to get the CNN broadcast signal out of New York and down to Atlanta. Our studio was at the very bottom of the World Trade Center. The satellite dish was on the roof one hundred and ten stories above. At one point, I had tried to move the studio to the hundred and tenth floor. Mike Kandel thought I was trying to get a panoramic shot of the New York Harbor, and I was crazy because the top of the World Trade Center is usually shrouded in mist. He didn't understand that I was trying to save money. It costs a hell of a lot less to cable one floor than it does to cable one hundred and ten floors. In the end, we couldn't get the space, and we had to run the cable.

I knew an electrical contractor from my days in Newark. His company had the right to work for the Port Authority in any of its locations. His men were union, but the New Jersey rate was somewhat less than the New York rate. I gave him the contract to wire the building. We used New York electricians, but they were paid at the New Jersey rate, and they were perhaps not working at full speed. Mary Alice used her contacts to speed them up. The job got done just before we went on the air. We had saved a lot of money, but those hundred and ten floors still put CNN $100,000 over budget.

For the assignment desk, I recruited Richard Roth. Roth was another WPIX employee who had helped us at ITNA, but now he was working at AP radio in Washington and seemed content. Over the years, Rick Brown and Jane Maxwell, who had already joined CNN, had stayed in touch with Richard. They were living in Atlanta at a motel we called, unaffectionately, "Sleazy Jim's," because it was sleazy, and it was run by a man named Jim. It was also the cheapest place in town, and within walking distance of CNN's temporary headquarters. Roth came down on a Saturday for what was supposed to be a one-day visit, but as night fell he was still wavering.

Rick and Jane shared their room with Richard to give us another day to convince him. The trouble was, at Sleazy Jim's, you got only two blankets per room. There was no blanket for Richard. Ted Kavanau, who had a room to himself, had two blankets. Jane called him and he came over and gave one of them to Roth. But Ted couldn't just leave Roth with the blanket. He had to make his own recruitment speech.

Brown says Kavanau defined CNN like this: "We're gonna knock on people's doors and knock on them. And if they don't answer, we're gonna keep knocking, and if they still don't answer, we're gonna knock some more, and finally our guy is going to turn to the camera and say, 'These people who refuse to come to the door are accused of—' You name it, rape, murder, arson, embezzlement, or doing brain surgery with a butter knife."

Kavanau left. Jane and Rick and Richard wrapped themselves in their blankets, got into their one bed, and went to sleep. Jane giggles as she remembers it as "the only time I ever slept between two Dicks."

Kavanau's recruitment speech had been counterproductive. Richard Roth did not want to spend his career knocking on people's doors, accusing them of rape or murder. That's not to say Roth did not have on-air aspirations; he did. But he was young, skinny, awkward, and wore glasses. It was unlikely he could work on camera for a broadcast station. Still, he had a great voice, was very smart, and would grow up. I promised him that if he came to CNN, he would get his chance. That outweighed the Kavanau tirade. He joined us, grew up, and, no longer skinny or awkward, he's worked on air all over the world and is now CNN's UN correspondent.

Round 19: **Grab 'Em by the Throat**

When Ted set up his own sales department for WTBS in 1977, he made a conscious decision to hire the ten most aggressive salesmen he could find, whether they'd worked in television or not. They were hired for tenacity, not intellect. George Babick was the house intellectual, but the rest of the guys were supposed to be thugs. Bill Gantley, head of TBS sales, told his salesmen, "We will grab them by the throat. And we will shake them until they buy. Our philosophy is 'buy or die.'" That's how they sold TBS for two years.

Proctor & Gamble, the largest advertiser on TV, had been Turner's most intractable nonbuyer. For two years Ed Plowden, their head of media, saw—correctly as it turned out—that CNN and the other cable networks would fragment the market and make it much harder for P&G to reach the enormous audience it needed. Commercial time on the three networks was so expensive that no small company could afford it. Only the big companies—like P&G, General Foods, GM, Ford—were able to reach a national audience on television. Moreover, the network monopoly made it possible for advertisers to reach very large audiences very easily. Cable advertising would make life more competitive and more complicated. Plowden wanted no part of it.

Gerry Hogan, a Turner salesman who later became vice chairman of TBS, had a friend who had a friend whose name was Jack Wishard. Wishard was head of all advertising at P&G. Plowden reported to him. Hogan talked to Wishard. Wishard was open. He suggested a face-to-face meeting. Turner was there, Hogan was there, and Plowden was

there with a group of his people. Wishard opened the meeting by saying, "I know you've had a number of meetings. Today, I want you to
address this subject from only one point of view. Why *should* we do
this?" One of Plowden's aides spoke. He began with a negative spin.
Wishard cut him off. "I don't think you heard me," he said. By the time
Plowden and his people left the room, they knew that from then on they
were going to advertise on cable networks, and particularly on TBS.

Plowden was righter than right about the future of advertising, particularly for P&G. Hogan quotes Peter Seely, formerly of Coca-Cola: "In
1967 P&G could reach 80 percent of all the women in America with
three spots on daytime soap operas. In 2000, it would take P&G 190
spots across all of national TV to accomplish the same thing." Yeah,
some of it's sociology—so many women work, so many are single
mothers—but a lot of it is so many channels to watch, so little time to
watch them.

George Babick was head of advertising sales for CNN. Ted Turner is
still a hero in George's eyes. He thinks Ted is the world's greatest salesman. First, Ted sold George on taking a job at TBS, then he sold him on
moving to CNN, which everybody knew was going to be a very hard
sell. George said he couldn't refuse Ted anything. But George also
believed in the CNN product: "I'd seen a diagram of how a satellite
worked so I was sold on cable. I was also sold on news, and mostly I was
sold on Ted Turner."

I didn't know why CNN could never get McDonald's as a sponsor.
Then I heard a story from the old TBS days. Ted had accompanied a
Chicago salesman on a visit to McDonald's. The McDonald's buyer was
a beautiful woman, the daughter of a famous Chicago broadcaster, who
knew how to buy advertising time. She was the only woman in a room
full of men. When Ted was introduced, he walked up to her, commented
on how attractive she was, reached out, and grabbed her breast. She
stepped back, the room was in shock, but nobody said anything. Needless to say, McDonald's did not buy time on TBS or CNN. When I confronted Babick, who was in the Chicago office at the time, with the
story, George's only comment was, "Ted was very decent about it. He
never beat us up on why we couldn't get McDonald's to buy airtime."

That grab was a problem for me. I wasn't in the room when Ted did
it. I wasn't even working for him. I never asked him about it, but after I

heard the story I wondered what I would do if I ever saw Ted pull a stunt like that. Nobody in the Chicago sales office quit after Ted made his grab. Would I quit? I didn't last long enough to find out.

I asked Gerry Hogan, who worked his way up to vice chairman of TBS, how he dealt with Ted's antics. He says he made a virtue of them. "Ted is not a fool or an idiot. Every move he makes is calculated. He can appear outrageous to the world, off the wall to his clients and the people he works with, but he is sensible and responsible when he speaks to Wall Street or a CEO." Only in private conversation did I ever see the sensible and responsible Ted. Otherwise, he was always putting on a show, and I never knew for whose benefit.

The most important client CNN picked up was Bristol-Myers. They committed $10 million to us publicly even before we went on the air. Marvin Koslow, executive vice president of Bristol-Myers, supervised all their media buying as well as the creation and production of special Bristol-Myers programs. Among other things, Bristol-Myers was heavily into over-the-counter drugs. Drugs are bought by old people. News is watched by old people. Marvin bought a lot of time on news programs, but he demanded quality. Bristol-Myers also produced Clairol. Since he wanted women viewers, he was one of the first advertisers to support women's tennis for television. He made sure to vet the quality of anything Bristol-Myers supported. In tennis, he worked very closely with Billie Jean King. He had worked with Ted Turner on CNN, and now he wanted to meet me. I explained our strategy and took him through our schedule. Marvin made it clear that he had no political bone to pick. He told me that he was the first advertiser to refuse to use the *Red Channels* black list. For years a supermarket operator in upstate New York had checked into the backgrounds of people working in television. If he decided they were communists or communist sympathizers, he put their names in *Red Channels*. Once listed, they were unemployable, because sponsors would not buy time in programs to which their names were attached. Marvin said Bristol-Myers would not use *Red Channels*, and other advertisers followed suit. Marvin was delivering a message, and I got it: He would not bow to political pressure. On the down side, Marvin wanted to be involved in whatever he was sponsoring.

Marvin planned to be the sole sponsor of a CNN medical segment, and he wanted the presenter to be an MD. Now we were getting close to the line; you cannot let your sponsor choose your talent for you. Marvin said we could choose the doctor. That's okay. Next, Marvin wants "positive" medical news. "Ah," says I, "you want the Wonders of Modern Medicine. I can give you that. But I'm going to do tough medical stories too." Marvin's advertising spots would not appear on those reports. What he wanted to do was make sure that his spots played only around positive stories. That was okay too. All the airlines pull their spots off the news shows on the day of an air crash.

Marvin and I understood that we were both reasonable men. CNN will not go out of its way to cause Bristol-Myers problems. Marvin would not go out of his way to cause CNN editorial problems. Nevertheless, Marvin wanted to see a tape of the doctor we chose before we went on the air. That could have been a problem, since Marvin could have nixed our choice, but he didn't. No problem. Marvin wanted to see some sample stories. That was okay so long as he understood that we would run them even if he didn't like them. We would just remove his advertising. Again we agreed. We were both betting there would be no conflicts, and there weren't. Marvin and I became good friends.

Satisfied with me, Marvin and Ted held a press conference to announce that Bristol-Myers had bought $10 million worth of advertising on CNN. They did not say over how many years. Marvin became the godfather of CNN within the advertising community.

Ted was just as effective selling other clients. I remain amazed that anyone was able to sell time on a network that didn't exist with a product that had never been tried before, with not even one marketable name attached to it, except of course Ted Turner. At this moment he was selling "Ted Turner against the world." His courage, his tenacity, his ferocity was our product.

Just as network arrogance helped me with news guys, network arrogance helped him with advertisers. Ted and George Babick took American Home Products to lunch at the New York Yacht Club—Ted was host, attended by AHP's media chief and four of his aides. Showing his guests around the club, Ted stopped in front of the glass case that held the America's Cup he'd won on his boat *Courageous*.

Babick says, "Ted was in his element. He led the way upstairs to a private dining room, and everyone sat down at a wooden conference table that had been polished so many times the dark wood seemed to have the depth of a mirror. Ted said it was too warm, and took his jacket off. He looked at the AHP media boss. The boss slowly took off his jacket. The four aides took their jackets off, too. Ted loosened his tie. The AHP boss loosened his tie. His assistants followed. Now Ted had them.

"By then, he was walking around the tabletop and stopped in front of the vice president of American Home Products. Ted said, 'I understand you've just signed a deal with NBC. Wasn't it $250 million over five years?' The vice president said the figure was in the ballpark.

"'Did the President of NBC call you to say thanks?'

"The room was silent. Ted spoke again. 'You are now the biggest client NBC has and the president didn't call? . . . Who *is* the president of NBC?'

"'Fred Silverman,' somebody mumbled.

"At this point, the executive heads are turning in unison as they follow Ted around the table. Ted walks faster. 'Fred Silverman. It makes no difference who their president is because he's gonna get fired anyway. But'—Ted paused and smiled—'no one is gonna fire me because my name is over the door. And I'm asking you guys to work with me to sell your products so you won't have to pay such outrageous prices to NBC.'

"He had them in the palm of his hand," Babick says. "We got a big order."

Not all sales went that well for CNN. We had trouble in Detroit. Before we went on the air, David Koff, our Detroit salesman, tried the big three. GM and Ford passed. Chrysler, teetering on bankruptcy, wanted us but couldn't afford us. They had cars they couldn't sell. We had airtime we couldn't sell. It was a marriage made in heaven. They gave us a half-million dollars worth of cars and vans, for our bureaus and cameramen. We gave them one thirty-second spot every two hours for a full year.

By the fall of 1980, Koff had still failed to bring in hard cash from the automobile industry. Ted flew into town with Jim Trahey, his ace sports salesman, who knew all the automobile guys. Koff remembers driving Ted and Trahey through a pouring rain to Chevy's advertising agency. Koff and Trahey were in front, Ted alone in the back seat. The atmosphere was tense. Ted was beating up on the sales guys. "What's the matter with you guys. We're putting out a good product. We're getting more homes. And you can't sell it." Finally, Ted quieted down. Koff tried a joke he thought would break the tension. Trahey laughed. Ted went crazy. "You think it's funny? You guys are laughing, and you can't sell a dollar's worth of advertising in Detroit? You're fired. You're both fired."

It was still pouring rain. Koff pulled over to the side of the road. He looked at Ted and said, "Get the hell out of my car." "You can't do this," said Ted. "You just fired me, and this ain't the company car," said Koff. "Get out." They were on a superhighway, circling Detroit in the midst of a rainstorm. Ted knows when he's beaten. "I didn't mean it," said Ted. "You know I didn't mean it. I'm always firing you guys." Koff relented but not until he got Ted to give him and Trahey an extra hundred dollars a month on their car allowance. Chevy did not buy.

Koff said he couldn't sell CNN until he got the *1981 Pocket Piece* based on the ratings in the CUBE system in Columbus, the only city in which homes were metered. CNN finally had evidence that it was getting ratings somewhere between a .5 and a 1. Koff could sell that.

In 1982, right after I left the company, Ted made another trip to Detroit. This time he visited Ford, where he saw Phil Caldwell and Don Peterson, the chairman and president. They were complaining about "the media." In 1982, Japanese cars were cutting deep into the U.S. market. American cars were soft, inefficient gas-guzzlers. Japanese cars were lean, mean driving machines. That's what the media said. Some of it was true, but it was not as true as it had been in 1980 and 1981. Caldwell and Peterson complained that the media never covered the improvement in U.S. automobiles. Ted promised to open a bureau in Detroit that would tell the Detroit side of the story. CNN had no money. It could barely afford its own bureaus, let alone open new ones. Caldwell and Peterson were impressed.

As they left the room, Koff asked Ted, "Are we going to be able to do this?" Ted adopted his abashed little boy look and said, "I don't know. I should never have said it." Koff said, "If we don't do it, I may as well close the Detroit office and look for another job." Ted found a way out. He went back to Atlanta and assigned Peter Arnett to a documentary about the U.S. auto industry. It was balanced and responsible. Ted had not gone overboard. He owes Peter a lot for that documentary. It bought him nine months before he had to open the bureau.

Today Koff is still in Detroit, now selling time for CNN's strongest rival, CNBC. He says his job has gotten easier. Since the late eighties, CNN has been seen as "the Ted and Jane Network." It is now sneeringly called "the Clinton News Network." I am sure that Koff uses that line whenever he calls on a client.

Round 20: **The Greed Factor**

At ITNA, I had struck up a relationship with Lew Young, managing editor of *Business Week*. Young reminded me of Ed Asner: broad, stocky, bald, and authoritative. We used him as our business expert at ITNA. When Ted and I made our deal, I called Lew, and offered to coproduce our business programs with *Business Week*. CNN would build its bureau, complete with studio, in *Business Week*'s offices in the McGraw-Hill building. We would produce the business shows with our own anchors and producers, but we would use *Business Week* people as reporters and analysts. The benefit to the magazine was a twenty-four-hour presence on CNN, promoting McGraw-Hill journalism. It was a fair deal, and Lew was enthusiastic.

With that deal in my back pocket, I decided to visit the *Wall Street Journal*. *Business Week* was a weekly; the *Journal* was a daily. If CNN set up its bureau there, we'd have access to more reporters, more bureaus, and a steadier flow of general business information. I met with Bill Dunn, the *Journal*'s general manager. He was an ex-marine, and in a nest of journalists he was an extraordinarily practical and farseeing man. (It was he who created the *WSJ* satellite network and made the deals that enabled the *Journal* to become a national newspaper.) Bill understood CNN immediately; there was no need for mc to do a sales job. But he had one question: "Who is going to have editorial control of the financial segments on CNN?" I said we would, we knew television. He said they knew business news. I said the product was television, and we had to be in control of our product. He asked if the *Journal* could buy the half hour on the network and do its own financial program. I asked if we could buy the *Journal* front page and do our own financial newspaper. He laughed. I laughed. No go. We shook hands, and stayed friends.

I went back to Lew Young at *Business Week.* We were ready to do the deal. But Lew asked for another meeting, at which we were joined by Paul McPherson, the president of the magazine division. They heard my presentation, accepted it, but had to clear it with the proprietor, Harold McGraw.

McGraw-Hill also owned a group of television stations, good ones in medium-sized markets, run by Norman Walt, who had come over from CBS. CBS did not like Ted Turner. Norman Walt, in particular, did not like Ted Turner. Walt was advising Harold McGraw not to deal with CNN. It was another case of "Do we want this man as a partner?"

Unfortunately, Ted had left his enemies a lot of ammunition. When Walt and McPherson met with McGraw, Walt won out. *Business Week* said no. I called Ted and told him that we had to add a million bucks to our budget to build our own financial bureau and find our own reporters. Ted said, "Good. I never wanted partners anyway."

Lew Young was crushed. I asked him if he wanted to be our vice president and run the financial programs. He was not ready for that. I told him that I was thinking of calling Dan Dorfman, ex–*Wall Street Journal* "Heard on the Street" columnist. Some establishment financial journalists distrusted Dorfman. They thought of him as a "stock tout." Dorfman did suggest that some stocks were good buys, but, to my knowledge, he always had good information when he made his recommendations and he had never profited from his stock tips.

I think his stories were straight, but while he was at the *Journal,* several lawsuits had been filed involving the paper. (I once talked to a lawyer who said he had built a wing on his house that he called the "Dorfman wing" because he'd earned the money by representing the *Journal* in Dorfman-inspired lawsuits.)

Young implored me not to hire Dorfman. He strongly recommended Mike Kandel, the financial editor of the *New York Post.* Previously, Kandel had been financial editor of the *Herald-Tribune,* a universally respected newspaper, defunct in 1980. Kandel's credentials would give CNN credibility with Wall Street. Dorfman would give CNN credibility with the "man in the street." I figured I'd hire them both.

First, I went after Dorfman. At the time, he was doing a column for the *Chicago Tribune* syndicate. During the New York newspaper strike he had appeared on WCBS, and I'd seen him on television. There never was a less prepossessing television personality than Dorfman. He had a face made for radio, and his voice was squeaky and rasping. I took him to lunch at The Palm, a newsman's steakhouse on Second Avenue, and offered him a three-times-a-week, on-air column for CNN. CNN would pay him $100 a column. Dorfman hemmed and hawed, but finally he accepted. He wanted television more than he wanted money. He made one additional request. He asked me to pay for voice lessons. I told him, "Not only will I not pay for voice lessons, I won't hire you if you take them." So far as I know, he never took them, but if he did, they didn't work.

Next, I went after Mike Kandel. I needed a full-time financial editor who I hoped could also be our financial anchor. I always tried for two-for-one. Kandel remembers saying he would "consider the job. . . . I had been on television panel shows maybe three times; I had no ambitions in that direction. Reese is persuasive."

I suggested an on-air test and sent Ted Kavanau to New York to work with Mike. According to Mike, Kavanau sat him down in a room with a desk, two chairs, a filing cabinet, and a camera in the doorway. Ted told him to talk naturally, read something, then interview him. Kandel took out a copy of his column and read it, told Ted who he was, and asked questions, including Where is this crazy guy Turner getting his money from? Kavanau said thanks, they'd get back to him. "On my way downstairs," Kandel said, "I met two guys I knew coming up. They were financial reporters, and they were both younger and better looking than me."

When Kavanau brought back the Kandel tape, he, Reinhardt, Zelman, and I viewed it. Kandel would never be an anchor, but he would be a terrific editor. I lost my two-for-one, but I gained a partner. Kandel says I told him, "What you don't have in television graces, you make up for with sincerity, knowledge, and credibility." Twenty years later, Mike Kandel was named one of the ten greatest financial journalists of the century by the Silurian Society, the organization of financial journalists.

I invited Mike down to Atlanta to make a deal. I showed him "Techwood," where we were building our headquarters. Mike had a moment of déjà vu. "When I was a kid, I spent two weeks in Atlanta and my uncle took me to the Jewish country club, and we went to the steam bath, and they turned a high velocity hose on you, and it was great. I was standing there, remembering this guy with the hose, and now, thirty-five years later, I look down at the tile floor and ask Reese, 'What was here before?' He said it had been the steam room of the Progressive Club." I often identified our studio as the old downtown Jewish country club. Ted heard me one day. That afternoon he sent a memo to all executives that henceforth the CNN site would be known only as "Techwood."

I offered Mike a one-year deal, but he was smarter than that. He said, "I'm going to put all my expertise into this job, and I don't want to be in a position where a year from now, Ted Turner says, 'I have this idiot nephew and he can do the same thing.'" I thought Mike had a good point. I gave him a contract that guaranteed two years with an option his way. He could get out at the end of year one.

When Mike first met Ted Turner, Ted told him, "We go on the air June first, and we don't go off until the world comes to an end." Then, pausing dramatically, he pointed a finger at Mike and added, "If that happens, I expect you to stay on the job and cover the story." Mike says he thought, "Wow! That's terrific, that's really great. Later I heard him say it ten more times to ten different people. It was still good, but not quite as good."

Mike was further enlightened about Ted five years later. One of his Atlanta relatives, who knew Ted pretty well, told him, "Ted has three goals. He wants to be the richest man in America, he wants to fuck every pretty girl he can find, and he wants to be president." Mike said, "He's not the richest, but he's pretty rich, he's done well with the second goal, and as for the third, he still has hopes. . . ."

I was still looking for a financial anchorman. I went after Louis Rukeyser, who did *Wall Street Week* for PBS. It was the only successful stock market program then on television. Rukeyser was by far the best-known name in financial television and maybe in all of financial news. His work was first-class, and his presence would've gone a long way in establishing CNN as a first-class network. He was worth stock options. I hired Mel Tarr, a financial PR man introduced to me by Kandel, as a consultant. Through Tarr, I was able to get through to Rukeyser. I called Lou, and made my pitch. Before I got very far, he said, "You know,

Reese, when you talk to me, you're playing on a very fast track." At that moment, I decided that talking to Rukeyser was the wrong track. I called Tarr and asked him to get me tapes of other anchors.

Tarr gathered the tapes, and Mike Kandel brought them down to Atlanta. As Mike remembers it, Sam Zelman, Burt Reinhardt, Ted Kavanau, and I were in my office viewing on-air candidates. Mike says, "It reminded me of sitting in the Colosseum . . . when the Roman Emperor would turn his thumbs up or down. They [Sam, Burt, Ted, and I] would say 'Oh this guy looks like a used car salesman' and 'This guy looks like a mortician.' These guys were fine journalists, but we were looking for an anchor." None of them worked, and we kept looking.

In March of 1980, three months before launch, our financial staff still consisted of only two people: editor Mike Kandel and columnist Dan Dorfman. Then Kandel got lucky. He says, "We came across this fellow Lou Dobbs in Seattle and Lou writes a letter to me, and I tell him, 'Mel Tarr will call you.' . . . We get a tape from Dobbs . . . big hair and all." Mike sent the tape down to Atlanta. When Sam Zelman saw it, he knew Dobbs was the guy.

I'll say it again: Sam Zelman had the best eye for talent of anyone at CNN. At the time, Dobbs was working in Seattle, as weekend anchor and reporter at KING, the NBC affiliate. He projected warmth, heartiness, and authority. I believed his resume was perfect for Wall Street. He had been smart enough to graduate from Harvard, but dumb enough to play football there.

Kandel interviewed Dobbs and was duly impressed. He was going to be Dobbs's boss, and he thought they'd make a good team. It was one of the few moments at CNN when I knew we had found a round peg for a round hole. No need for protracted negotiations; an offer from me, an immediate acceptance by Dobbs.

Lou fully perceived the opportunity that CNN provided. He would be the first national financial anchorman on commercial television. He had enough confidence in his talent to believe he could make a career of it. In fact, he did. Wall Street traders came to love him, moguls confided in him, and Ted Turner valued him highly.

Howard Kurtz writes in *The Fortune Tellers*, his book about the influence of television on capital markets, that Dobbs started *Moneyline* with Ted Turner. He says that when Dobbs joined CNN he asked

Ted what kind of a program he wanted. "That's up to you," Turner said. Hell, when I hired Dobbs, he didn't even talk to Ted Turner. He worked for Mike Kandel, and Mike worked for me. Mike and I designed and named *Moneyline.* Kurtz also says, "Dobbs had hired Dan Dorfman, the nation's best known financial columnist, as a regular commentator." As reported above, Dorfman signed up with CNN months before we found Dobbs.

Howard Kurtz now hosts a CNN show called *Reliable Sources.* Not this time, Howie. Howard says his source was either Dobbs or Dorfman. I'd be willing to bet which one.

After Dobbs signed on, all we needed was a morning anchorman. Kandel kept searching. He heard about a guy in San Francisco, Stuart Varney, who had a two-hour-long early morning program about the stock market. Varney would interview business people while the stock ticker ran along the bottom of the screen. Bill Donahue, the man who recommended Varney to Mike, said, "Varney is the best interviewer I ever met, but he has an Australian accent." I got Varney's tape, and the accent didn't bother me. We invited him to Atlanta, he flew in on the red-eye, and we hired him over breakfast. Later Kandel asked me why I hired so many Australians and New Zealanders. I said, "Americans think BBC journalists are smart. With these guys I get the same accent for half the money."

When the financial unit was put together, I told Kandel the roles I had planned for each of the correspondents. I said to him, "You're New York, Dorfman is Brooklyn, Dobbs is America, and Varney is the rest of the world. Dorfman is the 'greed factor.'" For years, *Wall Street Journal* readers had followed his tips. Now they were going to get them three days a week on CNN. I wanted viewers to believe that they could not afford to miss *Moneyline* for a single night; if they didn't hear what Dorfman and Kandel and Dobbs said, it could cost them money.

Mike said, "Dobbs is going to be our star." I said, "I think it could be Varney." Mike said, "Varney is very good, but Dobbs is going to be the star." Kandel was dead on, and I was 30 percent off. Twenty years later when Dobbs quit, CNN made Varney the *Moneyline* anchor. Since then *Moneyline*'s ratings have gone down by 30 percent. Mike Kandel beat me by a hundred thousand viewers.

Round 21: **Washington**

Washington was a problem. Washington is always a problem. At any network, at any newspaper, the Washington bureau believes that what it is, what it does, what it thinks, is more important than anything that is happening anywhere else in the world. Except maybe in wartime, when all the Washington correspondents want to grab their helmets, go to the front lines, and get their pictures taken.

If it's true that Washington, D.C., is the seat of world power, then the press corps is its rectum through which it passes its excrement onto the rest of the world. The Washington press corps spends most of its time commenting on the odor, color, and other qualities of the excrement. Rarely does it discover the few grains of truth it contains. As for the press corps itself, it believes its excrement does not stink.

Despite their attitude, Washington journalists are inevitable, and occasionally they do good work. When important things do occur in Washington, the Washington powers usually try to hide them from the public. The better journalists look under the rug, read the fine print, and try to let Americans know what their government is really doing.

CNN's Washington bureau was built on a foundation laid by Stan Berk, who had once been news director at WTTG Washington before becoming an agent. I'd tried to hire him for CNN, but he was more interested in representing the likes of Erma Bombeck and Jack Anderson. He found CNN all of its columnists, from Bella Abzug to Phyllis Schlafly, from Barry Goldwater to Frank Deford, as well as Steve Kritsick, our star vet.

Berk's attitude would have been perfect for CNN, but he still didn't want a job. So he became our Washington fixer. For almost a year, he and I worked together to get Washington going. He bargained for office space on Wisconsin Avenue and made a deal that worked. He brought his successor at WTTG, Jim Schultz, over to us as our assistant bureau manager, the hands-on guy. I was looking for an executive vice president/bureau chief, but no names surfaced that pleased everybody. Then Sam Zelman told me that George Watson, vice president and bureau chief of ABC Washington, might be available. George played in the big leagues. There was no way I could say no if he wanted to come.

Roone Arledge, who loved stars, had replaced Watson as bureau chief with Carl Bernstein of Watergate fame, even though Bernstein had never worked in television. Roone wanted George to move to New York. George didn't want to move, his wife was pregnant, and he was sick of Roone Arledge. He was also stunned that Arledge thought that Bernstein could run the Washington bureau or that George couldn't.

George flew down to Atlanta, we spent a morning together, and he signed on. He later said of me, "I met a man who had a vision of what could be done in TV. He seemed to me a shining intelligence who could deliver me from Roone Arledge." Maybe I could, but I couldn't deliver to George the things he needed the most. I couldn't protect him from the demands of the more freewheeling producers in Atlanta, and I couldn't guarantee the acceptance of his news judgment on all political stories.

Our problem was integrating a group of reporters, producers, and desk assistants who had worked at ABC and who had been hired by Watson with an Atlanta production group, most of whom had worked only at local stations. In 1980, local news was not the "crime and grime" it is now, but local producers wanted short, fast, punchy human interest stories. It didn't hurt if a little sex and violence just happened to be included. The network alumni needed more time to tell stories "in-depth"; they wanted to produce stories that fit Washington standards of importance, whether or not the rest of America appreciated their relevance.

The networks were not very concerned about "relevance" in 1980; they covered the stories they and they alone thought important (usually the AP daybook or the front page of the *New York Times* or *Washington Post*). CNN's Atlanta producers had been infected by "relevance" when they produced local news.

It was a classic battle: elitist versus populist. The Washington people were prescriptive; they "knew" what was best for the audience. The Atlanta producers were populist; they adjusted their programs to what they thought the audience wanted. Since CNN was a twenty-four-hour network, I believed there was room for both. We would have elitist programs, we would have populist programs, but the elitists and the populists refused to live together. For both sides it was all or nothing, and I was refereeing. I wasn't successful, but maybe nobody could've been.

George Watson was the best newsman, the best reporter, the best writer, the best thinker, and, I think, the noblest soul at CNN. When I hired him, I told him I did not think I would last more than three years with Turner, and I hoped he would get my job. But George was an elitist. He was the purest of pure newsmen. If Watson could not tolerate Roone Arledge, there was no chance he could abide Ted Kavanau and Alec Nagle, who were producing the news programs in Atlanta.

Watson said, "There was a kind of friction over editorial judgment. Rude and uninformed is the kind of style I associate with New York." I am ashamed to admit it, but Atlanta was worse, and I couldn't stop it. Kavanau and Nagle thought Washington correspondents were windy ramblers. Watson thought they needed time to tell the stories right. Neither side was correct, but I needed a super editor to make the decisions, case by case, and I didn't find one until too late.

By the time George came aboard, CNN had already hired and assigned some people to Washington, not the best way for George to start his new job. He should have been able to pick his own staff, but it was not to be.

When Ed Turner was hired to be in charge of CNN's small bureaus, a job already filled by Pete Vesey, we had to find a job for Pete. We sent Vesey, the former news director of the Pulitzer station in St. Louis, to Washington with the title of bureau chief. Watson became executive vice president, with Vesey reporting to him. It was an awkward situation. "I didn't know Pete," Watson recalls. "When I got to know him a little, he was okay, it's just that he wasn't my guy."

Others in the Washington bureau before the start-up were Bernie Shaw and Dan Schorr. George hadn't chosen Schorr, but he respected him a great deal. Davey Newman, formerly of ABC, was Watson's number two, and I had hired a guy named Mark Walton from Channel 5 Washington to be the White House correspondent, but the rest of the staff was put together by George.

Kirsten Lindquist (she later became a CNN anchor) was to cover the economy, John Holliman had the farm beat, Bob Berkowitz was the fireman. Dave Browdie was to cover the Pentagon and Dan Brewster was to cover Capitol Hill.

Holliman's farm beat didn't work out, so he went on general assignment, and he's best remembered as one of the stars of Baghdad. Browdie had come from New York local stations.

We couldn't afford too many experienced journalists, so most of the people we hired came from radio, either RKO or AP. They needed a leader, and Dave Newman was it. Newman had been an ABC executive producer, one of their best. He had just come out of rehab, but he was enormously talented, a terrific writer, with the grizzled look of an experienced newsman. Davey seemed the perfect teacher for the young kids who were going to do the work.

Watson was willing to make any kind of logistical sacrifice for the new company. "At first," he says, "I was running the bureau out of my house. There was a new baby, just born, and a new network, not yet born." Resumes were being sent to him from everywhere in the world. Everyone wanted to come to CNN, and he was looking for the diamonds in the piles of stuff.

George was keen on Bob Berkowitz, who was working for AP radio; he thought radio reporters were inviting targets, because they didn't have high expectations, they were accustomed to ad-libbing, and they had some degree of poise. "We were accused of raiding ABC, but we were being raided even before we got the Washington bureau up and running," Watson insists. "I had a handshake with David Ensor, of PBS, and ABC turned around and hired him. They were coming after people I was going for. (Ensor wound up at CNN twenty years later.)

"Mike Halberstam was my doctor in Washington. He was also a terrific writer, fascinated by television, so I asked him if he wanted to do some medical pieces on TV." George found Katie Couric through his secretary, Wendy Walker (now the executive producer of the *Larry King Show*). When it became known that Watson was going to CNN, Wendy suggested people to him. Katie was a desk assistant at ABC, and became a desk assistant at CNN, not a big step up for her. Katie was all of twenty-three when she dropped ABC in favor of CNN. Most people came to CNN because they got a big promotion or their career at ABC was at a dead end. Katie came to CNN because she saw the opportunity and knew she had the ability to take advantage of it.

Neither she nor George knew that within a few months the morning Washington producer would be putting desk assistant Couric on the air as the morning news anchor. Desk assistant/anchorwoman was not a job description even at CNN, or so I told the producer who first put her on the air.

Ted Turner still didn't have much grasp of journalism. During the prelaunch period, when Ted was in Washington making a speech to a blue ribbon group of public broadcasters, an extremely right-wing guy, Lester Kinsolving, came up to him and said, "I want to be on the air."

"Sure," said Ted. "Go talk to George Watson." So Watson asked me, "What do I have to do with this guy?" I said, "Absolutely nothing."

Our publicist had come courtesy of Ted. "She was," to George, "also hopeless, the only person I've ever seen literally fall into the soup from overindulgence." What George didn't know was that the lady in question was married to an important cable executive.

George knew everyone in Washington who mattered and was respected by everyone he knew. When CNN went on the air, we had an hour interview with President Carter. Some thought it was Ted Turner who arranged for the interview. It was George Watson.

Watson's virtues included an ability to bring in the best of a new generation. The people he hired in Washington were his kids. Most of them were a couple steps ahead of the video journalists we hired for Atlanta. They had worked in television a little bit, they had covered news a little bit, they were connected to politics, and/or they came from very good schools. Dan Brewster is a good example.

Dan is the son of a former Maryland senator. He had gone to Georgetown. He had worked at *Rolling Stone,* and he had been a very junior producer for Barbara Walters. Dan tells of George Watson's coming to see him and saying, "We've got this guy in Atlanta who is going to start an all-news network. It sounds interesting, why don't you come talk to me about it?" Watson's talk worked.

Brewster came on board, and he said he was on top of the world. The bureau was still a work in progress, some of the phones weren't yet working. But it was all esprit de corps, and Dan was exhilarated. "We were willing to work way beyond reasonable hours. We were passionately committed to fair coverage of the subject we were reporting on. We were all interested in the process, we were all enthusiastic about the new medium, we were the talk of the town and in time we made CNN the talk of the town."

Since Dan had reported on Congress as a print reporter, he was given the job of covering the House. He considered the Washington bureau the news-gathering hub of CNN, a hard news organization with a national conscience, providing real-time news on important subjects. "It wasn't so much how you looked on camera, but how good an understanding you had of the subject you were covering."

Brewster was not a guy who had to worry about how he looked on camera. He had the makings of a matinee idol, he talked well, and he was smart. In the end, he was smart enough to get out of the news business, and he now runs the Bertlesman U.S. publishing unit, which includes *McCall's, Woman's Day, Parents,* and others.

Sandy Kenyon was just a couple of years out of Princeton. His parents had founded *Food and Wine.* He'd been the boy producer of a celebrity radio show aimed at his generation that had run for two years and was cleared by over a hundred stations on NPR. Kenyon was the kind of kid who couldn't be stopped.

Sandy wanted CNN because he felt CNN was the one big chance of his generation. He typed out a hundred letters and sent them to a hundred people because he couldn't get anybody on the telephone. And when he finally did get people on the phone, every one of them told him to send his resume to somebody else. Finally, he sent a letter to George Watson in Washington. Wendy Walker called him back. She said she had good news and bad news. Mr. Watson was intrigued by his resume, "but we go on the air in less than a month, and we are all staffed up."

Refusing to take no for an answer, Sandy borrowed fifty dollars, took a train from New York to Washington, and walked into a very small newsroom. Its energy seemed right. He met George Watson and Davey Newman. Kenyon remembers, "George said to Dave, 'This is the boy we are thinking of as a writer/producer,' and Davey looked really dubious. What had happened was, we'd hired a real writer/producer who wrote the news for Channel 7 in D.C., but Channel 7 had simply offered him more money to stay, and he'd stayed."

CNN needed a writer/producer for Bernie Shaw, but they didn't want to hire anybody without checking with Bernie, who was in Nicaragua covering a revolution. ABC was upset that Shaw was leaving, and they were working him up to the last hour of his contract. Newman said, "Come with me." So they went into his office, Sandy sat on a packing crate, and Newman sat behind a desk and said, "Now, tell me your experience."

Sandy was twenty-two, looked sixteen, had never taken a journalism course, had no training in news, and couldn't type. He opened his mouth to tell Dave he'd been to the White House when he'd had a college part-time job in the Counsel's office, and he looked up, and there was Bernie Shaw.

"He was back," Sandy recalls. "And someone shouted through the door, 'The British have just stormed the Iranian embassy in London,' and even though we weren't yet on the air, we were doing rehearsals, and it was, 'Try to act as if we're on.' Bernie pounds on the table and says, 'You come with me, we're going to write copy.'" Sandy was hunting and pecking on an old manual typewriter, and Shaw was working very fast, and he looked at what Sandy wrote and said, "I can tell you have experience in doing print journalism. We do things a little differently here on the broadcast side, but you'll get used to it." Sandy adds, "I thought, this man will help me, and the only way I can make this work is to be indispensable, and the only way I can be indispensable is to come in early and stay late. Because the level of confusion there was so high that my screwups could get lost in the shuffle, provided Bernie was on my side."

Sandy likes to say he went to Bernie Shaw journalism school. He remembers one day when the place was about seven-eighths built, and Bernie was showing some people around. There was a phone all in pieces, a mass of wires on the floor, with the mike from the handset exposed and twisted at a crazy angle, and Bernie said with a very theatrical gesture toward the debris, "When I started at CBS, it was like that."

"What we had at CNN Washington," Sandy says fondly, "was a group of people who were young and had no time for anything but CNN. My shift on a regular basis when I worked for Bernie was thirteen hours. Minimum. He used to call me regularly and say, 'What are you doing now?' and I would say I was doing my laundry, and he would say, 'Good, get back here, because Carter has just broken his rib.'"

Sandy was beeped all hours of the day and night. There was nothing he was doing from being in the can to being in the sack that precluded being beeped and told to get there immediately. Sandy says, "There was a lot of working hard and a lot of drinking hard and playing hard.

"At the first Washington Christmas party, I can remember Cissy Baker (Senator Howard Baker's daughter, Everett Dirksen's granddaughter) trying to do a flip, and landing on her back, breaking three ribs, and going on dancing. People just went nuts. I don't think you'd find a lot of sober people today who could remember much about it. We were a bunch of people who fought a war together."

Despite her senatorial pedigree, or maybe because of it, Cissy played it tough. She was short, broad-shouldered, and exuded strength, which isn't easy for a twenty-four-year-old. She had Washington connections, and she is very smart. Smart, connected, and tough equals the perfect assignment editor. She tells her story better than I can:

"Jim Schultz, an assistant bureau manager, hired me. I had interned for him when I was in college, and he'd been at Channel 5 here in Washington. He called and asked did I want to help launch an all-news network? I said no, I had a job in Nashville at a CBS affiliate where I was making $10,000 a year. He offered to double my salary. So I started work at CNN in March of 1980, before we went on the air. I was twenty-four years old, and I was going to be the assignment editor.

"I showed up to meet Schultz, and we went to the not yet built-out bureau on Wisconsin Avenue, and I freaked. It had a cement floor, no furniture, cables dangling from the ceiling, which had no tiles on it, exposed pipes; there was nothing."

Baker was in the front line from the beginning. At twenty-four, she was not just assigning stories but teaching reporters the ABCs of their beats. First, she worked on Kirsten Lindquist. "Kirsten was supposed to be the economics reporter and I was supposed to be looking for economics stories for her, though neither of us knew anything about economics. I called one of my college professors, and he gave us a crash course. He taught us, and we quizzed each other. What is the GNP? What is the CPI? We learned.

"Kandy Stroud came on board to cover the State Department. She had been at *Women's Wear Daily*. From *WWD* to our chief diplomatic correspondent—that was a hoot. There was real spirit," as Cissy puts it. "Everybody was eager to do his job and make something of this upstart network. The day we went on the air, I remember it was a Sunday, I wrote in my journal, 'The Cable News Network went on the air nationwide today. Forever.'"

Round 22: **The Sporting Life**

I had always been my own sports editor. I grew up loving sports, not as an athlete, but as a fan. I knew the Yankee roster, I knew the Giants roster, baseball that is, and I can still name a lot of guys on the original Knicks. I covered sports stories, Hank Aaron, Willie Mays, Tom Landry, Sugar Ray Robinson, Floyd Patterson, the stars of another era. I used to choose the Movietone All-American Football team.

Of course, my choices were substantially influenced by the player's performance on the games we had covered that year. If it was ever a toss-up, we picked the guys who had the best plays in our film vault. I covered the 1958 Giants/Colts NFL championship game, maybe the greatest game ever played. I still feel the rush. From Movietone to ITNA, I ran the sports department.

I planned to do the same at CNN. Then I ran into the Ted Turner problem. As I've said before, Ted was not in the good graces of his fellow baseball owners. At ITNA, I had been getting sports rights from Major League teams to take game excerpts directly from satellite. No such luck at CNN.

Ted's problem with the sports establishment was the Superstation. He owned the Atlanta Braves and the Atlanta Hawks, and he put them on his national satellite network. You could see the Braves in Los Angeles. You could see Hawks games in Chicago. His teams were stealing audience from the local stations. The other owners said Ted was poaching in their territory. Additionally, he was regarded as a clown, an invader, and a renegade. Broadcasters and owners tried the courts, they tried the FCC, but in the end, they discovered that Ted had found loopholes in the regulations. There was no way to stop him. There was, however, a way to stop me and CNN.

Nothing in the regs commanded the offended owners to give CNN access to their baseball or basketball games. That's when I called for help. I added a hundred thousand dollars to the budget, created a vice president of sports, and named him MacPhail. Bill MacPhail, as I've mentioned, was the father of television sports. He had been with CBS from the fifties to the seventies. At CBS, he was an innovator. He was the first to cover the Olympics, he was the first to put pro football on a national network, and everybody loved him.

MacPhail hadn't been best man at Pete Rozelle's wedding for nothing. Rozelle was NFL commissioner. One phone call from Bill to Pete gave CNN the rights to use NFL football. Phone calls to the various Major League teams gave CNN baseball rights. Who was going to turn down MacPhail, the son of the man who invented night baseball and the brother of the president of the American League? Hockey would do anything to get national television exposure, and then the NBA had no choice. Nobody could say no to Bill.

Bill and I made one deal that was too good to last. HBO agreed to give us the rights to use up to two minutes of their live fights on our sports shows. Shortly after we went on the air, there was a Norton heavyweight championship fight that lasted two minutes and forty-four seconds. We used two minutes. That didn't leave much to the imagination.

Lou Falcigno, the promoter, had sold broadcast rights to ABC for their weekend show. Now CNN had shown 80 percent of the fight before ABC. ABC was screaming at Falcigno, wanting to cut his price in half. Falcigno was telling HBO they had to make up the difference. How could they give away what he owned?

Ordinarily, HBO would have given CNN a hard time, but they couldn't bring themselves to give Bill MacPhail a hard time. They *had* given Bill permission; it was their mistake. ABC agreed to pay Mr. Falcigno most of the money in his contract. He agreed to eat a few dollars. HBO cut our access down to one minute, and everybody was happy, sort of. Everybody had started out furious. MacPhail turned us all into gentlemen. If it had been me, the lawsuit would still be going on.

Years earlier, when Bill was head of CBS Sports, and had acquired the rights to most of sport's major attractions, he wanted to take the World Series away from NBC, which had owned the rights since radio days. After years of trying, Bill was able to bring baseball to the table. Baseball would consider an offer from CBS.

MacPhail and Bob Woods, then president of CBS, had lunch with Bowie Kuhne the commissioner of baseball. MacPhail said the lunch went well, CBS had a chance to get the World Series. Before Bill could make his final pitch, Woods intervened, "By and large, television is a cutthroat business with the exception of the long relationship between major league baseball and NBC. From the beginning of broadcasting the World Series has been carried by NBC. It's a wonderful tradition and CBS will not interfere."

Woods turned to MacPhail and apologized: It would be wonderful business for CBS to broadcast the series, but this time tradition must override business considerations. Bill was disappointed but pleased at the high road CBS had taken. Everyone at the table was impressed. I'm a lot more cynical than Bill. I thought that Woods had a different motive. I think Woods was saying, "Listen guys, we're not going to get into a bidding war with NBC over the World Series." So long as NBC didn't bid against CBS and CBS didn't bid against NBC, they kept the price of sports under control. I never exposed MacPhail to my cynicism, I was afraid it would shatter his dreams.

In the sixties, ABC got into the live sports business and the prices went way up. Then Fox got into it, and the prices went out of sight. Now all four networks bid against each other, and all of them whine that they're losing money.

MacPhail was also a pretty good judge of talent. He's the guy who found Pat Summerall, still the national anchor of NFL games. In his CBS days, MacPhail was looking for a play-by-play broadcaster for pro football. He called Charlie Connerly, the former New York Giants quarterback. Summerall was Connerly's roommate. When MacPhail heard his voice he said, "Pat, you have a pretty good voice. Why don't you come down and audition too?" Forty years later, Pat Summerall is still doing play-by-play, but now it's on Fox.

MacPhail found the sports talent for CNN, again with Sam Zelman's help. Sam knew Nick Charles. Charles had worked for WRC in Washington when Sam was there. Charles was smooth on camera and knew everything there was to know about boxing and horse racing. A man after my own heart and MacPhail's, too. MacPhail liked anybody who knew what he was talking about. He didn't go for the pretty boys; he wanted character. Charles had that. Later Charles saved CNN's ass on the Air Florida crash, but that's another chapter.

We found a couple other more than serviceable sports guys. And then, just before launch, desperate for a fourth sports anchor, we stumbled on Fred Hickman. He was a little green, but he had great presence and lit up the screen when he went on camera. He was making only

$18,000 a year, so we got him cheap. Best of all, to make it three for three, he was black. Charles and Hickman are still at CNN and now CNN/SI, so MacPhail's good judgment lives after him.

He picked only one loser, and that wasn't his fault, because CNN lost her to love. On this one, it's no names please. It is sufficient to say that during the baseball strike, the press was at a Manhattan hotel, waiting for negotiations to end. At about one in the morning, the talks broke down; there was going to be a strike. Everyone in the lobby was looking for our reporter. She had disappeared.

Phil Griffin, the producer, did a "phoner," no pictures. I called him. "Why don't we have pictures, where's the reporter?" Griffin did not tell me that she was up in a hotel room with a TV anchorman who was later to become her husband. He said that we didn't have a satellite truck on site. I believed him, so I didn't fire her. Thanks to Griffin, her job was saved, and we didn't fire the anchorman, either.

The sports department filled its lower ranks with video journalists and young kids from CBS. A year and a half into CNN, Bill hired Jim Walton as his assistant. Walton was the same kind of guy as Bill, just thirty years younger. When Bill retired, Jim took over sports. He was so successful that he's now head of all CNN networks in the United States. He's as competent as MacPhail and as decent as MacPhail. CNN is very lucky.

Round 23: "For Every Drop of Blood I Shed, You Will Shed a Barrel"

Early in 1979, there were four people I was talking with about starting the twenty-four-hour news network: Turner, the *Washington Post*, Scripps Howard, and the Univision Television Network, which was owned by Emilio Escaraga. The *Post* and Scripps Howard were public corporations. They couldn't get their act together; too much research, too many fiefdoms, too much due diligence. CNN was an act of faith.

Turner had faith, but Escaraga had faith, too. Turner had a transponder; Escaraga didn't. Therefore, I went with Ted. And then Ted lost the transponder.

The RCA satellites had twenty-four transponders. A transponder is like a bundle of phone lines in the sky. At that time, it took a full transponder to transmit CNN to cable systems. Some transponders were dedicated to phone service, others to data. Only a few were dedicated to video, and they were tough to come by.

The RCA Satcom III satellite was the "cable bird." It was the only satellite that reached the entire cable industry, and it was full up. RCA was about to launch a second satellite, also fully booked; CNN had one of the bookings. That satellite was our lifeline to the world. On December 6, 1979, our lifeline ruptured. RCA launched its new satellite, and it blew up. No satellite, no CNN. NBC News distanced itself from RCA, its mother company, reporting that there were "a lot of red faces at RCA." On CBS, Walter Cronkite shed crocodile tears. He read a poem that ended with, "You can't win 'em all." For CNN the problem was, we might have lost it all.

This was the one moment in all my time at CNN when I doubted its success. I had bet twenty years of news experience on Ted Turner and his transponder. I had hired dozens of people, spent millions of dollars of Ted's money, and called in twenty years of personal favors to structure this grand enterprise. Now, RCA had blown it all up in my face. When I heard the news, I threw everybody out of my office and thought, What could I do? I had been used to solving my own problems. I was solving all the CNN problems, but there was no one I knew who owed me a transponder. This one was up to Ted.

RCA had covered its ass. Their contract for Satcom III expressly stated that all transponder reservations were "subject to a successful launch." An explosion is not a successful launch. RCA owed us nothing. They had another satellite in reserve, and that would be launched in time to meet CNN's June 1 deadline, but they had devised a whole new set of rules for that satellite.

RCA said that all previous reservations were cancelled and potential users would have to reapply. Since there were six applicants for four slots, RCA decided that the only fair way to choose between them was to draw lots. CNN's whole future was about to be decided by someone putting his hand into a fishbowl and pulling out a piece of paper. Everything was up in the air except the RCA satellite.

We figured that we had sunk $34.5 million into CNN. We had dozens of cable operators signed up, and we had a fixed date. We were all dressed up with no place to go. Then Bill Bevins, the CFO, called me. He told me we had a chance. Terry had found a clause in an old contract that gave us some rights. "Terry McGuirk?" I asked. "No," Bevins snorted. "Terry McGuirk never read a contract in his life. Terry Bridges found it." "Who's Terry Bridges?" I asked. "A lawyer at Troutman Sanders," Bevins said. Bevins continued to appreciate Terry Bridges. Seventeen years later, when he left Turner to go to work for Ron Perelman, he took Bridges with him as his chief operating officer.

Riding to the rescue out of our past came Will Sanders. Sanders had been the Turner CFO in 1978, when Turner sold a satellite uplink to RCA. Bridges had been his lawyer. Sanders had inserted a clause into the sales contract that granted Ted rights to first refusal on two more transponders on the original cable bird. RCA had never given Ted "first refusal" rights, and Terry Bridges remembered this. He thought the old Will Sanders clause might give us some leverage.

We flew up to New York to face RCA in their lair high atop Rockefeller Center. Bridges had found the appropriate clause, but the wording was not all that clear. Still, it gave us a leg to stand on—maybe a spindly leg, but we were hopeful. Ted brought Tench Coxe and Terry McGuirk with him to the RCA meeting. I had Bill Henry with me. He was a former FCC chairman and CNN's attorney. On the RCA side, there were, among others, Andy Inglis, the president of RCA Americom, and Jay Ricks, RCA's lawyer.

We sat around the table. Tench Coxe presented our best case in equity. "CNN ought to be granted a transponder on the equitable ground that CNN's unique cable news programming is more important to the television viewing public than the programming which the other programmers proposed to offer viewers." We all knew that "equity" didn't mean anything. Then we hit 'em with breach of contract. They had denied Ted the chance to exercise his right of first refusal. They scoffed. Then Ted became Ted. He told Ricks he was going to sue, and he advised Inglis to sell his RCA stock because, "When I get done with you, it ain't gonna be worth a dollar a share!" He got up from the table, walked across the room, and glared at Andy Inglis, the man who ran RCA Americom. "Sir," he yelled, "does your chairman know what you're doing? Does he realize where this is going to end? I'm a small company, and you guys may put me out of business, but for every drop of blood I shed, you will shed a barrel!"

Ted knew he was an owner. The difference between an owner and somebody who works for somebody else is, an owner can do what he wants. But Andy, the guy he was yelling at, had to worry about what his boss said. His boss, the chairman, could fire him and probably would if Ted did what he said. Ted was swearing that if he fell on his sword, he was taking half of RCA down with him. Andy Inglis's career was vanishing before his eyes.

At which point, the lawyers went into another room with the two principals, and an agreement was hammered out. CNN would be assigned a transponder on Satcom I for six months while a court decided what RCA's contractual obligations were. If RCA won, we had to move to another satellite (but in six months we'd be on the air, and it wouldn't matter). If Ted won, he'd keep CNN on Satcom I. The RCA lawyers wouldn't give us the transponder unless we sued. If they did, all other transponder applicants would be screaming bloody murder and calling in their own legal teams. RCA said, "Sue us."

They gave us a wink and a nod and assured us that they would not fight our claim too hard. They were even willing to give us home court advantage. We could file suit in Atlanta, and they would not ask for a change of venue. We would be presenting our case to the judge of our choosing. When we won, RCA would be able to tell the world: "The judge said we had to give them the transponder. It's not our fault."

Ted was exuberant. We got into the RCA elevator. It was full of people who worked for NBC, but Ted could not keep his mouth shut. "They're going to throw the case, Reese," he said. "They're going to throw the lawsuit. They're going to let us win." Tench Coxe was muttering, "Shh, Ted, shh, come on Ted." Ted could not shut up. He crowed all the way down to the lobby. I couldn't blame him. Ted blustered, but no one will ever know if he bluffed. If I were Ted, I'd have been shouting it from the rooftops. Single-handedly (or single-mouthedly) he had, all by himself, beaten one of the great corporations in America. It was not a bad moment.

The rest is anticlimactic. CNN won the case in the northern district of Georgia and won the proceedings before the FCC. Competing networks filed appeals. They lost. CNN launched June 1, 1980, and 1.7 million Americans were watching.

Round 24: The Ten O'Clock Follies

The 10 p.m. show was designed to be the network's centerpiece—a serious one-hour discussion of the day's leading news story or stories with guests, call-ins, and CNN reporters joining in with a solid, attractive host. The host would know something about everything, make his guests comfortable, and be willing to defer, at least occasionally, to a CNN reporter who might know more about a particular area than he did. The position was going for a mere $80,000 a year. This was not going to be an easy job to fill.

No one had done a national live call-in television show before this. No one had ever done a one-hour television hard news talk program before this. It seemed to me the natural follow-up to *Prime News 120,* which ran from eight to ten. On *Prime News,* we told you what was the most important story of the day. At ten o'clock, we wanted the most important player in the most important story to be on our air, to talk to our journalists, and to be available to take questions from everybody in America. It was not necessarily a celebrity show. The most important person might be a relatively obscure figure, or even just a civilian involved in a situation that had grabbed front pages everywhere.

My first choice for host was David Frost. He had been doing it all his life, first as satire: (*That Was the Week That Was*), then as a straight 11 p.m. talk show for Group W. Westinghouse Broadcasting. Frost read newspapers without anyone telling him to. He was funny and he controlled an interview. He came down to Atlanta with Jim Griffin, the William Morris agent, we had lunch, toured the Techwood studios, and then went up to Ted's office. David Frost was too big a star for Ted to miss. I also counted on Ted to charm Frost into submission.

At the time, all we had to show David was the tape of the contributors we had signed up: Barry Goldwater, Bill Simon, Bella Abzug, et al. One of the contributors was a dud from Dudsville. Everybody groaned. Not Ted. "Even Jesus Christ couldn't pick twelve men without one bum in the bunch," says Ted.

Griffen, Frost, and I talk deal. Frost will not do five shows a week, he doesn't want to live in Atlanta. He says, maybe three. I need a five-day-a-week guy. We never get down to talking money, but Ted at least brought Frost to the table.

Another early candidate was Charlie Rose, who was married to a local Atlanta anchor. He wanted to work for us. He was bright, he was charming, and he would've been okay about money. But Sam Zelman insisted that Rose was "dull, dull, dull." Rose is the only guy on television who manages to be charming and dull at the same time. I didn't want to turn Charlie down hard, so I offered him $45,000 a year, which I knew he wouldn't accept. He didn't, and I kept on looking.

I talked to Maury Povich, but not for this job. I wanted him to be our lead sportscaster. His father, Shirley Povich, covered sports for the *Washington Post* for sixty years. I first met Maury when he was a sports anchor at Channel 5 Washington, and I thought he was in a class by himself, one of the best sports journalists on television. He was young, good-looking, passionate, and extremely knowledgeable about sports.

I met him for lunch in New York. He walked in exhausted. He explained he'd been up until three in the morning watching the L.A. Lakers go into overtime on cable. We talked about the game for fifteen minutes. I talked to Maury about the sports job. I offered him $100,000 a year. He didn't want to do sports, but he'd take $80,000 if I'd give him the ten o'clock call-in show. I didn't believe that Maury had the same passion for news that he did for sports. I didn't believe I could keep Maury awake till three in the morning to watch a hard news event. I didn't take his offer seriously. I kept coming back to him about sports. He kept coming back to me about news. I made a classic mistake: I didn't put him on hold. Never say no to anyone until you find someone better.

Geraldo Rivera's agent called. Geraldo was working for ABC, he had an out on his contract, but ABC had a right to match other offers. I was not naïve. I knew Geraldo was fishing for another offer. I knew NBC and CBS had shown no interest in him. I did not think he was particularly fitted to the role of the ten o'clock host; his ego was not likely to have suffered the presence of other CNN reporters on the show. But I am a broadcaster, and I knew Geraldo's worth as an anchor. I also knew that as a reporter, he had exposed the horrors of New York State's mental institutions, forcing the state to implement major reforms.

He and his wife came to Atlanta and seemed sufficiently interested to drive around the city, looking at real estate. I made him an offer including options on 100,000 shares of TBS stock. I took him into Ted so Ted would see what he was getting for his money. I signed the offer sheet. Sure enough, Geraldo showed it to ABC, they improved their deal, he accepted, and CNN heard from him no more. Geraldo's current agent tells me now that his client deeply regrets his choice, as well he should.

On the day the AOL/Time Warner merger was announced, Geraldo's stock options would have been worth about $180 million. Geraldo is now on CNBC, doing his version of the show I offered him twenty years ago. He competes head to head with Larry King. King beats him regularly.

After Geraldo, I turned to Linda Ellerbee, or, to be more accurate, she turned to me. Linda had been one of the first and best women to work as a street reporter in New York. She worked for Channel 2, the CBS local station, then moved to NBC network. By 1979, Bill Small, who had been second in command at CBS network news for a generation, had gone over to run NBC news. Linda's contract was up, and it seemed that Small was not going to renew her.

Not only was she smart, she was funny and passionately committed to news. When her agent called, I would've signed her on her reputation alone. She flew down to Atlanta. We talked money, we talked options, she seemed receptive, and we were going to discuss details with her agent. Of course, she had to go back and talk to Bill Small.

Now that CNN was interested, Small made her an offer. That was all she really wanted, and she accepted too fast. She should have thought twice. She was out in a year or two. (Statistics show that only 50 percent of employees who use outside offers to get their jobs renewed last more than two years.) Linda now produces programs for children, which show up on Nickelodeon and some of the broadcast networks. I know she's doing good work, but I believe she'd have been doing better work hosting the ten o'clock show. I am absolutely sure she'd be getting better ratings than Geraldo.

I had talked to Larry King about a job at CNN early on. I wanted him to do our 1 a.m. Hollywood show, *People Tonight.* He wouldn't move to the West Coast, so the talks never got anywhere. I felt about him as I felt about Povich. Larry King was the best of the celebrity interviewers, but not as strong for hard news. Larry King was Walter Winchell; Edward R. Murrow he was not.

King, Rose, and Rivera have all wound up doing one-hour prime-time news talk. The line is: You can go on the Larry King show and interview yourself, or you can go on the Charlie Rose show and listen to him interview himself.

There is method to King's madness. When guests interview themselves, they sometimes say things they wouldn't say to other people. When they do, they make news. Walter Sabo, a radio guru, told me that Howard Stern wears shades on the radio because people look into the eyes of the person they're talking to to get a reaction. If you hide your eyes, your guests may just keep on talking. Sabo adds that one of King's great strengths is that he does not need shades, he's got the deadest eyes on television.

We continued our search, and made a brief, unsuccessful run at John Johnson, an elegant black news reporter for WABC. Then I tried Pat Mitchell, who had hosted a successful talk show on Channel 5 Washington before going on to politics, working for David Garth and Boston's mayor, Kevin White. She was ready to move, but she wanted to move to Los Angeles, where her romantic interests lay. Fifteen years later, she moved to Atlanta to become head of Turner Productions and in 1999 she became president of PBS. I think she's the only talk show anchor ever to became president of a network.

Speaking of PBS, I called Jim Lehrer, who had switched from news executive to anchor the PBS coverage of the Watergate hearings. At first, he was nervous and tentative on the air. By 1979, when he was partnering in the *MacNeil/Lehrer News Hour,* he had become smooth, but not overly smooth, and would've been perfect for CNN. He was, however, joined at the hip to Robin MacNeil. He wasn't going anywhere.

Forrest Sawyer, a local Atlanta radio host, pitched the job. He would've worked for an Atlanta salary. I passed. I didn't want the critics to say we were giving our most important program to a local radio guy. I was snobbish and dumb. Sawyer later showed his ability on *ABC News* and *Nightline.*

Toward the end of the search, Sam Zelman, who, I will say for the umpteenth time, knew more about talent than almost anybody in broadcasting, came up with a name I hadn't heard, Oprah Winfrey. She was a local anchor in Baltimore and had a talk show there. Sam thought she had a bright future. I thought again that hiring a relatively inexperienced anchorwoman from Baltimore would give television critics too easy a chance to take a shot at CNN. I didn't even look at the tape. One thing I know now, don't worry what the critics are going to say about credentials, take a look at the talent.

June 1 was fast approaching. We had no host. Another woman I hadn't heard of, Sandi Freeman, called me. She was cohosting *AM Chicago,* a local morning show on WLS, the ABC-owned and -operated station. She really wanted to work for us and sent her resume, which consisted of a Jules Witcover column from the *Washington Star* characterizing her as "a pleasant looking blonde woman with one subject on her mind, and the determination to get answers about it." Witcover claimed Sandi had done a better job of pinning Ted Kennedy down about what she called the "Joan Factor" than anyone else on television.

The Joan in the "Joan Factor" was Joan Kennedy, Ted's wife. Ted was notoriously seeing other women now that he and his wife were separated. When Sandi asked Ted about the "Joan Factor," he talked of Joan's problems with alcohol and her need to rebuild her life, as if this was the sole cause of their separation. Sandi wouldn't let him get away with the answer. She kept asking him about his role in their marital problems. He avoided and left the studio furious at Freeman.

Sandi's tapes showed that when she interviewed ordinary people she was extremely kind and warm. Seeing her tough on big shots and sympathetic to ordinary folks, I thought I could make her a star. Her agent tried to improve her deal, but Sandi overrode him and accepted our offer. We were set. The 10 p.m. show would be *Freeman Reports.* Little did I know that I had really been set up. More about that later.

We still had to find one more executive producer. CNN's table of organization called for four executive producers: one for hard news, one for sports, one for financial news, and one for the talk shows. Mike

Kandel was running financial, Rick Davis had sports, Ted Kavanau had hard news, the talk shows were a problem.

I tried Brooke Bailey, now Brooke Bailey Johnson, who later became head of programming for A&E and the History Channel. She had worked with Sandi Freeman in Chicago and for whatever reason would not do so again. I had known Jane Caper when she was producing *Panorama,* the WTTG talk show in Washington. She'd moved to WCVB Boston, where she was producing the *Janet Langhart Show.* In between, she'd worked for ABC and produced Peter Jennings's *Good Morning America.* If you worked with Jennings, you had to know news, and if you coexisted with Jennings, you had to know how to handle talent.

Langhart did a morning talk show, very soft and featurish. She was also enormously kind to her guests. Caper saw CNN as a chance to get back to hard news, to get back to a national network, and a great career opportunity. In addition to her credentials, she had a piece of videotape that proved one of the major points of the CNN credo. Our 10 p.m. show was going to take calls from the audience *live,* no seven-second delay the way the networks did. Whatever our caller said went on the air. There was no opportunity for censorship.

Jim Kitchell, the ex-NBC executive who was head of operations at CNN, was horrified. His credo was, "If it hadn't been done at NBC, it couldn't be done at all." NBC was afraid of everything, especially losing its broadcast licenses. Therefore NBC always used a seven-second delay in case somebody said something naughty. I reminded Kitchell that cable didn't have licenses to lose. He sulked anyway.

Then Caper came down to Atlanta with her tape. Langhart had interviewed Lauren Hutton live. Her introduction to Hutton went something like this: "Lauren, every year millions of girls are born in America, and they all hope to grow up and be models. Maybe a thousand make it; you were one of them. Those thousand all dream of being cover girls. Maybe ten of them make it; you were one of them. All of those ten hope to become spokeswoman for a major product, and that happens once every five or ten years. You did that, too. Tell me Lauren, how did you do it?" And Hutton answered, "Oh, I fucked around."

Hutton said this live, on the air, on a licensed television station. Bob Bennett, the general manager of the station, raced out of his office, screaming, "I'm gonna lose my license! I'm gonna lose my license!"

But what was done was done. Bennett expected the worst, but there were no phone calls, no letters, no FCC problems. I hired Caper for her talent, and for her tape. From then on, if anyone mentioned "seven-second delay," I played the tape, told the story, and the discussion ended.

Kitchell had another problem with the show. He did not come to me with the problem; he went to AT&T. I had ordered a 1-800 number to encourage callers to phone in. Kitchell scared AT&T: There had never before been a national call-in show. There was no way to measure potential response. Suppose we swamped the entire phone exchange. Within that exchange was Piedmont Hospital. People could die because the hospital phone lines were jammed.

AT&T refused to give us a 1-800 number. They did not like "has never been done before" situations. I tried to reason with them. We were going on the air with only 1.7 million homes, far fewer than the New York City market or the L.A. market. AT&T grants 1-800 numbers in those areas. They were adamant. Finally, I ordered more regular long-distance lines. The caller would have to pay to voice his opinion. Would callers pay just to talk to Sandi Freeman? The concern vanished immediately: Our lines were always busy. Lots of people would pay for a phone call to express their opinions to a national audience. Thanks to Kitchell, we saved $5,000 a month on 1-800 numbers.

Round 25: Ted Panics

I should have been ready for it. Bunky Helfrich, the CNN architect and Ted's navigator on *Courageous,* warned me. When Bunky and I heard about the disaster at the Fastnet yacht race, before we knew Ted had survived, Bunky said, "I hope Ted is locked in his cabin. He goes crazy in a storm. We used to call him Captain Panic." As it turned out, Ted hadn't panicked; he had outrun the storm and won the race. Ted knew everything about sailing. CNN was different; he had a lot to learn about news.

It was May, a month till launch, Ted's anxieties were rising. He had little understanding of what CNN was going to be, and he had no idea of how it would be received. Ted's chief contribution to CNN until then had been, aside from the money he spent on it, the blaze of publicity he brought to it. If I started a news network, it would have gotten four paragraphs on the television page of *Variety*. When Ted Turner did it, it was full-column, front-page *Wall Street Journal*. That fact had a down side. If CNN failed, Ted Turner would fail on every front page, on every network news program in America.

ON May 1, Ted was in New York City making a speech to the big guys about CNN. He wasn't sure CNN would be ready. People in Atlanta were still hammering nails and laying cables. He could not foresee how it would all come together. But there he was, standing before the New York Academy of Television Arts and Sciences, proclaiming the greatness of CNN. Even worse, most of the audience was the "enemy," broadcasters.

Look at it from Ted's point of view: He was going into a business he had never liked, and about which he knew little. He had every right to be scared. Hell, I was scared, and I knew what I was doing.

When Ted is scared, he lashes out. His speech that day was all lash-and-smash, a Turner tirade complete with exaggerations, inaccuracies, and old wives' tales. It was amazing, it was arousing, and, to much of the audience, it was offensive. Coming from that "good ole boy" Ted Turner, it was fun; coming from the proprietor of CNN, it was trouble for me. How could I make it clear that the opinions expressed by Ted Turner did not reflect the views of CNN or its journalists? I had to build a wall between our product and our proprietor.

Anyway, Ted opened his speech by offering a solution to the Iran hostage crisis: The U.S. could, in exchange for getting the hostages back, rotate fifty volunteers who would remain in Iran for two weeks, then be replaced by a new group; Muhammad Ali had already volunteered, and Ted was prepared to do the same. "They can't do anything to me over there that the networks and the National Association of Broadcasters haven't tried to do over here," he proclaimed.

What a segue! He went from a hero who's rescuing hostages to a victim of those cruel, evil "broadcasters" he was addressing.

Next, he told the broadcasters that the reason he'd gone into television was that they were doing "a pretty bad job," ranted on at great length, and concluded by calling the state of television "an absolute tragedy."

Now he turned to his real target, the TV news programs. He thought network television was slow to report the good deeds of senators and congressmen and quick to report catastrophes. He implied that somehow CNN would be different: "With cable, you will see on June first just how good television news can be." He then proceeded to attack, again at some length, an organization of which he was envious: the Cox empire, with its reputation for good newspapers and great television stations. His specific target was WSB, the Cox outlet in Atlanta, which was in the midst of a possible acquisition by General Electric. He accused the station of tabloid journalism to the max, ending with, "And this is WSB, with the white columns on Peachtree . . . they ought to have their license taken away in my opinion."

It was absolutely outrageous. Here was the owner of a dinky little UHF rerun station suggesting that the FCC revoke the license of one of the great American television stations.

But Ted wasn't done. He excoriated Hollywood for fomenting violence and predicted that, unless America cut back on welfare and put the money into weapons, the Russians would liquidate every single one of us. Finally he closed with a CNN promo: "As you know, we've gotten my transponder squared away. I would have had a hard time making this speech two weeks ago . . . but it looks now like we're not going under, so CNN will . . . be ready to go June 1. I think you are all going to want to see it because you are all interested in television or you wouldn't be here. I mean, this ain't a damn sailing group, thank God."

Gabe Pressman, New York's most recognized street reporter, was in the audience along with Mark Monsky and Jim Coppersmith, the news director and general manager of WNEW, where Pressman then worked. Pressman challenged Turner to define good local news. Ted was stuck for an answer and asked Pressman where he worked. Gabe identified himself as Channel 5 WNEW.

"That's a tabloid television station, and you're a yellow journalist," Ted lashed out. Monsky, Pressman's news director, yelled at Turner, "You're talking about the most respected reporter in New York." Coppersmith stood up and attacked Turner's news on WTBS. It turned into a grand furor, and it was thought to be the most exciting luncheon in the history of the academy. And no one was injured.

A few weeks later, Ted was back in New York, and this time I was with him. We were going to have lunch with the editorial board of the *New York Times*. The lunch had been arranged by Les Brown, the television writer for the *Times* and one of the most influential journalists ever to write about television.

On Brown's recommendation, I had hired Ben Kubasik, formerly PR man for CBS news, to handle CNN public relations. When Fred Friendly resigned from CBS news, claiming that the news division was suffering from corporate interference, Kubasik walked with him. He was thought by the TV critics to be the only PR man who had ever quit anything as a matter of principle. He was respected, even revered, and his integrity was unquestioned. The press knew Ben wouldn't flack for bad journalism. Having him on our side would help overcome journalistic prejudices against that "wild man from the South."

For all his bravado, Ted wanted my help when he faced the *New York Times*. Most people who came to these lunches recognized them as very serious business. Les Brown told me that guests at these luncheons, even the most powerful of men, ordinarily arrived in awe, paid obeisance, and left somewhat humbled. Ted reacted differently. As we walked in, he stared at Kubasik and demanded, "What the hell am I doing here? . . . Who got me into this?" Kubasik introduced us. As we sat down, Ted went on the attack: "Don't you know we are going to bury you?" he asked of the assembled *Times* editors. "You are putting out a paper tomorrow, and we're putting our news out for today."

We ate, and when the questions began, they were directed toward me. There were questions about schedule, talent, point of view, all comfortably handled, but nothing not previously known. The editorial board members recognized names like Kandel and Klensch, who had come out of the newspaper business. They all knew Dan Schorr, but after that, they knew nobody. It seemed that they didn't pay much attention to television.

Finally, John Nordheimer, an assistant managing editor, asked what we were doing that the networks had not done. I said, "We're going to do live news and more live news like it has never been done before." Nordheimer asked, "Won't you be covering a lot of one-alarm fires?" I replied that, until the fire is over, no one knows whether it's a one-alarm fire or the fire that burned down Chicago.

I'm sure that the *Times* editorial board did not grasp the revolutionary nature of live television or the twenty-four-hour news schedule. In terms newspapermen would understand, we were advancing the news cycle by at least twelve hours. Later, Les Brown told me that the *Times* people were absolutely terrified, but they were terrified of Ted Turner, not of CNN.

When the lunch ended, Ted was much relieved, he thought we had done good.

Les Brown wrote a long piece on the lunch, hoping it might get a few paragraphs on the front page and then carry over into the television section. Abe Rosenthal, then the editor of the *Times,* told Les the piece was too positive, CNN wasn't even on the air yet. Les toned down the story, Rosenthal killed it anyway. Looking back, I suppose that if you tell the *New York Times* you're going to bury them, maybe you shouldn't expect much space in the paper.

Ted's final anxiety attack, at least prelaunch, occurred in Atlanta. In late May, Ted Kavanau called me: Come down to the floor, come down to the floor. There on the floor of the newsroom, with the carpenters hammering and the electricians wiring, was Jim Kitchell with a sheaf of white papers. Kitchell, CNN's in-house doubter, consistently fed Turner's anxieties. Now he was distributing a one-sheet "call to blackmail" to every CNN employee he could reach. Kavanau and Pat O'Gorman walked behind him snatching up the papers as Kitchell passed them out.

Kavanau showed me one. Kitchell was asking every employee of CNN who had ever worked at a network to tell him every bit of dirt we knew about that network. Turner had commissioned a documentary about network practices that he wanted to run on CNN. He thought he could documentary the networks to death. I told Ted that CNN didn't need to do it and wouldn't do it. Ted seemed to calm down, we gathered up the papers and destroyed them, the project vanished. (Shortly after the launch I fired Kitchell, and Ted hired him to work for TBS.)

After that, it was too late for panic. It was put-up-or-shut-up time. Either I put up or Ted shut up. And so we waited.

Round 26: **Finding Homes**

It was May 1980, and two guys whose names I barely knew, Don Lachowski and Gerry Hogan, showed up in my office. I did know that they were advertising salesmen and they were selling spots to advertisers based on certain subscriber guarantees that CNN had made. First we guaranteed 5 million homes on launch date. When Ted saw that was unobtainable, he reduced it to 3.5 million.

Then these two guys barged into my office. I didn't consider Hogan a friend of ours, since he was the one who begged Ted not to start CNN, saying he would be "putting the whole company at risk." He had also put up the sign in Ted's office that read, "Don't do this to us Ted."

Hogan and Lachowski told me, "CNN doesn't have 3.5 million homes." I said, "Bullshit. Of course we have 3.5 million homes." "How do you know?" they asked. "Terry McGuirk says so," I said. They said, "There is only one guy in this company who will tell you the truth about affiliate subscribers, and he is Don Anderson. You go see Don Anderson, and you'll see how many homes CNN is in. He'll give you the straight numbers."

I stormed out of my office in the former rehab building, went next door, and stormed in on Anderson. I was convinced that Lachowski and Hogan were trying to sabotage CNN and that this man, Anderson, was fronting for them. Then I confronted Anderson, and he looked the soul of integrity. He had snow-white hair, a craggy face, and a New England accent. I blustered, "What do you mean, we only have 1.7 million homes?" He said, very quietly, "Look. Here's a list. It comes to 1.7 million homes, these are the homes you are going to have when you go on the air June first. If you don't believe me, take it to McGuirk or to Roy Mehlman." Mehlman was the man Ted Turner had hired to do the heavy lifting when it came to getting affiliates. I told Anderson, "I'll talk with you later," and walked away with the list.

I called Mehlman to my office and showed him Anderson's list, expecting bad news. I said, "It comes to 1.7 million homes. Where are the others?" He looked at the list, he looked at the list, and he looked at the list. *"Where are the other homes?"* I demanded. "They're coming," he said. "So is Christmas," I said. "How many homes are we gonna have when we go on the air?" He said, "1.7 million."

I grabbed Lachowski and Hogan and the three of us rushed up to Turner's office. I was convinced that McGuirk was a lightweight, carrying Ted's briefcase, but what I did not know was that Ted had special feelings for Terry. He was like another son to him. Years before, Terry had told Ted that some of the guys working for him in his Charlotte station were skimming. It was true. Ted fired the guys, and the station turned profitable. Ted loved and trusted Terry ever after.

Anyway, being innocent about any of this, I walked into Ted's office and showed him Anderson's subscription roster. I told him that Roy Mehlman accepted Anderson's numbers. Strangely, Ted shut up and listened without comment. Then he called Anderson and went over the list with Don. Ted nodded. Hogan, Lachowski, and I left his office.

I was not aware that I had stumbled into a political swamp. Gerry Hogan and Terry McGuirk had been rivals for Ted's affections for years. It seemed as if I was siding with Hogan against McGuirk, when what I was doing was fighting for CNN. Looking back now, I know two things: Ted loved Terry, but he knew Don Anderson told the truth.

Ted reacted within days. McGuirk was "promoted" to handling international development of TBS, and Nory LeBrun, head of affiliate sales for TBS, was put in charge of CNN affiliate sales as well. McGuirk was a smoothie, LeBrun a fighter. He was a man who would go into the trenches and battle for subscribers. But LeBrun had not picked his staff; Turner and McGuirk had picked it for him. Their working boss, Mehlman, was a man for whom I harbored a particular dislike. At one point, he'd run the UPI still pictures commercial department. The commercial department took pictures of chief executives and ribbon cuttings and other ceremonial events for companies that wanted to preserve their special moments.

Mehlman developed a new line of business. When antiwar demonstrators held sit-ins at the University of Chicago in the sixties, Mehlman hired out to the university. He sent commercial photographers with UPI press passes dangling from their necks into the dorms and classrooms to take pictures of the demonstrators. The pictures were turned over to the university administration. Later, the students were disciplined, some expelled. UPI was paid, and then the story broke in the press. Every legitimate UPI newsman suffered. We did not shoot "fink film." Mehlman did.

I'm sure Ted didn't know the University of Chicago story when he hired Mehlman, but I did, and I had little faith in his ability. Mehlman had brought with him another UPI sales veteran, Frank Beatty. Beatty was better. McGuirk and Mehlman added several young, relatively inexperienced guys to the affiliate sales staff, and that was the team that was supposed to deliver the 5 million subscribers. Nory LeBrun, who succeeded Terry, said that the sales force was not entirely at fault. "The cable industry had little faith in Ted as a news provider," Nory says. "Cable veterans, fairly sober businessmen, were saying, 'Take a look at Ted, there is no way this guy can pull this off. There is no way I'm going to tie my cart to his tail. This guy is looney tunes.'" Ted reaffirmed those doubts every time he acted up. In Nory's view, Ted was making it tougher for everybody.

That's where McGuirk was helpful. He had the contacts to overcome that perception. He knew the top guys at the MSOs (multisystem operators). Companies like Time-Life, Teleprompter, and TCI. According to Nory, McGuirk was able to convince people like Tryg Myrhen, head of what is now Time Warner Cable, that "McGuirk carried a lot of weight with Ted and if Tryg felt that Ted was being too outrageous, Tryg could call McGuirk and McGuirk could get Ted to cool his jets a little bit." McGuirk was playing the same role with cable affiliates that Gerry Hogan had played with advertisers. He was cleaning up after Ted.

Turner had set it up so that there would be two affiliate sales groups, one to call on the cable operators for TBS, the other for CNN. That's why he'd hired Mehlman and Beatty. LeBrun says, "It ended up with everybody tripping on each other. It made very little sense." So he combined the CNN affiliate team with the TBS team. The same salesmen pushed both networks to the same customers. They could make combination deals, they could use the leverage of one network to help the other. Everybody in the cable industry works that way now.

Before LeBrun took over, McGuirk took me along with him on calls to the major players. In Denver, I met with TCI's John Malone for an hour, then had lunch with Tryg Myrhen. They were concerned about Turner's news credentials, or lack thereof. They queried me on my credentials. I had to convince them that I would make CNN a respectable news service that would bring honor to their industry. Malone and Myrhen bought in. They would carry CNN.

At the TCI meeting, I met with John Sparkman, who had final authority on what networks were carried by his cable systems. There was one system with more than enough capacity to carry CNN. The local manager wanted it, and Malone had given CNN the corporate okay. I asked Sparkman why we were having trouble getting a contract. He told me that TCI was petitioning for a rate increase in the local community. (A lot of subscribers wanted CNN.) Sparkman would tell the regulators that he couldn't afford to give them CNN unless the regulators gave TCI a rate increase. CNN would get on the TCI system when TCI got its rate increase. Other MSOs adopted the Sparkman strategy. CNN had become a valuable commodity. The systems used it as a bargaining chip in their regulatory negotiations.

We tried to meet in New York with Dan Ritchie, who ran Teleprompter, the Westinghouse cable system, then the largest in the country. Ritchie would not meet with us. Westinghouse had pioneered all-news radio, and they believed we were stealing their birthright when we launched all-news cable. Ritchie refused to put CNN on the cable system on Manhattan's West Side, a vital area. It later turned out that he was saving it for his own news service, Satellite News Channel, which launched in 1982. It cost him a $100 million before Ted Turner forced him into submission.

Given Ritchie's attitude, we had to get CNN on Time-owned Manhattan Cable, which covered most of the upscale parts of the city. That's where the advertisers lived and where the advertising agencies had their offices. If advertisers couldn't see their spots, they wouldn't believe that anyone was seeing them. That's the way it works. "If I don't see them, they don't exist." Manhattan Cable was headed by Jack Gault. Gault didn't want to spend fifteen cents a month on any service. Here's where the McGuirk/Myrhen connection paid off. Myrhen was Gault's boss, and he laid it on the line. He told Gault to stop bargaining and put CNN on. One Manhattan home was and is worth five homes in any other city. Manhattan is whence ad dollars flow.

When LeBrun took over, things changed. He put in a younger, stronger affiliations team. Mehlman left to join Westinghouse Broadcasting, where he would shortly attempt to compete with CNN. Frank Beatty switched over to TBS.

The Nielsen company required a universe of 13 million homes before it would rate a network. They regarded anything less as too small to sample. Even that number was a Ted Turner accomplishment. When Ted got into the cable business, Nielsen required 30 million homes. It took a long hard campaign for Ted and Bob Sieber to get Nielsen to come down. Sieber, the best research man I've ever known, kept producing numbers that showed Nielsen that 13 million was enough. Nielsen had its own reasons for accepting the lower number. They got more network subscribers sooner, and sooner meant a lot more money to Nielsen.

Advertisers pay much less, maybe 50 percent, for networks that are not rated, so Ted's efforts doubled his advertising rates two years earlier than if he had to wait for the 30 million homes to come aboard. Turner's efforts helped not only him, but the entire cable industry. It's not a widely recognized contribution, but Turner's achievement has resulted in billions of dollars in additional revenue for all cable programmers over the past 20 years.

The CNN contract proposed that the operator pay a monthly subscription fee of fifteen cents per subscriber. Cable operators did not want to pay fifteen cents a month for any network. Broadcast affiliates of CBS, NBC, or ABC were paid to carry network programs. Cable owners wanted the same treatment. Nory had to convince them, monopolists all, that our programming was of such value that they should surrender one of their precious channels to carry CNN, and pay us for it.

By June 1, 1980, Nory, Ted, McGuirk, and I had been able to convince cable owners who controlled 1.7 million homes to put us on their precious air. Bob Wright at Cox, Al Gillaland of Gill Cable, Malone at TCI, Myrhen at Time-Life, Bob Miron of Newhouse Cable, and Bill Daniels carried us from day one. As for the rest, if we had offered them a twenty-four-hour channel on which God Himself appeared accompanied by the full heavenly choir, they would still have asked, "How much will you pay us to put that guy on the air?"

Once we were on the air, Nory and his troops had a product to point to in their battle for carriage. I thought of it as a holy war to bring news to the American people. On a day-to-day basis, it was down and dirty. If a cable owner had a relative who wanted to be in the news business, we would put him in our training program. If there was a good story in the cable owner's hometown, we'd find a way to cover it. Finally, if all else failed, Nory would even "surrender my body." The only thing we wouldn't do was make price concessions.

Occasionally, when local systems managers wouldn't say yes, we went over their heads to corporate; Ted and I would make the calls. Ted had arranged a meeting with the local managers of all the Cox cable systems. The meeting would include Bob Wright, then the president of Cox Cable. Ted delivered his sales pitch. With me in the room, he included in his pitch a promise to the Cox cable managers that since CNN is in the cable business, it will protect the interests of the cable industry against broadcast and government opposition. He said we would be on cable's side on every issue.

Then it was my turn. I opened by saying, "Ted is right, CNN is in the cable business, and we will protect the interests of the cable industry on every issue where we think cable is right. CNN will report the news fairly and objectively on *all* issues." The room was hushed, even Ted. I made my pitch to Cox: "CNN is a good service, it deserves carriage." My comment didn't cost me or CNN any points with Bob Wright. Cox became a major CNN supporter, and ever since, Bob Wright has been my friend.

Ted never again brought up the Cox meeting, but he has a long memory. Looking back, there's no question that I had failed at company politics. One does not contradict Ted Turner in public, and maybe not in private either. To put the frosting on the cake, Dee Woods, Ted's most trusted secretary, had been romantically involved with one of the affiliate relations salesmen who had just been eased out of CNN by Nory LeBrun. When he was fired, Woods did not forgive me. Between the Hogan/McGuirk rivalry, and the firing of Dee's boyfriend, I had managed to alienate two of the people closest to Ted before we were on the air six months.

We had underdelivered our audience, but Ted did not try to hide it. He came clean with all the advertisers. A week before launch he went up to New York and told them that CNN's number was 1.7 million subscribers, not the 3.5 million we'd promised. Dancer, Fitzgerald & Sample (DSF) was our lead advertising agency. They had brought eight accounts to CNN. Beverly O'Malley was their media guru, and she had pushed for us. Betsy Frank, then a researcher, now an exec VP at Nickelodeon, had backed her up. They had risked their jobs on us.

Ted walked into DSF accompanied by George Babick. George quotes Ted, "You know, I bought a plantation in South Carolina, and I spend my weekends there. When I'm down there, all I think about is CNN. One cloudless night I went for a walk and I looked up at the sky, and I saw 3.5 million stars. That's how I made my subscriber estimate." Everybody laughed. Ted promised "make-goods" (extra spots to advertisers) to make good the shortfall. Dancer was satisfied; not only were they going to get their money's worth, they had a story to tell their grandchildren. Ted's personality redeemed CNN's performance.

Round 27: **CNN College**

At CNN it was "earn while you learn," minimum wage, maximum opportunity. We hired kids just out of school, and we called them "VJs," video journalists. For six months, they rotated through the newsroom, spent time on the studio cameras and in the editing room, loaded tape in the control rooms, fetched for the graphics department, ran copy for the writers, and answered phones on the desk. They mastered the basics of a network news operation.

That's the thing CNN offered that the networks didn't. If you worked at a network, you did one job, and God forbid you help somebody on another one—the union would have you written up. There'd be a grievance. You could be fired. A network was a one-path place. At CNN, you could discover your own path and follow it. The unions failed when they tried to sign up CNN. When you're twenty-three years old, you don't think about retirement benefits.

Phil Griffin, a former VJ who is now executive producer of *Hardball* on MSNBC, sees his training experience this way: "One of the things I learned was never bother to study television in college. You can learn it in two weeks on the job. The same things we talked about in that first month—taking video live on air even as it's being fed in, going places live, God, the exact stuff we were doing then, the networks are still trying to get right twenty years later."

As they went from department to department, the VJs discovered which area they liked best, and we discovered what job they did best. At the end of six months, they'd either get a fifty-cent-an-hour raise and be assigned a function or wouldn't get the raise but could stay on as a floater. If they didn't get the raise, the real message was that they didn't have a future at CNN.

Ted Kavanau, Jim Kitchell, and Pat O'Gorman came up with the idea of CNN College. They wanted to start training the VJs before we went on the air. Orientation began at the end of April 1980. Before it was over, almost all CNN employees went through it, including reporters, bureau chiefs, writers, technicians. The course lasted a couple of weeks for the kids, three or four days for the professionals we brought in from other bureaus. They were there to learn CNN procedures, of which there were few.

Kitchell arranged for the technical training; the head of the department was Guy Pepper, who became our best director. Pepper went on to NBC to direct the *Today Show,* then the evening news, then *Dateline.* He became head of "look" for NBC and designed MSNBC and redesigned CNBC. He also designed, with a Microsoft partner, the MSNBC website. His Microsoft partner joined a website startup and became worth hundreds of millions of dollars. Guy decided that was the path he wanted, and he is now CEO of ByeByeNow.com, hoping to survive the Internet fallout.

Guy was another twenty-four-year-old with great promise. He laid out the CNN College curriculum. "We broke the VJs up into groups, and we had little busses and vans that would take them to the field shop, to the library, to the video tape. The tapes were running out, things were getting all jammed up, and they had no clue what they were doing. They wanted to learn so badly, and they had the greatest feeling about this place."

Guy met Phil Griffin at CNN College. Phil remembers Guy taking him to a 1-inch tape machine, and asking, "'Phil, do you know how to rewind one of these things?' 'Sure I do,' I said, and I turn it on and there's tape flying all over the room, and Guy tells me 'Hey, Phil, you know what? You're never going to be a technician. Don't ever touch a tape machine again.'"

Pat taught editing, not technical editing but content editing. How you put pieces of picture together to make a story. She and the kids invented a news story. They imagined the tape that the cameraman brought back. Then they would edit the pretend tape in their heads, including all the best pictures. After that, the editors in training would write a script to fit the pictures. In most newsrooms, the writer writes the script first, and then the editor matches pictures to the writer's words. That's why so much television looks slapdash.

Pat had grown up in the newsreel business, where you made the best pictures first, and then let the writer write to it. At CNN, this was going to be a very important skill, because tape was coming in live all the time and had to be written to instantly. The editor and writer talked about it, then the editor cut it, and the writer wrote it. It usually matched at the end.

Pat also taught tape library. She'd gone up to New York and acquired film and tape libraries for us. She taught the kids how to library visual material, and how to find it once they'd libraried it. They practiced cutting obits. They cut real stories about elderly people of note, and Pat saved them for when we would need them.

Pat's star pupil was a guy named Derwin Johnson. He was just out of Boston University, but he had already worked two years at the Newhouse station in Syracuse. He says, "I was paying my way through school with the Newhouse job, and they had identical equipment to the equipment at CNN. One day I just said, 'Hey, look, guys, I've been editing on these machines for two years, I know how to use them.' The next day, Pat called me. 'Could you teach it?' So my second week, I was teaching other VJs how to edit on one-inch tape machines."

John Hillis came to work in March, about a month before CNN College began. He was twenty-five, had worked in television for a couple of years, and was already an experienced producer when he arrived. He remembers "the scene was like an invasion was being mounted." The Techwood renovation project was the dirtiest and dustiest he's ever seen. It seemed a wonder that any of the equipment functioned. From beginning to end, CNN was built at crash course. The place was being constructed in such a hurry, everything was being done at once. It could never have happened in New York City, a union town with city inspectors hovering.

At one point, according to Hillis, Ted Turner was wandering around, speaking loudly to no one in particular. John was in the pit, Eric Shepherd was directing, and Jim Shepherd (another producer) was just hanging around watching. Turner's talking broke everybody's concentration, and Jim Shepherd yelled, "Will you shut up?" and then turned around and looked at the guy he'd just told to shut up. Eric Shepherd turned around and said to Turner, "That was Jim Shepherd. I am Eric Shepherd."

Jim Shepherd later told John that Turner came up to him and said, "Jim, you did right by telling me to shut up. Now I've got something to tell you. You're fired. Now we've surprised each other, go back to work."

Turner made a second manifestation. Guy Pepper was working with bureau chiefs and correspondents, people who had given up good jobs at the networks and come down to Atlanta, thinking that they might meet Ted. Guy promised he'd be coming in to offer some encouragement and welcome them to CNN.

"About two in the afternoon, Ted walks through the door. Now here were these bureau chiefs and correspondents, and they're starstruck." Pepper goes on, "'Everybody, here's Ted Turner. Ted, do you want to say a few words?'

"Ted starts walking around the room. 'Let me just tell you something,' he says. 'We are going to beam this shit all over the world. And you know what? We are going to beam this shit to Russia too, because you know what? One day they are going to bomb our asses.' He stops, briefly. Then: 'But I don't know if they all speak English,' and he walks out the door."

Jaws dropped to the floor. Pepper swears you could see people looking at their watches and thinking, I wonder if it's too late to call my agent.

"Well," Guy announced, "there you have it. That's Ted Turner, everybody."

Round 28: **College Life**

The kids had a life of their own, and I tried to know as little about it as possible. We brought down about a hundred people to Atlanta, all under twenty-five, threw them together, gave them very little money, and, with the exception of Pat O'Gorman, who was everybody's mother, left them pretty much to their own devices.

Guy Pepper recalls it as "going to camp at CNN. Nobody made any money, so at the end of the day, they'd rush over to Harrison's. It was 'Oh My God, come on, happy hour is almost over.' Atlanta bars were great. They would have all kinds of food if you got there for happy hour. That's why everybody was drunk after work. Happy hour was the favorite dining experience of the video journalists because at Harrison's you could eat the buffet for one dollar. . . . CNN was a party place. It was a hotbed of sex, drugs, and rock and roll."

Pat was the one person who couldn't ignore that. And it made for some very colorful scenes. The phone rang one night at 3 a.m.; a bunch of very drunk VJs were in jail, so they called us to get them out. We called the company lawyers, and the kids got out of jail that night.

Then there was an editor Pat loved dearly who was at our house quite a lot. Pat told a friend, "My God, he goes to the bathroom more than anyone I know." And the friend said, "Boy, you are the dumbest woman I ever met. Didn't you ever hear of cocaine? What do you think he's doing in that bathroom?" Pat called the boy's father and said, "Your son needs you." It didn't work. When the father visited, the son said, "Nah,

I'm fine." The father said, "He's fine." And that was the end of it. The son drifted off to oblivion.

Conversely, there was a girl in the New York bureau with a large drug and drinking problem. Pat called her father. They were both grateful. She went into rehab, and her life has worked out. When the unions came calling on CNN, Pat's mothering was worth a hundred votes.

The Washington bureau, of course, was the same story, but with an older cast. Again, the long work day, the close collaboration, the constant pressure. Cissy Baker says, "There was no time for anything else in the beginning, so the people we worked with became our family. We worked together, we ate together, we partied together, and sometimes paired off together. . . . Every feeling was intense, whether it was a relationship, or partying, or working."

Cissy was dating two guys in the bureau, John Holliman and Sandy Kenyon. Holliman kept a sailboat tied up on the Potomac. One night, Cissy and Kirsten Lindquist stole the sailboat. "It was like three in the morning," she recalls, "and we stole it because it was parked in Alexandria, and we'd been partying all night, and it was fun. I fell into the Potomac." She and Kirsten showed up for work on time the next day.

Holliman was married but ready to leave his wife for Cissy. As the world works, she preferred Sandy and was seeing him pretty steadily. Then one morning, Sandy was late for work. Cissy called him and, again, as the world works, a woman answered. Cissy hung up, and the relationship ended.

Sandy Kenyon remembers that another CNN Washington reporter was dealing dope out of the bureau. The bureau got word that the Feds were closing in, and everybody dispersed in the nick of time. I didn't know the story at the time, but the reporter in question must have been using too much of his own goods because he was doing a lousy job, and we fired him for incompetence.

New York wasn't much better. There the dealer was a tape editor, who became notorious when one of his prize customers, a major network anchorman, was caught with the goods. The anchorman was fired. The editor cleaned up his act, and he now edits tape for one of the major networks.

No one had a chance to meet anybody who didn't work for CNN or know somebody who did. New York's most important anchorman divorced his wife and married a CNN sports reporter. The dope dealer married a producer's best friend. The best tale has an assistant producer coming back to work on a Friday night. She had already started on her weekend when she was called in to handle a breaking story. As Chris Chase remembers it, the poor girl spent most of the night bombed out of her mind, wandering through the newsroom barefoot and overalled, sobbing, "I love my job."

Sandy Kenyon says, "What you had in those days was an atmosphere of working hard, and playing very hard. What was unusual was the intramural aspect; you would be literally working with someone one day and sleeping with them the next."

The Washington bureau vets report they've gotten through rehab successfully. They still work very hard at it, but they've been sober for years. Sandy is now the entertainment reporter for CBS Radio and Hollywood.com. Cissy Baker is bureau chief of the Tribune Broadcasting Washington bureau. John Holliman got sober on his own, remarried happily, had a family, starred for CNN in Baghdad, became the space correspondent, and was about to take the first chair with Walter Cronkite supporting him at the *Orbiter* launch. On the Sunday morning before the launch, he drove to the store to buy syrup for his pancakes. On the return trip, a car crashed into him and he died.

I suppose Sandy, Cissy, and John Holliman could've gotten into trouble, even without CNN and me to help them. All of them survived the CNN early years. Looking back as I write this book, I keep wishing that I could have done some things differently. I was on a news crusade. I didn't stop to ask myself what crusaders were doing in their spare time.

Round 29: **L.A.**

L.A. is a lousy news town. If it wasn't for Hollywood, you could cover it with one crew and two small boys to answer the phone: one day shift, one night shift. Yeah, I know, Rodney King, but the best video on that was shot by a civilian. There was O.J. Simpson, too, but hell, the O.J. story would have been back page if he wasn't a star and it wasn't Hollywood. Nevertheless, you had to have a bureau there, and we did. But we never got it right.

I had hired a bureau manager: former KTLA news director, knew the town, well liked, good contacts. Unfortunately, he did not cotton to Ed Turner and took a job at NBC instead. In the next three years we went through five bureau managers. None of them lasted.

The bureau itself was jinxed. While we were building it, burglars broke in and stole all our cameras and equipment, hundreds of thousands of dollars worth. I called RCA. They made lousy cameras, but they gave good service. They sent us two cameras on loan, and insurance covered our losses. Bill Bevins insisted that all employees with knowledge of the cameras take lie detector tests. The L.A. bureau did not take kindly to this seeming lack of trust. I took the test, too. Luckily, it turned out that I had not committed the crime. Nor had anyone else we tested.

When CNN went on the air, Bill Zimmerman was covering the presidential primary in California. The bureau was barely working. Zimmerman says, "There were guys running around changing little wires during the whole time I was out there. I'm not sure I had a producer. When our first cut-in made it on the air, there were cheers and hugs all around. Not because of the content of the cut-in, just the fact that it made it on the air."

On the big stories, we always flew people in from out of town. When the Las Vegas fire broke, Mary Alice Williams and Jim Miklaszewski, our Dallas bureau reporter, went in. That was typical. We knew L.A.'s limitations.

L.A. was supposed to produce one live hour of television every night. It was a breakthrough idea. I wanted to recreate the Walter Winchell column on television. I wanted to steal opening night, play or movie; I wanted to steal "society news," I wanted to steal "gossip" from the morning newspapers. I wanted to move that up one full cycle. I called the show *People Tonight.* I couldn't name it *People* because that was the Time-Life magazine, I couldn't call it *Tonight* because that was the NBC show. But if I stole both names and put them together, I was in the clear.

The show ran at 10 p.m. L.A. time, 1 a.m. in the East. It was hosted in the L.A. bureau, with reporters in L.A., New York, and Washington, and guests live in the studio. There were to be nightly satellite feeds. Each night, Chris Chase, the New York critic I'd hired, was to review whatever opened that night. She would write her copy, stand in front of the theater, and tell the world whether the show was good or bad; she was also supposed to pick up and report on the doings and the gossip of New York "café society." Washington was supposed to cover the night life of officialdom, tell who was seen with whom at Pamela Harriman's parties. Meanwhile, L.A. was supposed to be staking out Hollywood celebs all day long, and booking guests to fill the hour.

It was, and still is, a wonderful format. Unfortunately, we couldn't afford it. Every night the crews would be hijacked to cover a hard news event. The reporters were always off on another beat; although I'd hired Kandy Stroud from *Women's Wear Daily* for the job in Washington, she wound up as our State Department correspondent.

The one guy who worked out was Robin Leach. It was his first television gig, but he was a natural, and I was getting him cheap. Leach did his pieces from New York, always with a pretty girl on his arm, and always at some fabulously cheesy party. Every once and a while, he would swing out to L.A. and be a guest on the show. He'd do his gossip thing, and there would still be a pretty girl on his arm.

Our host, Lee Leonard, had been a sports announcer in New York, was terrific on radio, and, I thought, looked good in the Walter Winchell role. He could play New York tough. The problem was, we didn't have the money to make proper use of him. Most of the show was live interviews from the studio. Have you ever tried to do a talk show at ten o'clock at night on a start-up network over cable, when cable can't be seen in most of L.A.? Guests were not lining up at our door.

If CNN was a school for television, *People Tonight* was kindergarten. Executive Producer Eddie Madison was one year out of Emerson College. Eddie saw *People Tonight* as the perfect opportunity to show that he could do things that had never been done before. "We were blind with ambition," he recalls. "We had no sense of limitations. We would call anybody and ask them to do anything, and sometimes, some of them did."

Eddie's intern, Doug Herzog, had to go back to Emerson the next year to finish college. Between the two of them, they weren't forty-five years old. John Kalish and Myron Wilson filled out the producing staff.

Three guys and an intern did an hour of television five days a week and it was not bad. Doug Herzog, who went on to become president of the Fox Network, still says, "I'll take the CNN days anytime. We were all young guys together. It was the most fun I ever had."

The studio was next to the elevator shaft. Whenever anybody got on or off the elevator, we heard it on the air, so one of the breaks of doing this show at ten o'clock was that there wasn't much traffic. There were only two cameras in the studio. One was an RCA that was used as a field camera during the day. If there was a late-breaking story, we sometimes did the show with only one camera. It was not technical perfection.

Then we got a break. The Screen Actors Guild, led by Ed Asner and Charleton Heston, went on strike as we went on the air. Every night members had to be told where the next day's demonstrations were going to be. Although we weren't seen in L.A., we were carried in the valley and Asner and Heston used CNN as a communications tool. They were names, and Lee Leonard could talk to them for fifteen minutes. Ernie Borgnine was another easy "get." His wife, Tova, had a line of cosmetics. So long as we let Tova come in and plug her product, he'd be there, too.

The not-yet famous Tom Cruise did his first television talking on *People Tonight*. Tom Hanks, who had already starred in *Bosom Buddies*, loved doing the show. We even had his home number. He told Herzog, "If anybody ever cancels, you call me." Once he showed up with his wife and their little kid in pajamas.

Leonard put together a roster of regulars, Pee-Wee Herman, Howie Mandel, Gary Shandling, all guys on the rise. We got Joyce Jillson, the astrologer to the stars. Frankly, most of the guests were either too young or too old. But together Madison, Herzog, and Leonard always filled the show.

I made their job harder. Sam Zelman's buddy, Jim Bacon, the AP Hollywood reporter, was also Frank Sinatra's buddy. Bacon could get us a full half hour of Frank when he played South Africa. Just a couple of bars of music; the rest was the tour, a Bacon interview, and a look at the gambling dens of Lesotho. Getting Frank on television was a coup, and we grabbed it. Sinatra's lawyer, Milton Rudin, laid down one stipulation. We could play the tape for one week, and then we had to send all copies and the master to him. No librarying of Frank's material.

Frank's PR representative, Lee Solters, called me for a tape. I told him to call Rudin. He said, "I represent Frank." I said, "So does Rudin. Rudin says no tapes to anybody but him." We went through this two or three times, and Solters said, *People Tonight* will never get one of my people again." I said, "You mean your first-string people. I'll be sure never to book one of your second-stringers who you are dying to get on the air." We huffed and puffed at each other. I was not sure that *People Tonight,* in its desperation, did stop booking Solters's second-stringers. Before we worked anything out with Solters, I was gone from CNN. It was then Burt Reinhardt's problem, and I'm sure he handled it well.

Upon occasion, Ted Turner also made everybody's job harder. Liz Wickersham, Ted's girlfriend, was doing a show for TBS. Every once in a while she'd show up, and she'd want to use a crew to do a story. Once Myron Wilson managed to get Stevie Wonder on a Saturday night at the L.A. Forum. We had a crew booked when Liz turned up and hijacked it. Somebody came up to Doug Herzog and said, "You've got to let the crew go, we've got Stevie Wonder waiting." I said, "You know what? *You* tell Liz Wickersham she can't get a crew." Myron saved it. He said, "Our crew was in this accident. One guy was hurt, we couldn't get to the Forum." What do you do when you're in trouble? "You lie like a dog."

After I left CNN, Ted gave Liz more than a camera crew. He gave her her own show. The funny thing is, she got pretty good at it. She would've been the perfect Hollywood reporter for *People Tonight,* and I'll bet Ted would've found the money in the budget so we'd finally get a Hollywood reporter.

We weren't on the air six months when *Entertainment Tonight* started up: Paramount had seen what we were doing and thought they could make a half hour of it for syndication. They now knew they could syndicate the show on a same-day basis via satellite. Our satellite provider, Bob Wold, became their partner along with Cox Broadcasting, and thus a television staple was born.

Paramount raided our staff. First off, they wanted Robin Leach. I had Leach under contract, but they offered him 50 percent more than I was paying him. I never believed in holding anybody if I couldn't match the other guy's offer. I let him go. After they got Leach, they came after Herzog and John Kalish, and got them both.

When it came to getting guests, Kalish says Paramount made deals that CNN never would have. They allowed PR companies to decide what questions could be asked and to reserve the right to change answers. By now, it's gone so far, ET cannot show a still picture of Tom Cruise without his permission.

The quaintness of the bureau had its own charm. Kathleen Sullivan's mother, who lived in Pasadena, couldn't get cable. We had cable in the lobby of our building. Several times a week Kathleen's mother would come into the building and sit in the lobby, and watch *Prime News 120*. Kathleen herself showed up occasionally. She'd file a story out of the bureau. Herzog says, "I was completely smitten. She was smart, beautiful, and swore like a sailor. The first time she was in the office working, she yelled, 'Who the hell do I have to fuck to get a pencil around here?'" Herzog wished it were him.

At the end of our second year, Huell Hauser went to Hollywood as a reporter. He was a Southern boy who had worked at CBS. His first assignment was the premiere of *Nine to Five*. Kalish was his producer, and gave him his outline for the piece, which Hauser disregarded. He walked straight over to his old friend Dolly Parton, and began an interview that went on and on. Rogers and Cowan, the PR people for the movie, had Lily Tomlin and Jane Fonda standing by. Kalish tugged at Hauser. "Talk to Jane, talk to Lily." Hauser kept talking to Parton. Rogers and Cowen got angrier. Tomlin and Fonda were still waiting.

Finally, Hauser concluded. He asked Kalish to bring the other ladies over. Kalish was relieved. Rogers and Cowan were relieved. Hauser put Dolly Parton in the middle, Fonda on one side, Tomlin on the other. Then he stood in front of them and did his intro. He used Fonda and Tomlin as backdrop. Kalish was crushed. Rogers and Cowan would not be his friends. Ten years later, Fonda became the third Mrs. Turner. I'm sure Huell Hauser would not have ignored her then.

This was 1980, before the PR ladies had taken over Hollywood. I wanted to do a show that would reveal the real Hollywood, not filter it through a studio promotion department. We didn't grow fast enough to make it happen. Now it's impossible. All the television news outfits are run by companies that own movie studios or television shows. God forbid you tell a story that offends a star. He'll never work for your studio again, and you won't be working for your company the next day.

Round 30: **Ted and Louise: Rome**

If the hub of the news world isn't New York, it's London. So why did we put CNN's European headquarters in Rome? Because BBC and ITN would not give us access to the Eurovision news feed in London. RAI (Italian television) would, so we wound up in Rome. It was too bad because our London bureau under Françoise Husson was one of the three bureaus that understood what CNN was supposed to be. (Miklaszewski's Dallas and Weine's San Francisco were the other two.)

Françoise learned the business working for Ken Coyte and Burt Reinhardt. She believed head, heart, and soul that news was a "cause." She thought the Third World, particularly the Muslim Third World, was ignored. She was right. She thought Americans didn't understand what was going on abroad, because the U.S. networks covered foreign news superficially and stereotypically. She was right. She thought that American networks, with their twenty-four-minute news shows, neglected foreign news. She was right.

When Françoise heard about CNN, she wrote to Burt Reinhardt for a job. She was working for NBC London, and she wanted to trade in a twenty-four-minute day of news for a twenty-four-hour day of news. When Burt got her letter, he checked her credentials, flew to London, and signed her up. She started work on March 1, 1980.

Through Vittorio Boni, I had gained access to the Eurovision (EBU) news feed. But to gain local access, we had to attach cable through a Eurovision member to the Eurovision network. In London, neither the BBC nor ITN would let us hook up: BBC because they were snooty, and we were upstarts; ITN because its EBU representative was the twittish Hugh Witcomb, who had personal ambitions elsewhere. I was then and am now a close friend of Sir David Nicholas, head of ITN and Witcomb's boss. He gave us nonexclusive U.S. rights to all ITN material. I gave him the right to use CNN in England. Still, he couldn't overrule the twerp who was his board representative at the EBU.

Although London couldn't be headquarters, we still had to have a bureau there. We had too much news to cover, and the flight schedule was too good. Through the efforts of Coyte at WTN and David Nicholas, we got a one-room office a block away from ITN, in north Soho, amidst the London thread trade.

Before that, we worked out of Françoise's house. We didn't get her the office until May. Zelman found a London reporter, Richard Blystone— AP radio, good voice, Vietnam War reporter, terrific writer. Husson loved him. He cared about foreign news as much as she did. No pretensions, he carried the cameraman's equipment. On major interviews, Françoise joined them and ran sound. She had even been able to get the EBU feed delivered, despite the ITN twerp. Our office was in the same building as Brazil's TV Globo and Canada's CTV. ITN couldn't cut us off without cutting them off. The twerp tried it one time, and I don't think he ever dug his way out of the doghouse.

The London bureau had three desks. One for Françoise, one for Blystone, and one for a secretary/researcher. Four months later, when Derwin Johnson came over as cameraman, Françoise put a door over a couple of file cabinets, and called it his desk. Johnson recalls, "There was a little workstation with a soldering iron so you could repair cables. There was a machine that brought in the UPI wire, there was a television set. This was the CNN London bureau." Françoise adds, "Everything was cheap, and if we could actually find it in the street, all the better. I bought used tapes, used furniture, but we covered 'new' news. Now CNN buys new tapes, new furniture, and puts out 'old' news."

According to Françoise, the Brits and the other European news broadcasters were terrified of us. All of a sudden, CNN was raining down upon them. Almost all of them were government employees, with enormous staffs, political positions, and all kinds of power. Françoise says, "They didn't want to introduce a new kid on the block who would break up their cushy lives." If CNN succeeded, they might lose their jobs; it would certainly change their lifestyle. Margaret Thatcher had just become British prime minister. She was beginning her battle against government broadcasting monopolies, against union featherbedding. It was the start of the free market revolution. Françoise says that's why the EBU members fought us so hard.

I asked Françoise why, if all this was true, Vittorio Boni supported me. Françoise says that he, like us, was a "man of the future." He also had another agenda: He and his allies within EBU, the French, and the

Swiss, were eager to establish a non–Anglo Saxon worldwide news agency. Vittorio hoped CNN could help them.

Françoise thinks there was a lot of infighting within the Eurovision camp. Some, especially the government broadcasters, saw that CNN was representing a news philosophy that was going to change broadcasting forever. It would change functions, job definitions, and methods. They were right. Within a few years, CNN had changed the hardware and the software of television news all over the world.

The Atlanta desk thought Françoise was difficult, and maybe she was for them. She had better news sense than they did, and it was always tough to get them to listen. Still, she could pull off miracles. She would get us pictures out of Europe when everything was blocked. Once, during the Polish crisis, when all lines out of London were preempted, she fed us live out of Brussels. Time after time, we beat the world on major European stories because of her. She was Europe for us.

We still had to set up Rome. I handled it as if it was a U.S. bureau. Thanks to Boni, RAI agreed to provide us with an office, technicians, and lines into Eurovision, and to connect us to Telespazio, the Italian satellite uplink. They even gave us desks and chairs. Our bureau chief was Dennis Troute, who had been working at WFAA Dallas. I'd used his work on ITNA, and I knew that he was a different kind of television reporter. When he was covering the Vietnam War for WFAA, he'd written articles about it for *Harper's*. Writing for *Harper's* made him a real journalist, and working at WFAA had turned him into a solid TV professional.

Burt hired our bureau manager, Louise Priestly, in part because her sister worked in the NBC Rome bureau. The sister was famous for her competence. Louise was not quite as good. She had no experience on television, but she had been married to Tom Priestly, an NBC cameraman, whose abilities are legendary. As we say in the trade, she had learned television by injection. She did well by us. She got along with RAI, she got us help from NBC, and she somehow kept us clean despite the intricacies of Italian tax law.

Mark Leff became the voice of CNN Rome. He'd been the voice of Visnews for ITNA. He was a tall reedy guy with a deep tubby voice. Every day he wrote scripts to voice over the material that CNN took from the EBU feed. He was "one take." That means that he wrote well to tape, read at the perfect rate so that the sound track matched the picture, and sounded good. We never had to do a refeed. Guys like Leff are hard to find. He never wanted to leave the studio, he didn't want to go out in the field as a reporter. But leave him with a typewriter and a half dozen stories, and he'd have 'em ready for you in an hour.

Getting money into Rome was a problem. Patrick Marz, our head of business affairs, who'd worked overseas at ABC, suggested that $10,000 a month in cash be carried in and kept in a cigar box to handle travel and expenses. It was standard network procedure, but Troute said no. He had seen too many guys get fired, either for good reason or for no reason, because nobody could figure out what happened to the money in the cigar box, and somebody had to be blamed.

For months, Troute financed the bureau on his American Express card, but Marz was slow to get the money back to him. Amex canceled his card when he ran it up to $22,000. Troute didn't mind. He claimed it was a privilege to broadcast the news, and he was willing to pay for it. That's how we all felt at the beginning of CNN.

A month after start-up, we sent Dave Tyson and John Moore to Rome as the camera crew. Troute remembers them as two Southern boys who had never been farther north than North Carolina. They adjusted quickly. Almost immediately, Troute got a half hour interview with Anwar Sadat, then they did Lech Walesa, and they became regulars at the King Hussein press conferences. Hussein was the first head of state to send out four network invitations to his events rather than three. Troute says that getting on the Hussein list moved him a couple of notches up in the estimation of his professional colleagues.

Just as the bureau was running out of money, we got lucky, or maybe Ted Turner got lucky, or both. Ted came to Rome to visit the bureau and to see the sights. Louise Priestly, our Rome bureau manager, became his guide. She and Ted had a wonderful three days and three nights together, and after that, the checks always came on time.

With the money coming in, the bureau hired an American accountant in Rome to handle the tax situation. Some of the employees used him for their personal taxes as well. Then the Rome taxmen grabbed the accountant, went through his books, and put him away for a while.

Troute says it was lucky that the whole bureau wasn't sent to jail, but he was out of the country by then.

Round 31: **Rehearsals**

In the middle of May, two weeks late, we were finally ready to go into rehearsal. I must have been the only one at CNN who knew that it would work. Everybody else was worried stiff, but after putting ITNA together, I thought two weeks of rehearsal was plenty of time. I thought things were going fine. I thought I wasn't worried. My assistant, Diane Durham, disagreed. She gave Pat some Valium and told her to put it in my orange juice. Pat stopped after a week, because she and Diane agreed it hadn't made a difference.

Our rehearsals were going fine, that is to say they were a mess, but less of a mess every day. Our lifeline to New York and Washington, our AT&T land line, hadn't been completed. The producers were scared. How were they ever going to fill up their shows without New York and Washington? Then, out of the blue, or rather I should say out of the black, the Washington newsroom popped up on the monitors. The producers stood up and cheered. The run-through stopped. Everyone went to look at the picture. It was as though the producers were saying, "Oh my God, there really is a Washington bureau." But the New York leg had not yet been completed.

Producers are by nature candy-assed. They expect everything to be delivered gift-wrapped so that they can then make thirty magical minutes of television. Now CNN was showing the candy-asses that we really could deliver Washington news to them. But the twenty-five-year-old kids didn't believe they could fill an hour. They continued to find fault. The line to New York wasn't finished. Neither was the plumbing. There were no indoor toilets; only Porta-Johns out back. Some people went out and found a tree. This did not please the candy-asses either.

My producer children were in a panic. They were rookies, but Ted Kavanau was the top sergeant, and he would not let them fail. They were young; they couldn't get through a rundown without a glitch. Their morale was failing. Every night they'd wander over to Harrison's, drink, and tell each other, "This is not going to work." Kavanau made sure it would.

Two weeks before launch, he dragged all his producers into an office behind the newsroom. John Hillis reports that there were seven kid producers under the gun. Kavanau got up on a crate and yelled at them for an hour. The gist of the rant was: "I understand what you are saying among yourselves, that the whole thing is so hopelessly screwed up that it is never going to get off the ground. Well, that may be true for the rest of this damned organization, but I will not let you producers fail. If you don't want to work under those conditions, get up and leave this room right now." Nobody left. They were scared to death. According to John, "They thought they might get shot." John believed that he and Kavanau were "in a foot race for a nervous breakdown."

Washington was having a nervous breakdown of its own. Cissy Baker was running the assignment desk from the top of a construction crate. She used a dial phone that had just two lines. In the middle of May, as the camera crews started to report for work, I called her and told her it was time to "practice the news."

Cissy remembers: "All the reporters showed up. We sat in a semicircle on folding chairs. There was real spirit and everybody was anxious and eager to make something of this upstart network. I introduced myself. The reporters introduced themselves. Unbeknownst to me, almost all of them were radio reporters. They had good voices, but they didn't know how to hold the microphone or look into the camera."

Cissy gave them instructions and assignments. They were to go out, cover a story, do a voice track on a different tape, and ship the tapes to us via Delta Dash. It was like my old days at Movietone News. Shoot and ship. Then our Atlanta producers would have to edit the tape and put it in their programs. When we started rehearsal, Washington didn't even have an editing setup. As the rehearsals proceeded, Washington got its edit bays, and by the time the AT&T line reached Atlanta, they were able to edit their own stories.

Regardless, panic prevailed in the Atlanta newsroom and in Ted Turner's head. I knew that everything would be all right. They didn't. These were the times that tried men's souls, and a lot of the troops were diving for foxholes. Turner made his speech to the Television Academy. We visited the *Times.* The *Wall Street Journal,* the *Washington Post,* and the *Atlanta Constitution* visited us. Ted tried to tell them what we would do. Sometimes he got it right, sometimes he didn't. This was the moment I had to tell the *Washington Post* that we wouldn't be giving the betting line on ball games because bookies didn't take bets after the game started.

A year earlier, we had told the world at the 1979 cable operators convention that we would launch CNN on June 1, 1980. It was time for the 1980 cable convention, and we were in the midst of rehearsals. I flew down to Houston for two days. Ted was there, Nory was there; we had a booth. We were trying to get cable operators to sign up, and now, one year after we announced, we could show our product.

We had rehearsal tapes on monitors. Cable operators crowded around. Of course, we had chosen the rehearsals with the fewest glitches. The cable operators were really impressed, because we were really real. Our customers had seen us. Nory LeBrun could begin to take orders.

Les Brown of the *Times* came over to the booth, saw the screen, and told me it looked like regular television. He thought we were going to do something different. I told Les, "We are going to do something different. The best way to introduce something different is to put it in a conventional package. The viewer is comfortable. On his own, he will discover that the package has different contents." I am very proud of my quote, particularly because it is true. It never appeared in print. Les still cannot get a story about CNN in the *New York Times.*

When we got back to Atlanta, advertisers and cable operators were streaming through the CNN news plant. Ted would take them on walking tours of our construction site. They would emerge covered with sawdust, certainly no wiser, and probably no more confident than when they arrived.

Bureaus in Chicago, Dallas, and San Francisco were coming along on schedule. Los Angeles was in a shambles because of the stolen cameras.

We were committing a revolution, holding press conferences, wiring and hammering, and taking lie detector tests because of those damned cameras. It was a helluva rehearsal.

Twenty years and five start-ups later, John Hillis, now the president of Newschannel 8, Washington's twenty-four-hour news service, leaned back and said that it was there he had learned that run-throughs are designed to expose the weaknesses in the system, even if it leaves you feeling like you're just getting slugged daily. Even in 1980 Hillis knew: "Watching the pieces fall into place, you could see that notwithstanding all the obvious errors, it was going to pull together as actual hours of television."

The American Newspaper Publishers Association was meeting in Atlanta the weekend we went on the air. Bill Dunn, my friend from the *Wall Street Journal,* asked for a guided tour. It was Saturday, the last day before we went on the air. He saw the activity, the combination of construction and production. I walked him through the newsroom, showed him how it worked: The assignment desk way in the back, the satellite desk cojoined, writers and producers halfway forward, graphics on the left, editing rooms on the right, the anchor desk facing forward, cameras pointing back, and out in the open in a slightly recessed pit, the control room.

Directors, video men, audio men, and producers sit facing the back of the room. Anchors, writers, assignment desk face forward. The cameras shoot everywhere. The editing rooms are glassed in, open to the cameras. Activities merge. Anchors read their lines while carpenters hammer under their feet. The technical director pushes buttons while electricians are wiring the buttons.

Dunn sees it, Dunn gets it, Dunn knows we will be on the air the next day.

Then the eleventh-hour crisis hits. When I picked June 1, I hadn't realized it was a Sunday. Since no news happens on Sunday, we hadn't produced any shows for Sunday daytime. We would look empty. So, I had changed the starting time. We would go on the air at 6 p.m.

Ted loved it. It made for a better party.

Round 32: **Opening Day**

When you're done, you're done. On Sunday, I stopped being the creator. I was an operator. At that moment, there was nothing more that I could or should do. The feeling was unreal. In the next few hours, I would discover—and so would the rest of the world—whether what I'd been doing for the past twenty-four years paid off. Would the damn thing work? CNN's fate was in the hands of the writers, the producers, the directors, and the talent. No longer was I an architect, no longer was I a dealmaker. I was a newsman.

The newsman got a break. On Saturday, the day before launch, Vernon Jordan had been shot while jogging. The accused shooter was a notorious racist who traveled the country picking off blacks. Jordan was wounded but alive in a hospital in Fort Wayne. Out of nowhere, we had major news for opening day. We could look good. All we had to do was cover the story and get it on the air.

Ted was throwing a lawn party. There had been some drizzle earlier in the afternoon, but the weather cleared, the grass was green, the place was crowded and very festive ("very festive" is wire service for everyone was getting loaded). There was music, there were banners, the UN flag flapped in the wind, along with the state flag of Georgia and the Stars and Stripes. You've seen those Kentucky Derby pictures where the women are walking around with big hats, men in seersucker suits, and the mint juleps are flowing? That was the scene.

Ted knows how to spend money the right way, but Burt Reinhardt must've been flipping out. He'd been trying to save every nickel, and here's this lavish party going on. There were three hundred guests, two huge tents, and the fountain in front of the former Progressive Club had been reinvigorated, spouting water ten feet high. Three military bands marched throughout the afternoon. The Marine Corps Band contributed "Nearer My God to Thee." TBS taped it. Ted sent a copy to his redoubt in the hills of Tennessee. He would save it there, deep underground, in a bombproof shelter, so that the moment might be preserved forever.

Ted had another use for it. Years later, when Cissy Baker became the assignment editor in Atlanta, her boss, Earl Casey, told her that there was a copy of the tape in a drawer in the assignment desk. CNN editors had looped the tape so it would play over and over again until the picture wore off. It was there because Ted had told Earl, just as he was telling everyone else, "We will stay on the air till the end of the world and then we will cover the story and sign off playing 'Nearer My God to Thee.'" Ted made sure the tape was still in the drawer, "just in case." Earl said to Cissy: "When the world comes to an end, play it or Ted will fire us."

The tape is no longer in the drawer. It mysteriously disappeared when CNN moved its headquarters from Techwood to the Omni. However, it has been rediscovered. It now rests in Master Control, where a phone call from Ted or anyone else in authority, and a push of a button, will send us all off to eternity, comforted by the strains of "Nearer My God to Thee."

Back on the great lawn, I was waiting for the revolution to begin. To those invited, it may have seemed a garden party. But I knew that from this day forth, presidents and kings, prime ministers and foreign ministers, the Pentagon, Congress, the media, the public, would have to adjust to CNN.

The guests included cable operators, advertisers, dozens of representatives from the press, a few CNN commentators, agents who represented on-air talent, and the VJs. Pat had sent them out in shifts onto the lawn so that they might join the celebration of their efforts. Pat herself was talking animatedly with our commentator Phyllis Schlafly about the fate of babies born to mothers who were refused abortion. I was working the lawn, making nice to the cable operators, selling the advertisers, giving sound bites to the press, telling the agents their talent was terrific, thanking the VJs sincerely, and trying to bring peace between Pat and Phyllis. Then it was 5:40 p.m.

Rows of white lawn chairs had been set up facing the porch of the Techwood Studio. Between the white pillars, a podium had been built. TBS, the Superstation, would carry the CNN opening live.

Ted and I were standing at the podium with a few others, including Bob Wussler (a Turner Broadcasting vice president) and Tench Coxe (the lawyer who had been so important to us). Wussler introduced us. I thanked Ted, I thanked the people working at CNN, from Burt Reinhardt to the VJs.

Ted welcomed the hundreds of guests and then offered what one reporter described as "an ode to himself," about acting on one's convictions and providing information to the American people. Then the "Star Spangled Banner" played, and he stood at attention, hand on heart, as trumpets blew.

With the last flourish, Ted forgot about CNN; he wanted to see who was winning the Braves game. When he found out the Braves were, he, like the baseball owner he is, bellowed "Awwright!!" and disappeared into the building. Minutes after the ceremonies concluded, I was back on "the floor" trying to get the Vernon Jordan story out of Fort Wayne.

President Carter was now in Fort Wayne visiting Jordan. Jane Maxwell was screaming bloody murder because she had arranged to take the Fort Wayne NBC station's live coverage of Carter at the hospital, but NBC was refusing to share the AT&T line with us. We had been through this dozens of times at ITNA. Kavanau was howling: "NBC fucked us." Jane checked it out: The networks were sharing the line amongst themselves. She invoked the rule of Reese: "A share with one is a share with all."

Alan Stasky, the NBC editor, didn't buy it. Stasky asked Jane how CNN got its material; Jane said, with sweet menace, "Your affiliate sold it to me. You're not telling your affiliates they cannot sell to us, are you, Alan?" Jane got a call back. Stasky said, "Okay, you're in the feed." Twenty years later, Stasky is working for CNN.

Kavanau, Sam Zelman, and Alec Nagle were more or less jointly overseeing the first hour of programming. Guy Pepper was directing. Right before we start, he told his crew on headsets, "Don't forget, in television, shit flows downhill." "We're nervous wrecks," he continues, "because we want it to be perfect, and we know the press is watching us our first time out."

On the set, coanchors Lois Hart and Dave Walker were waiting for their cue. Lois remembers that, moments before they went on the air, "there were these three guys standing a yard away from the anchor desk screaming at each other, 'What are we supposed to say to start this damn thing?' Sam Zelman, of course, wanted some lofty introduction to the world's greatest journalistic operation. 'You know, welcome to the new world, blah blah blah,' and some executive producer was fighting with Kavanau, they both wanted us to say something different. Dave and I were still sitting there wondering what the hell was going to happen here."

Dave claimed Lois and he actually made the decision on their own. Essentially, they opened with "Good evening," and at the end of the show concluded with, "The news will continue for the next hour, and forever."

CNN led with a package out of Fort Wayne. We were still waiting for the president to leave the hospital as we went on. In Connecticut, a man had gone on a shooting spree, someone in New York had fired a shot at Reggie Jackson over a parking spot, and Mary Alice Williams told both stories from our New York bureau.

"We had Mary Alice on videotape," says Guy Pepper. "We get into the show about five minutes, roll the tape, and the tape operator hits reverse. I thought I was going to have a heart attack. It was live television, just one of those things. Dave and Lois covered, and everybody got through it, and I said on the headsets, 'Well, that is the first mistake we are ever going to make. We did it, we got it out of the way, let's not make any more. Especially on my shows.'"

The news rundown continued. Not only were there enough stories for a Sunday, there were too many. We couldn't fit in all our commercials.

As CNN took its first commercial break, President Carter walked out of Vernon Jordan's room. We broke the commercial, went to Carter live. The president held a press conference and said Jordan was doing well and would survive. Killing the commercial was a moment of pride for Dan Schorr, Ted Kavanau, Ted Turner, and me. It was an easy decision. I knew we had plenty of unsold commercial inventory and could "make good" on that commercial in another show; it didn't cost us a cent.

I had scheduled a feed from Israel, where Sunday is a working day, just to show that we were international. We had bought the time on the satellite, and we had Jay Bushinsky, our Jerusalem correspondent, standing by. We broke early from the Carter press conference to go to him reporting on another political crisis in Israel . . . What else? Bushinsky was a seasoned radio reporter, but his voice and his looks were not great. Nobody in the world but me would have hired him to do television. In those days, CNN hired for knowledge and connections; the networks hired for looks.

For the last two weeks in May, I'd been looking for the live story with which we would launch. Mount St. Helens blew up before we got on the air. Castro's refugees were landing in Florida, but that was an old story.

With one week to go there was nothing better. I could choose between the Mount St. Helens aftermath and maybe get lucky and have it erupt again, or go to Florida and if we were lucky show some Marielitos coming ashore. My choice was made for me. The truck driver said his truck would never make it over the Rockies. It was Key West or nothing.

So there was Mike Boettcher standing on the shore in Key West with our one and only satellite truck, the first in the world. For $5,000 a month, Ed Taylor, whose company fed CNN to cable operators, had leased me an eighty-foot flatbed truck on which was loaded a five-meter satellite dish. The $5,000 covered five days' use. Any additional time was $1,000 a day. I had my reasons for this arrangement. I was forcing the assignment desk to find at least five days of live coverage every month. The five thou was "use it or lose it." We were certainly going to use it on opening day.

That first day it was nothing, except that Boettcher was caught picking his nose on camera; he had no IFB earpiece so there was no way he could hear us cue him. Worse than that, he had no story to tell. No one had arrived that day, but he was still there, way at the Southern tip of the United States, waiting. Subliminally, it was a promise to the viewer, stick with us baby, you're gonna see some action here.

Years later, a couple of guys wrote a book about Ted Turner. They said our first day was a mess: a cleaning lady walked through the set, a guy was caught on camera picking his nose. The audience saw both, and I didn't care. It showed that people we were working in the midst of reality.

You could have done focus groups on news forever and still not come up with CNN, because we were going to give people something they didn't even know they wanted. I needed to show that on Sunday.

Although we didn't recognize it, we had another great story going on June 1. Jim Miklaszewski, our Dallas reporter, was at Fort Chaffee, Arkansas. The Marielitos were being picked up by Immigration as they landed and shipped off to prison at the army stockade there. The night before, dozens had escaped.

The governor of Arkansas, one Bill Clinton, raced to the scene. So did Mik, but Mik got lost. The cameraman was driving, and he noticed a number of cars going the opposite direction on a two-lane road. He made a U-turn. Before they knew it, they were at the tail of Bill Clinton's motorcade driving into Fort Chaffee, which had been sealed off to media. The military guards waved them through. For the next hour and a half, they followed Clinton around as he was given a tour and the military was explaining to the governor how they'd lost the prisoners.

As Mik tells it, they even got inside headquarters: "The governor's people thought we were with the military. The military thought we were with the governor. We went unchallenged for some time. . . . Suddenly Clinton realized that we didn't belong there, and he just stared right at us. . . . It was the first time I ever got 'that look' from Bill Clinton. The military officers came over and escorted us off the base." CNN had a useful exclusive, not a headline, but useful. For Mik, it was his first story, and his first exposure to working television news and to Bill Clinton.

Fifteen years later, covering the White House for NBC and getting "that look" regularly, Mik talked with President Clinton about the night in Fort Chaffee. Clinton told Mik that he'd been defeated for a second term as governor not only because he'd raised the Arkansas vehicle tax, but also "because of the Fort Chaffee business." After that, Clinton felt he was seen as "a duplicate of Jimmy Carter" who had just blown the hostage situation in Tehran. He was still bitter about the incident, and he blamed the media.

As our first hour ended, Dave and Lois walked off the set. Hart says, "It took ten years off my life." Walker is matter-of-fact: "At first, we had some butterflies, but once we got into the newscast itself, that was all gone. There are fleeting moments of glory in a career."

Ted had not been witness to the glory. Pat O'Gorman bumped into him sitting in front of a TV set in a back office. He was watching the Braves. She says, "I put out my hand and said, 'Congratulations, Ted.' He said, 'Don't congratulate me, this is Reese's thing.' He was gracious, but not without a touch of resentment."

I wasn't as happy as I might have been. We'd gotten it on. CNN lived. The moment we started it rolling, people saw it was going to be okay. At the party, everyone was singing, but it was as if the air had gone out of me in the first hour. CNN didn't need me anymore, it had a life of its own. I could have left right then. I wondered if Ted was thinking that, too, as he sat watching the Braves game.

Lois Hart, however, remembers me kindly. "We all look back and say it was wonderful, but honestly lots of us had reservations about whether it would last. We were all exhausted, except for Reese. Without

Reese, it wouldn't have happened. Ted is really kind of brilliant, but he had no clue about TV news or journalism. But between the two of them—I think it was one of those moments in time, a brilliant collaboration that doesn't happen often."

The second hour of CNN was sports, again sticking to our regular schedule. There is no shortage of sports news on Sunday. At eight o'clock, we did our star turn. Thanks to George Watson, we had an exclusive one-hour interview with President Carter. Dan Schorr and Watson had an extensive, wide-ranging, non–headline making talk with the chief executive. It was on tape, there were no glitches, and it was ready to roll. We could all relax for an hour. It would be our last chance to relax for a whole year.

Round 33: **A VJ's Story**

I had a dream, and the dream had a system. The dream was I could turn kids fresh out of journalism school into super broadcasters. The system was throw a kid in over his head. For him it's sink or swim. If you picked the right kid, he'd swim. We picked a hundred kids. In the end most of them swam, and Derwin Johnson swam the best.

Derwin was recruited out of B.U. journalism school. One interview and a same-day offer, but he had another semester and a half until graduation. We called B.U. They agreed to give him credit for his work at CNN; all he had to do was write a paper. We gave him three days to get down to Atlanta. He says, "I don't know what made me say yes. Three days to pack up and move across the country, am I crazy? But three days later I was there."

Johnson began training in May. He'd never heard the term "video journalist" before. We told him that a VJ had to be omnifunctional. He would transfer from the studio to the newsroom to the editing rooms to the field, until he learned all the required skills. He was the VJ that Pat "picked out of the chorus" to teach editing after noticing he had some experience, garnered while working at a Syracuse television station. This was a week after he'd hit town. When he'd been in Atlanta two weeks, as he tells it, "I was teaching editing, shooting, whatever."

By the third week, Derwin was out on a major news story, the Liberty City riots in Miami. A black kid had been shot. They were burning up the place. The National Guard was called in. Johnson thought, "What the hell is wrong with us? Is Reese crazy? We're down here covering the story, we're not even on the air yet, and we can get ourselves killed." The producer on the story, Dean Vallas, was driving through all these National Guardsmen with the inside lights on in the car. The cops came over, Dean reached into his pocket. Derwin yelled, "Dean what are you doing?" "I'm getting out my I.D.," said Dean. "The cops don't know that," Derwin said. "I thought we were all going to take a bullet."

The next week ended June 1. Derwin was not scheduled to work; it was Sunday. He moped all through Saturday. Pat noticed. She asked him if he wanted to work Sunday. He remembers, "I had to beg to be put on the staff the first day we went on the air. I'll never forget that feeling, the first minute it came on the air . . . Vernon Jordan, Jimmy Carter." Johnson was unstoppable. He spent four months in Atlanta, doing everything, failing at nothing, and he adored working with Pat.

Then Françoise Husson needed a cameraman in London. Derwin was the obvious choice. Pat called him over, told him, "C'mon the big guy wants to talk to you." Derwin worried about what he'd done wrong. I told him I wanted him in London the next day. He needed a week to see his family. I gave him three days. His mother said, "What? You're going where?" His grandmother said, "Oh, I think that is so beautiful." He came back to Atlanta, spent two days, and Pat said, "Take off."

Françoise met Derwin at the airport. They knew each other over the phone and hugged warmly. Then they tried to get his equipment off the plane. Customs stopped them. Atlanta had given Derwin the wrong "carnet." Françoise said "Why does this not surprise me?" She found the shipper, jumped through a few hoops, produced substitute documents, got the gear released on the spot.

Derwin went to CNN College Euro-style. Françoise taught him satellites: how to get them and how to use them to beat the opposition. Blystone taught him writing. Françoise taught him how to edit Blystone's writing. Derwin thought Blystone was the Hemingway of television: an amazing writer and very funny. Nevertheless, Johnson, six months on the job, was going to edit Blystone.

Johnson also acted as Blystone's assistant producer. They were going to cover the French elections. Derwin had never been to France. Françoise gave him a contact list. He knew who to call about the story, he knew who to call to feed the story, and who to call to book the satellite. All he had to do was shoot the story, match it to Blystone's highly visual script, rough-cut the story, and feed it to Atlanta.

The networks' field crews had never seen a producer/editor/cameraman. They laughed at Derwin and CNN. Then they got calls from New York asking why CNN's pieces were better than theirs. They stopped laughing.

Blystone and Johnson worked Northern Ireland. They tried to cover the IRA's Bobby Sands on his hunger strike. Johnson says, "Miami was dicey, but Northern Ireland was scarier. One time, we got jumped by the Royal Ulster Constabulary. I was knocked down with the camera, Dick was pushed and punched. Dick handled it. 'We're out of here,' he said. And we left."

Nobody expects a news crew to do otherwise. I still remember how we got nothing for all my crew's "bravery" in the 1968 Lincoln Park Chicago Riots. Our other cameraman, the "cowardly" Jerry Small, had the good sense to hide his camera. He shot the only pictures that UPITN got, and CBS got nothing. We let them use Small's film.

Later, Blystone and Johnson covered Bobby Sands's funeral. It was a ceremony, nobody bothered them. Maybe the cops, the Royal Ulster Constabulary, thought Sands's death was their victory.

They went on to cover the Italian earthquake outside Naples. It was the first time that Derwin had seen death and destruction on a major scale. Blystone specialized in personal, human interest stories. He found a ninety-year-old man who'd been shopping for bits of food. Despite his age and the tragedy, his face was full of life. Derwin and Blystone followed him into a small concrete room with a single naked lightbulb hanging from the ceiling.

Derwin remembers, "There was a woman on the bed, his wife, who had broken her hip during the quake. They had a little burner, and he made coffee, and Dick interviewed them. They'd been married sixty years. Dick ended his piece by asking them where they'd spent their honeymoon, and the old lady's eyes sparkled. "In bed," she said.

In October, Sadat was assassinated. Françoise, Dick, and Derwin chartered a Learjet and flew out for the funeral. Bill Zimmerman joined them, and it turned into a CNN triumph. But our Cairo bureau chief was quitting to go to NBC. Derwin was to be his replacement. Dick and Françoise spent two extra days in Cairo talking him through his new job. Since he was going to be a reporter, Françoise worked on his delivery. She produced his first piece. As he recorded it, she told him, "Read this part again, change this paragraph from here to there." Then Françoise and Dick flew back alone.

In Cairo he picked up a much better lifestyle. His salary might not have gone far in Atlanta or London, but now he was living in a three-bedroom apartment with a balcony overlooking the Nile. In addition to running the bureau, Derwin was also producer, reporter, cameraman, and editor. Dean Vallas, the previous bureau chief, had hired a driver. Derwin kept him on and added a cameraman. Derwin says, "The guy had picked up a camera once or twice in his life; he didn't know how to shoot. He'd take a shot of a flowerpot, I'd say, 'What's this?' He'd say, 'It's a cutaway.' I'd say, 'It's a flowerpot.'" Fifteen months on the job and Derwin had a video journalist of his own.

Jeanee Von Essen, the foreign editor, kept complaining to me about the expense reports from "our mysterious Mideast bureaus." Derwin Johnson and the Rome bureau were turning out terrific work. A good executive knows when to look the other way. And what Atlanta didn't know wouldn't hurt Derwin.

For a year Derwin was CNN Cairo. A year and a half on the job, from video journalist fresh out of grad school, to London cameraman, to Cairo bureau chief, at twenty-four. No one can say CNN didn't move the kids right along.

There's a postscript to Derwin's story. A year later, after I was gone from CNN, a new bureau chief arrived in Beirut with a wad of CNN cash to pay expenses. Somehow or other, the new bureau chief's accounts came up $5,000 short. He said he'd given it to Derwin; Derwin said he'd returned it. Derwin didn't have any receipts and CNN chose to believe the other guy. I would stake my life on Derwin's honesty. He is also devoted to the trade, brave under fire, and extraordinarily capable in difficult situations. We lost him because he failed to get a receipt for some cash outlay in the middle of a war zone. Getting receipts in the middle of a war zone was not Derwin's first priority.

CNN offered Derwin a job back in the States. Derwin had an offer from ABC. Three years after he started at CNN, Derwin Johnson was the ABC bureau chief in Rome.

Round 34: **You Boettcher Life**

Day Two marked the opening of diplomatic relations between Fidel Castro and Ted Turner. Mike Boettcher was still on the beach in Key West. In his case "on the beach" was a good thing; it meant he was still gainfully employed. We were waiting for the arrival of the Marielitos and, lo and behold, at midday they appeared.

A rust bucket of a freighter slips over the horizon, sails right into our camera and drops anchor. All these lifeboats with all these guys rowing them are coming right into our lens. They wade ashore, the mangiest, scruffiest guys ever seen. They have just been released from jail; you can practically smell them. All that's missing are daggers between their teeth, eye patches, and bandannas.

Boettcher is reporting live. CNN is broadcasting live. It is exclusive. There isn't another camera within a hundred miles. At first, I thought I was the smartest, or the luckiest, guy in the world. Later, I figured it out: It was a Fidel Castro setup. Fidel sees the launch of CNN. He wants to end Cuban emigration to the U.S. because he was losing so many of his educated middle class. He has released the Marielito prisoners to force the U.S. to close its borders, but no one has paid attention.

Now Fidel sees an opportunity to take advantage of CNN and its audience. I could hear him telling the ship's captain: "Okay, stop there!

Now boats over the side! A little to the left! A little to the right." I see him as a director with a megaphone, setting up a scene that will make the headlines.

The minute the Marielitos popped up on our screens, the three networks in New York called their Miami bureaus. They ordered Learjets. They flew in crews, producers, and reporters. Boettcher was standing there on the back of the truck all alone, and we were beating their pants off. The networks did packages, flew them back to Miami, ran them in their 7 p.m. national news shows, hours after we did. Less than twenty-four hours after CNN went on the air, we were forcing the major media to follow our agenda (and Fidel Castro's).

Castro's ploy, if it was a ploy, worked. President Carter ended his invitation for Cubans to emigrate to the United States. Fidel was saved the embarrassment of closing off emigration, in effect admitting that half the people in Cuba wanted to come to the United States, and Mike Boettcher had earned a chance to go to Cuba.

Fidel's brother Raul was a friend of a friend of a friend of Mike's. Mike was invited to Cuba, covered a couple of stories, then called to tell me I'd been invited down. I told him that Fidel didn't really want to see me. If he wants to see anyone, he wants to see Ted.

I liked the idea, but it had its dangers. Fidel was notorious for inviting visitors and then refusing to see them. (The CBC had done a whole documentary called *Waiting for Fidel* after Castro stood up some of their emissaries for more than a month.) What if our fearless leader got to Cuba, and Fidel never showed up? I wanted guarantees. It was a full year before we could work out the details of the "summit."

Round 35: Carper's Hurrah

Our July triumph belonged to Jean Carper. We had found her through agent Stan Berk, who'd trolled triumphantly through the Washington talent pool for us. In her he discovered the perfect medical correspondent. Carper had been a freelance medical reporter for the *Washington Post* who gave occasional reports on television for WTOP Washington.

She possessed a sound skepticism about the American medical establishment, doctors, and pharmaceutical companies. She had worked with Ralph Nader. She wrote books and columns and had never been involved in a libel suit. Jean is a tiny woman, birdlike and sturdy at the same time. Her voice is chirpy, and she laughs as if she is enjoying every moment. She is a very serious reporter. She is not embarrassed by the word "muckraker."

The health food craze was just beginning. Carper had done a story about the Women's Cooperative Market, which was offering "nitrite-free bacon." Jean bought some, ran it through FDA testing, and discovered it had more dangerous nitrites than ordinary bacon. Even worse, one of the people who sold the bacon to the Women's Market was an FDA inspector. Jean's story was a local sensation, and it got her a job at CNN.

A month into CNN, Jean called me. She had just gotten a tip from a former FDA official teaching in Galveston that there was an epidemic of brain cancer in areas surrounding certain Texas chemical factories. Investigators were concentrating on Dow Chemical and Union Carbide. Jean wanted to know what to do next. According to Jean, I said, "Why are you talking to me? Why aren't you in Texas?"

Jean met a CNN cameraman in Houston. She talked to a toxicologist. He told her that glioblastoma, a particularly nasty form of brain cancer, was indeed showing up at an alarming rate among people who worked at the chemical plants. Jean interviewed some of the afflicted and their families. She walked with one of them through the streets near the chemical plants, interviewing him with the plant framed behind him. Then she tried to interview Dow and Union Carbide scientists. Neither company would allow her on their premises, but a Dow scientist walked to the chain-link fence around his factory and talked to Jean through the wire. He revealed little, but neither did he deny. He came off as a rather weak apologist.

When Jean was ready to leave, walking through the Galveston suburbs just to get a few more shots, she learned that a glioblastoma victim had died, and his funeral was scheduled for that afternoon. Jean and her crew raced to the cemetery. The family did not welcome the crew, but the crew recorded the event anyway. There was weeping, there were hymns, there was a benediction. Family and coworkers mourned, and Jean had transformed a "statistical epidemic" into a human tragedy. It won CNN its first Ace award.

The next week CNN ran the glioblastoma story as a five-part series. Then we put the pieces together and ran them as a half-hour documentary during the weekend. In the midst of the five-part series, the *Washington Post* caught on to the story and tried to catch up. They ran their catch-up story on the front page. I sent Jean flowers.

Dow Chemical sent their PR man. First he went to see Ted; Ted sent him to me. He was the Dow vice president for public relations, and he was clearly very unhappy. He had been in the hospital, and from his hospital bed, he had seen the story on the local cable system. He got out of his hospital bed, got on the Dow private jet and flew right to Atlanta. He told me that Dow had an absolute rule that employees were not to comment to the press without approval from headquarters.

How dared CNN talk to this guy in Houston when Dow had refused to allow us on the premises? "He made himself available," I said. "He was a new guy, he didn't know the rules," said the PR man. "Not our reporter's fault," I said. "She asked the questions, he answered them, and we used them fairly." The PR man still felt that we had done Dow wrong. He had a special reason to complain.

Dow's headquarters are in Midland, Michigan, a company town, and the PR man told me that Dow, considered a very, very conservative company, was largely responsible for getting CNN on the Midland cable system. Back then, Ted Turner was considered a very, very conservative man. Relying on Ted's reputation, Dow had broken its neck to get CNN on the Midland cable system, so that we might counteract network news. Now we were acting worse than the networks.

The PR man did teach me something of value: "A statistical epidemic" is not in any sense a traditional epidemic. If an average of four men in a thousand are dying with glioblastoma nationally, but in Galveston seven men in a thousand are dying, that's a "statistical epidemic." I do not think "epidemic" is the right word. In the future, CNN would not use "epidemic" in its true sense. AIDS is an epidemic. Glioblastoma is a tragedy of a different sort.

I did not tell Jean about the visit from the Dow PR man. I was afraid that it might inhibit her reporting. Looking back, I doubt it. I don't think anything could inhibit Jean. In 1981, Carper was the first national television journalist to look into right-to-life violence. Dr. Takei Crist, a Jacksonville, North Carolina, obstetrician, occasionally performed abortions. He estimated that they constituted about 3 percent of his practice. Antiabortionists threatened Dr. Crist's life. He took the threats so seriously that when he drove the North Carolina roads, he kept two guns in his car. He knew he was a hated target.

Crist remembers, "Press coverage of the charges against and threats made to doctors who perform abortions didn't begin in earnest until the late eighties or early nineties." Carper was there in 1981. Jean and the crew accompanied Dr. Crist along the lonely roads, with the guns beside him, as he went out to deliver babies. Crist still operates his clinic.

Then Carper went after quaaludes, then the drug of choice for teenagers, which Jean had found out was easily obtainable. Jean sent her producer, Keel Heisler, to an Atlanta doctor. He only had to tell the doctor he was nervous and stressed-out to get a prescription. Jean and Keel, who looked like a typical hippie, drove to Ft. Lauderdale and went to drugstore after drugstore, where Keel would pick up " 'ludes."

After CNN aired the story, one of the larger drugstore chains in the South stopped filling quaalude prescriptions until it could change its procedures. These were baby steps for CNN in establishing its journalistic effects, but if a CNN report, which might be seen by seventy thousand viewers, could influence a major commercial establishment to change its business practices, then CNN was beginning to have clout.

When the quaalude story was over, Carper asked Heisler what happened to the pills. He said he had put them all in my desk, except one. That one he saved for Carper. Jean had a flying phobia, and Heisler gave her the one last pill to use on the flight back home. She nibbled on it all the way through the flight, and got off the plane staggering from ataxia, a loss of balance, which the 'lude had caused. Everybody thought she was drunk, but Carper said she'd never had a better flight.

A month after I left CNN, Burt Reinhardt told Jean that she was "too valuable" to do in-depth stories. He needed her presence on the air every night. She should do breaking news. There are dozens of reporters who can do breaking medical news; most often they just pick it up off the wires. The reason Jean is special is that she never needed the wires;

she found her own stories. A year later she retired from CNN to write books, mostly about alternative medicine. They are all authoritative, and they're all best-sellers. Now she's featured on NBC's *Dateline.* Jean Carper now plays in a higher league than CNN.

Round 36: **Conventions**

If I were running a news network, political parties would have to pay to get their conventions carried live. I see conventions as political infomercials. Staged, scripted, manicured, cosmeticized. I'd edit them down to half an hour and package them between a couple of infomercials, maybe Richard Simmons's *Sweating to the Oldies,* and that perennial winner, *Buns of Steel.*

That's not to say I wouldn't cover conventions. I would. And when anything real—unstaged and unscripted—occurred, I'd cut live to the show. Otherwise, I'd advise my audience to go to the Web, read the minute-by-minute convention schedule, scan the advance text for the speeches, and then go to C-SPAN to watch whatever it was they wanted to see, if anything.

I'd covered conventions since 1960, and even that year, only the Democratic convention had any suspense. Some Democrats thought Lyndon Johnson might make a better president than John Kennedy. Some Republicans had thought Nelson Rockefeller might make a better president than Richard Nixon, but Rockefeller and Nixon had done a preconvention deal, and the only suspense left was how many right-wing Republicans would boo Nixon for talking to Rockefeller. It turned out to be a large number. The winner of every nomination since 1960 has been determined before the first gavel falls.

The political events that stick in my mind occurred off the convention floor. In 1964, the Republican convention met in San Francisco. Barry Goldwater, after winning the California primary, had a lock on the nomination, but hundreds of delegates were still committed to Nelson Rockefeller, and his name was also placed in nomination. The Goldwater forces, who were now running the convention, had scheduled Rockefeller's nomination for about 3 a.m. Eastern time. When Rockefeller's name was finally announced, his delegates, as is the political custom, paraded around the hall, waving their signs and chanting his name.

Suddenly, the parade became a bloodless riot. Goldwater delegates jeered at the "liberals," harassed and spat on them. I grabbed a cameraman and ran to the convention door. The New Jersey Rockefeller delegation emerged. It was led by a black man with tears in his eyes. I brought him to our camera.

His hair was grey and tightly curled, he looked as if he could have played the part of the butler in *Gone With the Wind.* Despite the tears, he carried himself with dignity. He was a gentleman.

I didn't have to ask questions. "They called me nigger," he said. "They spat at me. They burned holes in my coat." He showed me where cigar butts had been pressed into his jacket.

The faint smell of burnt cloth surrounded him. He was lit by the harsh glare of a Frezollini bulb, and as he lifted his face to the camera, we saw silver tears streaming down his coal black face: "I have brought up my children to be Republicans. I have told them that the Republican party is the party for people who study in school and who work hard in their lives. I told them we have a chance to prosper like everyone else. We can be Republicans, and now they call me nigger."

At that point, a white woman, a Rockefeller delegate, who looked like a cross between Millicent Fenwick and Christy Whitman, walked into the picture, put her arm around the delegate's shoulders. "They're using you," she said softly, pointing her finger at me and the camera. "Can't you see that they're using you?" She led him away. I'm not sure which was worse, the cigar burn or her condescension.

It was the middle of the night in New York. The film didn't get there for another thirty-six hours, and by then it was too late to use it. Just because it happened at three o'clock in the morning didn't mean it wasn't important. I hadn't imagined a twenty-four-hour news network in 1964, but I knew there should have been some way to get that story on the air.

The most important thing I learned in 1964 was that despite their journalistic protestations, the networks were in cahoots with the political parties. On the eve of the Democratic convention in Atlantic City, Burt Reinhardt, our cameraman Fred Lawrence, and I saw a tiny demonstration: three people on the boardwalk, facing the convention hall, each carrying a placard bearing the face of one of the three men who had been murdered by Klansmen in Philadelphia, Mississippi, that summer.

The lead demonstrator was Rita Schwerner, the widow of Michael Schwerner, one of the victims. The second was Gus Hall, the head of the American Communist Party, and the third was a black man, also as I recall, an American communist leader. No cameras were covering the demonstration. We sent Lawrence back to his car to get his gear. By the time he arrived, Hodding Carter III, a journalist from Greenville, Mississippi (later assistant secretary of state under Jimmy Carter), had joined the group. Rita Schwerner and Carter were debating. She was charging him with racism.

Hodding Carter, and his father before him, had fought the Ku Klux Klan in Greenville for thirty years when all about them Mississippians were bowing and scraping to white supremacists. The Carters regularly ran editorials in their newspaper, the *Delta Democrat-Times,* opposing the Klan. Everyday they walked the streets of Greenville or printed their paper, they were in danger of violence, but they held to their stand. Rita Schwerner had lost her husband, but Hodding Carter was not responsible. He had fought the same forces she was fighting, twenty years before she took up the battle. Now she charged him with racism. Had his family not owned slaves? Were they not responsible for hundreds of years of injustice to blacks? Hodding Carter, a very brave man, did not deny her charges.

Lawrence raced to get his camera up on the tripod. We were ready to shoot. A New Jersey state policeman, in his Smokey the Bear hat, stood in front of the camera and said, "You can't shoot this." "Yes we can," I said. "What about the agreement?" he asked. "What agreement?" I asked. "You agreed not to shoot any demonstrations on the boardwalk." "Not me," I said. "Not UPI." As we stood there the trooper radioed to headquarters. Within minutes, J. Leonard Reinsch appeared.

Reinsch was head of Cox Broadcasting. Every four years Cox Broadcasting loaned him to the Democratic Party to deal with television. Reinsch confirmed that the three networks had agreed not to cover demonstrations at the Atlantic City conventions. "We are not bound by that agreement," I said. Reinsch was embarrassed, the state trooper held firm. A compromise was reached. We would be permitted to shoot pictures but no sound. Of course that killed the story, but by then the story was almost over. Carter was walking away

By 1964, I had been in television for eight years. I had believed in CBS and NBC and ABC. I had believed in the world of Edward R. Murrow and in Huntley and Brinkley and Roger Mudd and Walter Cronkite. That night ended it for me. The U-2 lies had ended my faith in the inevitable truthfulness of the American government. J. Leonard Reinsch and a New Jersey state trooper eliminated my faith in America's networks. I was sure that UPI would not have entered into that agreement. For the first time, I thought that UPI was better than the networks.

Round 37: **Conventions, Two**

You'd have to be an idiot to open a ski resort on June 1. Likewise, you'd have to be an idiot to launch a twenty-four-hour news network in a quadrennial year. "Quadrennial year" is a news term applied to the year in which a president is elected. Such years are very expensive. There are primaries, conventions, and campaigns. They require great preparation and organization. The networks had teams of producers and researchers who spent the full four years between elections getting ready for the big events. Nevertheless, I had stuck CNN with a June 1, 1980, launch date.

Six weeks before the Republican convention, ten weeks before the Democratic convention, we had no election unit, no designated political correspondent, no designated researchers. Even while we were completing construction on our own bureaus, we had to begin construction on convention booths; even while we were finishing the construction of the lines and satellite links between our bureaus and headquarters, we had to begin arranging for lines and links from Detroit and New York, the convention cities, to Atlanta. It was an absurdity.

I could've launched the network on September 1, but that was when the networks introduced their fresh programming for the new year. I thought CNN would do better competing against the network reruns of the summer season. From a television point of view, it was a very professional decision. From a news point of view, it was a prescription for disaster.

The 1980 Republican convention was staged at Cobo Hall in Detroit. It was clear that Ronald Reagan had the nomination sewed up, but I ordered gavel-to-gavel coverage anyway. Although CNN was not going to carry the convention gavel-to-gavel, we had to be ready to go to the convention whenever events warranted. Jim Rutledge understood what I hoped to get out of the convention. He believes we could have owned them, but we didn't do enough color. "Reese always talked about color," Jim says. "Everybody can cover the bullshit inside the convention hall, but there was other stuff there, and we were capable of getting it, but we didn't."

That wasn't exactly true. There was one story we did that made our whole convention coverage worth it, but that comes later.

Cissy Baker and Guy Pepper had to bear the brunt of carrying out our convention plans. Cissy arrived at the convention center, headed up the main driveway, and confronted eight ABC News trailers, seven CBS News trailers, and a gaggle of trailers from NBC News. When she got to the entrance to the hall and asked the guard where the CNN trailers were, he didn't even know what CNN was, but he told Cissy there was one trailer down on the lower level next to the river.

"So I drove around the wall," Cissy remembers, "and there was a trailer set kind of sideways in a pile of gravel, with nothing in it. That was CNN, one trailer. We got desks and chairs and phones, and we finally got an anchor position inside the hall for Bernie Shaw. It was up in the nosebleed section on the highest floor of the arena, and we had no glass walls or anything."

I'll take responsibility for that. I intended to keep CNN the "open network." I didn't want us in glassed-in isolation. I wanted to have the sound of the convention all around us. I soon learned there were no microphones, or at least we didn't own any, that were sufficiently directional to prevent ambient sound (a kind term for a marching band over the noise of an enormous crowd) from leaking under Bernie's voice. (Leaking under is also a kind term; it was more like roaring over.)

Cissy's concern wasn't only the noise. "We were like the black sheep squadron," she says. "We didn't have anything." Cissy stole a golf cart so they could start bringing equipment into the hall. CNN never had a permanent repeater set on top of the convention hall to permit two-way radio communication between the crews, the control room, and the truck. In the end, Cissy put my son Orrin, who had signed up for a summer job, on the roof of the convention hall with two radio phones and used him as a "human repeater." If the signal didn't get from the trailer to the crew, Orrin would hear it and relay the message. That was the only way to get to the crews if we lost direct contact. "Worst of all, there was no back to our booth," Cissy reports. "We kept worrying that Bernie was going to lean backwards in his chair and fall out into the audience" one hundred feet below.

It was Guy Pepper's job to set up the technical arrangements for CNN Detroit. His crew consisted mostly of CNN Atlanta VJs, the children of our network. Their task was installing the CNN return downlink. Nobody had any idea how to do it. Guy remembers asking, "Anybody know how to put this together? We've got all these instructions in front of us, and we have people falling all over each other saying, 'I think this screw goes in here,' 'I think that bolt goes in there.' It was nuts." In the end, Guy got it put together, and we went on the air.

Most of the equipment had been driven up from Atlanta in the TBS mobile truck. Luckily, they didn't have Braves games to cover that week. The booth camera "was the oldest camera in the TBS arsenal," according to Kenyon. "It had aluminum foil, like from a kitchen, wrapped around the cords." Apparently, this camera was so ancient that microwaves would screw it up. Somehow the aluminum foil was going to help.

CNN did have its moment of glory, and it belonged to Bernie Shaw. It hadn't been easy for Bernie to adjust to CNN. This was the era of network news extravagance. Cameramen flew first-class. Everybody had limos; Bernie and his writer/producer, Sandy Kenyon, took cabs.

Even as Bernie arrived, he suffered his first slight. Kenyon says, "The only time I ever saw Bernie get angry was when we were waiting in line to enter the convention. He was standing in front of Ed Bradley and Walter Cronkite, and the guards wouldn't let him in." We hadn't arranged for proper credentials. "Bernie took his briefcase, slammed it down on the table, and they found the credentials for him real fast. He's left ABC News for a completely different venture, and here he is being humiliated."

Bernie's bit of superior journalism was set up by Kenyon. Detroit City cops had been handling most of the security in the press area of the arena, and Sandy had become friendly with the plainclothesmen assigned to the CNN booth. One day, another group of detectives arrived and informed Sandy that there would be a security sweep that afternoon, which meant that everybody had to be out of the auditorium for three hours.

CNN was different from the other networks. We were going live to Bernie Shaw for five minutes in each half hour, and he was updating us as to what was happening in Detroit. If Bernie was out of the hall, CNN would lose six cut-ins and have no Detroit presence. Sandy talked to "our cops," the guys who had been parked next to the booth, and went into his song and dance. "We have to be on live so is it okay if we stay? You know it's Bernie Shaw, and you know we're safe, and you have been so nice to us." The upshot was Bernie stayed put.

At this moment, Kenyon and Shaw are all alone in the hall where nothing is happening, there is no sound, no movement, no nothing, only an eerie feeling. Kenyon says, "Way below us, Ronald Reagan stepped out. Not Ronald Reagan the politician, Ronald Reagan the professional actor. Confident that only his handlers are watching, he starts giving notes. 'Move that key light just three inches to the left. I'm gonna stand here; my mark will be here.'

"Bernie tells me, 'Have them come to us,' and I scream to Atlanta, 'Bernie's got something, come to us, come to us.' And as the camera zooms in, Bernie says, 'This is a side of Ronald Reagan the average person will never get to see.' Sure enough, here is a man plying the mechanics of his trade, a movie star who knows how to make himself look good.

"Bernie hears the mellifluous tones of the president; he is rehearsing his acceptance speech. Lyn Nofziger, the GOP political strategist, is directing. His shirt is unbuttoned, his tie askew, he sees the camera is on, and he goes nuts. He shakes his first, he bellows. Bernie completes his report." CNN had taken one small step for political truth. We had shown how carefully prearranged these 'spontaneous events' were. For the Detroit cops, it did not go as well. Kenyon says, "When it was all over every single one of those friendly security guys, the Detroit detectives, had been replaced."

Most of the rest of the convention coverage was a mess. John Hillis, who turned out to be the most competent television professional we hired at CNN, refers to Detroit as a "four-car pileup." Sandy Kenyon avers that guests didn't want to do CNN because they didn't know what it was. He'd call somebody and say, "Hi. I'm from CNN," and they'd say, "Oh, we can't get cable where we live." Most potential guests thought he was trying to sell them cable. Once after a lot of work, he got Coleman Young, the mayor of Detroit. Then the Atlanta producer said, "Fuck Coleman Young. He is not going on my air." Everybody was embarrassed.

I should have stepped in sooner. I don't know who the producer of that segment was, but I know he didn't own the "air" he claimed. It was CNN's air, and whether Coleman Young was a good guest or a bad guest, he had been invited by CNN, and the CNN producer had to put him on the air out of ordinary politeness.

The Atlanta versus Washington problem set the stage for George Watson's departure from CNN; Watson's final straw was the Republican convention. Henry Kissinger was scheduled to speak on the last night. It was a long speech, Kissinger was a dull speaker with a German accent to boot, and I saw no reason to carry the speech from beginning to end.

George, on the other hand, saw enormous significance in the Kissinger address. He was convinced that it represented the surrender of power of the Eastern Republican establishment to the West Coast-Southern State coalition that controls the Republican Party to this day. Watson viewed the speech as Kissinger begging for a role in the new administration. It was Kissinger delivering his resume.

I hadn't seen the text of the speech, hadn't perceived its significance, but even if I had, I wouldn't have carried it full-length live. I think George should've culled the sections of the speech that most obviously exemplified the Kissinger surrender and plea. If Kissinger was going to humble himself before Ronald Reagan, we should've been ready for it, and at the key moment have Dan Schorr and Bob Novak ready to comment. Schorr might have said Kissinger's kissing Reagan's ass and Novak reply, "It's about time the Eastern establishment realizes what the American people want, and realizes where the power is."

That might have been informative and, more to the point, interesting television.

With a speech as dull as Kissinger's, you have to follow an old Movietone adage: "Tell 'em why it's gonna be important, let 'em listen to what's important, and then tell 'em why it was important." Then maybe they'll pay attention to a tedious address and actually learn that sometimes it pays to listen.

I can best sum up the convention on a personal note. At the convention's end, according to Cissy Baker, "When the gavel went down, we all went back to this puny little trailer and got as drunk as we could on champagne. All of a sudden we heard the little two-way key up. It just went *brrr*. We'd forgotten we left Orrin on the roof, and the door to the roof was locked. We looked at each other and went, 'Oh Shit.' We ran up and we got him. He was fine." George Watson wasn't fine. The next Monday he resigned.

Round 38: **Horatio at the Bridge**

Ggeorge Watson had left ABC because of his disappointment with Roone Arledge. Now he was disappointed with me. I would like to think that my task had been impossible. I was trying to meld two cultures—the Ivy League gentleman, George Watson, and his gentlemanly Washington bureau, with the street toughs who had grown up at independent stations or in local news. I'd been born in Newark; I'd gone to Dartmouth. I thought I could bridge both worlds. Not a chance.

Ted Kavanau and Alec Nagle were abusive, wise-guy bullies who were used to shouting matches and verbal put-downs. Watson, and particularly Davey Newman, the Washington executive producer, who was most often on the other end of the phone from Kavanau and Nagle, were gentlemen. That is, they were gentle men. They would not tolerate overt disrespect. Watson would call me, I would tell Kavanau and Nagle to tone it down. A week later it would be as bad as ever.

The Republican convention in Detroit had been critical to George. My refusal to carry the Kissinger speech live was the final straw. The president of CNN was overruling George Watson's news judgment. Looking back and seeing it from George's point of view, I was his last hope for a better network. If I were like Kavanau and Nagle, then CNN was not for him. Had I realized the Kissinger speech was so important to George, CNN would have carried the speech. I would have carried ten dull Kissinger speeches to keep George Watson.

When Watson left, Davey Newman went with him. The Washington bureau was leaderless. Jim Schultz, the assistant bureau chief, was operational, not editorial. Jim Rutledge, who sat on the assignment desk, understood my strategy better than anyone else in Washington, but neither he nor Jim Schultz had any recognition in the Capitol. The ABC contingent, still loyal to George, wanted a leader with inside-the-beltway clout. I flew to Washington for an open meeting with all the CNN employees, some of it hostile.

The summer of 1980 was a very hot summer. I had ordered a satellite whip-around from all our bureaus. I wanted our correspondents to find a location showing how hot it was in their city. We would go live from bureau to bureau with each reporter doing thirty or forty seconds, including a brief interview. It was to be a demonstration of CNN's national presence and its ability to report live from everywhere. One of our Washington reporters felt it was beneath her standing to do a weatherman-in-the-street story. She was meant to cover "serious stories." I had to spend five minutes answering questions about whether she would ever again be assigned to a weather story.

Other reporters and producers had their own gripes, but most wanted to know who their new boss would be. I couldn't tell them. I hadn't seen it coming, I'd never thought about a replacement for George. I tried to be calming, reassuring. I asked for time for us to find the right person, someone they would respect, who they would be proud to have lead them.

Questions were still coming fast and furious when Michael Halberstam spoke. Halberstam did a medical column for us and was Watson's doctor and close friend. He had been standing quietly against a side wall listening hard. He spoke softly, concisely, in simple, well thought out sentences. He told the group that he had been hired by George Watson and that he recognized Watson's virtues. Then he suggested that the bureau give me a chance.

He reminded the staff that I had immediately flown up from Atlanta, had stood there for ninety minutes answering their questions, some of them difficult, courteously and responsibly. He wondered how many other network news presidents would have faced the bureau in this situation. Halberstam was fifteen years older than most of the people in the bureau. He was very good at what he did as a doctor and on the air. His words carried authority. After he spoke, there were fewer questions, and they were softer. I walked about the room, offering whatever comfort I could to George's people. There were no further resignations.

I called Ted Turner in Newport to tell him what had happened. He asked if there was any hope of getting George back. I said I had done my best, and I doubted it. He asked me if I would like George to come back. I said, "You bet." He asked, "Should I call him?"

"Give it your best shot," I said.

Although Watson had gone to Harvard and been an editor of the *Crimson,* he was originally from Birmingham, Alabama, which was Ted's wife's hometown. In Ted's mind, he was a Southern boy. Watson remembers the phone call going something like this: "'You and I are manning the barricades,' Ted said. 'We're Southerners, holding off the Yankee hordes.' He recited 'Horatio at the Bridge' from *The Lays of Ancient Rome:*

> I, with two more to help me,
>   Will hold the foe in play.
> In yon strait path a thousand
>   May well be stopped by three.
> Now, who will stand on either hand,
>   And keep the bridge with me?

He told me that his baseball players could not just abrogate their contracts and run off to play for someone else," Watson recalls. "He said I was deserting him in his hour of need."

If Ted felt deserted, I felt bereft. George may have been Ted's Southern brother, but although I may be elevating myself, I thought he was my brother in his respect for news. After Watson's resignation, we never had a top-of-the line bureau chief in Washington. We tried twice. One guy was a great newsman who didn't understand television, and the other a great writer who didn't work very hard. Their failure dogged the rest of my time at CNN.

We moved on to the Democratic convention in New York. It went a little better. At least we had a bureau in town, and we could offer better support. There had been no time to correct my Detroit mistake. We were still broadcasting from an open booth, and there was no way to control ambient sound. I don't think anybody cared; I don't think anybody wanted to hear what they were saying. The convention was dull beyond dull. Jimmy Carter, who was not the most exciting president the U.S. had ever had, was going to be renominated. Everybody knew that. Nothing important was going to happen at Madison Square Garden.

Our best moment at the convention was a Ted Kavanau "special." Sandy Kenyon, who had come up from Washington with Bernie Shaw, remembers, "Kavanau is listening to his scanner early in the morning, and he discovers that the president of the United States, the leader of the free world, is jogging in Central Park. Kavanau flips on the radio. It was like something out of a movie. 'Calling all crews, calling all crews, converge on Central Park,' says Kavanau. So all four of our crews descend on this huge area," says Kenyon, "and by God, someone gets lucky. They got the shot of the man himself, running." If this was the high point of the New York convention, "fuggedabout" the rest of it.

The conventions themselves are contrivances, calculated reconstructions of an earlier and more vigorous era when open battle waged on convention floors, when no one could predict what would happen next and no one knew for sure who would emerge as the party candidate. I felt it was CNN's job to demonstrate the obsolescence of a system that held its conventions after everything of importance had been determined.

It is television itself that has turned the conventions into staged formal occasions. Grown men do not wheel and deal when everybody is watching. The deals, the side deals, the trade-offs will not be made in full view. Idealists thought that television would end the deals, the side deals, and the trade-offs. Instead, practical men made their deals elsewhere and arrived at the conventions with nothing left to decide. I wanted CNN to find a way to cover wheeling and dealing. It hasn't happened yet.

Round 39: **Road to Damascus**

In 1958, when I was a writer for UPI, I went to a party thrown by a couple of women I'd known at college. Among the guests were a hearty, friendly Russian, a member of the Soviet delegation to the UN, and his wife. The only remarkable aspect of the encounter was that it was the height of the Cold War and I'd never before talked with a real live Russian communist. A couple of days later, the Russian invited me to dinner. I remember that we sat across from each other in a booth with a red and white checkered tablecloth and we both ordered roast beef. (Many years later I discovered that all Russian diplomats posted in the U.S. exist on roast beef and lobster.)

The diplomat informed me that American planes were regularly flying over the Soviet Union, then showed me a picture of a plane carrying a United States Air Force insignia. It was a medium close-up, and he explained it was shot from a MiG flying alongside the U.S. plane. I said the photo could have been shot anywhere. He suggested certain topographical features would prove it's Russian.

I said, "Look, if you're going to tell me that some hotshot American pilots fly into Soviet airspace and play tag with Russian planes, I don't doubt it, but not under government orders."

"These are U.S. planes flying over Russia to take pictures for the CIA," he said. I told him flat out it wasn't true. I didn't believe the U.S. government would, as a matter of policy, fly over Russian airspace. At twenty-six, I had the arrogance of innocence.

A year later, the U-2 story broke, Gary Powers was shot down. The U.S. admitted the CIA had been flying spy planes over Russia, there was a showcase trial, and Powers was dispatched to a Russian dungeon.

If I had believed the story, checked it out, and then been able to convince UPI to print it, it would have changed my life. In one way it *did* change my life; I never again believed the CIA or the Pentagon.

On September 19, 1980, I hear that a Titan II missile had blown up in its silo on a missile farm in Damascus, Arkansas, and the Pentagon is denying the presence of any nuclear material. I call Jim Rutledge in Atlanta and tell him to send the satellite truck, a six-wheel semi with a parabolic dish that will have to be assembled panel by panel on the bed of the truck and that will then feed our pictures live to Atlanta.

Jim Miklaszewski has already flown up to Damascus with the crew. Mik says that when he arrived on Friday the military, briefing reporters at a community center near the missile site, refused to confirm or deny the presence of nuclear warheads. They had given Mik the impression that there was no danger, the story was over, and the newsmen should go home.

Miklaszewski calls Rutledge at the desk and says, "The story is over." He has sent his tape back to Atlanta, there is nothing more to report. Jim tells Mik, "You better find something, Reese has just sent the live truck to Damascus. Reese said, 'Anytime I hear the words air force and nuclear in the same sentence, I want a live truck.'" At that time, Mik didn't even know what a live truck was.

So the live truck makes its way over the back roads of the South from Atlanta to Damascus. After killing a cow and buying the corpse from a farmer, we arrive at the scene by noon of the next day.

Our first pictures look like a scene out of *The Grapes of Wrath*. The county sheriff is leading a bunch of people who look like sharecroppers down the road. They are toting bags with sticks on their shoulders bearing more bags. Mik asks the sheriff what's happening. The sheriff says, live on camera, "I don't know, I just been ordered to get them out of here." The air force had announced there would be no further evacuations, yet we see civilians walking out. Mik's suspicion deepens. On site the air force tells him there has been a liquid fuel spill; it is dangerous but not nuclear. The air force in Washington, in keeping with its policy, refuses to comment, except to say there are "no nuclear hazards."

We have parked our truck on a dusty two-lane road looking toward a hill on which the missile site is perched. Miklaszewski is to do five-minute live reports every half hour. We set our camera up at ground level and watch the air force clean-up begin. Even as we start shooting, the air force moves two blue step-vans into position to block our cameras. Every time we go live, the air force moves the step-vans and tries to block our view. Finally, we move our camera onto the top of the truck, and we see a cluster of men in hazmat (hazardous material) suits, looking like Buck Rogers, with Geiger counters in their hands. The air force brings in bigger trucks.

By luck, as we are shooting, a telephone lineman appears to install temporary phone lines for us. Earlier in the day, he was called onto the missile site to install phone lines for the military. He has seen what's going on and tells us that in fact there is a weapon on the ground. He has seen it and been told by the air force it was a nuclear warhead. Mik talks to a county supervisor who tells him that the military is being very evasive, they won't give him a flat denial. They won't deny it to Mik either. He too suspects that there was a warhead. Based on that information, an eyewitness, and no denial, we report that there is a warhead out there on the ground.

The telephone lineman is using a cherry picker to put up our phone lines, and when he sees that our cameras are blocked, he lends it to us. Now we can see into the missile base over the trucks. The men in the Buck Rogers suits are still there. For the rest of the afternoon, Mik does live voice-overs as we watch the air force try to get its mystery package covered up.

Mik remembers the whole process: "The bulldozer digs a ditch, then a flatbed lowers a canister into a hole, they push the device into the canister and they use the bulldozer to push the warhead into the canister. They buttoned up the canister and as the day light was absolutely failing. . . . the last picture you saw was of the air force personnel ratcheting this canister down on the flatbed truck, and they chain it down."

Throughout the weekend, the Pentagon continues its non-denial denials. On site, an air force general invades our truck. He tells Miklaszewski that radiation from the truck is "cooking his pilots" and demands we shut down. Miklaszewski says he doesn't have the authority to do that but if the general wishes, he can talk to headquarters in Atlanta. The general does not so wish. Several times over the next few hours air force personnel try to convince Mik that shutting down our live feed is in the interest of national security. Mik refuses. Atlanta insists that pushing warheads into a canister is not a matter of national security. It is a matter of public safety.

Our Pentagon reporter, Dave Browdie, suddenly appears on the screen from Washington saying that there is no nuclear material present. I go ballistic. "Who put *him* on the air?" I ask. Ted Kavanau says he did. We have words. He accuses me of censoring our reporters. I inform him I am editing our reporters and will continue to do so. I call Bernie Shaw in Washington and tell him to correct Browdie's report.

CNN knows that nuclear material is present. In addition to everything our camera has seen and everything Miklaszewski has told us, a high Pentagon official has been calling us to confirm our story. He says we're "right on." He wants us to "keep it up."

Browdie will not give up. He calls back in tears. He says, "They're laughing at me Reese, they're laughing at CNN. They flat out deny the story. CNN is the only one going with it and we're looking like fools." Browdie is a sucker. His air force handlers have razzed and conned him into committing a cardinal sin: denying the report of another CNN journalist. Kavanau has done even worse by putting Browdie on the air contradicting Miklaszewski. If CNN is telling two different stories, how is the audience to know which one is right?

By now the viewers have seen Miklaszewski showing the men in Buck Rogers suits with their Geiger counters and the sheriff evacuating his civilian charges. Everybody at CNN knows what's happening, everybody except Ted Kavanau and David Browdie.

Throughout a long summer weekend when there isn't much other news, CNN has the only camera watching the air force, live, as it attempts to cope with and cover up a potential nuclear disaster.

The *Washington Post* reporter on the scene in Damascus is watching CNN. The *L.A. Times* guy does him one better. He climbs into our truck and watches our coverage from the monitor. He sees stuff that he could never get standing on the road. When he learns that his motel has CNN, he tells Miklaszewski, "I'm going to my room, I can cover the story better from there."

On Monday, a CBS camera arrives. The other networks never show up at all. CBS gets there just in time to see a flatbed truck with a container lashed to it drive through the gate. The capsule is shipped to Pantax, in Amarillo, Texas. Pantax is the company that handles hazardous nuclear materials. The story is finally over.

I learned one thing in Damascus: how hard it was to merge live news into dead news. The explosion had occurred concurrently with high-level disarmament talks in Moscow. Our Titan missiles were obsolete, but our negotiators wanted to use them as a bargaining chip. Maybe we could get the Russians to give us something valuable for something we were about to throw away anyway.

Within the Washington beltway, diplomatic news is a hot topic. It's the kind of story that foreign policy wonks love to dither about. "We will give up two ounces of *x*, if you will give up one ounce of *y*, and how many angels can dance on the head of your pin, sir?"

Our Atlanta anchor asked Mik, who was standing in the middle of a dusty road in Damascus, Arkansas, with an air force general hassling him and not even a producer to help him, "So Jim, how do you think this will affect the nuclear arms discussion in Moscow?" Mik had the good sense not to respond. That was Mik's method. He says, "If I get a really dumb question, I just pretend my IFB (radio earpiece) went out."

At that moment, I realized CNN would need two reporters on live stories like Damascus, a play-by-play reporter like Mik and a "color" man, maybe Dan Schorr. It's like football: One guy will tell you what you're seeing as you see it. The other will tell you "what it means in the big picture." We should have had Dan Schorr there. He was always a big-picture guy.

The payoff on the story did not occur until 1985, after Mik left CNN for NBC to be their Pentagon correspondent. The air force invited him to lunch, and laughingly admitted that after the Damascus story, they had changed its PR policy: In a case where the public safety or security was an issue, they would no longer deny the presence of nuclear material, but they wouldn't confirm it either.

They told Mik he was the first reporter who had ever made the air force change its PR policy on anything.

Round 40: **Piracy on the Caribbean Sea**

Shortly after the launch of CNN, I got a phone call from a colonel in the Panamanian army. He praised CNN. He exclaimed over what a difference it had made to journalism in Panama. He told me how difficult it was to get objective news in his country. Then he made his pitch. Would I give him the exclusive rights to market CNN in Panama?

CNN was carried on a U.S. domestic satellite. We couldn't sell our service across international borders, but CNN's domestic signal was strong enough so that it could be seen throughout the Caribbean and in much of South America. I explained to the colonel about the legal problems and said, "I can't sell CNN to you."

He was surprised. "How does my friend Colonel So-and-So in Colombia get the rights to CNN?" he asked.

"Who is Colonel So-and-So?" I asked.

The colonel said, "Thank you very much," hung up the phone, and went into business for himself.

Round 41: **The Ayatollah Holds an Auction**

Ted Turner wanted "investigative reporters." I don't like investigative reporters. I wanted beat reporters who could find "original stories" and then report on them. For the most part, investigative units just provide a convenient mail drop for whistle-blowers or malcontents to drop their droppings. Still if Ted wanted one, I'd get him one.

Ted Kavanau knew a couple of guys we could afford, Joe Pennington and Stanley Pinsley. Pennington had been a local station reporter with an okay record on investigations. Pinsley was a New York researcher whom Kavanau had used at WNEW. He had never gotten the station sued.

In the midst of the Democratic convention in New York, the Pennington/Pinsley team told me they had evidence that President Carter was secretly negotiating with Ayatollah Khomeini in an arms-for-hostages deal. The middlemen, the Hashemi brothers, were well-known Iranian expatriates, thought by some to be arms dealers, by others to be dope dealers, but certainly the kind of characters who would and could do business with both sides in this kind of operation.

The Pennington/Pinsley story made political sense: Jimmy Carter knew he was in trouble in the 1980 presidential election unless he could get the U.S. hostages out of Iran.

In the spring Ted Kennedy and Carter were running neck and neck for the Democratic presidential nomination in the Wisconsin primary. On April 1, the day of the primary, Carter held a 7 a.m. press conference to announce progress in "resolving the hostage crisis." It was the lead item on the morning news shows. Of course, the hostages didn't get out, but the phony story helped Carter beat Kennedy. It was Jimmy Carter's April fool's joke on Ted. I'm sure it disappointed the hostages, too.

In the long run, the person it hurt most was Jimmy Carter. He had shown the Republicans the power of the hostage issue. Moreover, he had demonstrated his willingness to use it for political purposes. Carter had put himself in a tough spot. He had to get the hostages out if he wanted to win the election, but he couldn't be seen paying "ransom" to their Iranian kidnappers.

In Wisconsin Carter had been blowing smoke; now he had to build a fire. First, he tried to rescue the hostages by force. On April 24, he sent eight helicopters into the Iranian desert. Three were damaged in a sandstorm. No one could fix the choppers. Eight Americans died. The hostages stayed in Iran.

That's how things stood when Pennington/Pinsley came to me in New York. Carter was desperate. He was dealing surreptitiously, through the Hashemi brothers, with the ayatollah himself. The Hashemis were thought to be all-purpose middlemen—guns, oil, drugs. Now they added hostages to their inventory. Pennington claimed that Carter was offering money, arms, and continuing support to the ayatollah, in exchange for the captives' release. Pinsley showed us documents, official government papers stamped Top Secret. They indicated that Pennington had the story right, and according to Pennington, the Hashemis had already received advance payments on the deal.

Pennington was pleading to go on the air "now, if not sooner." He swore that a *Washington Post* reporter was working on the same story. (I have never known an investigative reporter who didn't say that there was another reporter working on the same story, and if we didn't go with it, we'd be beaten.) It was a race, and we had to get on the air before they got it into their paper.

We wondered where Pennington's documents came from, but in our business, you don't ask a reporter for his sources. If a source was feeding stolen government documents to Pennington, it was because he trusted Pennington. That didn't mean that he trusted CNN. We ran the documents past our lawyers. They were satisfied we would use them.

Pennington and Pinsley pushed harder and harder. Then the *Washington Post* ran a Hashemi story not in the paper, on their wire service. The *Boston Globe* and the *Atlanta Constitution* picked it up. The story was different from ours, but it too implicated the Hashemis.

Our story was ready. We had checked it out, we believed it, and we put it on the air. It was not picked up by the rest of the press. (The FBI, on the other hand, seems to have believed it. Shortly after it aired, the FBI requested permission to install a surveillance system in Cyrus Hashemi's office.) The Hashemi brothers immediately sued both CNN and the *Washington Post* in Atlanta Federal Court. The *Post* withdrew the story. We did not. Now we stood alone in federal court, with Hashemi all over our face.

We called in Pennington and Pinsley. We cross-examined them. We needed to know more about the documents and where Pinsley had gotten them. He gave us no names. He said they had come to him through the Executive Intelligence Report (EIR). I gulped. The EIR was funded by and associated with Lyndon LaRouche, a demi-fascist crank who was running for president against Carter and Reagan. The documents EIR supplied came from the Pentagon and the State Department and appeared to be authentic, but if we fought the suit, we would have to admit publicly that we had been accepting information from a highly contaminated source.

When we ran the Hashemi story we believed it to be true. Nothing had changed. If it was true before, it was true now. CNN couldn't back away. We would contest the suit. Not only would we live with any embarrassment, we would continue to investigate.

Our problem was Pinsley and Pennington couldn't produce anymore information. Pennington said the advance payments had been deposited in a Cayman Islands bank. I wanted Pennington to follow the money. Pennington was afraid to go. He said the Caymans had the most secretive banks in the world and people who ask too many questions are apt to disappear permanently. He wanted to know what kind of security we would provide him. I began to suspect that no matter where I sent him, Pennington was unlikely to find out anything more unless the EIR gave it to him.

With the *Washington Post* out of the story, CNN out of information, and a lawsuit pending, the Hashemi story died a natural death and the hostages remained in captivity. Ronald Reagan won the election. The Atlanta federal judge hearing the Hashemi case dismissed the suit. I thought of it as a minor victory for the First Amendment. We had stuck to our guns and won.

What I was not aware of was that Pinsley/Pennington might have stumbled onto one of the biggest stories of the past twenty years. The Carter administration had indeed been dealing with Iran through the Hashemis. The administration had been prepared to release $12 billion in Iranian funds that were frozen following the shah's overthrow. It had also been prepared to deliver to the Iranians spare parts for military equipment that had been purchased by the shah before his overthrow. It seemed likely that some money had been paid to the Hashemis, but the Hashemis had been unable to deliver the hostages. Carter was dealing through rug merchants to rug merchants, and the ayatollah had said no.

Now it seems that Republicans, alerted by Carter's use of the "hostage crisis" against Ted Kennedy, had also been dickering with the Iranians. They wanted the ayatollah to keep the hostages in Tehran until after the election. The Hashemis had been involved with them as well.

In 1991, Gary Sick, Carter's chief Iranian negotiator, wrote *October Surprise,* a book about the dealing and double-dealing during the presidential campaign. He claims that negotiations between Reagan campaign aides, including William Casey and Richard Allen and the ayatollah, had been going on since the spring of 1980. The Carter administration knew nothing about them.

Sick says that even as he was bargaining to get the hostages out, Allen was bargaining to keep them in. The Hashemi brothers were participating. Ayatollah Khomeini was holding an auction, high bidder becomes president of the United States. Reagan won. The hostages were released moments after his inauguration.

Looking back, we'd missed our chance. CNN had found and reported a major story that no one else had, but we couldn't follow through. Jimmy Carter outfoxed Ted Kennedy, but now it seems that Ronald Reagan outfoxed Jimmy Carter, the ayatollah raked in the pot, and CNN had not broken the story. An eighty-year-old Muslim fundamentalist, sitting in Qum, Iran, had determined the "leader of the free world," and we hadn't reported it.

The press, the networks, CNN in its meager way, had covered the race in traditional fashion. We had assigned reporters to follow the candidates state by state. We had reported on the issues, the high interest rates, the economic downturn. We had contrasted views on abortion and taxes. It was only the weekend before the election, that we discovered the obvious: 1980 was a one-issue campaign. That issue was the hostages.

Round 42: **Sandi Freeman**

Media critic Arthur Ungar of the *Christian Science Monitor* was watching television at 4 a.m. on the morning of October 1, 1980, the morning after the United States Supreme Court limited abortion on demand. Ungar wrote in his paper, "Only a few hours later, now, on national television via satellite, I was seeing the rerun of an unexpectedly informative discussion program covering all aspects of the decision and its impact on all levels of our society. It was *Freeman Reports,* a nightly discussion show hosted by a superb reporter named Sandi Freeman."

Ungar's exhilaration knew no limits. He extolled the satellite interviews, and the two-way discussion with guests from opposing sides of the abortion issue. He praised the intelligence of the questions and the responses. He was impressed when the program was broken into for live news bulletins and reports, which kept the coverage up to the minute. He went on to say that "a few hours later, when the local daily morning newspaper was delivered to my door, I found myself a full half-day ahead of the print story. I was able to realize that something extraordinary was going on."

It was a great moment for me as an inventor. Someone, a newsman, a television critic as knowledgeable as Ungar, understood that we were doing something new, that CNN had indeed invented something. Ungar had become a convert.

He thought that CNN was committing a revolution: "Might it be that commercial television programming has been completely off base? Maybe, instead of twenty-four hours of entertainment, interrupted occasionally by news, what television should really be is twenty-four hours of news interrupted occasionally by entertainment. I talked to CNN President Reese Schonfeld, who asked 'What makes you believe the news should be interrupted *at all* by entertainment?'"

On Monday, June 1, for the very first Freeman show, we had tried to arrange an interview with Ted Kennedy. It was the day before the Super Tuesday primary. Carter and Kennedy were still contesting the Democratic nomination, even though Carter seemed a sure winner. We had had Jimmy Carter on the air for a full hour on Sunday. We wanted to give Ted his turn.

Kennedy was still so angry at Sandi for her "Joan Factor" interview that he would not speak with her. Dan Schorr would do the interview. But Kennedy kept changing travel plans. After three changes, he agreed to do the interview on a plane ride from Washington to Cleveland. Dan and two crews flew with him. The flight lasted an hour and thirty minutes, we got somewhat less than an hour of tape. We brought it back to Atlanta, edited it, aired it, and then Sandi and Schorr reviewed Ted Kennedy's last-gasp campaign.

The situation was awkward. Sandi was not comfortable with Schorr. He had gotten the interview, she hadn't. She was not ready to share the spotlight, no matter how it might benefit CNN. I wanted CNN to open with Carter and Kennedy. If Schorr could deliver Kennedy, he had to be on the air. CNN was proving that even with only 1.75 million potential viewers, we could deliver the biggest names in news.

On the show Arthur Ungar had watched, Freeman was doing the job we'd hired her for. She was taking the lead story of the day, expounding on it, bringing in guests, doing what a newspaper does when it prints a backgrounder right next to a hard news lead on the front page. CNN was reporting the news first and reporting about reaction to the news first. We were beating Ted Koppel.

I thought Sandi was a star. Evidently, she didn't believe me. Rather than do the hard news for which she'd been hired, Sandi acted like a groupie. She wanted "big names" on her program, prebooked, uncancellable. If the U.S. had declared war, and Sandi had booked Eddie Fisher, Sandi would have insisted on sticking with the Fisher interview. She was intransigent.

We tried three or four producers to help keep her head on straight: a soft Boston lefty who wanted to book shows about the Trilateral Commission; a tough lady from Washington who is now an executive vice president of CNN and who asked off the show because she couldn't deal with Sandi; Karen Sugrue, now a producer at *Sixty Minutes,* who swears that Sandi gave her lessons on how to deal with network anchors, but that Sandi was worse than any of them; and finally a sweet but intimidated Washingtonian who would do whatever Sandi told her. That's the way Sandi wanted it.

Granted, Sandi had her moments. The best show she ever did ran on December 30, 1980. That day the Court of Appeals ruled that Bob Jones University had lost its tax-exempt status by discriminating between black and white students. For instance, unmarried blacks would not be accepted for admission, but unmarried whites were acceptable. Sandi had booked a forgettable guest, the best she could get on the night before New Year's Eve. I told the producer to cancel the guest and get Bob Jones, Jr., and Julian Bond. Atlanta was Bond's hometown. All we had to do was send a car to pick him up. Jones, outraged by the court's decision, flew down on a private jet from North Carolina.

Entering the studio: Julian Bond, the Supreme Court winner, a black man, gracious in nature, polite by habit, and Bob Jones, Jr., the loser, a white man, outraged in defeat, irascible in habit. All Sandi Freedman had to do was stay out of the way. On this occasion, she showed she could genuinely be a newsperson. She was gracious. Despite her grace, the situation itself was so charged that what began as a polite discussion ended in almost personal attack. We were observing the Ungar dictate of staying a half day ahead of everybody else, broadcast and print.

The Koppel show had been scooped. The next week they booked our same two guests. By that time, Bond and Jones were so angry they would not appear in the same studio: one sat in the ABC bureau in Atlanta; the other was miles away in ABC's Atlanta affiliate. Their remarks were much the same, but now, separated by distance, the face-to-face electricity had vanished. Koppel looked like a timid repeat of the

Freeman Show. It still did not please Sandi. Her goals were different from mine. I wanted the show to make news. She wanted the show to make friends. Emily Post dictates you never cancel a guest.

Sandi had a special touch for interviewing "ordinary people." Once on a slow news day, I found a guest off the op-ed page of the *Washington Post*. A forty-year-old woman had been raped in her own home by a gang of thieves. Her husband had been tied up, heard what was going on, but could do nothing about it. The victim wrote frankly and sensitively about the experience. Without hesitation she agreed to appear without disguise, full-face, on the Freeman show.

The interview might have been sensational tabloid, but Sandi let the guest tell her own story her own way. She was sympathetic. She seemed to feel her pain. I felt her pain. I was sure the audience also felt her pain and her bravery.

Once again, fifty minutes into the show, Sandi had to be Sandi. Her producer had been so concerned that the rape victim might be a dull guest that she had booked a minor TV/movie personality as a backup. Sandi felt compelled to give him the last ten minutes. It was not a smooth transition.

One reason Sandi did well with "ordinary" people was that, by television standards, she was "ordinary" herself. She was from a working class family in St. Louis. I wasn't sure if she had a college degree. She was married to an ABC studio cameraman, who had stayed behind in Chicago, with their kids. The husband was very much a regular guy, and the family was a regular family, but Sandi brought with her a feeling that she was the least educated person in the newsroom. She was terrified of the competition.

Sandi had been lucky to get into television at all. After her marriage, she had worked as a singing waitress at the Chicago Gaslight Club. Gaslight Clubs were a national chain, two steps above Playboy Clubs. At the Playboy Clubs, the waitresses were bunnies. At the Gaslight, they dressed as French maids, but they were respectable.

One day, her husband, who worked at WLS, the Chicago ABC station, noticed an open call for a female "second banana" to work on *Kennedy and Company*, WLS's morning talk show. He talked Sandi into auditioning. She got the job.

On local television, every host fears his sidekick might replace him. He makes sure the sidekick never looks too good. Sometimes Sandi was treated like a dumbbell, with Kennedy using her for decoration and laughs, à la Vanna White. Sandi was better than that. She fought through Kennedy and gradually emerged as a personality of her own.

When Kennedy left the show, Sandi worked with Steve Edwards, who had done *Good Morning, L.A.* They became partners. When Edwards left, he was replaced by Rob Weller (later of *Entertainment Tonight*), and it was Weller who was playing sidekick to Sandi Freeman. I was probably the first guy who'd hired her for her mind, but she never understood that. I thought more of her mind than she did.

Six months before my departure, I had given up on Sandi. As a matter of fact, that was the reason for my departure. Sandi wanted to do a personality talk show. I wanted to do a news talk show. We never could agree, and I fired her. She didn't leave the company for another three years, but that comes later in the story.

Since CNN, Sandi has completed law school, but hasn't worked regularly on television. She could have been a contender.

Round 43: **MGM, Grand for CNN**

During my first CNN talks with Ted in September of '79, as we conversed about Dan Rather, satellites, and the program formats, I explained to him the advantage of doing CNN my way, the live way, rather than the four half-hour wheel Ted had been thinking about. My example was the hotel fire. I told him, someday there's going to be a fire in some big hotel, and there'll be smoke billowing and people trying to get out, and we're going to be there live, showing that fire, all over the world.

On November 21, 1980, the MGM Grand in Vegas went up in flames. I was in Columbus, Ohio, speaking at a Time-Life cable press conference.

Ted called. It was the only time in my two years of running CNN that he had ever called about a story. Ted had a long memory. "Are we going to have the fire?" I laughed to myself, if we didn't have the fire, I'd be fired, but I was confident. I told Ted, "Yes."

I called Burt Reinhardt. "How we doing on the fire?" "We got it," he said. KLAS, the CBS affiliate, was a CNN station. It was the best news station in the Vegas market. They gave CBS the first five minutes of the fire. The rest they gave to us, and we were live and running with it.

Stations all over the world were calling for our coverage, particularly the Japanese. This was 1980, and lots of Japanese were just discovering Las Vegas. In Tokyo, this was almost a local story. It was early morning in Japan, and people were just waking up. NHK, the Japanese national network, was carrying CNN live. Our logo was on NHK air. By 9 a.m., everybody in Japan had had a chance to see it.

In Vegas, helicopters were circling the MGM Grand roof, attempting to rescue guests. KLAS stayed live. We were the only ones sticking with the story. We were live all over the U.S. and around the world. It was the perfect international story. A fire is a fire, no matter what the language. Great pictures are great pictures. Live is live. In every country where CNN was available, we had made our first major impression.

By the second day, Mary Alice Williams and Jim Miklaszewski were in Vegas. Second-day fire stories are never much, just crawling through the ashes. Mik found us an angle. NBC had brought in a San Francisco fire chief. The fire chief was touring the MGM Grand site, along with Vegas fire officials and Mik. There was nobody around from NBC, so Mik interviewed the San Francisco expert.

It had been suggested that Vegas casinos occasionally pumped pure oxygen through their vents in order to keep gamblers awake. Las Vegas fire officials had denied that this was a factor in the fire, but, according to Mik, "The San Francisco fire guy said the fire was so hot and furious, it was such a fire ball that raced through the casino, that he suspected it was fed by an accelerant like oxygen."

We had this story on the air before NBC, even though NBC had flown the fire chief in from San Francisco, put him up in Caesar's Palace, and was paying him a fee. This was CNN's way: Let NBC pay a fortune and we'd beat them on the air with their own story. Mik had become the CNN fireman, the guy I sent to the hot story.

Round 44: **The Great Debate**

In 1960, the broadcast networks had staged the Kennedy/Nixon presidential debates. After that, the FCC introduced "equal time" rules, and for sixteen years there were no more debates because the networks would have had to allow all candidates to participate. In 1976, the networks, and the League of Women Voters contrived a solution. The League, as a private organization, could invite whichever candidates they chose to debate, and the networks would cover the League's debate as an event of general public interest.

To maintain some appearance of impartiality, the League agreed that they would honor the polls and that any candidate with 15 percent of likely voters would be included in the debate. That standard effectively barred fringe candidates like the demi-fascist Lyndon LaRouche or the Socialist, David McReynolds. So in 1976, the debates resumed, and the only participants were the Democratic and Republican candidates, Jimmy Carter and Gerald Ford.

In 1980, there was a third-party candidate, a moderate Republican named John Anderson, who exceeded the 15 percent bar. At one point, the polls showed him with more than 20 percent. Under the League's guideline, John Anderson had to be invited to the party. Neither President Carter nor Ronald Reagan wanted to appear on the platform with Anderson since they weren't sure which side his votes were coming from. They also weren't sure they could outdebate Anderson. Consequently, no debates had been scheduled.

Finally, toward the end of October, Anderson fell below 15 percent. He was no longer entitled. The League of Women Voters, the Democrats, the Republicans, and the three networks agreed to stage a single debate on October 28. Anderson had been excluded, but I had a plan. David Garth, a political acquaintance of mine from New York, was managing Anderson's campaign. I told David that CNN could and would inject Anderson into the Carter/Reagan debate—if Anderson would cooperate.

CNN would find the appropriate venue, invite the appropriate crowd, install the appropriate podium, and, thanks to the wonders of videotape, permit Anderson to reply to all the questions to and statements by the other candidates. If they talked to each other, he would have a chance to comment on their remarks. If they were permitted time for rebuttal, he would have time for rebuttal. Yes, it would be on tape, but we would try to make it look real.

David Garth is a very smart man, and a clever political operative. He knew that CNN was in only 3.5 million homes, so he peddled our idea to other networks. The equal time rule scared them off. However (and I've always wondered if it was at David Garth's suggestion), PBS said that if CNN ran the event, and gave PBS permission to use it, they would rebroadcast it immediately following the other presidential debate. CNN would be responsible for equal time. Garth got what he wanted. The Anderson debate would be seen in CNN's 3.5 million homes and PBS's 75 million homes. Anderson was in business, we were in business.

Preparations for our event had gone well: We leased Washington's Constitution Hall, selected Dan Schorr as the moderator, and arranged to fill the hall with college kids. The Reagan campaign was helping us, because their latest polls showed that Anderson was taking votes from Carter, not Reagan.

Dan Schorr had a friend in the Reagan entourage who sent him a diagram of the layout of the Carter/Reagan debate. He told us that the background curtain would be dark blue and how high the podium would be. He told Dan where the Carter/Reagan moderator would stand; Dan would stand in the same position. We built our set.

The technical requirements were a nightmare. When Roone Arledge invented tape replays at ABC sports, he spent months getting the technique right. We had days. Roone Arledge had a pool of skilled technicians from which to choose. We had a bunch of kids. I knew we couldn't do it internally. Our director of operations chose our best director, our best tape editor, rented a truck from an educational station in Pennsylvania, and tried to teach them what to do. Unfortunately, he didn't know himself.

Our version of the debate would open at the Reagan/Carter site. The network moderator would introduce the Democratic and Republican candidates, who would then make their opening statements. At that point, CNN would cut to Constitution Hall, where Dan Schorr would introduce John Anderson, and Anderson would make his opening statement. Meanwhile, in the truck, CNN technicians were taping the Carter/Reagan debate. When Anderson finished his remarks, we were supposed to roll the second tape from the "real" debate. The tapes weren't ready. Anderson and Schorr had to "fill."

The next tape wasn't ready either. We fell further and further behind. Anderson and Schorr improvised, and improvised, and improvised. To put the best possible face on the event, it was a fiasco. It took us three-quarters of an hour to get it right, and we never caught up. We finished forty-five minutes behind the network program, but at the end we were getting it right. A half hour later, PBS rebroadcast the CNN version of the entire event. Now the whole country would see us fuck up. Nevertheless we survived the debacle.

The next day, the *Washington Post* was uncomplimentary but relatively gentle: "From the start almost everything possible went wrong. The twenty-four telephones that Anderson had installed for the press did not work . . . and the telephone company yanked them out before the event began."

Then it was CNN's fault. "Entire questions were lost, only to reappear in confusing order. . . . Strange noises crackled."

After that Anderson discovered that NBC had screwed up, too. The *Post* reported that Anderson's people had purchased time to run a five-minute commercial on NBC before the debate. The commercial never ran because of "what a [NBC] network spokesman described as 'human error.'"

After the technical glitch–plagued program ended, Anderson's press secretary, Tom Matthews, mused, "This is more than curious. Maybe we have a return of the dirty tricks." I don't know if dirty tricks did in the phone company or NBC, but I do know that dirty tricks did not affect CNN. We screwed up all by ourselves.

All was not lost. The *Post* reporter praised Anderson's performance and concluded, "It seemed somehow almost fitting, considering that the debates featured John B. Anderson, the maverick independent presidential candidate, and was sponsored by Cable News Network, the maverick television system."

Cissy Baker, our Washington assignment editor, was heartbroken. She says it was her worst experience in the twelve years she spent at

CNN. Her journal entry after the debate reads, "went home and got drunk, so ashamed I almost quit."

Cissy had worked in broadcast news, and she expected the highest possible technical standards. She didn't understand that at that point in CNN's life, "The Great Debate," despite its great disgrace, was a greater success. It showed that we would try to do things never done before. Maybe we wouldn't do them well, but we would keep on trying.

One small victory: I had solved the equal time problem. I would claim that the FCC rules apply only to broadcasters, not cable. CNN was a cable service. Then I was spared even that battle. The debate was on a Monday, October 28, 1980. The LaRouche campaign demanded equal time from PBS on Wednesday. On Thursday, PBS informed the LaRouche camp that they had merely rebroadcast a CNN event. On Friday, the LaRouche campaign called CNN and demanded equal time from us. I got back to them on Monday. The election was on Tuesday. LaRouche had no time to go to court. The issue was moot.

Round 45: San Francisco

I never visited the San Francisco bureau. That means it worked perfectly. The squeaking wheel gets the oil, and San Francisco never squeaked.

The bureau was located, like all our other bureaus, in the same building as the Western Union uplink to the satellite. For the first sixty days, the San Francisco assignment editor would put a tape replay machine on a shopping cart, wheel it to the elevators, ride up to the top of the building, plug the machine into the satellite feed, push a button, and CNN Atlanta would get the story.

Ed Turner had hired the original bureau chief, Donna Sykes, from CBS in Atlanta, but the San Francisco bureau was not up to network standards, and Donna didn't stay around long. Luckily, Tami Weine, our assignments editor, was ready to run the shop. Tami had worked for

CBS San Francisco. In San Francisco there was no culture. It was all counterculture, and Tami was familiar with it.

At CNN Tami had to feed a ravenous news machine. She was expected to transmit stories to Atlanta everyday at noon, 4:30, and 5:30 p.m. San Francisco time, which meant San Francisco had to produce three or four stories every day.

Her reporter, Jeff Levine, had been working at the Sacramento ABC affiliate, the weakest station in the market, and he was happy to move on. So happy, in fact, that after getting married on May 31, he took a one-night honeymoon and showed up for work at ten o'clock the next morning. On June 1, he did a piece on kite flying, his contribution to CNN's first day on air.

Levine was a one-man reporting staff. If Tami was going to produce three or four stories a day, Jeff had to report two or three stories a day. Together they invented the ideal CNN system. Jeff would arrange a 9 a.m. interview, shoot it, do a stand-up, and then, in the car on the way to his next story, he would write a script on his portable typewriter and then voice-over the story into his tape machine. When he got to his next story, he would hand the tapes, accompanied by editing instructions, to a courier. The courier took it back to Tami, who would edit and feed to Atlanta at 12:30.

As Levine points out, this kind of schedule is possible only when you are able to produce your story without prior script approval. To operate that way, Atlanta must trust the bureau chief and the bureau chief must trust the reporter. As a fallback, Atlanta can screen the story once it arrives to guard against grievous error. Otherwise, it's shoot it, voice it, cut it, feed it, and air it.

The alternative procedure, the way the networks have always done it, is to have a bunch of editors sitting around a big desk every morning, telling reporters what to cover. The reporter covers the assignment, reads a proposed script to his New York producer, who edits it, maybe rewrites it, and tells the reporter what to read and what to say about his own story. It's probably a terrific system, if you want to get one story every two days from a journalist. To me it makes no sense.

The networks may say it makes for better quality, that it's better journalism, it's more thoughtful, that you will make fewer mistakes. I just don't believe that guys reading copy in a city three thousand miles away know more about a story than the person who covered it. Give me a good bureau chief and a good reporter in every town, and I'll run rings around network "collaborative journalism" anytime. That's what San Francisco did for two years.

San Francisco ran on such a tight schedule it covered a lot of early morning stories that otherwise might not have seen air. Jeff remembers covering the kite-flying clubs and the early morning surfers, but his favorite remains the "Sisters of Perpetual Indulgence."

The "Sisters" were comprised of a half-dozen transvestites in clerical habits, with glitter makeup, white stockings, and high heels. Among them were Sister Fred, who espoused the missionary position, and Sister Sadie, the Rabbi Lady. One morning, the Sisters demonstrated at the Palace of the Legion of Honor, protesting something or other the Jesuits had done at the University of San Francisco Law School. Their performance was lacking in respect. The piece ran three times, including prime time before it was yanked. I wish I'd known about it. If I had, it would still be running.

Levine also covered the Oakland Hell's Angels trial. They had been brought up on RICO conspiracy charges but were acquitted because the judge ruled they were too disorganized to form a conspiracy. Stories like this in prime time introduced the counterculture to a mass audience who had never seen anything like it. It offended some viewers, but it attracted many more. It was one of the things that brought us fans like Frank Zappa. And for CNN, with our two-hour *Prime News 120,* you had to be outrageous from time to time, or two hours would seem very, very long. Tami's counterculture contacts got her unique, exclusive interviews that met our needs.

At the time, there was a group of IRA prisoners in Ulster taking part in the Blanket Protest who refused to wear convicts' clothes because they demanded to be treated as prisoners of war. They had gone for months unwashed, unshaved, unclothed, with only blankets to cover them. One of them had escaped, turned up in San Francisco, and went to the CNN bureau on a Saturday. Tami and the crew worked for nothing just to get the story. No one else had it.

A few days later, the FBI came in. How could they get in touch with the "blanket men"? "Don't you have some numbers?" they asked Tami. "They always call me," said Tami. She was unable to help.

Another time, Steve Tenzakas, a leading Filipino dissident, showed up at the bureau. Again Tami got a long, exclusive interview. Again the FBI showed up. Without identifying themselves, they asked, "Is Steve Tenzakas here?" "Why would he be?" asked Tami. "We saw him on television," said the FBI. "That was two weeks ago," said Tami. The FBI men identified themselves. "Do you know how we can get in touch with him?" they demanded. Once again, Tami was unable to help.

Tami could occasionally be unable to help her bosses. Ted Kavanau once called the bureau and screamed to Tami that someone had contacted Atlanta to say there was an atom bomb planted in San Francisco. "Get a crew there," he yelled. Tami refused. "There are only two choices," she says. "Either there's no bomb, in which case there's no story, or there is a bomb, and we're all dead. In either case there's no pictures."

Tami and Jeff led CNN to the AIDS story before there was an AIDS story. Over the years, people have asked me how we got such a head start on that story. The fact is, I was letting the bureaus decide what stories to cover and, of course, CNN had a lot of time to fill. CNN should still be running that way. It proves to your bureau chiefs that you trust them, and that you don't pretend to know more about their hometown than they do. Then your bureau chiefs get you stories that nobody else has.

The AIDS story started as local news because San Francisco has such a large gay population. The newspapers printed stories about it before anyone else did. Jeff and Tami read the newspapers and also had great contacts with the San Francisco medical community, who didn't yet know the disease was AIDS. They shared their lack of knowledge with Jeff and Tami. They told them the cause of the illness had not yet been identified, its prognosis had not been established, and treatment was years away.

Atlanta was just reading about it. Tami and Jeff saw people dying of it. Tami and Jeff were living amidst a plague.

San Francisco was in a panic. Jeff reported on it. He did story after story about the mysterious disease then regarded as the "gay plague." He reported about the effect of gay-related immune deficiency syndrome, or GRIDS, as it was then called, on the restaurant business. San Franciscans wouldn't go out to eat, they were afraid of the gay waiters. Restaurants were going out of business.

Tami knew people who were getting sick. She saw them going back and forth to the hospitals. She saw them improve and then relapse, improve and then relapse. The hospitals gave her press releases. She covered the hospital press conferences. Jeff interviewed doctors. Still, nobody knew nothing.

Back in Atlanta, the story was a newsman's dream. It sounds heartless to look at a plague as a good story, but all newsmen do it. Maybe that's the reason we become newsmen. We disassociate ourselves from reality and look at everything either as a good story or it ain't no story at all. It does protect one's emotions. I remember that after JFK was killed, I didn't cry for three days—until I had the story under control.

What I knew sitting at my desk in Atlanta in 1981: There was a disease striking mostly gay men, and it had something to do with the failure of the immune system. I knew that if I were writing a tabloid headline, it would be, Mystery Plague Strikes Gay America. I knew if I were writing a *New York Times* headline I would write, "Medical Uncertainty Continues in San Francisco Deaths."

Nobody knew how to handle this story. On one side, there was the possibility of a catastrophic scourge. People were dying, and doctors couldn't tell us why. Some people believed that AIDS would react like other diseases. People would be stricken, they would be pumped full of antibiotics, they would get well, and they would go back to work. All they had to do was stay off the subways so they wouldn't pick up any more germs.

Anyway, I saw "the gay plague" as major news, and I wanted everything about it that San Francisco could deliver. I also asked Jean Carper in Washington to cover the doctors and scientists in the major research centers who were working on GRIDS, to find out who was investigating it, who was working on its cause, and who, if anybody, was looking for a cure. Early on, Jean learned of the rivalry between laboratories in Paris and Bethesda. She understood the politics and the infighting, since scientists around the world wanted to be the first to discover the cause of the plague and win a Nobel prize.

French television visited us. They wanted to use our material. Thanks to the Paris labs, GRIDS had become a big story over there. Still, Tami and Jeff were the only news people who were regularly providing stories about the people who were suffering.

For a while, it seemed that only homosexuals were being affected; then the sickness started spreading into the general San Francisco population. People were getting it from blood transfusions, from shared needles, from heterosexual sex with an infected person. The panic mushroomed.

Ambulance technicians refused to pick up injured gay men. In some areas, the police didn't want to deal with the gay community. It was a classic news dilemma. CNN had to cover the story, not because the public had a "right to know," but because, if the public didn't know, nobody would do anything to prevent it. At the same time, every time we told one of the stories, we fed the panic, and public fears became irrational. To this day, the NBA doesn't permit a basketball player on the floor with an open cut. He's got to go to the bench and have his cut bandaged before he can return to the game. Despite legitimate concerns, we stuck with the story all the way. By 1982, we owned it.

Then began the breakup of the San Francisco bureau. Levine was promoted. He was going to be CNN's Bristol-Myers's medical reporter; in other words, Bristol-Myers had given up on wanting a doctor to do the "Miracles of Modern Medicine" stories. They recognized that a good presenter is more important than an M.D. degree. We picked Jeff. Tami wanted to replace him with an experienced local reporter, a woman. Ted Kavanau favored a hunky guy, Steve Walsh, and persuaded us to hire him. Tami thought Steve was not up to the job and that she should be able to pick her own reporters. She was right on both counts.

Next, Tami found out that she was earning $10,000 a year less than her interim predecessor on the job. She asked Burt Reinhardt for a raise. Burt said, "Pete is a married man with a family." No excuse. Tami was not satisfied.

Finally, Tami called me to say she had the opportunity for exclusive coverage of Abbie Hoffman surrendering to the police. Hoffman, one of the founders of the "yippie" movement, had been on the run for seven years after trying to sell cocaine to an undercover cop. One of our free-lance technicians was an unindicted co-conspirator in the Chicago Seven trial at which Hoffman had been an indicted conspirator, and they'd remained friendly. The technician could get us the pictures. We would have to pay "transportation money" to get the crew and Tami to Hoffman's hideout.

I thought transportation money was a euphemism; I thought some of the money was going to Abbie Hoffman. I said no. Tami swears the money was really just transportation money, and she still holds it against me. She thought the interview might have made her career. It was a scoop for Barbara Walters when she got him on the air, and that was after we had passed. Tami admits the technician told her that Walters had paid Hoffman a lot of money to do the interview. I don't know, Barbara Walters still maintains she's never paid anybody for an interview.

By 1982, Tami was tired—not of the work, but of the environment. She didn't want to be underpaid any more than the other bureau chiefs were being underpaid. Now I never see a special "San Francisco story" on CNN. San Francisco is a great news town. Tami Weine is a great news producer.

Round 46: **Reagan Wins, CNN Loses**

From ancient broadcast days, the classic competition between network news departments occurs every four years at political conventions and on Election Day. Conventional wisdom suggested that whoever "won" those events will dominate the nightly news for the next four years. It was the networks' time to strut their stuff.

After 1972, the conventions were a meaningless ritual: WNEW New York would get 20 rating points by running *Casablanca* on convention nights. Elections were not quite that bad. Despite heavy polling and heavy exit polling, there were still elements of possible suspense in some elections. Nixon-Kennedy was very close, so was Nixon-Humphrey. In both cases, the polls predicted the winner.

In October of 1980, the Carter-Reagan polls were close. Carter had a tiny edge in the Republican polls, but the election hinged on the hostage release. Looking back, if CNN wanted to cover the 1980 campaign, it should've had crews in Tehran, in Washington, and wherever else the secret negotiations were going on. The last place we needed them was on the campaign trail.

At the last minute the Carter campaign made another desperate attempt to bring the hostages out. It was leaked that the hostages would be released just before Election Day. I sent Dan Schorr and Jane Maxwell to Wiesbaden, Germany. We were told the hostages would land there. Once again, Jimmy Carter was suckered. The ayatollah turned down his last-ditch offer. No hostages were released. Jane and Dan came home.

Carter's last misfortune was coincidental. November 3 marked the one-year anniversary of the hostage taking. On November 2, the president went on television to deliver a gloomy report about the state of negotiations. Next day, the newspapers and television ran one-year retrospectives on the hostages. It was rubbing salt in an open wound.

By the evening of November 3, it was all over. Polls showed the president losing votes at a rate of half a percent per hour. By the end of the day, he'd lost six points. On Tuesday, it was Reagan by a landslide. CNN should've declared him the winner and forgotten about Election Night.

We were not ready for network-style Election Night coverage, but the polls had given us an easy out. I didn't take advantage of it. On Monday night, CNN should've said, "Reagan is the winner, Senate and House races are still in doubt; we'll keep our eye on them for you, but for local results, best watch your local station."

We had one more chance. On Election Day afternoon, the exit polls confirmed the previous numbers. Reagan was way ahead. Right then, CNN should have gone on the air, declared him the winner, and quietly exited the Election Day coverage race. We didn't, and we lived to regret it.

No one likes to kill Election Day suspense. Everybody remembers 1948, and the *Chicago Tribune* headline, "Dewey Wins." Next day, Harry Truman beat him, and the *Tribune* has yet to live the headline down. I was afraid that might happen to CNN. So CNN reported indications, trends, but we never said that Reagan was the winner. If we had, I could've played Election Night as the formality it was and avoided head-to-head confrontation with the broadcast networks. If we had made the definitive "call" early, their coverage would have seemed overblown. We would have come off ballsy.

Instead, I allowed us to get sucked into the gigantic ego battle among the networks over who was going to get the most results the fastest. We didn't have a prayer. Originally, we had planned there would be no special Election Day coverage at all. The regular news anchors on their regular news shift would tell the election story along with the rest of the news. The early presidential results would have made that plan pretty good. The critics might knock us, but some part of the audience would have been happy to find something on their television sets that didn't sound like, "With one-hundred forty-seven precincts remaining to be heard from, Smith is beating Jones by a thirty-seven-thousand vote margin. . . ."

We would have been following our basic strategy, counterprogramming. It would have been our news coverage against their election coverage. We would have followed the basic CNN tenet, "Don't try to beat the other guy at his own game."

Ambition had overridden reason. We were reckless. The Washington bureau and the New York bureau thought we could report the election in depth, much as the networks did. We set up a special election desk in addition to the main news desk. The news desk would handle news stories, the election desk would handle results. You can't be a little bit pregnant.

We'd been on the air only five months, only a half-dozen of our people had ever covered a national election, and we were unable to spend the kind of money the networks spent. The networks had formed a collective that gathered results from around the country. It delivered the numbers fast and accurately. It was very expensive. CNN could not afford it.

UPI offered a competitive service; much less expensive, but it was first time out of the box. We bought it; it failed. We lagged far behind the networks nationally and state by state. They would declare winners, we didn't even have starting times. The two-desk system didn't work either. It was sloppy.

The only good thing was that there were very few witnesses. We had gone head-to-head against tradition. We lost, but nobody was looking. On Inauguration Day, I would damn well do things differently.

Round 47: **Reagan Wins, CNN Wins**

Inauguration Day, January 20, dawned cold and cloudy. By noon, the sun broke through and the temperature reached fifty-six degrees. It was one of the warmest Inauguration Days on record. For CNN, it was easy. The pool was doing the work. All we had to do was add Bernie Shaw's voice to the pool feed. In the newsroom, we hung over the wires. When would the ayatollah free the hostages? Dennis Troute and the Rome crew were in Wiesbaden awaiting their arrival. So was Dan Schorr. Two huge medical transport planes stood on the ground. We booked a twenty-four-hour satellite channel, Wiesbaden to Atlanta, and we waited.

The inauguration begins. Ronald Reagan has one hand on the Bible, the other raised. Chief Justice Warren Burger is about to swear him in. UPI is carrying an "unconfirmed" report that the hostages have been released. I call for a split screen: half inauguration, half the plane standing by in Wiesbaden.

Ronald Reagan brings his hand down. He is now president of the United States. Still no confirmation from UPI. I take my chances. I order a red, white, and blue banner across the bottom of the screen. The white crawl reads: "Hostages released. Hostages released." Maybe it reads, "American hostages released," I don't remember. I do remember the banner, red border over blue, blue border over red, whatever, and the white words crawling across the screen, and the banner flashing on and off, on and off. Inauguration bands are blaring in the background, it's wonderful television, and I'm betting everything on an unconfirmed UPI report.

I had learned my lesson on Election Day. This time I would be bold. Take my chances, bet on my gut, be right, or resign. Every time I make a call like this, I put the credibility of CNN on the line. If I'm wrong, I fall on my sword. I was not wrong. The hostages were on their way.

Derwin Johnson remembers the stillness in the newsroom in Atlanta. "There were yellow ribbons tied around the poles, and the ribbons were sort of swaying, and everybody was quiet."

In Germany, Dan Schorr is on the ground next to the airplanes. We bring him in live: "What is happening in Wiesbaden, Dan?" Nothing much, but Dan can talk about nothing for two minutes and make it sound good. We are advancing the story. We are looking good. So good that ABC, which does not have a satellite from Wiesbaden, calls Jim Rutledge on the CNN desk.

Stan Optowsky, the ABC news manager, is on the line. I am in the newsroom. Rutledge shouts to me, "Optowsky wants to share our satellite. What do I tell him?" "Tell him to go fuck himself," says I. Rutledge does not translate. "Reese says, go fuck yourself," Jim tells him. I have learned another lesson. No more colorful suggestions to Jim Rutledge.

On the air, CNN looks better and better, but on the ground in Wiesbaden, we are outmanned. Dennis Troute calls Jeanee Von Essen, the foreign editor. "CBS has a hundred and twenty-five people here," he says. "We have three. What do you want from us?" "We want everything they get," says Jeanee. Troute is also having trouble with Dan Schorr. Every time a feed comes up, Schorr reaches for the microphone. Sometimes it's Troute's turn. Schorr reaches for the mike anyway. Occasionally, the camera comes up on the wrestling match.

The hostages are not flying directly to Wiesbaden. It's Tehran to Algiers, change planes, then Algiers to Wiesbaden. CNN was prepared. We had sent Dean Vallas to Algiers. We get the hostages changing planes. Early the next morning, midnight U.S. time, we pick them up in Wiesbaden. Dan Schorr reports from the military hospital on their medical condition. He and Troute provide hourly updates. The hostages spend four days in Wiesbaden. Our twenty-four-hour satellite link pays off time and again.

On Sunday, the hostages leave for the U.S. They will make one stop at Shannon Airport, outside Dublin. Jeanee has spoken to Irish Television. The 6 p.m. Irish news will lead with hostages at the airport. We will take Irish Television live and lead our 1 p.m. show with the story. As it gets close to one o'clock, Irish Television pops up on the control room monitor. They are showing the program lead-in.

At CNN, there is a conflict. The producer does not take the Irish TV feed. He wants to come in "clean," when the hostage story begins. CNN's style is show the viewer what you're doing. Do not hide the seams. Jeanee Von Essen understands the style. She tells the producer to take the story. He will not do it. She tells me. I yell to Jeanee, loud enough for the producer to hear, "Tell the fucking asshole take the feed, now!"

I want the CNN anchor to say, "We are now watching Irish Television. In just a few moments, we will be bringing you pictures of our hostages as they walk through Ireland. We're taking these pictures live from RTE. This is their air. The news is coming up." Let the audience wait with us for the news film. The producer has heard my yell, he takes Irish TV. It is on the opening commercial. The CNN anchor says, "Now to Irish Television."

Some of my yell had leaked onto the tape. No viewer ever complained about it. Neither did the FCC nor the press. But the videotape heard it faintly. The ever-troublesome Jim Kitchell grabbed the tape. He dubbed and redubbed it, boosting its sound. Then he delivered it to Ted Turner. Ted kept it in his drawer, just for the record. I loved the moment. So did Jeanee. It was one more small victory on a day of triumph. But Ted kept the tape for another reason. He regarded it as evidence of "volatility."

From Shannon, the hostages flew to West Point. While they were in the air their families went to the White House to meet President Reagan. We get the families going in, the families coming out, but miss the families talking with the president. The pool gives us that shot. We were still perfect.

At West Point, we had more than usual network interference. AT&T reported that the networks had booked all six lines from West Point to New York City. We would have no way to get our signal out. I called the satellite truck in Atlanta and told them to start driving. They could make it in time, but we needed FCC permission to transmit. It was Saturday, and the FCC was shut. I reached Bill Henry, CNN's lawyer, the former FCC chairman. He found an FCC commissioner at a Saturday night party. With the sound of ice tinkling in glasses and cocktail party chatter behind him, the commissioner told Henry, "You've got your license." The truck was in business.

By Sunday afternoon, we had staked out a prime position. Our camera would have a better view than the network cameras. There was also a pool; we would have those pictures too. Once our truck got there, the networks discovered that they did not need all six lines. They dropped two of them. AT&T offered them to us. We didn't need them either. The satellite truck had enabled us to position our cameras in the best locations. We had the best pictures.

Mary Alice Williams was the West Point presenter. She did it all with spit and mirrors. We had sent fifteen people up to the Point, the networks had sent three hundred. Mary Alice did a live report every half hour. CNN did two packages every day and covered the entire parade from start to finish. Since we had no switchers, two CNN technicians plugged and unplugged wires by hand as the parade went by. Bob Lily says, "Our fifteen kicked the network's butts, all three hundred of them."

Tuesday was the payoff. The hostages were to visit President Reagan, and he would speak to them. Again it was no problem, the pool was doing our work. It had been a week full of hostages, a week full of triumph.

From first moment to last, CNN had every picture, pictures the networks didn't have, better angles on pictures they did have, better interviews than they delivered; it was the first time that CNN, with its meager army, had beaten the networks on a major running story.

Round 48: **Katie Couric**

In the midst of the hostages' return, our camera crew had missed the hostage families with President Reagan. Katie Couric was the field producer, and I called to bawl her out. In my best Lou Grant imitation, I growled, "Katie, you got foreplay, you got post-coitus, you missed the climax!" Katie said, not missing a beat, "You mean all I got was a quick feel, wet sheets, and a cigarette?" I knew that Katie was destined for greatness, but I thought she'd find it as the president of a network, not as on-air talent.

Katie recalls that I once told the Washington 6 a.m. producer, "Never put her on the air again." I don't remember it quite that way: One morning at the very beginning of CNN the morning anchor didn't show up. The only two people in the bureau for the six o'clock national cut-in were the producer and Katie, the writer/associate producer. When I woke up in Atlanta and turned on CNN, I saw an ashen Katie Couric, looking all of fourteen, trembling through five or six minutes of national news. From my bed, I called Washington. "Who put her on the air?" I asked. "I did," said the producer. "Never put anyone on the network without asking me or the producer in Atlanta." I wasn't picking on Katie. I was telling the producer who it was who controlled CNN's air. Of course, if anyone had asked me after Katie's audition if she would become anchor of the *Today Show,* I would've said, "Not in my lifetime."

Katie fooled me and a lot of other people because she was eager to learn from anybody who did good work. When she noticed the work that Jean Carper did, she volunteered to work with her, even while she was working for the news desk. She researched for Jean, she wrote for Jean, and Jean began to use Katie as her producer. She told me that Katie was a very good writer.

One afternoon Katie showed up in Carper's office, shattered. Stuart Loory, the bureau chief, had just fired her. Loory was a superior newsman, but clearly no judge of television talent. Carper called me, told me the story; I spoke to Katie, and offered her the assistant producer's job on *Take Two,* the Don Farmer/Chris Curle noon program. Guy Pepper was the director/executive producer. It meant moving to Atlanta, but Katie said yes immediately.

When Katie got down to Atlanta, she won the hearts and the support of Farmer, Curle, and Pepper. She knew how to read a wire, she knew what a story was. She charmed guests, she was eternally helpful, and, as Carper said, she was a very good television writer. But, when *Take Two* went on a Texas tour with Houston as its first stop, there was Katie on the screen once again.

This time she did a package on Gilley's, a nightclub made famous by John Travolta's *Urban Cowboy,* which featured a mechanical bucking bull. *Take Two* devoted six or seven minutes to Katie's report. The idea was good, the visuals were great, but Katie was still unready. She looked more frightened of the camera than the bull.

Katie and Guy Pepper had fallen in love on *Take Two,* and when I saw Katie on the air, I suspected the worst. I was doing my best to make sure that CNN did not become a "girlfriend's network." Since I had kept Ted Turner's girlfriends off the air, I couldn't put Guy Pepper's on. So I sent a note to Pepper, Farmer, Curle, "No more Katie till further notice." It's bad enough to have been dumb once . . . .

Despite my aversion to the casting couch, I was not averse to girl-friends if they showed promise, but seemed to need on-camera confidence. But I only put them on the air at four in the morning. For a few weeks I used one of Ted's friends on the air at that hour and gave Katie a few weeks on the show as well. Both Katie and Ted's friend were scared of the camera. You saw it in their eyes when the light came on. Ted's girl-friend never overcame her fright; Katie did.

Katie spent eleven years working her way to confidence before she got on the *Today Show*. She spent four at CNN working her way up to field producer, and she practiced and practiced and kept asking for an on air try-out. By then I had left CNN, and Ed Turner was screening talent. When Ed seemed more interested in the size of her bosom than her on-air ability, Katie decided to look elsewhere. She sent her tapes to local stations and in 1984 WTVJ Miami grabbed her. She left Atlanta reluctantly. She loved CNN, and she loved Guy Pepper. When she left, there were tears and promises of phone calls and letters, but absence makes the heart go wander, and Katie and Guy found other people to love.

WTVJ was the strongest news station in Miami, Katie's work was noticed, and she moved on. In 1987, WRC, the NBC-owned and -operated station in Washington brought her in as a local reporter and fill-in anchor. Unlike Ed Turner and me, NBC knew what they had. She moved to the network as a correspondent in '89. By then she looked as though she had been born to the camera. The *Today Show* noticed and paired her with Bryant Gumble. When Gumble left, Katie became the star and now gracefully shares the spotlight with Matt Lauer.

Couric is an inspiration to anyone who has ever suffered from stage fright. Someone always says "just be yourself." It's not helpful. Being yourself is what you're scared of.

When Katie first went on our air, she suffered that agony. It took her years to overcome it. She stuck with it, she practiced, and now she's the most "natural" personality on television. When you see Katie on the *Today Show*, what you see is what you get.

What I got out of all this was a chance to go on *Oprah Winfrey*. Katie had made the story of my rejection of her first time on air part of her standard biography. When Oprah did her Katie interview, her staff called and arranged to tape me confessing my error and apologizing to Katie. I obliged happily. When you're involved in the young career of a superstar, it's better to be remembered for making a mistake than not remembered at all.

Despite her stardom, I think Katie's wasted on the *Today Show.* She's too smart to be an anchor; she could be president of CNN by now.

Round 49: **Strawberry Fields**

Two months before Ronald Reagan's inauguration, Mary Alice suffered through her first live-from-the-truck CNN story. It was baptism under fire. On December 8, 1980, John Lennon was shot outside his home across the street from Central Park. These days, there'd be a media frenzy. In 1980 we were the only ones with a live truck on site. The truck had been delivered just days before, and this was our first chance to use it on a major event.

When the story broke, Bob Lily ran down to the bureau. He'd been drinking. He ran into Mary Alice. She'd been drinking, too. Lily stayed in the bureau. He was to edit and feed. Mary Alice grabbed the live truck. They fought the traffic all the way up from Wall Street to what is now Strawberry Fields in Central Park. Mary Alice climbed onto the roof for her live shot. She was surrounded by a mob who mourned Lennon by crowding around Mary Alice and shaking the truck. She had written her piece, but she couldn't deliver it.

Mary Alice climbed down from the truck. She crouched on the ground and spoke to the crowd, telling them that if they jiggle the van, the story can't be transmitted, that this is the very first live transmission ever by CNN New York, that she has to hit a satellite 250,000 miles out at thirty-two degrees. "If I don't hit the satellite," she announces, "we can't send this story to the world. I need your help to commemorate the death of John Lennon." Mary Alice says the crowd miraculously parted.

By now, it was close to midnight. For the East Coast, the story was over. Once again, we had time working in our favor. In California, it was nine o'clock, prime time. Mary Alice stayed on the truck and continued her reports. Bob Lily stayed in the bureau cutting packages. On the West Coast, people watched tomorrow's news tonight. In Europe, it was 6 a.m. the next morning. Eurovision was calling us. They wanted our story. Mary Alice Williams, a cameraman, a driver, and two editors, in a tiny room in the fishbowl studio, sent "Strawberry Fields" out to the world.

It was six months and eight days since CNN went on the air. We were in the process of inventing live television, and the opportunities seemed infinite.

Round 50: **We Never Killed Jim Brady**

On Monday, March 30, 1981, Cissy Baker was sitting at the assignment desk in Washington. According to her journal, "it was a rainy spring day, not much news. Suddenly I heard on the radio scanner, 'Reagan shot.' . . . Early reports said the President was fine . . . Suddenly we heard on the scanner that Nancy Reagan was arriving at George Washington Hospital. Shortly after that, it was confirmed that Reagan had been hit. He had been shot in the left side of his chest, the bullet penetrating his left lung."

It is a tenet of television that certain news events so override the ordinary that network performance on those events will determine the viewing habits of the audience for decades. In 1963, when John Kennedy was assassinated, ABC, just starting out as a national news source, totally screwed up the story. It took them ten years and Harry Reasoner to recover.

The shooting of Ronald Reagan was such an event. Everyone in America was watching television. Most viewers would be looking at the networks, some would be watching CNN, and some would surf. We had to look as good as the other guys. We had to capture the surfers. If we looked bad, we'd lose viewers forever. We ended up looking good, but it wasn't easy.

Our White House crew had been inside the Hilton hotel covering Reagan's speech to the AFL-CIO. The president was hit as he left the hotel along with a D.C. policeman, a secret serviceman, and his press secretary, Jim Brady. We had no crew outside. There was "pool coverage," but we didn't get it. ABC did not deliver it to us. The networks went on the air with their coverage. I said, "Take it, tape it, and run it." We did.

Bob Lily in the New York bureau calls it one of his "fondest memories." "The networks tried to bar us and CNN just grabbed the material off their air, threw it on our air, and said, 'Okay, go ahead, sue us.'"

After the shooting, the president was shoved into his bullet-proof limo, and driven away. No one at CNN or any other news company knew that Reagan had been hit and was going to the hospital. For the next ten minutes or so, the story was outside the hotel. What would happen to the other victims? We, like all the other networks, kept running tape of the shooting again, again, and again. Bernie Shaw was on the anchor desk. He was holding the bureau together, producing and anchoring at the same time. He called for the information that he needed, that the audience wanted to know. You could see the people in the background, scurrying to find what Bernie was calling for.

CNN reporter Scott Barrett arrived at the hospital with the rest of the White House press corps. They were there to cover Jim Brady, but as Scott walked in, he heard doctors say the president had been shot. For years the networks have argued over which one was first to report that the president had been shot, rather than just shot at. The first to report it on the air was Scott Barrett.

Bernie Shaw took Barrett's call from the hospital live on the air. "Bernie," Scott said, "the president has been shot. He is wounded." "Are you sure?" said Bernie. "Well," Scott said, "maybe I better check it out before I put it on the air." *"You've just put it on the air,"* Bernie said. "Check now."

Bernie sat there for thirty or forty seconds, whatever it took, waiting to hear back from Scott. "We are waiting to hear back from Scott Barrett as to whether or not the president has been wounded." Who could have turned it off? You had to keep watching to find out: Was Reagan shot or not?

I thought it was one of CNN's great moments. I still think it was Bernie's best moment. He proved in front of a live audience that he was going to double check everything before he reported it.

CNN did fine at the hospital. According to Cissy Baker, "CNN got the picture of him walking into the emergency room. . . . The president was in surgery for two hours. Afterwards, his condition was stable and good. Jim Brady is another story. On and off all day, there were conflicting reports that he was dead. . . . Brady was shot through the head. He was in surgery seven hours. I doubted he would make it."

There was so much doubt about Brady's condition that the other three networks reported that he had died. CNN had the same information; in fact we had it first. The story of Brady's death had come by way of Senate Majority leader Howard Baker, Cissy's father. Baker had called Cissy, and then the three networks, to say he'd been told Jim Brady had died. Cissy passed the information to Sandy Kenyon, who was sitting at Bernie's feet under the camera, typing feverishly and passing information to Bernie. When word reached him that Brady had died, Bernie refused to kill the man without corroborating evidence.

Citing a "top-level congressional source," Bernie repeated the story, but added, "We are not sure, we have no official confirmation." Meanwhile, the other networks continued to pronounce Brady dead. Kenyon kept handing Shaw pieces of paper with messages like, "Jim Brady is dead, say ABC, NBC, CBS and CNN sources." Bernie won't read them.

Dan Rather had taken to the air on CBS and asked his audience to observe a moment of silence in honor of the departed press secretary. Still Bernie wouldn't get on the band wagon. He wasn't going to say Jim Brady was dead without confirmation. Kenyon remembers people coming up to him in the newsroom and saying, "What is wrong with our guy? What's the matter with him?" And Bernie continues to caveat everything he says. "This is only one report, it is a confusing time, the man in fact may be alive—"

Other information starts trickling in. Kenyon claims it was "like a huge train that has been going forward, and then starts to back up. I've been sending Bernie increasingly desperate notes, and then the train just backs up and backs up and backs up. Now, Frank Reynolds is on ABC, pounding his desk, boom, boom, boom, and saying, 'Let's get this right!' And everybody has to say the man isn't dead, he's still alive. Everybody except Bernie." Bernie had it right all the time.

After twenty-one hours straight, Shaw and Kenyon went out for a drink. Kenyon felt he had witnessed something incredible; he had seen a newsman in his absolute prime and in absolute control. Walking down to the bar in the dark, Kenyon asked Bernie, "Why wouldn't you declare Jim Brady dead?" And Bernie answered, "Howard Baker wasn't at the hospital. He was a secondary source of a high order, but he wasn't in the room."

Earlier in the afternoon, I had put Dan Schorr on the anchor desk with Bernie. I thought it was a terrific idea; Bernie was the news guy, Dan was the analyst. Once Dan starts talking, you can't say, "cut." He won't shut up. After a half hour or so, I pulled him off the air and sent him to the White House to talk with Alexander Haig. This was the day on which Secretary of State Haig declared himself president of the United States. What with Reagan being in the hospital, and Vice President Bush being out of town, he thought he had a fair claim on the title.

Atlanta called the bureaus asking for man-in-the-street reactions to the Reagan shooting. New York sent out the live truck. Bob Lily says, "We had our truck on lower Fifth Avenue, with Joann Lee as the reporter. Joann walks up to someone in the street and says, 'President Reagan has been shot, what's your reaction?' And the woman's reaction is, 'Well, I think whoever shot President Reagan struck a blow for poor people around the country.' In New York, the phones started ringing. 'No more live shots!' they're screaming from Atlanta. 'Move the truck away!'"

It turned out that the man who struck the "blow for poor people" was John Hinckley, a twenty-five-year-old from an affluent family, who had wanted the actress Jodie Foster to notice him.

Ted Turner never recognized CNN's success on the story. Two years later, in a *Playboy* interview, he was asked why CNN had not been first on the air with the Reagan shooting. We had been, but he didn't know that. His answer was an excuse. He said CNN was "young and lean." Now, if Ted is asked about the rotten ratings, I guess he can say that CNN is old and fat.

Round 51: **Everybody into the Pool**

I'd been fighting network pools since 1963. The networks made up their own rules as they went along, and I was forced to battle over every issue. At CNN, I thought it might be easier. We were prepared to bear the burdens of a full pool member. That meant we would cover the White House, for the pool, one month out of four. NBC, CBS, and ABC would also cover one month out of four. We would have a regular spot in the pool rotation.

The network unions threatened to strike if we became a pool member. They told the networks that they would not handle tape that CNN shot, since CNN was a nonunion company, ergo the tape was nonunion tape. The networks themselves didn't want CNN in the pool, and they were certainly not prepared to fight their unions for us.

I tried reason. I met with the network news divisions, attempting to work something out. Ralph Goldberg was, at that time, the chief lawyer for CBS News. He still remembers the meetings. "Inside CBS everybody thought Reese was a pain in the ass." They were the giants, and they did things their own way, the expensive way.

CNN had designed a better, more efficient system. We didn't want to pay a quarter of their inflated pool costs. We wanted to pay our share of the pool in kind, while they were insisting we pay in dollars. They thought we were just trying to get pool material on the cheap. We knew that we could do better than they could, at half the price.

At ITNA I had been spending about 1 percent of their budgets and matching their coverage on the stories that mattered. In defense of their old methods, they had to believe, or at least claim, that I was cheating. To be fair, many of their reporters were better than ours, many of their stories were better written than ours, all of their 7 p.m. news shows were more elegant than ours, but we got the same stories they did, and we had an audience. The networks were livid. Inside their newsrooms, they regarded CNN as a tacky purveyor of tacky news. They also regarded CNN as a threat to their lavish lifestyle.

In ITNA days, Gordon Manning, the operating boss of CBS News, was particularly outraged by our pool demands. He wanted nothing to do with ITNA or me. As our ITNA meetings grew more frequent and the situation more serious, Goldberg needed Manning. He wanted newsmen in the room when he was negotiating. Goldberg remembers that he would go to each meeting surrounded by a couple of other lawyers and a couple of news executives. ABC and NBC would likewise. He says, "Reese would come into the meeting all alone and there would be fifteen guys from the networks sitting around the table."

Under those circumstances, I always came into the room with a winning hand. I was certain of the facts. I knew that if I made any mistakes, my credibility with the network lawyers would end. Every time I complained of a network violation of a pool agreement, the lawyers would turn to the newsmen. "Did you do that?" the lawyers asked. "I don't know, I'll get back to you," the news execs would say. I'd never hear from them again, which meant they couldn't deny it, and the lawyers would call to give me access to whatever it was I was complaining about.

Lawyers are constantly ambushed by their clients. There is an old German saying, "Beat your child everyday; if you don't know what for, he does." Lawyers should treat their clients the same way.

Manning had continued to resist meetings. According to Goldberg, when my name came up, he would go on a tirade. Schonfeld is a this, Schonfeld is a that; he's done this, he's done that; this guy says this about him, this guy says that. Goldberg finally told Manning, "Look. Come to the meeting. This is your big chance. Now you can tell him off personally." Ralph says that at the meeting Manning "never said a word." ITNA got its pool deal. We would pay a hundred dollars for ninety seconds of pool stories, and we would all stop bothering each other.

CNN was different. I didn't want to pay money, I wanted to provide tape. I wanted our camera crews to take our turn in the pool rotation. This the networks could not allow. Our meetings were fruitless, the nets would not allow CNN in the pool. Finally, I took it to the White House. When it comes to pools, the White House makes the rules.

Ronald Reagan was president. As a Republican, he supported "right-to-work" and the "open shop." He should have been on our side. (Reagan had been president of the Screen Actors Guild, and SAG was a closed-shop union. His position on unions was somewhat hypocritical: "Unions are good for me, but nobody else needs them.")

In any event, Reagan refused to take on the networks and the unions. We were arguing principle, he was playing politics. We had asked, begged, petitioned, and still the White House refused to take action. Reagan's decision disturbed many of his most ardent supporters. Various right-to-work groups offered to support CNN if we chose to take action. We said, thanks anyway. If we were going to take action, we had to do it on our own.

When President Reagan was shot, we were barred from the pool; the pool had footage, but they didn't give it to us. We took ABC's footage off the air and ran it. "You stole our material," screamed ABC. "You didn't deliver the pool material," said CNN. The issue had been forced. CNN sued ABC, CBS, NBC, and the president of the United States, demanding admission to the pool as a full-fledged member.

Ted had been attacking the networks left, right, and center for ten years. By suing the networks, I was giving him the chance to put his money where his mouth was. The sheer outrageousness of suing the three networks and the president was right up Ted's alley. He went along.

When we filed the suit, the networks went nuts. Neither was the White House pleased, although I did detect some grudging admiration from their side. They did not like the networks, and they were pleased to see that we were embarrassing them. The networks, the proclaimers of First Amendment rights and Free Access, were now refusing to give CNN access to the White House. We were too immature, our cameramen weren't good enough, and they and couldn't rely on us, they said.

We had solid business reasons to bring the lawsuit. Our crews cost us about $60,000 a year. Networks crews cost more than $150,000, and the networks always padded the bill. At pool events when the network people ate together, the saying was, "The pool is picking up the check." If we paid for our pool participation in dollars, rather than in kind, we would be forced to absorb part of a network salary structure and network expenses that could have put us out of business.

It seemed to me that we were certain to win the case. We would either be admitted to the pool or, as a backup, the networks who barred us from participating would have to give us the pool material for nothing. I estimated that if they permitted us into the pool, we would've saved $2 million a year, and if they had been forced to give us pool material for nothing, we would have saved $4 million.

Our suit bore fruit immediately. The network lawyers took charge. We had accused them of breaking antitrust laws. We said that they had combined with each other in an attempt to put CNN out of business. We said that they shared stories with each other and that they didn't offer them to CNN. The network lawyers instructed their newsrooms: "Don't do this anymore, if you've ever done it." That's lawyer's language for "stop doing it you dumb bastards, you could cost us our licenses." The instructions helped. Thanks to them, ABC bailed us out when Anwar Sadat was assassinated.

Dean Vallas, our one-man bureau in Cairo, was in transition since NBC had hired him to work in Beirut, and he was merely serving out his time. He didn't think Sadat's appearance at a military parade was worth covering. CBS did. They got a great story, and they got it out first. ABC got a good story and got it out second. CNN stood naked in the storm. As it turned out, so did NBC.

ABC must have owed NBC something; they gave their Sadat tape to NBC. I got an unprecedented phone call from Roone Arledge's office. In a grudging tone, I was informed that ABC's Sadat material was now available to us. If they shared it with NBC, they had to give it to us too. It was lawyer dictate. We may have been naked going into prime time, but by 6 p.m. we were fully clothed.

The lawsuit became serious. They took my deposition. The White House lawyers went first, then ABC, then NBC. Our counsel, Jack Dalton, a wise man and a remarkable litigator, warned me that the networks had just been warming up. The next weekend, CBS was due, and their lead counsel was the much feared (but not yet famous) David Boies. Dalton explained the network strategy. Boies would have a week to study my answers to the other lawyers and then he would probe for weakness or contradiction.

Dalton told me what all lawyers tell their clients: "Keep your answers short. Don't volunteer information. Look him in the eye. If he sits waiting after your answer, just wait him out. Remember, you will never be up against a tougher lawyer than David Boies." (In 1999, Boies took on Bill Gates and the whole Microsoft legal team. He proved Dalton right.)

So, on a bright Saturday morning, under hard florescent light, I faced the enemy. Boies asked questions, many the same as the other networks', but better framed. It was harder to give him short answers, but I did. Following some answers, Boise would sit there with the back of his hand flat on the table, curling his fingers back and forth, encouraging me to say more. I kept my mouth shut.

When it ended, I told Jack that I thought I had done pretty good. Jack laughed, and said, "Boies was just getting a look at you. He wants to know what kind of a witness you'll be at the trial." He also told me that the curling finger motion was a good sneaky lawyer trick. If he had verbally suggested that I go on, his words would appear in the transcript. If his finger curls had extracted additional words, it would seem as if I was volunteering additional information.

In the meantime, Ted was orchestrating his own seduction. Bob Wussler, who served as executive vice president of TBS, had been a long time CBS employee, and at one time was its president. He still had many friends there, and he arranged a meeting for Ted with Tom Wyman, then Bill Paley's number two.

Wyman and Ted hit it off. At the meeting, as the story was told to me, Wyman threw his arm around Ted's shoulders and said, "What can we do about this lawsuit? Schonfeld's driving us crazy and we're both spending a fortune. Can't we settle this thing?" Turner came back to Atlanta and ordered me to settle the case. At the settlement meeting, I was accompanied by Bob Wussler, whom Ted had appointed my keeper to make sure that I settled peacefully.

As an old poker player, I knew we held the cards, and that the networks were four-flushing. We had the networks beat, but Wyman had suckered Ted. Now, I was following Ted's orders. We made a deal: We would be permitted into the pool, but only on pools outside of the country, where union rules are not in effect. In the U.S., we were still banned. We'd get a cut rate, but we had formally accepted something less than equal. Ted had been conned; I had to pay the price. To this day my gorge rises. The son-of-a-bitch had sold me out.

Karen Sugrue was one of those who had to bear the burden of our capitulation. She had been the executive producer at CNN New York, the right arm of Mary Alice Williams. She was with Mary Alice when the union goons attempted extortion. She was a stand-up lady. When she became deputy bureau chief in Washington, she stood up for better journalism. She also worked as Washington pool producer.

Her first pool assignment was accompanying President Reagan to the Berlin Wall on Air Force One. As she walked down the aisle, she was greeted with snickers of "Chicken Noodle News." No one, neither the other networks nor the White House, gave her pool material or notice of pool meetings. After all, we had just forced them into a settlement of a lawsuit, why should they abide by its terms?

A couple of hours out on the flight, Karen noticed that the network pool producers and their talent, including Sam Donaldson, were no longer in the back cabin. Karen moved forward through a closed door, and there sat the other pool producers and their anchors. The White House was briefing them. As Karen entered, Sam Donaldson looked up and said, "Oh, let us not forget to introduce the new pool producer from Chicken Noodle News."

Karen still feels humiliated. She wishes she had made a comeback. She says, "CNN was a cause to all of us who worked there; we were younger, they hated that. We represented cable, and they hated that. But we could do our job, and they still called us Chicken Noodle News." Karen is now a producer on *Sixty Minutes*. I guess the networks finally recognized her abilities.

As tough on us as the settlement was, the lawsuit wasn't a total loss. Six months earlier, it had gotten us the Sadat assassination tape.

Round 52: **The Ass Backwards Company**

It was a "Hollywood movie set." The scene was Cape Canaveral, and the event was the launch of the space shuttle *Columbia* on April 13, 1981. It was the first time in six years that America had sent men into space. Eighty thousand people had been specially invited to the event. Those uninvited had to rely on the three broadcast networks and CNN.

We arrived at Cape Canaveral with a guerilla cadre. The networks had sent hundreds of people; we sent a dozen. Our dozen proved superior to their army. We had airtime; the networks didn't. Our trump card was our anchor and leader, Bill Zimmerman. He was the best all-around newsman at CNN. He could anchor, he could report live, and he could produce excellent "packages." He had never been a space correspondent, but like the best of journalists his character was to know everything about everything. By the time he got to Cape Canaveral, he knew as much about space as the guys who'd been covering it for years.

Zimmerman was one of Watson's boys and shared George's standards. He said that for him "moving to CNN was like moving from first class to steerage, and fomenting a rebellion after you got there. We started an uprising against the people in first class, the networks." Watson had been unable accept the rudeness of CNN life. Zimmerman would fight it.

Bill understood what I was trying to do, what Ted was trying to do. My strategy was to creep up on the networks while they slept, and let them discover the next morning that we had taken over the news business. Ted's idea was to blare out our arrival, club our rivals over the head, and drag them off into our cave. Zimmerman was gentler, a classy fighter, but he knew we were in a fight, and he was out to win.

Once, when Zimmerman was on the air, something happened in Iraq. The assignment desk found somebody at the Baghdad airport. Kavanau told Zimmerman, "You gotta do this right away. Now, take this phone call." Zimmerman took the phone call and told the viewers he would be talking to an eyewitness.

"I started asking this guy questions," Zimmerman says. "He was speaking Japanese. He didn't understand the questions, I didn't understand the answers. The control room told me to keep going. It was a total farce on live television. When the show ended, I took off after Kavanau. I was shaking my fist and calling him a son-of-a-bitch across the newsroom, and he was running away from me. I was so mad, I didn't even care that he was the one that was wearing a gun on his ankle."

Bill understood that there were two factions at CNN, the network guys and the independent guys. He was a network guy, but he was willing to fight for his standards. Zimmerman worked with the young journalists all the time. He improved their writing, he helped with their news judgment. They were learning the high end from Zimmerman, the down-and-dirty from Kavanau.

Just before June 1, 1980, Kavanau asked his young producers to choose their candidate for CNN's strongest anchor. Don Miller, a handsome, deep-voiced Canadian, was anchoring one hour of *Prime News 120,* Zimmerman was anchoring the other. There were twenty other anchors to choose from. The producers voted for Miller. Six months later, Kavanau took another poll. Zimmerman won unanimously.

For the space shot, each of the three networks had a special three-story set that they brought in. The sets were so large that huge cranes had to be transported to the site just to install them. A crane would lift the set up high and drop it down into its proper place. The top level of the set was the network space studio. Beneath that sat the executives, experts, and technicians. The first floors even had reception desks. Everything was air-conditioned. It was beautiful.

When the ABC crane operators dropped their building in, they did it backwards. The ABC studio was facing the parking lot. Their cameras had nothing to shoot at but cars pulling in and out. It's a kind of stupidity that is only possible in a big bureaucracy. ABC had to call the crane back, lift the building up again, and turn it around so that it would face the launchpad.

Rick Brown was at the Cape with Zimmerman producing satellite feeds and doing anything that needed doing. As Brown walked away from our trailer, he noticed that Roone Arledge was standing in the parking lot, seeming stupefied. As Rick passed Arledge, he spoke. "Phew," he said. "We thought we were in trouble. We thought maybe ABC knew something we didn't know. Maybe NASA was going to launch *Columbia* from the parking lot."

Arledge was not amused. I was. For two years, ABC had been calling CNN "Chicken Noodle News." For two weeks, I called ABC the "Ass Backwards Company."

CNN had taken its satellite truck to the Cape. It was the only one there because in April of '81, the nets were still tethered to AT&T long lines. We had rented an RV—just a regular trailer, the kind your grandparents take on the road—put a wooden platform on its roof, placed two camera cases upright on the platform, covered the whole thing with a tabletop, and draped a cloth over it; it was our anchor desk.

Janet Northrup, Pat O'Gorman's assistant, was directing the shoot. Kevin Sanders, our science reporter, worked in the field. All we had on the ground was our little RV. But somehow, "This crazy little thing we built was perceived as cool," Northrup says. "The guests had to climb up the skinny little ladder on the back of a trailer to get to the roof and be interviewed by Zimmerman. Senators, astronauts, it didn't matter, they all had to climb."

Each network had an astronaut assigned to it for expert commentary. We got Sally Ride, a smart and charming woman. It was a perfect match. Ride and CNN were breaking in to the "old boys club" at the same time. The guests came to us happily because we were covering the story all day long. When they talked to us their material got on the air. When they talked to the networks they were cut into sound bites, if they were used at all.

Zimmerman sat in a lawn chair behind the desk during his interviews. The guests sat in folding chairs next to him. Northrup remembers, "Whenever we went on the air, we yelled to the technicians downstairs in the trailer, 'Don't walk, don't walk.' Every time they stepped down hard, the platform would tremble, the desk would tremble, the chairs would tremble, the camera would shake too."

In addition to directing, Northrup produced, shot, and edited a lot of the packages on that trip. The most popular was our "potty package." Everyone wanted to know how the astronauts performed bodily functions in Space. We interviewed the NASA authority on toilets. NASA, PR conscious as ever, loved it. Kevin Sanders won NASA points when he did a long piece on the civilian benefits of the program, stressing the technology and Tang, which had been developed as a drink for the astronauts. NASA could see its budget growing.

The launch was delayed. Zimmerman sat in his chair, ten hours one day, eight hours the next. When it rained, he put up an umbrella. In the midst of the wait, there was a flare from the launching pad. The rocket seemed to be spewing flames. Zimmerman had done his homework. Bill, alone on the platform, spoke calmly to the viewers. "This happens," he said. "It's not unusual and it won't create an enormous problem." Within minutes, our crew had an expert on top of the trailer. He confirmed everything that Bill had said.

We had to depend on what our journalists knew. We didn't have briefing books and researchers running in and out. We needed one intelligent guy on every story who could stop, think, and then tell the story. Our anchors often had to act as managing editors. Zimmerman and Shaw were the two best at that.

Nineteen years later, Northrup remembers Zimmerman's words just before liftoff. "As the rocket is vibrating, you hear it in the background. It is as though humanity is trying to escape." Fifty-four hours later the *Columbia* landed at Edwards Air Force Base, California. It had returned, a combined spacecraft/airplane that was supposed to open the way for regular space travel. NASA said, "Everything looks perfect." Everything looked perfect on CNN, too.

Round 53: **The Pope Gets Shot**

The spring of 1981 was not a bad season for news. First the president was shot, then the space shot, and on May 14 the pope was shot. CNN was lucky. Since we'd been barred from London by the BBC and ITN, we took our main international feed from Rome at noon Eastern time. RAI had a tape of the shooting ready for us. We sent it out hot-live to our cable subscribers and beat everyone. Hot-live means we're sending it out even as we're receiving it.

I was in the bureau in New York when the story broke, and I made a major mistake. For once in my life, I was a nice guy. I permitted the other networks to stay on the line as our feed came through so that they might feed their own material next. They didn't bother with their material. They just took ours, turned it around, and fed it to their stations. If I'd thought about it, I'd have extended the CNN feed, included loads of feature stories, and kept them off the air for an hour. I didn't think of it. I didn't do it. That's why nice guys finish last.

As the feed ended, Jim Miklaszewski arrived from Rome where he'd been filling in. Mik says, "I had just arrived in the bureau at the World Trade Center. I had my suitcases, I came back from Rome, I put 'em on the floor, Reese was in the bureau. The bells go off on the UPI machine and he walks over, looks at me, and says, 'Go to Rome now.' I said 'Okay,' picked up my bags, got out to the airport, flew back to Rome."

Dennis Troute and Ron Dean were waiting there covering the story, which was mostly medical bulletins. "The pope's condition is improving. The Holy Father has spent a quiet night." Crews have to be at the hospital. It is the daily grind of the news business. You don't expect anything to happen, but still Dennis Troute had to spend a lot of time there, just in case.

Miklaszewski was assigned to Mehmet Ali Agca, the shooter. Ali Agca was being taken from one prison to another, and CNN got there late. We were stuck in a bad position. The networks clustered around the spot where the police said they were going to bring Agca out. Mik says, "As they were bringing him out, it turns out that they pulled the police lorry right up next to us. So, Agca walks right into our camera. We were literally ten feet from him, and he was shouting at the network reporters across the piazza as he got into the van."

In Rome, all the networks fed material out of the same place, Telespazzio. We fed our story first, and then George Lewis, the NBC correspondent, fed his. Lewis said, "Even in custody, the suspect shouted in defiance." But all you could hear on the NBC tape is *owwah wah mah-wah* because they were so far away. Mik told Lewis that our tape caught Agca's voice clearly, and what Agca said was, "I'm sorry two tourists were hurt." He shouted it twice.

Mik played the tape back for Lewis, "Oh my God, he wasn't shouting in defiance, he was apologizing to the tourists," Lewis said. He went back in and changed his track. Mik had corrected a footnote to history. Agca was not defiant, he was apologetic. If it hadn't been for Mik, the NBC archives, eternal silicon history would have had it wrong. By the way, that's what news does to history—if the reporter doesn't see it right or hear it right, history has it wrong forever.

For most of the reporters, the good ones, at CNN, the first two years were the best years they ever had. They were allowed to do their own thing, report what they saw, the way they saw it, and they didn't have New York or Atlanta rewriting their material to coincide with the wire services. Mik remembers, "When we were one against many and it was just us—we had the freedom, I'll say it again, we had the freedom to go out and cover the news and not worry about what everybody else was doing."

Round 54: **The War That Doesn't Happen**

Ted Kavanau had a friend, a journalist named Martin Abend. When Ted was running WNEW, he'd used Abend as a commentator. Abend was conservative. Ted was conservative. Abend was Jewish. Ted was Jewish. In the sixties, they may have been the only two Jewish conservatives in New York. In 1979, when Kavanau was down and out, it was Abend who gave him a couch to sleep on. Now Ted was bringing Abend to see me, because he wanted me to hire him.

It should be clear by now that Kavanau was one of those guys—you couldn't work with him, you couldn't work without him. When he ran WNEW, which was the thing he loved most in the world, he was crazily opinionated. He screamed, he wore that gun on his ankle, he changed shows at the last minute just to energize the troops. Worse still, he and the anchorman, Bill Jorgenson, didn't get along. Jorgenson was a little crazy himself. Once he and Kavanau had a fight about who was going to get the station couch to sleep on. The loser got the floor.

In May of 1981, Kavanau introduced me to Abend, since Ted's successors at WNEW were no longer using him. Ted thought he'd fit at CNN, but CNN had plenty of conservative columnists. We had Novak and Evans and Phyllis Schlafly and Barry Goldwater—if anything, I needed a liberal. Unfortunately, there weren't any good ones around. Abend was local, not known, and looked strange on camera. There seemed no reason to hire him.

Then Abend, who was very well connected in the Middle East, offered me a scoop so good that it could earn him a job. He was positive the Israelis were scheduled to invade Lebanon in the middle of June. I knew that Abend had contacts in Israel's Begin government and I acted on his information.

Bill Zimmerman knew everyone in Beirut from having been the ABC bureau chief there so I sent him to Lebanon. No American journalist had better contacts with the Israeli government than Dan Schorr. I sent Schorr to Jerusalem. I alerted Bushinsky in Tel Aviv. He laid on staff and satellite time. Zimmerman restored his connections at the Commodore Hotel, the center of journalists and fixers that would enable newsmen to work in Beirut in some safety. We had cameras, technicians, and facilities on both sides of the border.

We were ready for war, but war never came. When it didn't, I didn't hire Abend. He had been wrong, and guys who are wrong don't get hired.

A year later, almost to the day, Israeli troops invaded Lebanon. I now considered Abend genuinely an expert. The invasion might well have been planned and set to roll in 1981, but someone powerful in the U.S. government might have nixed it. The same guy might have okayed it in June 1982. By then, it was too late for me to hire Martin Abend. I was gone from CNN.

Round 55: Kathleen Sullivan

In 1983, a year after Kathleen had left CNN for ABC, where she had been homogenized and cosmeticized so that she looked like any ordinary anchor, Frederick Barthelme wrote in the *New Yorker*, "Kathleen Sullivan is back on CNN, a guest on a call-in interview show about the boom in news . . . the callers are all men. . . . Tonight she is wearing one of her old purple outfits, and her hair is messed up as it used to be. A caller who says his name is Toby from Tennessee says that he doesn't think she is the real Kathleen Sullivan, that the real Kathleen must have died and gone to heaven." She hadn't. The real Kathleen had gone to hell, or ABC, as it is occasionally known.

From day one, Kathleen was the sweetheart of CNN. Sam Zelman found her working in Salt Lake City, of all places, when Sam was still at CBS. She was a news anchor and a sports anchor. She had hosted Spartacade, a precursor of Ted Turner's Goodwill Games from Moscow. She was a Pasadena girl, a tennis player at USC, and well-traveled though still under thirty. Unfortunately, she had never covered hard news in the field. Fortunately, she was aware of her shortcomings and eager for loving support.

I picked Alec Nagle as loving supporter. His wife Dial had not yet arrived in Atlanta, so in the evening, he would take Kathleen out for a drink and hold her hand through the start-up. It was never more than that, but when Dial came, Alec asked that we not tell her about the "Kathleen assignment." He didn't think Dial would believe that any man could have a platonic relationship with Kathleen.

We sent Kathleen to Nicaragua to cover backgrounders we would run after the launch. We hoped she would gain confidence in her ability to handle hard news, but it became clear that Kathleen didn't enjoy covering Third World stories.

Once we launched and put her on the air, nothing else mattered. The camera loved her, every man in the audience (and most of the women) loved her. She worked hard, she wrote her own copy, and she did not resent—in fact, learned from—helpful editing. She read very well, her timing was great, and something about her said, "Look at me sitting up here reading the news, when I would much rather be in bed with you" to every male viewer.

Kathleen did not shy away from sexual conversation. She had known Bob Wussler in her previous life, she had worked for him in Moscow on Spartacade. After she had joined CNN, Wussler was hired at TBS. She was asked if she'd had to "screw Wussler" to get her job. "No," she said. "He had to screw me to get his."

On our first New Year's Eve, Kathleen was anchoring with Don Miller. Miller extended a mistletoe twig and kissed her gently. From her side, Kathleen hauled up a mistletoe bush and asked, "What do I get with this?"

At CNN Kathleen dressed herself, there was no clothing allowance. There was no wardrobe woman, and for the most part she did her own makeup. According to Roz Abrams, a black anchorwoman, there was just one makeup person who applied the same shade of powder to the faces of all the anchors, man or woman, blond or brunette, white or black. Her job was best described as avoiding sweat on anchor faces. There was little hope for a cosmetic upgrade.

Kathleen wanted better treatment, a clothing allowance, and a more attentive makeup artist. We couldn't afford them; besides, I loved her the way she was. Every night when she went on the air, I wanted it to seem as if she had just gotten out of bed and there was a run in her stockings.

Lee Strasberg was once asked why women thought Greta Garbo was the most glamorous woman in the world, but men thought the title belonged to Marilyn Monroe. Strasberg supposedly replied, "Marilyn Monroe seems available." Kathleen Sullivan seemed available. The show she anchored, *Prime News 120,* was a two-hour roundup of all the day's news, scheduled from 8 to 10 p.m. From the beginning, it was the network's major effort, as highly produced as we could afford.

Every day Alec Nagle found a mildly erotic or scandalous or reasonably salacious item and assigned it to Kathleen. Kathleen rewrote it and read it at the 9 p.m. break. She read it with obvious relish. The audience loved it, the ratings on the show were 20 percent better than the network average. I attribute the rise to Kathleen. I thought she was the only anchor on the network who actually brought viewers to CNN.

At CNN, Sullivan had created her own presence, but she didn't want to be unique, she wanted to be like the glamour anchors at the big networks. Every week or so I would get a call from Jimmy Griffin, her agent at William Morris: "What about the clothing allowance? What about the makeup person?" We had promised Kathleen an office of her own. We had provided her with a large cubicle that passed for an office at CNN. One night Kathleen walked into her "office" and found a male anchorman astride a producer upon Kathleen's desk. Griffin called again. He was entitled. We began a search for an office for Kathleen that had a door.

Kathleen starred for us when she covered the July wedding of Prince Charles and Lady Diana. Kathleen went over with Jane Maxwell and a few technicians to anchor our coverage. All the American networks were getting the same pool feed from the BBC. Kathleen's aura put an edge on our story. Di was the virgin bride; Kathleen was the eternal "other woman." Her narration gave CNN a quality wholly different from the networks. For a moment Di and Kathleen even appeared together. When the newly married couple came out on the palace bal-

cony, Kathleen was doing a stand-up. She picked up the picture immediately, told the story as it was happening, and we split the TV screen.

To top it off, Nancy Reagan, who attended the wedding as the president's representative, was an old friend of Kathleen. After the ceremony,
Kathleen stood on the cathedral steps with her cameraman, wunderkind
Derwin Johnson. Kathleen shouted, "Mrs. Reagan, what are you going to
tell the president? Do you miss him?" Johnson says, "That was all it took.
Nancy Reagan walked right over to our camera with all the other hundreds of cameras there, and did an exclusive interview with Kathleen."

"When we got back to the bureau, Françoise Husson grabs me, kisses
me. She hugs Kathleen and says, 'Oh my God. All the other networks
have been calling. They want copies of the tape. You were great.' We
viewed the tape. There was Nancy walking straight into our camera."
We didn't give the other networks the tape. They didn't give us no
respect, we didn't give them no tape.

Roone Arledge coveted Kathleen for ABC. He and most other television professionals appreciated her talent and understood that she was
the first star CNN had created. Arledge had made Jim Griffin aware that
ABC had a standing offer for her services. I had other plans for Kathleen. Her interview with Mrs. Reagan had given me an idea.

In 1889 when Joseph Pulitzer owned the *New York World,* he sent his
star reporter, Nelly Bly, around the world in eighty days. (She did it in
seventy-two.) I was going to send Kathleen around the world in eighty
hours. With Rick Brown, our head of satellites, and Jane Maxwell, head of
special events, we were scheduling Kathleen to fly from Washington to
London to Moscow to Delhi to Los Angeles and then to Washington. At
each stop she was to interview the most important women in the country.

Through our contacts, we thought we would be able to snag such
women as Margaret Thatcher, an important Russian lady official, at
least a deputy premier, and Indira Gandhi. In Los Angeles, we would
have our choice of reigning movie queens, and Mrs. Reagan would do it
for us in Washington.

Rick was arranging satellite feeds, Jane and I were arranging airline
schedules and interviews. I was even going to give Kathleen a large
clothing allowance. This was one time we wanted Kathleen to look
great. This wasn't news—this was publicity: Kathleen as the guest on
the other network's morning talk shows; Jane Maxwell with her to

explain the logistics, how close the schedule was, how difficult the feat, how important the interviews were going to be. CNN, of course, would carry Kathleen live at each arrival and departure.

Could we get heads of state to come to airport VIP lounges so that Kathleen might interview there? Or would we have to do the setups from their homes or offices? How could we arrange schedules so that Kathleen would always arrive at times convenient for our subjects. Charles Lindbergh took off all alone from Long Island. By the time he arrived in Paris, he was the most famous man of his time. We hoped that by the time Kathleen returned to Washington, the whole world would be waiting for her.

Alas, fate and Ted Turner intervened. I was fired, the plan was scrapped, and to this day Joseph Pulitzer's Nelly Bly still holds the record. When Nelly Bly returned, she married a multimillionaire. Kathleen would have done as well.

Kathleen was not a conventional glamour girl. She looked her best when her hair was messed and her lipstick smeared. Her hair showed signs of gray, but her blue eyes gleamed, and when the lights came on, her face glowed. She had a half-dozen laughs, from naughty to a roar. She licked her lips when she told a particularly scandalous story. She enjoyed news and she enjoyed herself as she was telling it. That's what Barthelme and Toby of Tennessee missed when they said the real Kathleen must have gone to heaven. Barthelme reports that in reply to Toby, Kathleen said, laughing prettily, "It's still me, I look all right now, don't I?"

But Kathleen never looked all right on ABC. I don't think she's been all right since CNN. But then I may not be all right, either.

Round 56: "He's a Dictator, Just Like Me"

In 1981, Mike Boettcher renewed the idea of a Ted Turner-Castro visit. I wanted Fidel to tell Mike that he would agree to meet personally with Ted Turner. The best we could get was a guarantee from his top aides . . . for whatever that was worth.

We take the chance. Ted flies down with his girlfriend, Liz Wickersham. Turner and Castro become buddies. They, with their girlfriends, go hunting in a duck blind. They even manage to kill a couple of ducks. They enjoy each other.

Ted came home having undergone a conversion. The first words out of his mouth were, "Reese, Fidel ain't a communist. He's a dictator, just like me." His second words were, "I'm the only American who's come that close to Fidel with a gun in his hands in twenty years."

Ted had wanted to interview Fidel. I said no. Boettcher would have to do the interview. Ted had asked me, as we were starting CNN, whether he might do some interviewing, I had said yes. I remembered William Randolph Hearst's "interviews" with world leaders. Hearst would travel with Bob Considine, and Considine would then write stories based on the interviews and credit his boss with the questions. That system wouldn't work on television. After being around Ted for a year, it was clear to me Ted was not able to do an interview. He'd never hung around CNN long enough to learn the technique.

We tried to interview Castro a year later, but this time he wouldn't cooperate. *Take Two*, Don Farmer, Chris Curle, and Guy Pepper, had wanted to broadcast live out of Beijing. We wanted to be bold, but the People's Republic said no. As second choice, we picked Havana and used the CNN-Castro connection to get us there. Mike Boettcher went through his friend of a friend-of-a-friend connection, and the Cuban government gave us permission.

CNN was making history in Havana. It was the first time an American network had been on the air live from Cuba since the revolution. Guy Pepper, *Take Two*'s executive producer, knew how to make television with no more than a camera, two sawhorses, and a flat board. The anchors of the show, Curle and Farmer, could go with the flow. Boettcher was their reporter, and he knew the drill. They brought with them Katie Couric as associate producer and Gail Evans to book the guests; that is, whatever guests the Cuban government said we could have.

As a business matter, *Take Two* had to pay for all Cuban services in advance. It was cash or travelers' checks only. Guy had to sit in the lobby of the hotel, each day, signing travelers' checks for the satellite uplink. The same for the remote truck. They say, "You pay every day or you don't go on the air."

One night before we went on the air, two Cuban officials knocked on Guy Pepper's hotel door at two in the morning. They said, "We have something from Fidel for you." Then they brought two giant boxes into his room and said, "This is a gift for Ted Turner from Fidel. Please take them back with you." Next day, Guy dragged Katie into his room and said, "We have to look into these boxes. Who knows what's in here? We open the boxes, and there they are, two stuffed ducks that Ted had shot while he'd been out hunting with Fidel. They were huge."

Havana accommodations were not perfect. The food in the hotel was awful and there were no toilet seats, but the biggest problem was the weather. We had an open air set, and rain would've killed us. A tropical storm raged for two days before we aired. Pepper paced in his room, Katie Couric said she would kill me. But when day of air dawned the sun was shining in the sky.

Pepper had picked the Moro Castle, a sixteenth-century ruin, high on the water overlooking Havana as his set. The Cubans supplied the remote truck and the technical crew. Pepper's problems were political and directorial. There was a commissar and an interpreter standing between him and the technicians. When a Russian warship sailed through the harbor, Pepper shouted to the crew, "Get that shot!" His interpreter did not hear him. The commissar shook his head no. "We were fighting," Pepper says. "I'm screaming, 'Take the ship!' and these guys are not going to do it. Thirty guys on the truck are saying, 'No, no, no.'"

We had to get official permission for everything that we shot on location. When Boettcher wanted to go into the streets and talk to ordinary people, the commissar would say, "No, no, no." If Boettcher argued hard enough, and they let him into the street, they would pick the people he could talk to. Everything Mike heard came through translators, and all we would ever have on camera was, "We love Cuba, it's the best place ever."

Despite it all, *Take Two* in Havana was a terrific program. Never before seen is never before seen, no matter what. The supporting cast, ordinary Cubans, Cuban artists, Cuban writers, was perfect, and we waited for the star. First, Boettcher's sources said, "Fidel will show up on Wednesday." Then, "He'll show up Thursday." "No, no, now he's going to show up on Friday." He never showed. According to Boettcher, Fidel had finally decided not to show up because "when he speaks, he speaks with a message, and he is not ready to deliver his message to the American people."

Pepper remembers Cuba as a "great time, an adventure. . . . We were making history, we were doing something important, we wanted to get it right, and everyone felt proud that we were able to do this thing. But, when it was time to go, we were ready. We'd had it with the food, we'd had it with no toilet seats."

When they came back, Pepper and Couric dumped the ducks in Ted Turner's office. Last I saw of them, they were in a place of honor. Ted has kept on Fidel's good side for twenty years, and CNN was the first American network to get permission to open a Havana bureau. The bureau sits high up in the old Hilton hotel with a beautiful view of the harbor. CNN could air a terrific program from there now, but all they do is inserts.

Round 57: **God and Ted**

I never inquired into Ted's politics. I knew when I met him they were somewhat right-wing, how far right-wing I did not want to know. I figured I would do news my way, and, if Ted didn't like it, he could fire me.

Within a couple of months, Ted wandered into my office and said, "I've been getting mail from the Eagles." The Eagles are the heavy hitters in the Republican party. In those days Eagle wings came with an annual donation of $10,000. In his previous life, Ted had been an Eagle. He'd campaigned for Barry Goldwater, and he'd met his second wife Janey when they stuffed envelopes together at Goldwater headquarters. Now, the Eagles were writing Ted and complaining that CNN was too liberal. Ted said, "I don't care, Reese. You just keep on doing what you're doing." It was good to hear. CNN news did not seem liberal to me, but then it would've had to be pretty far right to satisfy the Eagles.

Similarly, I never inquired into Ted's religious beliefs. I knew that Ted's Charlotte station had helped launch the Jim and Tammy Faye

Bakker evangelical show, and I heard that Ted had been close to both of them. Still, I ordered up a documentary on television evangelists, including the Bakkers and Pat Robertson. I have always felt partially responsible for Pat Robertson. While I was working for TVN, the Coors brothers' news service, the brothers had arranged for me to meet with Robertson and his broadcast aides to instruct them in the basics of satellite technology and costs. The aides took me to lunch, gave me a cellophane-wrapped paperback copy of Robertson's basic book, sent me home, and soon thereafter launched their satellite television service, the Christian Broadcasting Network.

I thought that had earned me the right to take a hard look at the doings of the televangelists. I gave producer/reporter Jim Clancy his head, and he turned in a strong hour. The part I remember best was an interview with an elderly black woman in Texas who tithed monthly to Robertson from her social security check. She was virtually impoverished and lived in a bleak trailer. I thought that in most churches she would be receiving charity. Instead, she was sending money to Virginia.

Clancy's hour was objective but hard-hitting. Again, Turner came wandering into my office. He had heard about the documentary, watched it, and loved it. He suggested that CNN continue doing documentaries like it. I remain unsure of his motives. I don't know if, given his lifestyle, he objected to televangelists in general, or to Pat Robertson in particular, because they were both Southern boys competing to get a piece of that satellite pie.

One day when I was in Ted's office, he took a call from the Reverend Donald Wildmon. Wildmon was not a televangelist. He was chairman of the Coalition for Better Television (CBT). He crusaded against sex and violence on television, particularly sex. He was also one of the religious zealots involved in the battle over Procter & Gamble's logo. P&G products had featured a crescent-shaped "man in the moon" symbol since 1882. A Minnesota fundamentalist identified the logo as a sign for a witches' coven. Christian groups, including Wildmon's, took up the cause. P&G thought the complaints ridiculous. Then, the Christians organized a boycott of P&G products, the boycott hurt sales, and P&G dropped its trademark.

In 1981, Wildmon went after network programming. He attacked sponsors and networks. P&G was again a prime target, and P&G once again conceded. It produced a list of fifty television programs it would no longer sponsor. The network Wildmon picked on was NBC. That surprised me. NBC was the least venturesome of the three networks, it never pushed the envelope. There was less sex or violence on the Peacock Network than on either of the others. In the early eighties, it was also the weakest network, crippled in its competition with CBS and ABC. ABC had captured most young viewers, CBS owned the older audience. NBC was drifting hopelessly through the middle. In the network herd, it was the wounded buffalo.

Nevertheless, Wildmon kept hammering away at NBC, monitoring NBC programming carefully. At the least semblance of sexual activity or violence, he would encourage his followers to send postcards to the network. Many did.

One day, in Ted's office, I hear him talking on the phone with Wildmon about strategy in the CBT attack on NBC: What is Wildmon going to do next, how can Ted help him. It seems to me a conversation between coconspirators. Then I get it. If you're hunting networks, shoot at the cripple. Ted must be hunting NBC.

I began to understand that Ted's religious beliefs were motivated by business considerations. He didn't like Christians who competed with him for a television audience. He loved Christians he thought could help him take over a network. He had a special place in his heart for evangelists who bought time on TBS.

In the early eighties, Jerry Falwell bought time. When he visited Atlanta, Ted assembled a group of executives to meet with him. I was included. It was a pleasant meeting. Falwell seemed sincere. He was jovial and surprisingly soft-spoken. We spoke of things in general and then Ted and Falwell began to deplore sex and violence on commercial television. It was awful, they agreed. It was shameless, they agreed. It was destroying America and the American family, they agreed.

After all this agreement, the meeting ended. As Falwell rose, he lifted his hands and asked us to kneel in prayer. He prayed that the cloud of sex and violence on television would be lifted from the American people, with the help of those of us kneeling before him. Then, in the name of God and Jesus Christ, he said, "Amen." I did not join him. It is not a Jewish custom. Nevertheless, I had knelt before God and Jesus and this is not a Jewish custom either. I walked across the hall to my office. Falwell walked to the elevator with some of the other attendees.

Before I closed the door, I heard Ted shout to his secretary: "Jesus Christ, Dee. Get me a joint." I do not know if Jerry Falwell heard him.

Round 58: **Sadat**

Anwar Sadat was assassinated in Cairo while reviewing a military parade on October 6, 1981. CNN was not there. Neither was WTN, the television news service to which we subscribed. WTN was supposed to cover routine news stories, just in case. . . .

Our cameraman/bureau chief, Dean Vallas, was still in Cairo, one week away from starting a job with NBC, a job we didn't know anything about. He decided the military parade was not worth covering. Then the assassination happened, it was early in the morning EDT, and we had no pictures. For a twenty-four-hour news service, that's a disaster. All day long, from seven in the morning until six at night, we had to use still photos, interviews, and phoners to keep the story alive.

CBS had its own video and fed it from Egyptian television. ABC got its pictures out and broke into news programs with bulletins. We had nothing, and it looked like a prime-time disaster. It was then that the new pool rules bailed us out. At the instruction of their lawyers, ABC gave us the pictures. We got them on by 6 p.m. Half our audience never knew we'd missed the story.

Bill Zimmerman flew to the funeral. Françoise Husson, Dick Blystone, and Derwin Johnson flew down from London. Françoise and her crew got to Egypt on Françoise's initiative. She called from London and requested permission to charter a plane. It was the only way to get there in time, and the Cairo airport was about to be closed. While I was still hemming and hawing, Brazilian television booked a charter of its own and offered to split it with CNN. Without waiting for word from me, Françoise jumped on the plane. They arrived just in time. The airport closed right behind them, but by then we had Bill, Françoise, Derwin, and Blystone in place.

Zimmerman had interviewed Sadat a couple of times for ABC and knew the Middle East from his days in Beirut. Bill's Cairo friends brought important Egyptians to him for on-camera interviews. Blystone and Johnson went into the street to report on Cairo's mood and the attempts to identify the assassins.

Since CNN was CNN, our coverage did not start or end with the funeral. During the next three days, CNN presented the three elements of the story: the event itself, its likely consequences, and the search for perpetrators. We did it intelligently. We had four of our best people in the right place at the right time: Zimmerman the anchor, Françoise the producer, Blystone the reporter, and Johnson the cameraman. As it turned out, Zimmerman had a passion for Sadat, really loved the man. That all came through on the air.

At the funeral, CNN was stuck in an announcer's booth about the size of a closet inside Egypt TV. Bill was seeing Egypt TV coverage of the funeral on a small monitor and describing it on the fly to the CNN audience back in the States. At one point, the picture failed. The line from Egyptian television to our booth had been switched. Instead of seeing the funeral, Bill had a picture of somebody reading the Koran.

Françoise swears she will never forget Zimmerman doing a live commentary of the funeral procession blind. He was fluent and accurate. He had clearly done his research before he flew to Egypt. He did an almost in-synch commentary before we got picture back, and an excellent commentary afterwards. Only Zimmerman reported the small turnout for the funeral. It seemed that Sadat was not as popular in Cairo as he was in the West.

For Zimmerman, it was the opportunity of a lifetime, both professionally and personally. He says he came to CNN to have that opportunity. "I never would have been able to do that at ABC," he explains. "I'd be running out covering fires or a campaign. Only the ones like Walter Cronkite and Frank Reynolds had the chance to do those kinds of things at the network level."

After Zimmerman left Cairo, Françoise and the crew remained. Derwin had been named Cairo bureau chief to succeed Vallas. Françoise and Blystone gave him last-minute training. And from there on, Derwin Johnson was CNN's man in the Middle East.

Round 59: **Forebodings**

It is 4 p.m. on October 19, 1981, in Nyack, New York. Four figures wearing dark ski masks emerge from ambush, firing shotguns and automatic weapons. They steal $1.6 million from a Brink's truck, but they bungle the job. They kill a Brink's guard and two cops and wound three others. Two hours later, they are captured. I think, John Dillinger has struck again.

That evening Ted Turner called me at home, in itself an unusual occurrence. His voice was high-pitched, his words slurred. He was in Washington, scheduled to appear at a congressional subcommittee hearing on television violence the next morning. He wanted CNN to carry the hearing live. I did not. I told him that when CNN carried an event live, we gave it a special importance. Subcommittee hearings on television violence were not breaking news. CNN would cover the hearings, but on tape, and air it later. I also suggested it was unlikely that we had time to get a television line into the hearing room for live coverage.

I then called the Washington night manager and told him not to put in the line.

What I had not said to Ted, because slurred telephone conversations were not the best time to confront him, was "when an owner starts putting his face on his own network, particularly live, it looks as if he is turning his network into a vanity network, a whore's network."

At 9 a.m. on October 20, I was flying to New York to meet with Mary Alice Williams, the New York bureau chief. Ted Turner was awaiting his appearance before the subcommittee on violence. And CNN's New York bureau had been informed that the four ski-masked figures now sitting in a Nyack jail were not modern-day John Dillingers. They were left-wing terrorists.

At 10 a.m., I was still on a plane to New York, but Ted was live from Washington, on CNN, decrying TV violence. I was not aware of that. I was also unaware that the Brink's bandits had been identified as remnants of the Black Panthers and the Weather Underground. For the past year, they had been robbing banks and armored cars to finance their revolution.

Among them was Katherine Boudin, whose father was a famous left-wing lawyer. Boudin had been in hiding for more than ten years. She was notorious as a leader of "Chicago's Day of Rage" and a survivor of the New York bomb factory explosion on West Eleventh Street, from which she had famously fled naked through the streets of Greenwich Village.

By 11 a.m., I was landing at LaGuardia airport. Ted Turner had finished attacking the networks on CNN, but had ordered Ed Turner, whom I had recently named Washington bureau chief, to keep the hearings on CNN until they concluded. By now, Mary Alice had the whole story of the robbery—the ambush, the shootings, the victims, the chase, and the identities of the culprits. She had tapes of the crime scene, library tape of the bomb factory explosion, interviews with cops and witnesses. But she could not get her story on the air.

At 11:30 I was on the ground. I called Mary Alice from LaGuardia airport. She was in tears. Mary Alice knew a story when she had one, and boy did she have one. But she couldn't get it on the air. The congressional hearings were droning on and Ed Turner, following Ted Turner's orders, would not release the video line to Atlanta.

I called Ed from the airport. "Why are the hearings on the air?" I asked. Ed said, "Ted told me to do it." I said, "You don't work for Ted, you work for me. Put Mary Alice on the line, I'll take the heat." Then I asked Ed why he had put the line into the hearing room in the first place. His answer was the same. "Ted told me to do it."

At last Mary Alice got her story on CNN. It was perfect material for a twenty-four-hour news network. Hour by hour there were new developments. Boudin's parents visited her in jail. They announced that

William Kunstler, a left-wing lawyer even more famous than Boudin's father, would defend her. Kunstler was interviewed. The FBI held a press conference to update the story and pat itself on the back.

Mary Alice and her reporters did so well that in the end CNN owned the story. Although the New York local stations announced it first, Mary Alice had more than caught up because the network stations couldn't afford to carry the story live; they would have lost too much commercial revenue from their entertainment programs.

Ted Turner never spoke directly to me about the day's events. He had not followed my advice, but I had refused to follow his orders. When I'd agreed to start CNN, Ted had given me his word that I would control editorial format, content, and personnel. Even then I knew who Ted was and what, in the end, verbal commitments would mean to him. When I thwarted him on October 21, I knew I'd put my job on the line; and when I got back to Atlanta, I told Pat that it might be a matter of months.

Looking back, the Nyack raid was the final act of American left-wing terrorists. Now right-wing terrorists follow the Black Panther plan. Their militias attack armored cars, hold up banks, and use the money to finance their revolution.

The Brink's robbery has become the stuff of American mythology. Books are written, movies are made, television programs are broadcast. The happenings of October 20, 1981, mark, as well as any single event can, an end to the radical idealism of the sixties, and a beginning to the bitterness of the nineties. It is no longer blacks and women who take up arms to fight the establishment. Now the guns are in the hands of the white yeomanry.

To this day, Ted has never admitted the significance of the Brink's robbery. He claims that I took him off the air for "some crime story." If the Brink's story is just "a crime story," then Noah's flood is just the spring thaw.

Round 60: **Headline News**

By the end of November 1980, we all knew that CNN had made it. We had proved that we could do news twenty-four hours a day in an original and responsible way on a very limited budget. Ted was so sure of it that all he feared was competition.

"If we're gonna have competition, what would competition look like?" he asked me over dinner one night. "Short form," I said. "Headline news." Ted said, "Do a schedule and a budget." I asked why compete with ourselves? Ted said, "If we're gonna have competition, it might as well be us."

A few days later, I drop a budget and a schedule on his desk. He doesn't even look at it, just puts it in his desk drawer.

In July of 1981, we hear that Westinghouse Broadcasting (Group W) and ABC are going to announce their version of a twenty-four-hour news service. Marvin Koslow of Bristol-Myers had been approached about buying advertising, and he let me know about it. It would be called SNC (Satellite News Channel).

For years, Group W believed they owned the twenty-four-hour news format. They had developed it for radio and were the first to be successful at it. Dan Ritchie, Group W's CEO, deeply resented CNN, Ted, and me. He felt we had stolen his birthright. He had been searching for a national news partner for months and was about to join with Metromedia when he discovered that ABC might be interested. Ritchie talked with Herb Granath, ABC's cable boss. They came to an agreement.

Next, Ritchie called Leonard Goldenson, ABC's chairman. For years Ted had picked on ABC, always mispronouncing or misstating Goldenson's name. I don't know if that was the reason, but Goldenson and Ritchie shook hands on a deal immediately.

Ritchie, who had been an investment banker, knew very little about news. He called in the researchers to tell him what to do. The researchers discovered that the cable operators didn't want to pay for news—surprise, surprise. They also told him that cable viewers wanted to see local news. Ritchie came up with a simple plan. Since CNN was charging fifteen cents a month, he would give SNC away free. Since CNN offered no local news time, SNC would offer local stations six minutes per half hour. How the local stations were going to get the money to fill the six minutes does not seem to have occurred to him; neither did the rigid scheduling that would be necessary for his local partners to do their cut-ins.

Dan Ritchie's biggest edge was that Group W owned Teleprompter, then the largest cable owner in the U.S. They had the franchise that covered Manhattan's West Side. Nory LeBrun and I had tried every trick we knew to get Ritchie to put us on that system. Ritchie always said no, and now we knew why.

Even before the SNC formal announcement, Ted reached into his desk, pulled out my old plan, and said, "Do it." It was all the news in thirty minutes—headlines, business, features, sports, weather, and local. Then the cycle would start over. Since Westinghouse was offering SNC for nothing, we had to give away Headline News (then called CNN2). Since SNC was giving cable systems local time, we offered cable systems their own local five-minute news window at the end of each half hour.

I knew that our format would beat theirs, but we had to get on the air first. I called Ted Kavanau in Rome and told him to get back to town. Following the Damascus, Arkansas, battle, I had taken Ted off the desk and was using him as the executive producer on major live stories. He had handled a space shot, he'd handled medfly, a plague of fruit flies that threatened the California citrus crop. Then I sent him to Rome to cover the Naples earthquake and stay on as bureau chief. If we were going to do a headline service, we needed Kavanau. His moment had come.

Headline News was a double-edged sword. It had to be better than SNC, but not good enough to compete with CNN. Headline News was free, CNN cost fifteen cents a month. In order to make sure that cable operators wouldn't drop CNN in favor of Headline, I had to make sure that Headline News was an inferior product. That's when I called Ted Kavanau back from Rome.

Ted was the perfect man to manage Headline. He thought news functioned best when it ran like a railroad: everything on track and on time. He liked a "high story" count, which is a lot of short stories in each half hour. To make things tougher for him, I refused Headline News access to live news stories. That, combined with Kavanau's style, would make

Headline News a highly repetitive service. In television terms, Headline News would have high reach but low ratings, meaning everybody would watch it for a few minutes, but nobody would watch it for very long.

Ted and I discussed staff. Ted asked for CNN's best producers, best writers. I gave him second best. Ted wanted to introduce a crime section, I said sure. It's better for Headline to be a little tabloid.

Then we worked a miracle. Headline News had to launch January 1, 1982. It took us ten months to launch CNN, for Headline we had only five. I'd budgeted $18 million to cover the cost of construction and running the operation for a full year. Of course, that was $18 million that we didn't have, but Ted Turner knew CNN must meet the SNC challenge head-on. He told me he'll find the money. Bevins arranged a loan with GE Capital.

After that, we designed and erected a building, installed a studio, editing rooms, a computer system, a graphics system, and found the anchors, producers, writers, directors, editors, and technical staff to man it. Thanks to the CNN experience, everybody knew what to do. Bunky Helfrich designed the building. Pooch Johnson built it. Gene Wright, by now thoroughly familiar with news' needs, produced the schematics, bought the equipment, installed it, laid the cables, and resisted any Kavanau amendments that would increase costs.

Ted also found the anchors, the writers, the directors, the editors, and the technical staff. I give him loads of credit. With Sam Zelman's help and on a very small budget, he recruited future stars like Pat Harvey and Bobby Batista, along with other serviceable but nonmemorable readers. We had pulled off our miracle.

In December, Ted told me he had saved so much money in his talent budget that he could afford to buy sports anchors who would write their own material and take some of the burden off news writers and anchormen. I felt guilty. I had been deliberately using Ted to create a second-tier news service. I gave him a break and said, go ahead, hire your sports guys. It turned out that Ted hadn't saved any money. So Headline News went on the air already overbudget.

On January 1, 1982, we launched our second twenty-four-hour news service. Again there was a party, but much smaller this time because it was winter and there was no way to fit more than a couple of hundred people into our building. We had hired the Gruccis, America's first family of fireworks, to create a massive pyrotechnical display. And at midnight on December 31, as Headline News went on the air, fireworks lit up the sky over Atlanta, live on CNN.

By May 1982, CNN had an official Nielsen rating of 1.1. We got unofficial ratings for Headline News. Ted Turner told me Headline got a .5. It was CNN two-to-one, the perfect ratio. My strategy had worked.

For fifteen years Headline News consistently performed at half the ratings of CNN. When CNN got a .6, Headline got a .3. Now that CNN is getting a .4, Headline is getting a .2. CNN is still better than Headline, but neither is doing very well.

For the record, SNC launched on July 1, 1982, survived for a couple of years, and sold out to Ted for a pittance. It was a mercy killing.

Round 61: Stockman Goes to the Woodshed

David Stockman, Reagan's budget director, was running off at the mouth. On November 11, 1981, he was quoted in the *Atlantic Monthly* as saying that President Reagan's plan to cut spending and lower taxes had proved to be a fantasy. "We didn't think it all the way through and we didn't add up the numbers." The writer of the piece, William Greider, said that "Reagan's policy makers knew that their plan was wrong . . . but the President went ahead and conveyed the opposite impression to the American public." Greider was claiming the administration said one thing although it knew something else would happen. In other words, it was lying.

Democrats loved the story. They said Stockman had made a "devastating admission" that he, Reagan's budget director, was contradicting his boss's basic economic philosophy.

The next day, ABC announced it was making available a live feed of President Reagan cutting the ribbon of the new ABC bureau in Washington. It was scheduled for noon at the ABC auditorium. ABC employees would attend. Reagan and ABC president Goldenson would say a few words. Since it was a ceremonial occasion, no questions would be permitted. I knew ABC was indulging in self-promotion, but what the hell, it's live, it's free, and it has the president of the United States.

I decided to take the feed. Our noon show, *Take Two,* was coanchored by Don Farmer and Chris Curle. Farmer, who had worked at ABC as Washington's Senate correspondent, introduced the piece. Goldenson presented the president. The president cut the ribbon, said a few words, and as he stepped back, Sam Donaldson (it always pays to bet on Sam) shouted a question. "What are you going to do about David Stockman?" Goldenson seemed appalled; the president was not. He stepped back up to the mike and said: "Sam, when I get back to the White House, I am going to have lunch with David Stockman and I am taking him to the woodshed." The lunch had not been announced. It was not on the AP daybook.

I called the Washington bureau, got Jim Rutledge and told him to set up live in the White House Press Room immediately. I let him know what was going on and insisted we be live before lunch was over. I told the two o'clock news producer to be ready for the live feed.

I figured that our White House reporter would be first with the "woodshedding" story. We did better than that. As part of his punishment, President Reagan sent Stockman himself into the press room (always bet on Ronald Reagan); Stockman moved to the microphone, the press corps waited. It was David in the lion's den, and he was raw meat.

Stockman opened with a brief statement. "I have offered my resignation to the president," he said. The bells rang on the wire machines behind me. "Stockman resigns, Stockman resigns," they bulletin. Stockman continued, "The president has refused my resignation." The wire machine bells ring again, "Kill previous, kill previous." The news world was watching us, the wire services were following our lead.

For more than half an hour, Stockman stood before the White House press corps. He was humble, he was abashed, the press corps, sensing blood, ripped and roared. And it was all live on CNN only.

In the midst of all this, Tony Schwartz, the *New York Times* television critic called me. He said, "You have finally done it, the newsroom's stopped working, they are all watching CNN." He told me we are now "highly acclaimed." The *Times* had not acclaimed us previously. I thought Schwartz would toss us a bouquet in his television column. A few days later, he gave us a mention, no kudos. The *Times* still does not welcome competition.

Round 62: **The Tokyo Blues**

For six months, we had been exchanging news with NHK, the Japanese national network. They gave us Japanese news, we gave them the MGM fire. Everything worked fine. However, despite several invitations, neither Burt Reinhardt nor I had flown to Tokyo to formalize the deal. We had not had tea with the proper NHK executive.

The NHK bosses had no idea how valuable CNN's service had become to the working stiffs in the newsroom, the guys who had to put shows on the air. Their bosses felt disrespected. When my old CBS rival, Bill Small, by then president of NBC News, got there, he made a deal of his own. The NHK executives felt comfortable with him. He sold them on yesterday. He represented NBC, the network of David Sarnoff, the man who had practically invented radio and television. NBC had a long relationship with NHK, NHK and NBC were broadcast royalty; they had no need to deal with upstarts like CNN. By the time Small left Tokyo, NHK had entered into an exclusive news relationship with NBC.

Nobody told us. When a tornado struck in the Pacific, we called our contact at NHK Washington, who had continued to use CNN material, and asked him to arrange a feed for us. NHK Washington said, "Sorry, we cannot deal with you any longer. Tokyo has given NBC exclusive access." I asked Burt what was going on. I said that I thought we had a deal with these guys. Burt called NHK Washington and learned that no deal was final until it had been blessed by drinking tea with the bosses in Tokyo. NHK gave us one break. Since they had failed to inform us of the NBC agreement, they donated the tornado story to us as a parting gift.

I was scheduled to go to China with Chris Curle and Don Farmer, the *Take Two* team, to attempt to arrange a week of live broadcasts direct from Beijing. I tacked another week onto the trip and went to Tokyo to find a new partner.

The Beijing trip proved to be a disaster. Although Farmer and Curle had laid the groundwork with Chinese officials in New York, the diplomats' words carried no weight in Beijing. Red carpets were not rolled out for us. As a matter the fact, we were billeted in a hotel that was carpetless and had practically no hot water. To make it worse, it was winter, and each day was colder and grayer than the day before.

The television people with whom we met were second-rankers. We had wanted to talk to Chinese TV about producing *Take Two* live for five days, two hours per day, from their studio in Beijing. They wanted to talk about CNN carrying Chinese government programming in the United States. Neither of us was interested in the other's proposition. There was no basis for discussion.

I felt defeated. The Chinese either had no knowledge of or no respect for CNN. I flew to Tokyo on the Chinese government airline. I had a scotch, then another scotch, and then I realized that I didn't have to do business with China. Dispensing with CNN was their loss. By the time I arrived in Tokyo, I was in much better spirits.

John Lewis, the CNN bureau chief in Tokyo, had arranged meetings for me with the significant Japanese networks: NHK, TBS, Asahi, and Fuji. Lewis mapped out the terrain. We both knew that our visit to NHK would be a formality. As for TBS (no relation to Ted's Superstation), they had been partnered with CBS for a generation, little chance there. Five percent of Asahi was owned by ABC, so Fuji appeared to be our only realistic option.

Fuji was, at that time, the weakest of the Japanese networks, and it had an undistinguished news department. It is now the second or third largest Japanese network, and it produces successful, if somewhat tabloid-style news shows. Moreover, Lewis told me that his sources inside "Japan Incorporated," the informal cartel that coordinated much of Japanese industry, had determined that Fuji should be CNN's partner.

Lewis had arranged for me to stay at the Okura Hotel. It was five star, Henry Kissinger stayed there, and most importantly from Lewis's point of view, it carried Tokyo cable. As I walked into my room, Lewis turned on the television set and flipped to Tokyo's English language cable channel. Lewis said that from 7 p.m. until midnight the channel carried entertainment programs that it bought from the American networks. From midnight until 7 p.m., it carried English language news in print scrolled down the screen, white words on a black background, no pictures, no sound, with UPI providing the service.

It was 6 p.m. as we stood there, I watched for a few minutes, turned to Lewis and said, "There is no way I'll leave Tokyo until CNN replaces UPI on this channel." I asked Lewis who owned the English language service. "Asahi," he said. We were scheduled to lunch with the Asahi news director on the second day of our meetings. I knew what I had to do.

Then, Lewis and I went out to buy the bottles of scotch that were then obligatory offerings when visiting Japanese clients. We bought a case. We had to present bottles to everyone with whom we met, and we never knew how many people would be at the meetings.

Next day I made my first call, TBS. It was extremely pleasant. The TBS general manager asked about his old friend Bob Wussler, who was now working for Ted Turner at the American TBS. He had known Wussler at CBS, and he reminisced about him. I regarded it as a classy way of reminding me of the TBS/CBS connection, a gentle way of saying "no deal." John Lewis left the appropriate number of bottles of scotch, and we departed.

At noon, we met with Asahi. In addition to its television network, Asahi published *Asahi Shimbun,* the most independent newspaper in Japan. To my mind, the best Japanese journalists were Asahi people. The TV news director with whom we lunched was a newsman who had just missed out on his big chance. He had been promoted to program manager of the network. Then he purchased the Japanese rights to *Dallas* at an unheard-of price. The series bombed in Japan, and now he was back as news director.

I started our conversation by telling him how sorry I was that at the moment it seemed impossible for us to be partners, given ABC's small stake in his company. I expressed my great respect for Asahi journalists and for the independence of their news coverage. Then I threw out the bait. I said that I'd been watching the Asahi English language channel and that, if we were only able to deal with each other, we could replace seventeen hours of silent dull news scroll with seventeen hours of live worldwide news, with sound, and in color, from CNN.

The news director's eyes lit up. His demeanor changed. This was no longer merely a courtesy lunch. Now he began thinking like a businessman. "What would you charge us if we could do it?" he asked. I suggested we would give it to them for nothing if they bought the transponders to carry it from California to Tokyo. I added that they would, of course, have to give us access to all their material.

Two hours after the lunch ended, the news director called John Lewis and asked if I might be free for tea with his old boss, the senior programming executive. I certainly was. Tea was pleasant. The programming executive met me in traditional Japanese dress. He asked intelligent questions, listened very intently, and looked me over very thoroughly. Whatever he was searching for, I passed the test. Would I be free for dinner the next night with the vice chairman of Asahi? Of course. Before that dinner, I had to meet with NHK.

Lewis and I arrived at NHK News headquarters with bottles and bottles of scotch. We were escorted into a conference room on the first floor where a half dozen executives, apparently none of them newsmen, awaited us. The chief executive of the news division did not join the meeting. Since I had not traveled to Tokyo to meet him when we signed the Washington/NHK contract, he would not meet me now.

The executives offered apologies for the breakdown in our previous relationship. They were anxious to find a way to restore it. I suggested it could easily be done: All NHK had to do was agree again to share their material with us. They said that was impossible. They had made their deal with NBC. I asked if NBC might not be prevailed upon to allow NHK to share their news material with CNN. No, they reiterated, NBC will not share. They insist on exclusivity. Instead, they offered us other material, documentaries, feature pieces, access to their library.

I thanked them for their offer but told them that, while I placed great value on the material they offered, CNN had to have access to breaking news. I told them that although I knew CNN and NHK had little chance of reaching an agreement, I had wanted to talk with them in any case, because I valued their advice as to who would be a fitting Japanese partner for CNN. They immediately suggested "Fuji." John Lewis gave me the look. I gave him the nod. We thanked the NHK executives, picked up our bottles of scotch, and walked into the newsroom. We gave the scotch to the working journalists, and set out for my dinner with Asahi.

The Asahi vice chairman took me to an American restaurant. We ate steak—a good sign. He was meeting me on my gustatory turf. I'd learned beforehand from Lewis that the vice chairman had been a Japanese naval officer who, after the war, had worked with MacArthur in establishing postwar Japanese democracy. He recognized that our offer was of obvious value both to Asahi and to CNN. It looked like a win-win proposition. He said he didn't think ABC's 5 percent ownership would be a problem. We shook hands, I felt the deal had been struck. We had toasted it with tea. My meeting with Fuji was merely a postscript.

I flew back to Atlanta and told Ted about the new arrangement. His congratulations were somewhat understated. I got the feeling that he thought deal making was his job and only his job. We started our news exchange with Asahi immediately, but feeding seventeen hours of CNN to Asahi Cable was going to take a lot longer. Japan Inc. got in the way, and I was gone from CNN before it happened.

To this day, Asahi shares offices with CNN in Atlanta, New York, Washington, and London. It is now CNN's largest client and pays CNN $14 million a year.

Throughout the eighties and nineties, *Asahi Shimbun,* in a major break with tradition, published detailed accounts of incompetence and corruption in Japanese industry. Thanks to Asahi, Japan is a somewhat different country now. The Asahi/CNN relationship was one of the last favors I did for Ted Turner. The Asahi/CNN relationship honors both companies.

Round 63: The Hoower in the Sky

As CNN was starting, Solidarity was rising. Poland was moving towards freedom and the Polish revolutionary movement, led by Solidarity, had begun its confrontation with the Communist government in Warsaw. It was Dennis Troute's story. He handled it from Rome.

Troute and his crew were in and out of Poland three or four times in 1980–81. On his first trip, Dennis got the apparatchik tour of Warsaw. When he visited a museum, his Communist Party guide took him to look at the paintings that showed Poles fighting Russians, explaining that he was providing background to current Polish conditions.

Solidarity was making steady progress. Troute interviewed Lech Walesa, a welder from the Danzig shipyards who personified the movement. He was strong, dynamic, and confrontational. He was seeking a better life for Poles.

Troute interviewed Adam Michnik, the intellectual leader and pamphleteer for Solidarity. Michnik said off the record that his branch of Solidarity was seeking the end of Russian domination. We were giving both men more time on American television than they had ever had before.

On his next trip, Troute covered the signing of Solidarity's agreement with the government. After the signing, he slipped away from his minders and went down to southern Poland to interview Solidarity farmers. The farmers supported Solidarity as fervently as the industrial workers. The story went on CNN. CNN was seen in government buildings in Poland. When Troute was leaving Warsaw, the customs officials detained him. In those days, if you were in Poland and you weren't detained by the authorities, you weren't doing your job. They searched him and his baggage, seized his notes, and held him for hours.

Among the documents seized was a copy of the Solidarity government agreement, its last article providing for freedom of the press. Troute mentioned it to the secret policemen in charge. The cop smirked and said, "I know nothing of that." When it was at its best, CNN was teaching secret police all over the world something about freedom of the press.

Troute came back to Washington to become State Department correspondent just as all hell broke loose in Poland. Prime Minister Wojciech Jaruzelski, an army general, declared martial law, but the Russians weren't satisfied and threatened a takeover. Jaruzelski cracked down harder. Jim Miklaszewski, who was in Rome filling in for Troute, tried to get into Poland. When he couldn't do it, he spent two weeks in Vienna searching for another way to cross the border. He couldn't do that either.

Meanwhile, in Atlanta, Sam Zelman had found a correspondent to replace Troute—Tony Collings, a *Newsweek* reporter, with the looks and the voice and more than enough smarts for television journalism. He headed for Rome. That's when we got really lucky. Months before, CNN had applied to the Polish embassy in Rome for a visa. The visa arrived just as the confrontation reached its height. The Polish borders were closed, no Western television was present, and the just-arrived Collings had a piece of paper in his hand that says, "Come on in." It was pure coincidence.

On the appointed day, Collings and Ron Dean, his cameraman, arrive in Warsaw. Behind the Iron Curtain, papers are papers. Nobody questions Collings, nobody stops Dean. They have the proper credentials. For ten days, they cover the story, the only Western crew there. They witness the demonstrations and the confrontations with the police. Truncheons are descending. Dean hunches down in the back of a car, pokes his head up and shoots in short bursts. They get the only pictures. They hear the cops speaking Polish with a Russian accent. They think the "cops" are Russians shipped in especially to deal with the uprising. Collings reports it in his voice-overs and stand-ups.

Since shipment of videotape is not permitted, Ron Dean takes two cassettes, unwinds the tape from the spindles, and drops his pants. He winds the tape around his legs, pulls his pants back up, takes the train to Berlin, goes to the broadcast center, drops his pants, winds the tape back onto spindles very slowly, tightening it after every ten or fifteen feet, puts the tape into the tape machine and feeds the tape to CNN and all of Eurovision. It is the first tape, the only tape, out of Poland.

Dean returns to Poland and continues shooting, often from his hotel room. The still photographer in the next room also shoots from his window: One night, he uses a flash bulb; the cops are up within minutes. Ron has seen the flash. He pulls the tape-switch bit, stashes the tape behind a ceiling tile, and puts fresh tape in his camera. When the cops come, he tells them he hasn't been shooting anything. They don't believe him, and grab the tape in his camera anyway. They get the blank. Dean gets the story out.

Subsequently Dean is cautioned by friends that if he is ever caught and the cops beat him, to scream as loud as he can, as often as he can. It'll make them think they're doing their job well.

After Dean's first run, CNN finds other couriers who wrap Dean's tapes around their legs and take a train or an airplane to London. Some do it for money, some out of patriotism. Still-picture guys and free-lancers working for the other networks also use couriers.

Since no one knows when the couriers will appear, CNN and other networks wait for them at the terminals. The Polish embassy in London sends "watchers" to the terminals. When a courier approaches a man holding up a CNN sign or a CBS sign, the watchers take pictures. Françoise Husson, CNN's London bureau chief, says, "It was quite easy for the embassy to know who was smuggling stuff out." She felt bad about it, but this is the news business, the couriers knew the risk, and we wanted to get the story.

Thanks to Collings, CNN got first, more, and better reports out of Poland. We offered it to my old friends at Eurovision, who carried it on their feed. For most of the week, Europe and the rest of the world were getting their Polish news from CNN, and this was before CNN had become an international service.

All communications between Warsaw and London went by Telex. Our guys were allowed to send one message a day to the West, ostensibly to tell their families how they were doing. Françoise sat next to the Telex. When Collings finished sending, she jumped on to inform him in code whether or not the tapes had turned up. If she said, "Geraldine and Bernie were doing well," the coverage was reaching her.

The crew was concerned with equipment problems. Françoise had a code to tell them all the tapes looked fine. Collings wanted to know if he was appreciated in CNN Atlanta; Françoise had a code to let him know that everybody loved him. Françoise says, "They were working very hard in very dangerous conditions. It was important to them that their work was actually making air. Collings still talks about it, Poland and CNN at the Telex machine, where he is surrounded by censors and bureaucrats and getting messages about his children that really tell him that his stories are on the air and that his camera is working."

When Collings's visa ran out, I told Rome to keep him there. What was the worst that could happen? The Poles could expel him, but we might get a few more days' coverage. Collings, though, had had enough. The day his visa ran out, he left for Rome.

After Tony pulled out, we took our Polish coverage live off Polish TV. Françoise had arranged a satellite feed from Copenhagen, which we used as a listening post for Polish broadcasts. We all believed Copenhagen was a fiction, the material really came from West Germany, but the Germans, concerned about offending Russia, routed the broadcasts to the Danes.

When the Polish army killed Silesean coal miners, it was announced live on Polish television. CNN fed it simultaneously. We had hired a Polish interpreter to translate the broadcasts as they came in. The system was not perfect, the pictures were grainy, the translator's voice was not made for television, but the information was spectacular. No one in the world heard the story before we did. When the miners' deaths were announced, we got phone calls from three wire services asking us to confirm what our translator had said and what they had seen on CNN. That's what CNN was supposed to be all about.

I owe Tony Collings a debt of gratitude. His coverage helped me save CNN's membership in Eurovision. Vittorio Boni had been promoted. He'd left the EBU news group to become head of entertainment. CNN's enemies, the Brits, and the Belgians, were now in charge.

I spoke at an open meeting of the EBU news committee. I romanced them. I reminded them what we had done for them in Poland. I told them how our dauntless crew had resisted the Polish police. I extolled the bravery of the anonymous Poles who wrapped videotape around their legs and smuggled it across the border so that the world might see what was happening in Poland. I informed them that, although they had been unaware of it, most of the tape they had used on their air came from CNN. Then I explained how CNN worked, how we inhaled news from all over the world and then fed it out again. I compared CNN to a giant vacuum cleaner in the sky.

On the simultaneous translation in the background, I thought I heard the word "hoower." After my speech I said to Pat, who was with me, "My God, *they're calling us whores.*" Pat said, "Reese, 'hoower' is Hoover. It's what the Europeans call a vacuum cleaner!"

The EBU renewed our membership.

Round 64: **Air Florida: Favor for Favor**

In January 1982 WRC Washington, a station owned and operated by NBC, had stolen a CNN sports story. I saw Nick Charles, CNN's ace sports reporter, in the middle of WRC's eleven o'clock news. Charles, who had previously worked at WRC, had obtained an exclusive interview with Sugar Ray Leonard, the world welterweight champion. There it was on NBC air. If I called NBC headquarters, David Nuell, the WRC News Director, was toast.

NBC was always wondering where I got my news from, all but accusing me of outright theft. Now its flagship station in Washington had been caught stealing CNN news. But before calling NBC, I talked to Nuell.

Nuell knew New York could fire him. He was scared. He offered CNN access to anything on WRC air if we would forget the Sugar Ray Leonard episode. Our pool battle was being settled. I did not need to score any more points and Nuell was willing to trade all WRC's news coverage for one Nick Charles story. I took the deal.

On January 13, 1982, I called in my marker. Air Florida Flight 90 had taken off from Washington and crashed into the icy waters of the Potomac. It was a terrible but highly visual event, and CNN had no visuals. Ed Turner, still Washington bureau chief, didn't work any harder than he had to. He is a talented, funny writer, he is a great shmoozer, but when it came to covering a news story, Ed couldn't find his ass with both hands.

Dan Brewster, CNN's congressional reporter, got to the scene immediately, but Ed Turner could not get a crew there. It was 5 p.m., and everybody in America was on the way home, listening to the story on the car radio, and expecting to see pictures on the seven o'clock news. If we had the story CNN would be first because we did news at 6 p.m. I called the Washington desk and asked when they would have a live shot. They didn't know. I asked when they expected tape. They didn't expect tape. I asked, "What is WRC showing?" "The crash," they said. "Live?" I asked. "Live," they said. "Good pictures?" I asked. "Great pictures," they said.

I called Dave Nuell. I got a machine. I left a message. "I'm taking the crash. You will see it on CNN." Nick Charles's wife had been a WRC technician. She contacted her old friends in the control room, got the satellite address and the transponder number. She gave the numbers to me. I called our satellite desk. Within seconds, WRC's picture was on CNN.

For the rest of the night, we looked as good as everybody else, and after eight o'clock we looked better. By then, the networks had stopped showing the crash scene in favor of their entertainment schedules. CNN stayed with the story throughout the search-lit night. Shortly thereafter, Nuell left WRC to join *Entertainment Tonight* and our deal ended. It was too bad. I had looked forward to using WRC as a contributing station indefinitely. Trading Sugar Ray Leonard for Air Florida was a no-brainer.

The Washington bureau under Ed Turner was breaking down. Karen Sugrue, the executive producer, says, "Ed was never in the bureau and never gained its confidence or respect." State Department correspondent Dennis Troute quit because he felt, "Ed was backstabbing me and then lying about it."

Dan Brewster took the hardest line. Brewster was young when he arrived at CNN, but he'd worked at ABC, and he abided by certain rules. Early on, he'd gotten us a "scoop" by being the first to report that the Ted Kennedys were about to announce their divorce. He calls it "a legitimate one-line story, and I had it before anyone else, and I was live in front of the Capitol announcing it."

Ed assigned Brewster to do a follow-up story on the ups and downs of the Kennedy marriage, going into detail. Brewster refused. Ed called him into the bureau and said, according to Brewster, "'No reporter ever refuses an assignment.' I said that I understood that those were the rules, but I respectfully, strongly disagree. Later, Ed yells at me from across the entire newsroom, 'How was our gentleman journalist today?' I yelled back across the newsroom, 'Ed, you are the only person I know who considers the word gentleman to be pejorative.'"

Later, after I left CNN, Ed tried to get his revenge. Brewster had been awarded a Nieman fellowship at Harvard. There were certain conditions attached. CNN would have to make up any difference between his salary and the Nieman grant and would have to guarantee him a job when his fellowship was over. Turner refused. Dan threatened to sue.

Turner caved. Brewster never returned to CNN. He's now the CEO of Bertelsmann's U.S. magazine empire.

Ed Turner also had a hard time around women. He said things he shouldn't, and they came back to haunt him. His appraisal of Katie Couric's bosom got him in more trouble than he'd reckoned on.

Ed was working as Burt's vice president when Katie came to see him about becoming a correspondent. He was sitting at the head of a conference table, surrounded by a number of other people. He greeted Katie with something to the effect of, "Come on in here Katie and let me look at those beautiful boobs." Katie felt humiliated but mostly angry at herself because she just stood there and took it.

Many years later, Jane Fonda was appearing on the *Today Show*. On the air, Katie told Fonda the Ed Turner story. Later, during a commercial break, Katie said, "Jane, I've always wondered how I should have handled it because I felt there should be some retribution for what Ed did to humiliate me. I just don't know what to do." Jane said, "Don't worry, you just did it."

It was some time after that that Ed Turner finally left CNN. He spent a year, with WETA backing, trying to launch a local political talk channel in Washington. It never got off the ground. Now, along with Ted Kavanau and Bob Guccione Jr. he is trying to launch a twenty-four-hour California news channel out of Sacramento. It's a very good idea, but most such ventures lose more than $30 million before they break even. I hope Guccione has the money. Turner is also working with Peter Arnett on his own book about CNN. I think everybody should read it.

Round 65: "I'll Mortgage the House"

Headline News was a long-term necessity. In 1982 it was a financial disaster.

Ted could barely afford the $25 million a year it was costing us to run CNN. Now, we had a million dollars a month more to pay for Headline.

Even worse, we had no satellite transponder for it. Warner Brothers had a spare. Ted and Bob Wussler made a deal. Warner would lend us their transponder for a year or two. In return, Ted gave them the exclusive rights to sell advertising on CNN and Headline News (then CNN2). Ted was the world's greatest salesman, and now he couldn't even sell his own product.

Warner owned cable services like MTV and Nickelodeon. Their ad salesmen seemed to concentrate on Warner's own services, and our sales lagged. The Warner salesmen were delivering only 65 percent of their projected revenue. Now we had less money coming in and more money going out. It was a recipe bound to fail. Eighteen months later, Ted found another transponder and cancelled the deal, but by then I was gone.

Turner, Bill Bevins, and Paul Beckham spent most of the next three years looking for money to meet the next week's payroll. They got the Turner Field food concessionaire to pay Turner their 1981 season fees in advance (at a substantial discount), and for a month we ran CNN on hot dog money. Cable operators led by Cox Broadcasting paid their subscriber fees in advance, taking a 10 percent discount; CNN survived for a couple more months.

Five years earlier, when Ted had run out of money for his television station in Charlotte, he went "PBS," that is, he begged on the air. He personally pleaded with his viewers to contribute their dollars to keep the station alive. It worked. The station received hundreds of thousands of dollars. Later, when the station turned profitable, Ted repaid every donor he could locate. Now, Ted considers using the "PBS" strategy for CNN. Looking back I think that at that moment CNN had so many dedicated viewers it would have worked, but Bill Bevins had another solution.

Bevins arranged to raise funds through a public offering with Drexel Burnham, Robinson, Humphrey as the underwriters. Ted went along reluctantly, and then changed his mind. He didn't want to sell more stock in his company, and he had no intention of diluting his 80 percent interest in TBS. But the offering was already on the market.

The Securities and Exchange Commission requires that there be a "quiet period" about a company from the day it places a public offering until the day it is completed. During the quiet period, the company and its underwriters keep their mouths shut because they are legally responsible for the truth of every statement made by corporate officers. This means that if somebody talks too much and what he says proves to be false, anybody who bought the stock can at least get his money back and probably add damages to that. In addition to the company, the underwriters are also liable for any false statements because they have underwritten the offer's accuracy.

Ted wanted to appear on the Sandi Freeman show. He was well aware of what "quiet period" means, and he wanted to lie a little bit about TBS's prospects on the air. Ordinarily, Ted's appearance would be an attractive offer. It almost guaranteed a small boost in the ratings. But now, Bevins was panicked. He knew what Ted wanted to do. He told Ted, Sandi, and her producer what they should not talk about, but no one believed Ted would follow instructions. He is a loose cannon. I didn't think I wanted want him on the Freeman show, but there was no need for my intervention.

Ted was invited to appear on the *Phil Donahue Show,* where he could be a loose cannon before a larger audience. He didn't disappoint. On the Donahue show, he announced that CNN would make a profit the next year. This was not a realistic statement. The underwriters would not underwrite it. They withdrew the offering. Ted kept his 80 percent of the company. Now Bevins had no money, ergo, neither did I, and Ted decided not to go on CNN with a tin cup. It was all up to Bill Bevins.

We also had to pay off the First Chicago loan. Bevins made a deal with Citicorp. They lent us money against assets. We were able to make our bank payments, but Bevins and Beckham still continued their search for operating money.

Payroll checks began to arrive late. Pat paid the rent for some of the kids in Atlanta. In New York, when the checks didn't arrive, Mary Alice went to her savings account and cut checks for her kids who were living on $7,500 a year. In Los Angeles, the staff just waited. Sooner or later, everybody got paid.

Ted has never understood what "no money" means. In the midst of the Falklands War, we were beating up on the opposition, our ratings were rising steadily. The Falklands was a naval conflict, and Ted, a wannabe admiral if there ever was one, loved it. He walked into my office and asked, "Can we do more?" "Sure," I said. "What?" asked he. "Charter a boat and sail it right into the middle of the war," said I. Ted loved it. "What will it cost?" he asked. "A million dollars." "Do it," he said. "Bevins says we have no money." "Tell Bevins I'll mortgage the house," said Ted.

I called David Nicholas at ITN, who was outfitting a barge berthed in Southeast Brazil to sail into the war zone. We were going to have a helicopter fly from the barge and get footage of the British Fleet and any action in the south Atlantic. I told David that CNN would go halfies with him.

Then I walked down the hall and told Bevins to put a million dollars aside for the Falklands War. "Where are we gonna get the money?" asked Bevins. "Ted says he'll mortgage the house," said I. Bevins replied, "The house is already mortgaged."

The barge owner in Brazil said the mission was too dangerous and backed out. I was spared further embarrassment.

Round 66: "If They're Stealing It, Why Don't We Sell It to Them?"

Ted Turner found treasure in old TV sitcoms, in old Hollywood movies. He was uniquely able to find new uses for other people's products. Early in 1982, Ted drilled into CNN and struck oil.

CNN's news coverage had been erected upon a base of agreements with "corresponding stations." They covered their areas for CNN, we gave them exclusive access to CNN material for use on their news. All they had to do was watch CNN, record it on tape, turn it around, and it became part of their 6 or 11 p.m. news shows.

Our corresponding stations complained to Burt Reinhardt that other stations in their markets were pirating CNN material. CNN stories had proved so valuable, the other guys were stealing it. Our corresponding stations were killing their competition. The competition could not live with that.

First, we had to end the piracy. We put a "bug," the CNN logo, on the screen. The bug stayed up throughout the video, protecting our copyright and our partner stations. Ted Turner loved it. He strolled into my office and said, "Why don't we keep that bug up all the time? It will let them know what they're watching." Brilliant, thought I. The bug stayed up forever.

Nineteen years ago, the bug might have seemed a little pushy. Now, every network on the air puts up its bug, even CBS, ABC, NBC. CNN was the first one to do it, it was Ted's idea, and now in a world of seventy-five or a hundred channels, it's standard practice.

Ted saw the local station piracy as a business opportunity, and he took advantage of it. If they wanted CNN stuff so badly, let's sell it to them. Insights like this are the genius of Ted Turner.

When Turner hired a sales staff to peddle CNN, Burt Reinhardt, Jane Maxwell, and I were troubled. The CNN–correspondent station relationship worked. We were getting the best material from the number one news stations in markets all over the country.

I had originally started out making agreements with WCVB Boston, WFAA Dallas, and KLAS Las Vegas, every one the news powerhouse in its city. Then we added the Tribune stations, New York, Chicago, and L.A. When Jane Maxwell came on board we put her in charge of local station relationships, and she added another twenty before we went on the air.

As CNN developed, more and more stations wanted access to our material. Jane, who had begged in the beginning, who had cried in frustration as she got turndown after turndown, was being sought out. We had turned the game around; the stations were coming after us.

Now Ted was taking advantage of our desirability; he sent his salesmen into the field. They were asking everybody to pay for CNN, even the original corresponding stations. Salesmen are salesmen, they just wanted to bring in the money. They weren't concerned about the station's news product.

Maxwell and I had promised exclusivity to the stations. We had told them that it was to be a free exchange. Now, when our service had become a smashing success, we were walking on the deal.

Burt recognized we had been getting outstanding news coverage from our stations. He was afraid they might drop us, in which case

CNN would get weaker news material from the weaker stations who were willing to pay the money.

We were wrong. Ted's plan worked perfectly. Our stations didn't drop us. New stations wanted to join. In the beginning, we offered our original stations lower rates and gave them exclusive access to live events. Over the years, that's all gone by the boards. The corresponding stations pay the same as everyone else, all material is available to everyone, and the stations even give CNN the right to sell some minutes of their commercial time. The product is called News Source, and it's one of CNN's most profitable divisions.

From Ted's point of view, News Source was an easy decision. He hadn't given his word to anybody, and he's never been particularly grateful for past favors. As a businessman, he reached the conclusion that CNN must sell its material on a nonexclusive basis. Every local station needed a CNN type service to compete in its market. If we didn't sell it to them, somebody else would. As Ted said when we started Headline News, "It's better to be your own competition."

CNN, which had revolutionized cable, was now about to do the same for broadcasting. For twenty-five years, broadcast networks had provided their local affiliates with news feeds, but the feeds were strictly limited. They did not contain the top stories of the day. These stories were saved for the network national shows that followed the local news programs. The networks were afraid that if local news showed national stories, the audience wouldn't stick around for their programs; their own stations would scoop them.

The advent of CNN News Source broke the network news triopoly. Stations that bought CNN News Source got breaking news stories from all over the world, all through the day. Local stations could scoop the networks with CNN material.

The three networks had to compete. They began feeding selected bits of national stories to their affiliates even if the stories were going to be told on the network shows later. The boundaries broke down. It was hard to tell network from local so the networks became more feature-oriented. If they could no longer be first with the hard news, they would develop softer stories, featurish or sidebar, stories journalists call "back of the book."

Local stations were quick to take commercial advantage of the material now available. Local news expanded from half an hour to an hour, from an hour to an hour and a half, or even two hours. It became the most important source of revenue for local stations. Ratings became more important, local stations became more tabloid, and network news got softer and softer.

There's been a lot of talk about a "CNN effect" upon governmental policy making. I think CNN's major impact has been on television, and sometimes I think it's all bad. Local's gone tabloid, network's gone soft, and nobody watches CNN. That's a hell of a legacy.

Round 67: **El Salvador**

Miklaszewski was the living proof of CNN. From day one until the day I left, he was unstoppable. El Salvador was his greatest triumph. I sent him down in February 1982 to relieve Mike Boettcher. Eighteen years later, Mik considers it the best time he ever had in the news business.

The CNN crew initially consisted of Mik and a freelance cameraman from Miami named Howard Dorff. They taught their two Salvadoran drivers how to carry a tape deck and point a microphone. It was the four of them against the other networks, who each had at minimum of two correspondents and three or four crews and producers. Unless there was a specific event they had to cover on a given day, Mik's routine was to get up early and tour the countryside, finding the news.

Mik remembers, "After we kicked everyone's ass on a number of stories, the producers of the other three networks, ABC, NBC, and CBS invited me to breakfast one day. They asked me what my connections were in El Salvador, and they also asked if I ever got any 'rockets.' I said, what's a rocket? They were flabbergasted because I didn't even know what a rocket was."

A rocket, in fact, is a blast from headquarters telling producers and correspondents in the field that someone is beating the hell out of them. In El Salvador, the network guys keep getting them because Mik was beating the hell out of them. Mik's advantage was that he was able to go out into the field at 7 a.m. and find his own stories, while the other guys had to wait until after the New York 10 a.m. news meetings so New York could tell them what the stories were.

Mik understood CNN's place in the news universe. We were not going to follow the *New York Times* front page, we were going to *make* the *New York Times* front page. CNN was going to find reporters like Mik who knew what a story was and let them go off on their own. Jeanee Von Essen, our foreign editor, told Mik, "Look, we know you're outgunned. We know you're not going to be able to cover everything. Just do what you can and don't miss the big ones."

"As a reporter," Mik says, "that gives you a tremendous amount of freedom and flexibility because then you don't feel like you have to play cover-your-ass all the time. So you could go out and do what you are hired to do."

One day Mik and his men headed out towards eastern Salvador. The U.S. embassy, as was customary, had been complaining about "negative reporting." They had told Mik there was a bridge under construction that had been destroyed by guerillas. The locals were reconstructing it with the help of nonmilitary U.S. engineers. "We essentially went out there to do sort of a 'good news' story—U.S./Salvador cooperation."

The ground rules in El Salvador were that the U.S. military personnel were there only as "trainers," not even as "advisors." In the wake of Vietnam, Washington was afraid of U.S. involvement in another no-win conflict. The military were instructed not to leave their bases and never to go out into the countryside armed with lethal long weapons, although they were permitted to carry their own side arms for self-protection.

"Lo and behold," Mik recalls, "as we are standing at the bridge interviewing some Salvadorans, we see walking in the distance a man who was clearly American. He was in jeans and a sort of khaki color T-shirt, carrying an M16, and over the next five or ten minutes, we caught glimpses of him and more of these guys. They saw us and they quickly disappeared. They made sure that they were out of sight of our cameras. So we never did get a picture of them."

At that point, as the team was trying to shoot more pictures, word went out that the Americans didn't want them there. The crew of engineers working on the bridge sent Mik and company off to command headquarters about an hours' drive down the road to get permission. They got it from the local commandant and went back, thinking they'd missed their chance.

"We were sitting at the side of the road," Mik says, "actually at a stand off the roadway under a growth of trees, having a piece of watermelon, when these guys started marching down the road like ducks in a row. We hop back into our van, chase them; take their pictures for a while. They tried to avoid us so we followed them through a house . . . they went through somebody's house and burst through the door and went out the back."

The CNN team finally caught up with them again and tried to ask them questions. They refused to answer. As they were throwing their weapons in the back of the truck, one of them said, "Let's get the hell out of here." Mik asked if they were Americans and if they were military and the guy only repeated, "Let's get the hell out of here."

It was very late, and the thing that stuck out most in Mik's mind was that it was a Thursday, and he had to get the story out that night for the following day, before it lost some of its impact over the weekend. Mik relied on Jeanee Von Essen—who would automatically book satellite time for him everyday unless he called her to cancel it. So they knew that when they got to AT&T, they would have satellite time.

That night, they went straight to AT&T in El Salvador. It was an hour to two hour drive. They got there just in time, fed the tape, and did a track live over the satellite. Mik had done a stand-up. They fed all they had and got it on that evening.

"When we were in the field," recalls Mik, "we usually tried to strike up some kind of symbiotic relationship with one of the newspaper guys or still photographers, since it was impossible to cover the whole country with only four people. So when we went back to the hotel, I sought out Ray Bonner of the *New York Times*. He was out. I did find Chris Dickey of the *Washington Post*. He came into the room, looked at the video, and the next day it was the lead story of the *Post* . . . Friday morning."

The *Post* gave CNN a front page headline and a front page picture taken right off the television set. CNN got story and photo credit. Mik asked Jim Clancy, who was in the New York bureau that night, to call the

New York Times and give them a heads up. Clancy called the *Times*, got an editor on the phone and said, "CNN has got pictures of these American troops out in the field, armed with long guns in violation of U.S. rules of engagement in El Salvador."

The editor at the *Times* asked Clancy, "How do you know they are American troops?" Clancy said, "Because Jim Miklaszewski says they are." That wasn't enough for the *New York Times*. The *Times* said thanks and ignored the story. "That's the *Times*," shrugs Mik. "If they don't see it, it didn't happen."

When the *Washington Post* hit the street on Friday, there was political hell to pay. Congress was indignant, the president was embarrassed. The White House did not yet receive CNN. CNN White House correspondent, Bob Berkowitz, had to take a tape of the story into the White House, into the West Wing, and play it for them. Back in El Salvador, the embassy was catching holy hell from Washington. Mik says, "One of the U.S. embassy personnel came up to me the next day and said, 'Well, you think that is such a great story, I called my brother in Virginia to ask if he had seen it and my brother told me he doesn't even know what CNN is.' I looked at him and said, 'I don't care. The president of the United States knows what CNN is.'"

Once again Mik's pictures were giving the lie to official statements. That was the power of CNN, a world where portable cameras and satellites were making it difficult to conduct covert operations, secret wars.

On Saturday, the *New York Times* finally paid attention to Mik's story, two days after it had appeared on CNN, one day after it appeared in the *Washington Post*. By then, President Reagan was ordering an investigation into why "five American soldiers in El Salvador apparently violated United States policy by carrying M16 rifles in what may have been a combat zone."

The second paragraph read: "A video tape broadcast Thursday by the Cable News Network, shows several men identified by the camera crew as Americans in civilian clothes carrying M-16 rifles and .45 caliber pistols. . . . The video tape raises two key questions, whether the Americans were in a combat area . . . and whether they were soldiers sent into El Salvador in addition to the 49 military trainers already there."

The *Times* ran the story on page one, column one. I can't recall the paper running another CNN-based action story on its front page in the subsequent eighteen years—maybe Baghdad, but they had other sources there. For one day at least, we didn't have to pick up a story from the *New York Times,* they had to play catch-up with us.

The next day the colonel caught carrying an M16 rifle on Mik's tape was ordered to leave the country by the U.S. ambassador. Two other officers received oral reprimands. Before the week was over, the Reagan administration was taking another look at the regulations. Within a month, the U.S. had stepped up military aid to El Salvador, and the regulations were relaxed. This illustrates the power of the press. The press discovers the government is doing something wrong, the government then changes the rules and turns something wrong into appropriate procedure. It is the law of unintended consequences.

Miklaszewski was so hot that Roone Arledge gave up on his own people, and sent one more rocket. He assigned an ABC camera crew to do nothing but follow Mik around. Roone got lucky, because the next day Mik found José Napoleón Duarte, the president of El Salvador, and he wasn't even looking for him.

The presidential palace had been refusing interviews to the entire press corps. Way out in the countryside, Mik saw two Huey helicopters flying over his head very low, and said, "Lets go see who that is." It was Duarte. He had come to give a speech to the people in this small town. Mik interviewed Duarte and got him to talk about the upcoming presidential election. Roone's crew was there and picked up the interview, but they had to use Mik on camera; he was asking the questions.

The three networks' producers in El Salvador went crazy. They thought Mik had some terrific "in" with the government. Actually, he was just outhustling everybody. In those early days, that's what we did. We gave our reporters freedom in the field. We gave the bureau chiefs freedom in their cities. They got us the stories.

Mik remembers, "Jeanee von Essen's rule: you keep sending us stories, we will keep sending you money."

Round 68: **Falklands: Oh, What a Glorious War**

Mik's final triumph occurred in Buenos Aires during the Falklands War. Our coverage was a victory parade from beginning to end. Mik, and more particularly his wife, thought it was time for Mik to come in from the cold. After the Falklands, he was assigned to the White House. Two years later he went to NBC, first covering the Department of Defense, and then becoming White House correspondent, two of the least creative beats in television. Thus fell the best field reporter I've ever worked with.

Michael Grade, the British television genius, who was then at MGM and later ran Channel 4 in England, congratulated CNN in the *New York Times* and the London *Times*. British broadcasters, he said, could do worse than come to America and watch the coverage of the Falkland Islands crisis: "Not on conventional network news bulletins, where there is the familiar spectacle of hastily edited recorded speeches, short-hand headlines and abruptly truncated studio interviews. . . . No. The news revolution is happening on Cable News Network, a twenty-four hour, seven-day dedicated international news service. . . .

"With the flick of a switch, we are taken from press conferences at the United Nations in New York, to statements being made in Buenos Aires, to the Houses of Parliament. All live, unedited, and not recycled at a time more convenient for the program planners."

The war could not have been more convenient if I had designed it myself. London is five hours ahead of New York, so that by the time we went on at 6 a.m., there were next-day developments. Even Buenos Aires was a half hour ahead of New York time, so that early morning reports almost always had new information.

Richard Blystone was reporting from 10 Downing Street; Miklas-zewski and Dennis Troute were in Buenos Aires. Most importantly, my personal relationship with David Nicholas (later Sir David Nicholas), the CEO and managing editor of Independent Television News, enabled us to take their 1 p.m. and 10 p.m. news programs live onto our air.

Our best moment was 5 p.m. on a weekend afternoon in Atlanta. I had talked to the producer, and the first seven minutes of the ITN 10 p.m. bulletin *News at Ten* would tell the Falklands' story. The Argentines are reporting that the British flagship, the aircraft carrier HMS *Hermes* is hit, smoke is pouring from her, and she may be sinking. The ITN bulletin led with a live phone report from Mike Nicholson aboard the *Hermes*. Nicholson said the Hermes had not been hit, was not damaged, and was not on fire. Bells ring behind me, AP now bulletins: "ITN reports (no credit to CNN of course) that there is no fire aboard the *Hermes*. She has not been hit." It may have been ITN's story, but CNN delivered it to the rest of the world.

There was one hitch. When the seven-minute ITN report was over and we switched back to Atlanta, CNN opened its 5 p.m. news with our report about the *Hermes*. Reading from the previously prepared script, the anchor said something like, "Argentine naval sources report that the aircraft carrier *Hermes* has been hit and is reported to be sinking in the South Atlantic." We had scooped ourselves. The audience knew more about the story than our anchors did.

Mik went down to Argentina to replace the redoubtable Mike Boettcher, as had been the case in El Salvador. Boettcher had been competing with the big three networks in the field and in behind-the-scenes bidding for video. The Argentine military had barred journalists from Patagonia, the part of Argentina that faced the Falklands. Some of the more enterprising Argentine generals had set up their own video news service. They taped their side of the war and put the pictures up for auction. The big three were buying everything. There was no way CNN could compete, so Boettcher made his own arrangements.

The generals had to dub a copy of the material for the network that bought it. Mike's fixer was a friend of the engineer who made the dub. We paid the engineer $100 a tape, and he made an extra dub for us. We picked up the story before the network did, and since we were a twenty-four-hour network, Boettcher got his dub on the air before the network that bought it. He remembers, "When the Argentine submarine *Santa Fe* went aground, NBC paid an Argentine general almost $30,000 for it. CNN went direct to the dubber." For $100, Mike had it on the air six hours before NBC.

Boettcher also had to deal with the pool. They didn't want CNN to cover anything for them, which was fine by us because CNN had only two crews. Mike agreed to buy the beer and keep it cold. That was CNN's pool contribution.

Then Mike had to go home because of a family emergency, and Mik replaced him. He ran unfettered throughout the Falklands crisis— going wherever the story took him, whether Atlanta sent him there or not. Mik's cameraman in Buenos Aires, John Towriss, was one of the video journalists who had started their careers at CNN. He and Mik were constantly out in the streets toward the end of the war when it was clear that the Argentine military government was about to fall.

Needless to say, the Argentine generals were in a lousy mood. Armored cars were enforcing a curfew, driving everyone indoors. "We had pretty well finished our story," Mik says. "But John decided he wanted one more picture. So he stood there as one of the armored cars went right by us. The trooper in the turret leveled off with a shotgun and blasted right at him. Fortunately, the trooper was firing rubber bullets, but he was so close that the bullets penetrated John's jacket. The gun exploded right into our camera, and John and Joe Halderman [our producer/soundman] tried to run."

But they were running in the same direction as the armored car was rolling. John continued to roll tape, and the troopers kept shooting, over and over and over at the two of them. Finally, they turned around and ran back. They tore through some alleyways and made it to a thoroughfare where a very reluctant cab driver took $50 to drive them back to the hotel. He didn't want to get involved, because John and Joe were bleeding.

They got back to the hotel safely. Even as we edited the picture, Towriss was lying on the floor of the hotel room, and the house doctor was picking rubber bullets out of his skin. When they were finished, John looked up and said, "How's the videotape?"

"It was pretty powerful stuff," Mik recalls. "Here was a guy, wounded and shooting at the same time. He was screaming, 'I'm hit, I'm hit, I'm bleeding,' and there were sirens and gunfire, it really was some of the most dramatic video I'd ever seen. The other network cameramen came in to congratulate Towriss, and they all asked for copies of the tape. Just for their personal collections. Nobody else used it on the air."

Mik helped us in another area. Thanks to him and to Chris Chase, we were finally able to get *Freeman Reports* right—at least for a while. Chris was filling in for Sandi. Each night she talked to Mik by satellite. His reports were short, no more than five or ten minutes, but viewers were learning what it was like to be a journalist in Buenos Aires, even while they were learning what the journalist had seen. On *Freeman Reports* as hosted by Chris, Mik was delivering the color piece live to the audience, just after he filed the news piece. We had both sides covered before the morning papers.

By the time Towriss returned to Atlanta, I was gone, and Burt Reinhardt was running the company. Towriss had left Atlanta in May. In Buenos Aires, May is like November. John bought a new heavy jacket for $225. It was destroyed by the rubber bullets. Towriss put it on his expense account.

Burt Reinhardt claimed that the new, post-Reese CNN policy did not cover the cost of apparel. He said, just put it in as something else, make it a few extra dinners, some taxi rides. Towriss is a Mormon. He refused to lie, so he never got paid for his jacket. But the accounting department gave him a break. They let him pay it off a few dollars a week. John was making $8,000 a year at the time.

As I look back, I see Poland, Falklands, and El Salvador as all of a piece. It was the very beginning of 1982. For a year and a half, CNN had been walking. By January 1, 1982, we were running. On every one of those big stories, CNN was not just first, we looked different from, better than, any other network. When the Poles struck against Solidarity, only CNN had an American correspondent reporting and was the only news operation to get the tape out.

In El Salvador, CNN alone forced the *New York Times* to report a story on page one, column one, crediting us because they had missed it. CNN alone provoked a presidential investigation of military activities. And of course, CNN was the first news out of El Salvador every day. While the networks debated around their conference tables, Miklaszewski fed tape.

In the Falklands, we could use Michael Grade as our reference. We could use the Associated Press watching us and bulletining their thousands of subscribers all over the world. Or we could just remember Mik and John Towriss standing up to the Argentine armored cars, taking their bullets and firing back with their cameras.

In 1981, CNN's ratings were still unofficial, but we knew we were averaging a .7. By January of 1982, we were in the Nielsen books. Now, officially measured, we did better than a full rating point for the next six months. Good reporting on good news stories gets viewers. Period.

Round 69: **Labor Pains**

In the winter of 1981, Ted Kavanau asked me if I objected to his hiring a technician for Headline News whose father was a lawyer for Group W, the company that was launching Satellite News Channel. The tech's father was an old friend of Ted's. I asked Ted, "Will she make trouble?" Ted doubted it, he knew her father, but if he was clasping an asp to his chest, he wanted to make sure that I had approved it. I knew Ted valued loyalty above all other virtues. If Ted felt good about her, it was okay with me.

As it turned out, she was indeed an asp, maybe a cobra. Within a month, she began to organize a union. Ted was driving his people hard to get Headline News up to speed, but even he deserved a better fate than suffering her bite.

The people Ted hired for Headline News hadn't grown up in the CNN system. They didn't understand its benefits. All they knew was that it was a lot of work, and Ted was yelling at them all the time. Ted's whole life had been spent driving people hard. For him it was the ultimate test. He was the perennial drill sergeant. He believed training had to be tough. If they couldn't survive basic training, he didn't want them under his command. If they could survive Ted's basic training, they would believe they could survive anything.

Our asp picked up two adherents at Headline News and one at CNN itself. He, a Snopes type, was loyal to no one, had sucked up to everyone, and had never gotten a promotion. He felt that his talents were underappreciated. Her two adherents at Headline News were, like her, recent hires. They were fairly knowledgeable about television procedures, and therefore had little to learn at Headline. Thus was formed the "Gang of Four." Since Headline's launch, they had roamed the corridors of CNN, proselytizing, getting signatures on a petition sufficient to qualify for a National Labor Relations Board (NLRB) vote. The Gang of Four had gotten the support of the National Association of Broadcast Electricians and Technicians (NABET), and the NLRB ordered an election. Posters went up, literature was handed out, NABET professional organizers appeared, and the vote was on.

I wasn't overly concerned. Pat and I had kept in touch with the people who worked for us. We knew their sentiments. The staff we'd hired believed in CNN; they were committed to us. Bill Bevins was worried, he had to be. Potential lenders might be scared off if CNN had to pay union wages. Jim Kitchell, still at TBS and still the perennial doubter, was telling Ted and Bevins that his CNN sources said the union would win.

Predictably, Ted Turner panicked. He brought in a new TBS vice president for personnel and called meeting after meeting about strategies and procedures: What were the rules? What was CNN permitted to say to its employees? What was forbidden? None of it had to do with the kids themselves nor how they really felt.

On the studio floor, the battle grew vicious. The Gang of Four was everywhere, campaigning, complaining, bitching, and promising. My local Snopes was a technical director. He sat, skinny, mustached, hook-nosed, hanging over the switcher. He was so angry that every time he pushed a button, I thought he would take CNN off the air. The union organizers were more professional. They told the CNN kids how much money NABET members were making in New York doing the same jobs our kids did.

Pat was on the floor with the kids every day, talking to them. She had been a brilliant editor at CBS, a major network, a highly unionized network. Four documentaries she had edited won Peabodys. The kids respected her as a professional. They loved her as a person. Pat's best argument was "opportunity." Most of the kids had come to CNN to find out how to make television and then to discover what kind of television they'd like to make. Pat knew that unionization would end that opportunity. Pat could say honestly, and she did, that they were better off trusting CNN.

The day before the election, the lapels of Pat's kids, seventy of them, had blossomed with "Vote No" buttons. They were made by her people, distributed by her people, and worn by her people. They had trusted Pat, and now Pat trusted them. She told me we would win easily.

The next day, the NLRB set up a polling place. The kids streamed through filling out and depositing paper ballots. There were poll watchers from both sides. Out of nowhere appeared Jim Kitchell with his wife, Mary Jane. He was puffed up and wearing his best suit. She was prettified and wearing hers, along with a pillbox hat. He was glad-handing around the room. Jim is about six feet tall and must've weighed 230 pounds, packed and solid. He looked like a ward heeler checking the count. If we had lost the election, it would have proved to Ted that I had lost control of the people who worked for me. Jim would've gotten my job. Mary Jane was already auditioning for first lady.

Just before the polls closed, Ted's secretary, Dee Woods, said Ted wanted to talk to me right after the vote came in. Finally the polls did close. The NLRB counted ballots behind closed doors. Pat and I stood outside, next to Jim and Mary Jane. Jim seemed to be rooting for the union. When the vote came in, he was disappointed. CNN voted non-union 156 to 53. Our last memory is of Mary Jane turning on her heels, wagging her indignant ass and striding for the exit, Jim, lumbering behind her. I was surprised the building didn't shake.

I called Turner. "We won big," I said and gave him the numbers. He says now that he was delighted, but you couldn't tell it from the phone call. He used to call me partner. He didn't call me partner this time. I don't remember the word "congratulations." Even at the time, I wondered about Ted's disappointment; maybe he was looking for an excuse to fire me and unionization would've been it.

As for the Gang of Four, the asp and her two Headline News buddies left almost immediately for short-lived jobs at Satellite News Channel. The Snopes character was still at CNN, last I heard.

Round 70: **Friends**

I have just seen *Almost Famous*, Cameron Crowe's film memoir about his early career as a rock journalist for *Rolling Stone*. Lester Bangs, Crowe's mentor, warns the fifteen-year-old about the perils of journalistic friendship: "You're gonna have friends like crazy, but they'll be *fake friends*. . . . They'll buy you drinks, you'll meet girls . . . they'll try to fly you places for free . . . offer you drugs . . . I know. It sounds great.

But *they are not your friends.* These are people who want you to write sanctimonious stories about the genius of rock stars." Despite the warning, Crowe comes to believe they are his friends until he learns better later.

Even worse than believing they're your friends is writing about them like a friend. Doing them favors, plugging their pet projects, hiding their sins, or writing something for them because they're going to do something for you.

Ted Turner made instant friends. When a guy did him a favor, he wanted to do one back. When a major cable operator agreed to put CNN on his systems, Ted figured that was worth half an hour on *Pinnacle;* if the cable industry was in a battle with broadcasters, Ted wanted CNN to lobby for the cable industry. Since TBS was listed on Nasdaq, Ted wanted Nasdaq quotes on CNN, in addition to NYSE and AMEX (he was ten years ahead on that one). If Ted had a friend who was just a little kooky on the environment but spoke for his point of view, he wanted to give her a half-hour show. To all those things I said no.

I believed the journalistic establishment was lying in wait to brand CNN as a Hearstian enterprise spouting the whimsy of an erratic proprietor. I wanted no part of it. I knew they did the same kind of things themselves, but they were the big guys. They had their reputations made. We were trying to make ours, and I was being careful.

Bob Berkowitz, one of our White House reporters, told me that he had an exclusive: Frank Farenkopf was about to be dismissed as G.O.P. chairman. Farenkopf had spent over a million dollars of the party's money on billboards and TV ads meant to help Tom Kean become governor of New Jersey. The ads had never once mentioned Kean by name, and Kean had barely squeaked through.

"Who told you Farenkopf's gone?" I asked. Berkowitz had a new friend, a G.O.P. apparatchik who turned up at Berkowitz's door one night with a squash racquet under his arm. They became squash buddies. Berkowitz's new friend had given him the scoop. He wanted to go on the air right away.

I told Berkowitz I'd check it out. I called Rodger Bodman, Kean's chief of staff. Bodman laughed when I told him Berkowitz's story. The party money is "soft money," he said, and soft money is issue money. You cannot mention the candidate's name when you use soft money.

"Hard money." "Soft money." It was brand new in 1981. I didn't know the distinction, and neither did Berkowitz, but we should have. What Farenkopf did was right. I killed the story. Berkowitz's "friend" had planted it, because he wanted Farenkopf's job.

Years before I had asked John Corporon, then news director at WPIX, later chairman of the Associated Press Broadcasting Board, how to handle "friends" and "enemies." "Reward your friends, and give your enemies justice," Corporon had advised. It's good advice, provided you make no "friends," but there's another question: How do you treat the enemies of your "friends"?

I live across the street from the ABC studios in New York. One night in 1990, as I was coming home, I heard an ABC producer saying that *20/20* had just set up an interview with Baseball Commissioner Fay Vincent. It was a Barbara Walters piece, and she was going to hang Vincent out to dry.

In 1990, George Steinbrenner was out of baseball. Fay Vincent had investigated him, convicted him, and exiled him. George wanted to get even. He had prepared a counterattack against baseball and Vincent, and he had picked Barbara Walters to return the message.

Steinbrenner charged that the commissioner had investigated only him. There were lots of other bad guys, but baseball had ignored them. He claimed selective prosecution, did his own investigation, and came up with a list of suspects that included his nemesis, Yankee outfielder Dave Winfield (who denied the charges), other ballplayers, and a couple of Mafia figures. Steinbrenner was looking to plant his findings with some friendly journalists, and Walters was particularly friendly.

Walters and Steinbrenner had met in Cuba. She was there for a Fidel interview. George was secretly trying to arrange a game between the Yankees and a Cuban all-star team. Barbara's crew caught George at the Havana ballpark. George asked Barbara to kill the story. Barbara made sure it got on the air, and after that they were friends; George always respected someone who stood up to him.

They became an item in the gossip pages. They walked around New York together to see who was recognized by more people. She drank with George and his buddies at his East Side hangouts. But according to Dick Schaap's book *Steinbrenner!*, Barbara maintains they were "just good friends," and what's more, Schaap believes her. She defines their friendship as "an insult relationship." One way or the other, George and Barbara are "friends."

The ABC producer, who was talking in front of my house, mentioned the Walters/Steinbrenner relationship and said that Barbara was doing the piece to help her old friend. Both *Sports Illustrated* and *20/20* would treat George with kid gloves. To appear fair, they would speak to both sides, but Fay Vincent was in for the iron fist.

As I walked through the lobby of my building, I shook my head. When I got to my apartment, I called a man who knew Vincent pretty well. I suggested that he call Fay and give him a heads up. For a month, I didn't hear anymore about it.

In October, *Sports Illustrated* ran 5,900 words about George Steinbrenner's investigation of the baseball investigation. The story was so thin it was transparent, hearsay upon hearsay, elliptic quotes taken out of context, and thinly drawn inferences. The headline read: "BAD JOB BASEBALL . . . the commissioner [Fay Vincent] and his men ignored a mountain of evidence suggesting wrongdoing by others in the game."

SI admits that Steinbrenner got what he deserved but wants to know why baseball didn't look into gambling charges against Dave Winfield and others cited in Steinbrenner's investigation. Maybe because the accusations stem from Howard Spira, the man Steinbrenner had paid $40,000 in part to dig up dirt on Winfield. Spira, who had worked for Winfield's foundation as a gofer and hung out in the Yankee clubhouse, was an in-hock gambler with knee breakers after him.

Steinbrenner's investigation amounts to so and so "was an avid horse player," so and so "used to call me in my house and discuss football games with me," and so and so's chauffeur, who occasionally drove Winfield, too, "served several months in prison in 1974 for bookmaking." On that sort of evidence, based on the word of a two-bit extortionist, *SI* is demanding a full-scale investigation of gambling in baseball? Give me a break.

The *SI* article tells us what happened to the *20/20* piece. Fay Vincent refused the Barbara Walters interview. Don Thrasher, the *20/20* producer, told *SI* that when he confronted Richard Levin, baseball's PR man, and demanded an explanation, Levin's reply, according to *SI*, was an unofficial "You can go **** yourself."

ABC never ran Walters's story on Vincent. A spokeswoman for the network told *SI* the piece had been killed because it was not fully substantiated. *SI* discovered that Fay Vincent had called Barbara's boss, ABC president Daniel Burke. Did that have anything to do with the piece's being shelved? The spokeswoman said it had "no influence" on ABC's decision.

I bet it didn't.

ABC news people suggested to *SI* that ABC/ESPN's $400 million contract with Major League Baseball might have had something to do with the network's decision. I don't want to believe that, either. I want to believe that Dan Burke had better editorial judgment than anybody else in this smarmy story and didn't think that Barbara Walters should do what some might call a hatchet job on behalf of her "just good friend."

Of course, Burke might well have been a very good friend of Fay Vincent's, and Burke was one of the three people at ABC who had more clout than Barbara Walters.

Steinbrenner got his revenge without Walters's help. In 1992, baseball's owners fired Vincent. Ted Turner had promised Fay his undying support. At the baseball owners meeting, Ted voted against him.

Vincent survived. As a friend and adviser to Gerry Levin, Fay sits on the board of Time Warner right alongside Ted Turner. Time Warner owns *Sport Illustrated,* and had Gerry Levin's good friend Fay been sitting on the board of Time Warner back in 1990, I'll give any odds you want that *Sports Illustrated* wouldn't have run its story.

Barbara Walters survived too. Hell, she flourished. Well over seventy, she signed a $60 million, five-year contract with ABC. It's the biggest television contract ever given to anybody over seventy. Who says women over forty-five can't get a job on television?

At CNN in 1982, "friends" were not my problem. It was enemies I had to worry about so I turned my attention to Sandi Freeman, our would-be Barbara.

Round 71: **Caught in the Crossfire**

By 1982, it was clear that Sandi Freeman would not be a star on CNN. The ten o'clock show, *Freeman Reports,* was supposed to be live conversation with a guest and the call-in audience about the news of the day. She wanted a softer show, where she conversed with celebrities, booked days in advance. She was uncomfortable not knowing who her guest would be until the afternoon of the program.

Through a connection of mine, CNN was offered an interview with Jimmy Stewart, who was what is known in TV booking circles as a "very hard get." I thought that Sandi would jump at the chance. Stewart almost never sat for interviews; anything he said might make news. The interview was to be shot on tape, so that if real news broke, we could hold it.

Sandi and her producer flew out to Hollywood for the interview. For that night she had previously booked Orianna Fallaci, an Italian journalist who was then at the height of her fame. Now, Sandi couldn't do the Fallaci interview. Mary Alice Williams came down from New York to interview Fallaci.

As Mary Alice was coming down, Freeman's producer got on the phone and cancelled Fallaci. That was Sandi: Never give a potential rival an even break. Mary Alice had to scrounge up her own interview. I don't remember who she got, but she did fine; Freeman lost more points.

Sandi simply didn't "get" the rules of journalism. She made mistakes. When she interviewed Atlanta mayor Maynard Jackson, Jackson accused a former Atlanta police officer of corruption. The problem was, the officer had never been convicted. Sandi didn't pick up on that.

The ex-cop protested. I explained that the Freeman show was live, we had no idea what Jackson was going to say, and Sandi would set the record straight on her next program. She did. He accepted the solution.

Some of Sandi's shows were repeated on the weekend. Of course, I told her not to repeat that show. Of course she agreed, and of course the show was repeated anyway. The cop called again; now we were in trouble. Repeating Jackson's statements showed "reckless disregard for the truth." That's libel. So I invited the policeman to be a guest on the Freeman show.

He made his case on air for a few minutes, and he went away happy. National television exposure heals a multitude of wounds.

When our lawyers wanted to see the documents about the airing and re-airing of the program, Sandi's booker could not produce them. I was not surprised.

In my book, Sandi's days were numbered.

My first choice to succeed her was Tom Snyder, who was in the process of leaving NBC and therefore available. Sam Zelman suggested Orson Welles. Sam knew Welles; he would set up a meeting. Oh boy. Welles had credentials. He was a man of politics as well as of the theater. He'd been a journalist. He'd had a column in *P.M.*, a short-lived liberal New York newspaper, and in the early forties he'd regularly appeared on radio to debate conservatives. If I'd only thought of it, *Crossfire* should have been the Buchanan-Welles show. Would they ever have been worthy opponents.

We flew to California and met with Welles at Ma Maison. Ma Maison was Spago before Spago was Spago. Welles owned table six. We talked and talked. He was glib and wise, he was kind and caustic, and he knew everything about everything that had been in the papers that day. It goes without saying that he had style, but I'm saying it anyway.

There were only a couple of problems: CNN was a low-rent operation, and Orson Welles was not a low-rent guy. We also knew Welles was the walking, talking definition of "difficult." I envisioned him with by a twenty-two-year-old floor manager, being cued by a twenty-six-year-old ex-local TV station director. "Camera three, Mr. Welles," the floor manager might say.

"To hell with that," Mr. Welles might answer. "Dolly in on one, dissolve to two, and get the audience on camera three." The studio would have been more interesting than the show.

It was all moot. Would Mr. Welles move to Atlanta? Rush Limbaugh would move to Moscow first. For once I did not kid myself. Mr. Welles was not CNN material.

Then we went after Tom Snyder. Snyder's problem was his very Hollywood agent who played by Hollywood rules—which meant, play the game as if your client was unavailable whether he was unavailable or not. Keep shopping him to people who don't want him, avoid people who wanted him, rarely return phone calls, and keep potential buyers waiting. After a series of phone calls and one meeting, I got tired of waiting.

I called Stan Berk, my Washington talent scout, and asked what he knew about Pat Buchanan and Tom Braden. Braden and Buchanan were doing a highly successful call-in radio show on a local Washington station. WTOP, the *Washington Post* television station, had tried them at 11:30 p.m. They sat in the WTOP newsroom in shirtsleeves, collars unbuttoned, ties down, and talked about the news. The show did not work for broadcasting. The ratings were too low. For cable those ratings would do fine.

During the first two years at CNN, reading viewer mail, I had come to the conclusion there was no such thing as "objectivity." Viewer prejudices were so great that one set of eyes might see a story as Zionist propaganda, and somebody else might call it an Arab handout. I wanted to create a news program where the journalists admitted their biases going in. I wanted to put one guest between the journalists, and let the journalists battle over him as if he were a bone caught between two dogs.

I explained to Berk the program I intended to do, the show that would become *Crossfire*. Berk thought Buchanan and Braden might work, particularly in another time slot.

It was getting close to the end of Sandi's contract. I met with Buchanan. Within thirty seconds, I knew he was a television star. I also knew he was perfect for the new ten o'clock show. I suggested that Dan Schorr might make a better foil for him than Tom Braden did. Buchanan said it was the team or nobody. I signed the team to a contract for the ten o'clock program, a full hour, out of our Washington bureau. I was paying them $75,000 a year each.

When it came to matchmaking, Buchanan was probably better than I was. By 1982, liberals were on the run, at least on television. Battles between conventional liberals and Reagan conservatives seemed one-sided on the tube. It was like throwing lambs to wolves.

The battle for the soul of the Republican party seemed more interesting. It was still undecided, and *Crossfire* could help determine the winner. In one corner, the boxer, Tom Braden, a Rockefeller Republican, a former CIA executive, representing the best of the old Eastern establishment. And in the other corner, the slugger, Pat Buchanan, speechwriter, ideologist representing the new coalition, the West and the South. It was suave Republican versus raw Republican, with the winner in doubt. It made for great television.

Braden and Buchanan were going to admit upfront that they were not objective. I wrote, "On the left there is Tom Braden. On the right, Pat Buchanan. And tonight in the Crossfire is our guest . . ." I didn't name the show *Crossfire*. Paul Bissonette, the CNN PR man, now general manager of WPIX New York, gets credit for that.

Each night's show was designed to have just one guest. He or she was to present his or her point of view. Buchanan and Braden would try to win the guest over to their side of the argument. Fair fights are fine, but two against one is more interesting. The public would act as the referee. This was an hour show. There was plenty of time for phone calls, and I hoped that if the fight became one-sided, the public would call in to help the downtrodden—or the producer would choose calls in favor of the guest who was getting beaten up. I thought *Crossfire* would become CNN's equivalent of an op-ed page.

Back in Atlanta I told Ted I'd filled the ten o'clock slot. He didn't say much at the time. Two days later, he came into my office and asked me why I had hired "those turkeys." I told him that I was designing a new show around them, that they were first-rate on the air, and that Sandi Freeman wasn't in their league. Ted kept referring to them as "Reese's turkeys."

Two weeks later Ted and I were in L.A. for a cable convention. Ted invited me to dinner with Tom Snyder and/or his agent. Bob Wussler, Ted's number two at TBS, would be with us. It figured. Wussler had dealt with Snyder's agent since his days at CBS. I assumed he had set up the meeting. Desultory is not a word I ordinarily use, but I know no other to describe that meeting. It seemed pointless. I had already signed Braden and Buchanan. Ted never came out and asked if Snyder wanted the job, but it was clear that Ted saw no potential in Pat Buchanan and Tom Braden.

Whatever Ted's opinion might be, I felt my 10 p.m. problem was solved. *Crossfire* may not have been the hard news, newsmaker-of-the-day call-in program that I had wanted when planning CNN, but it was a helluva lot better than chatting with second-string talk show personalities. I felt pretty good about it. Then I got our first ratings book, the network was doing good, and Sandi's show was limp. I fired Sandi, felt better, and decided to take a vacation.

Round 72: **Ted Fires Me**

I'd gone to Martinique carrying CNN's first rating book. According to Nielsen, we had delivered a 1.1 rating for May. Two years before, we had promised our advertisers a 1 rating. We had overdelivered. We were heroes.

I lay on the beach, and once in a while sneaked a look at the beautiful data I was toting around. CNN's hard news was beating the *Today Show* and the *CBS Morning News* because the audience wanted hard news in the morning. We also had a very strong lead-in. We'd invented 6 a.m. television news, everybody else started an hour later. The early risers tuned in to CNN at six and stayed with us through the morning. Moreover, good reviews, raves, were beginning to trickle in. Within two years, CNN had become a major force in the news business.

With success came another problem. Ted Turner is the kind of guy who, once somebody does a difficult thing, thinks anybody, especially he himself, could have done it.

In the beginning Ted and I had been partners. I ran the editorial side; he ran the business side. He was the best partner a man could have. He left me alone, and I got the chance to do things the way I wanted them done. Ted was probably the only man in the world who would have given me the freedom I needed to put the pieces together. From ITNA I knew what was needed, and I knew how to get it. I knew the people to hire, the machines to buy, and the deals to make. And Ted let me have my way.

When CNN first went on the air, I spent a lot of money. I knew we had to get out there with a bang. When we were up and running, people were watching us and liking us; I wanted to cut back to meet budget.

Ted called me from Newport, roaring "It's too good. Don't cut back, I'll find the money." Boy, how I loved him in those days.

The best thing may have been that TBS didn't have a news department. If I had gone to any other network or even a local station group, there would've been guys in the news department jealous as hell and looking for ways to knife CNN at every opportunity. With Turner, I was building from nothing. There were no noses to go out of joint.

Ted gave me enormous editorial backing. He never came in and complained about a story, he never worried about displeasing advertisers. Sometimes he wanted me to put people on the air, but when I said no, he may have sulked, but he didn't resist. When CNN was launched, my wife, Pat, congratulated him. He said, "What are you congratulating me for? This is Reese's thing." By the second year, I was seeing signs that Ted wanted to make it his thing.

He hadn't seemed overjoyed when we won the unionization vote. He was beginning to feel that he knew talent better than I did. He thought Braden and Buchanan were turkeys. I was sure *Crossfire* was a major hit. We'd had that Hollywood dinner at which Ted was sniffing around talent. We weren't agreeing much about anything. Moreover, Bill Bevins was telling Ted we were running out of money, and Ted was saying spend more, spend more. I knew something would have to give.

Three years earlier we had agreed that I would be in charge of format, content, and personnel. He was to run advertising, affiliate relations, and finance. We shook on the deal, but never put it in writing. An oral contract ain't no contract at all.

When I returned from Martinique on Sunday, May 16, my phone rang. It was Ted Turner, calling me at home. He asked me to come down to his office right away. If I had been working for anyone else, given the Nielsen ratings I would've expected a moment of congratulations, shared glory, but Ted Turner did not like to share glory. Given Ted's signs of resentment, I was not optimistic.

I had not renewed Sandi Freeman. Another B-level anchor had demanded a large raise. I dropped her, too. They were both represented by the same agent, a man who later married Sandi. I knew he was whispering into Ted's ear. Ted listened. The agent said I hadn't been fair to his clients, that I was tough on all the talent. Ted listened. He was hearing what he wanted to. Any network president who believes what an agent says about his clients is a fool, but Ted owned the network. If he wanted to believe an agent, nobody was going to fire him for foolishness.

On the afternoon of May 16, I was sitting in my office with Burt Reinhardt, across the hall from Ted, waiting to discover whether I would be lionized or lion's meat.

I don't remember a lot about that meeting. I know I went in alone. I know Ted was as ill at ease as I was—and at least as nervous. We were both standing up. "We're going to make some changes, Reese," he said brusquely. "I've renewed Sandi Freeman and Marcia. They're going to report directly to me and Wussler. You can stay on till the end of your contract, and we'll find you an office."

I was numb. In a situation like that, you don't start bleeding till a week later when you realize what's happened. Ted said I was driving people too hard, and the talent hated me. It didn't really matter what he said, he didn't know what he was talking about.

I told him that Kathleen Sullivan's contract gave her the prime-time slot. If he was going to put his new star Marcia in prime time, Kathleen could walk. Ted shrugged it off. I knew ABC was anxious to get Kathleen. I kept my mouth shut. I just said Kathleen is better, she is as close to a star as CNN has, and you'll lose her. Ted said the other anchor was better.

There was no way I would work for a man with that kind of judgment; he wasn't even a semipro. Maybe I was just saying that to myself to make myself feel better, I don't know. I left Ted, walked back to Burt. "The son of a bitch fired me," I said. Then I filled him in on the details.

A couple of days later, Ted came back and offered me a three-year consultancy, no noncompete, and I could walk at any time. All I would have to do was be available for once-a-week CNN meetings. In July, Ted offered me the job back and said he'd hold the offer open for six months.

Many people tried to bring about a reconciliation between us. A couple of board members asked Pat what percentage of the company would it take to bring me back. Without consulting me Pat said 51 percent. I would've settled for less.

Ted had a long-term girlfriend, pretty and tenderhearted. She did her best to keep me around. "Reese," she said, "I kiss up to Ted, Bunky [Ted's architect and the man who designed the open newsroom that the rest of the world now uses] kisses up to Ted, can't you kiss up just a little bit?" The fact is I couldn't. Not about news. I know this sounds pretentious, but news is sacred to me, and I don't fuck around with it. Ted always had that sign on his desk, "Lead, Follow, or Get Out of the Way." Ted wasn't going to let me lead, I wasn't going to follow him, so I got out of the way.

I don't want to make too much of all this. From day one I knew what I was getting into. When I signed my contract, I told Ted I wanted money "and a lot of stock, because we're not going to last more than a couple of years together. You're gonna get in my way, or I'm gonna get in your way." Ted had shrugged. Thank God I got a lot of stock options.

Ten years later, Ted said he fired me because, "he [Reese] was making all the decisions, and most of the journalistic decisions, and really trying to do too much, rather than do the kind of delegating needed." But my decisions were working. We had a 1 rating. It's a strange time to be fired, right in the middle of a winning streak.

Ted and I were gamblers. He had bet on me, and we had won. There were a dozen men I could have been working for who might have resented my independence, but would have kept me around so long as I was a winner. Ted was different—he fired me right at the moment of our triumph. Maybe he figured our horse was so far ahead, he could be the jockey. Remember, he once named himself manager of the Braves.

Eighteen years later, CNN is CNN, one of the world's top brands, the world's number one news source. Occasionally, I remember that I had something to do with it, but to the world, it's Ted's accomplishment. Nobody remembers me except Bob Wright, the president of NBC. Whenever he gives a press conference, it's, "I was there in Atlanta when Ted Turner and Reese Schonfeld created CNN—."

Round 73: **Scorecard**

The closest thing I had to a long-range plan at the beginning of CNN was "stunt of the month."

Joseph Pulitzer and William Randolph Hearst knew that there would be occasional slow moments in news flow. They were always looking for stunts: the poor little paperboy who dives into the roaring river to rescue the drowning daughter of a millionaire; the little old lady practically a saint, who is separated from her ailing daughter by forty miles of snow; and the brave and handsome sled master who will risk death to bring her to her daughter's bedside. Pulitzer and Hearst put their names on balloons that might or might not succeed in flying from Tuscaloosa to Timbuktu, when necessary they promoted hostilities, and pushed the U.S. into war with Spain. When they needed news, they made news.

I was not willing to go that far, but I wanted one story every month that got other people to cover us. Some stories we created. At other times when big events brought millions of viewers, we had to do something so special that other media would be forced to report on us as part of their story. Sometimes it worked, and sometimes it didn't.

Once I sent Peter Arnett to Belfast with an alleged expert on Irish terrorism who lectured at Columbia University to chronicle seven days behind-the-scenes with the IRA. What I didn't know was that the expert's girlfriend was opening an art exhibit in Dublin that week; he just wanted to get there on our money. When we arrived, he offered to send Arnett to a street corner where he would guarantee a bomb would explode. That was nothing we wanted to know, let alone shoot. As for pictures of the IRA behind the scenes, we didn't have a chance. I wasted a lot of money.

On another occasion, we did an hour with Georgi Arbatov, the official spokesman to the U.S. for the Russian governments preceding Gorbachev. He was here for a series of cross-country speaking engagements, blustering and placating at the same time, a gun in one hand, a dove in the other. Arbatov was supposed to appear on the *MacNeil/Lehrer News Hour* one Monday night, but his visa expired on Sunday. The State Department refused to extend it. We could use him on Friday.

Gail Evans, then a booker, now executive VP of CNN, found him for me. We put him on the air with Bill Zimmerman, Stu Loory, and Dosko Doder as a panel. It was a terrific show. Arbatov was pleading for Reagan to end the arms buildup. When he finished, we all knew that the Russians couldn't keep up. As he left, he turned to me and said, "So Reese, what will you tell my good friend, Alexander Haig? I know, tell him you live in a free country. Ha, ha, ha," and he left for the airport.

Later on, Loory anchored *Moscow Live,* a short-lived one-hour, Saturday morning conversations between Stu and second-ranking Russian officials. We knew important people would show up only if they wanted to deliver a message. We also knew that Loory could ask tough questions about their message, so we wouldn't be smothered in propaganda. Ed Turner killed the series shortly after I left. It must have broken Ted's heart.

When Ted visited Fidel, that was a stunt. When *Take Two* broadcast live from Havana, that was a stunt. Every time Jean Carper did a story, it seemed to be in the *Washington Post* the next week.

The stunts themselves, month by month, offer a pretty clear snapshot of what CNN was doing over the course of our first two years. This was the period when CNN had to prove that it could live up to Ted Turner's hopes and Reese Schonfeld's promises. If we hadn't done our job in 1980–1982, you wouldn't be watching CNN now.

1980
June:
Mike Boettcher is standing on Key West waiting for Fidel Castro's Marielitos. They show up. CNN put them on live. The three other networks flew down to cover our story.
CNN earns an A+.   No Nielsen ratings available.

July:
Jean Carper plays Erin Brockovich. Covers cancer epidemic in Galveston. Dow Chemical goes crazy. The *Washington Post* covers our story.
CNN gets an A.   No Nielsen ratings available.

Bernie Shaw and Sandy Kenyon give us a moment of glory at the Republican convention, the rest was a jumble.
CNN gets a D+.   No Nielsen ratings available.

August:
Joe Pennington discovers that Jimmy Carter is offering to pay ransom for the Iranian hostages. Little press pickup.
CNN gets an A.   No Nielsen ratings available.

The Democratic convention. Our coverage was a little better.
CNN gets a C.   No Nielsen ratings available.

September:
Jim Miklaszewski forces the entire country to watch CNN when a Titan missile dropped nuclear debris over the Arkansas landscape. Press everywhere.

CNN gets an A+.   No Nielsen ratings available.

October:
The Great Debate. We inject John Anderson into the Carter/Reagan confrontation; almost every paper in America covers us. It is a technical fiasco. Loads of press coverage, not all of it good.

CNN gets an A for imagina-
tion, an F for execution.   No Nielsen ratings available.

November:
Election Day. Results late, studio confusion.

CNN gets a D.   No Nielsen ratings available.

Jane Maxwell beats the world on the MGM Grand hotel fire, *live.* Japan-wide press coverage.

CNN gets an A+.   No Nielsen ratings available.

December:
Mary Alice Williams live at John Lennon's assassination.

CNN gets a B+.   No Nielsen ratings available.

1981

January:
Hostages released in the midst of the Reagan inauguration. We're faster, better, more complete than the broadcast networks. Much press coverage.

CNN gets an A+.   No Nielsen ratings available.

February:
Bernie is remarkably correct when Reagan is shot. Cissy Baker gets everybody to the right place at the right time. We lose a point because the pool material is late. Otherwise, we're the best. We're mentioned in the press.

CNN gets an A–.

Jane Maxwell gets us five hours of Frank Sinatra testifying live to get a Las Vegas gaming license. Senators throng the gallery to watch the proceedings.

CNN gets an A.   No Nielsen ratings available.

March:
Washington sends troops to El Salvador. We anticipate and cover. The real war starts later.

CNN gets an Incomplete.   No Nielsen ratings available.

April:
Bill Zimmerman and company do everything right at the *Columbia* space shuttle launch. They get features the other guys don't have and they have more fun.

CNN gets a B+.   CNN gets a .6 unofficial Nielsen rating.

May:
The Pope is shot, we're first on the air. Mik gets another exclusive.

CNN gets a B+.   CNN gets a .6 unofficial Nielsen rating.

June:
Zimmerman and Schorr to the Mideast to cover the Israel/Lebanon war. The war doesn't happen until next year.

CNN gets an F.   No Nielsen ratings available.

July:
Kathleen Sullivan steals the royal wedding. Exclusive interview with Nancy Reagan. Sullivan interview gets press.

CNN gets an A.   CNN gets a .5 unofficial Nielsen rating.

August:
Jim Clancy does an unflattering hour on televangelism. At the time it's daring.

CNN gets an A.   No Nielsen ratings available.

September:
Clancy does a half hour on the business of journalism. *Newsweek* has said we are drowning in a sea of red ink. We tell the world their magazine, *Inside Sports,* is going broke. They close down; we do not.

CNN gets an A.   CNN gets a .7 unofficial Nielsen rating.

October:

Mary Alice and company swarm all over the Brink's truck murders, the last gasp of the sixties revolutionaries. We are late, but catch up. CNN gets a B–.

Sadat killed. We're not there. The pool saves us. Then Zimmerman, Françoise Husson, and company do a great job on the funeral.
CNN gets a C+.   CNN gets a .7 unofficial Nielsen rating.

November:

David Stockman goes off the reservation on the budget. Ronald Reagan takes him to the woodshed. We're the only ones there.
CNN gets an A+.   CNN gets a .7 unofficial Nielsen rating.

December:

Freeman interviews Julian Bond and Bob Jones, Jr. in the CNN studio. They're so angry at each other, they refuse to get in the same room with each other for the Koppel show a week later. We're first and we're better. We get local press coverage.
CNN gets an A.   No Nielsen rating available.

1982

January:

Tony Collings gets into Poland when nobody else does. Ron Dean smuggles the pictures out and they're carried worldwide.
CNN gets an A.

Air Florida crash. Ed Turner misses. WRC bails us out. Brewster stay live till late.
CNN gets a B.   CNN gets a 1.1 Nielsen rating.

February:

Mik makes the front page of the *New York Times* when he catches American soldiers out of position in El Salvador. The world picks up the story.
CNN gets an A+.   CNN gets a .9 Nielsen rating.

March:

GRIDS is an epidemic. Thanks to Tami Weine and Jean Carper we are first. We know more about it than anybody. French TV comes in, uses our material and credits us.
CNN gets an A.   CNN gets a 1 Nielsen rating.

April:
Argentina seizes the Falklands. Dennis Troute and Boettcher are in Buenos Aires. Richard Blystone is in London. We're on the air earlier than anyone else. We do cross-Atlantic colloquy. We get some press.
CNN gets an A.   CNN gets a .9 Nielsen rating.

May:
Britain grabs the Falklands back. Mik is on the scene. John Towriss takes a lot of rubber bullets. Mik talks to Chris Chase at ten Eastern every night. It is the CNN I dreamed of.
CNN gets an A+.   CNN gets a 1.1 Nielsen rating.

It was a helluva two years. Then I get fired. What the hell, you can't win them all.

Round 74: **Burt's CNN**

I stayed around CNN till the end of May, cleaning up loose ends. That was when Bissonette named the Braden and Buchanan show *Crossfire*. Tench Coxe, who was the TBS lead lawyer, called to tell me that Ted had informed Braden and Buchanan that he wasn't going to put *Crossfire* on the air; he would pay them off, but they weren't going to be on CNN. Braden and Buchanan were prepared to sue. Tench asked me if I had committed to putting the show in prime time. Yes, I said. Had I promised them a full hour? Yes, I said. He asked me to stand by for a deposition.

Ted Turner and I still talked occasionally. He asked me who I thought should run CNN. I told him Burt Reinhardt. He mentioned that both Bob Wussler and Jim Kitchell were gunning for the job. I snorted. Just two more old network guys who loved to spend money. Ted said he really didn't know Burt Reinhardt that well, but he knew Ed Turner. He asked me what I thought about bringing Ed down to be Burt's number two.

I thought that was a terrific idea. I knew that with Burt around, CNN would never get too bad, and with Ed Turner around, CNN would never get too good.

I had always been afraid of what Ted would do if he ever learned the real power of journalism. From day one, I'd been careful not to teach him too much. I knew that Ed Turner couldn't teach him anything. And Burt Reinhardt's strength was coverage, not editorial. There were a lot of people who would have been very dangerous sitting around running CNN, but Burt Reinhardt and Ed Turner were not among them.

In the meantime, I spent my last days helping my friends—the people I knew Ed Turner didn't like. When I signed Dan Schorr to a three-year contract, his agent, Richard Liebner, asked me to backdate it so it Dan could get a raise earlier. I let him know Ed Turner would fire Schorr the first chance he got. We dated the contract July 1. Ed Turner fired Schorr three years later.

Bill Zimmerman, best all-around newsman we had, was another guy sure to be fired, cause he was smarter than Ed. I gave him three years, too. By the time they fired him, I was running Channel 12 Long Island, and he got ten good years up there.

Faced with the *Crossfire* lawsuit, Ted—who was now running the CNN schedule—compromised with Buchanan and Braden. He gave them one half hour and put them on at 11:30 p.m. *Crossfire* was too hot for 11:30. The ratings were too good. Ted shipped them to 7 p.m., killing the early evening sports show. Buchanan and Braden did fine. They became the number one show on CNN.

The sports department did not fare as well. Until then, we had been running well ahead of ESPN. Now, with no competition from 7 to 8 p.m., ESPN captured the early sports audience, kept them through the night and became the first stop for dedicated sports viewers. In 1982 CNN had two-thirds of the sports audience at 11 p.m., now it has one-third.

From a bottom-line point of view, the new schedule was crazy. Turner had retained Freeman, given her a raise, retained her handpicked production staff, and let her broadcast regularly out of New York. Every time she used the New York studio, it cost CNN thousands of dollars in overtime. But no one besides Burt knew what the New York contract said about overtime, and Sandi didn't report to Burt. She reported to Ted and Wussler.

Turner was also paying Buchanan and Braden and their production staff on the basis of a one-hour program, but they were only on the air for half an hour. The sports department didn't fire anybody, although they had lost half their time on the air. CNN was paying for twenty-five hours of programming a day. Ted always found money for projects he wanted to do, and even Bevins couldn't cut him back.

At my first Turner-CNN news meeting, we had to decide what to do about Kathleen Sullivan. When she lost one prime-time hour, her agent, Jim Griffin, said we had breached her contract, and she could go to ABC. Jim said unless we gave her the full two hours, she was going north. At the meeting, Ted asked for opinions all around. Ted Kavanau knew television. He told Ted, "She's our star, she's the best we have. Keep her." Burt came down on the other side. Burt believed that "news" was the star. "We don't need her," he said. Ed Turner waffled as usual.

Ted turned to me. I said, "We had this discussion three weeks ago. I told you then that we should keep her, that she was better than Marcia. You said Marcia was better than Kathleen. If I was right, you keep her; if you were right, you let her go." Ted let her go. I thought I was doing Kathleen a favor.

I came to a few more meetings, but the other news guys, at least Burt Reinhardt and Ted Kavanau, seemed uncomfortable with me in the room. Ted Turner would make news pronouncements and they would nod, but behind Ted's back everyone but Burt would roll his eyes. I kind of liked watching it. I wasn't working there. I was just consulting. After a while, they stopped inviting me to the meetings, which continued for many years.

At one of them, years later, Tom Johnson suffered the Afghanistan embarrassment. CBS had sent Dan Rather, wrapped in bedouin headdress, into Afghanistan. The press called him "Gunga Dan." CBS got great publicity. Turner wanted to know if Tom had sent a reporter into Afghanistan. Tom said it was too dangerous. Turner went falsetto. "It's too dangerous, it's too dangerous for you, Tom." Tom said we're getting coverage from WTN. Ted was still falsetto: "It's too dangerous for us, but not for them, they can go there." Tom was squirming. "Do we send our reporters in?" asked Ted. Once again Tom talked about putting the reporters' lives in danger. Ted said, "That's what we pay them for." This time, no falsetto.

Sales staff were at the meeting, affiliate relations were there, PR was there. When the meeting was over, everyone knew Ted owned Tom's balls.

One of the problems with working for a Ted Turner is that he will let you make the decisions 98 percent of the time. He'll interfere on only 2 percent. But, since you don't know which 2 percent, you run scared all the time. Scared newsmen do not produce bold news.

In April 1982, I'd sent Stuart Loory to Moscow to cover Brezhnev's impending death. Brezhnev didn't die, but Stuart stayed on in Moscow and arranged special live coverage of a Soviet rocket launch, which he would voice-over. It was a first for an American journalist. Just before the launch, he was summoned back home. Ed Turner told him CNN didn't have the money. The reason given to Moscow was that, because of the World Cup, there were no satellite transponders available to bring the story to Atlanta.

Loory was embarrassed and angry. He'd been the *Herald Tribune* bureau chief in Moscow and used all his old contacts to get CNN access to the launch. After all the work and all the favors, he wouldn't be able to report the story.

Stuart went to Paris, and, using his CNN credit card, flew home on the Concorde, $10,000. When he got back to Atlanta, Ed Turner told him he had actually been called back because CNN was only three days from bankruptcy.

Somehow, CNN found the money to stay on the air and to pay for Loory's Concorde ticket. Ed Turner kept using bankruptcy as an excuse for his news decisions.

He wasn't alone. The news executives making changes at CNN used bankruptcy as an excuse to fire people or to kill projects they didn't like. Then they hired their own people and started their own projects. CNN was beginning to think of itself as a big company and such is the manner of big companies. Dan Brewster used to say that at Time Warner, "downsizing" was the best excuse to fire your enemies or your rivals. At CNN they used bankruptcy.

CNN's new leadership underwent its first test when Israel marched into Lebanon on June 5, 1982. It was Martin Abend's war starting one year later to the day. The year before, I had been ready. Bill Zimmerman was in Beirut, Dan Schorr was in Jerusalem. Both of them were familiar with the territory. Both of them had connections.

In 1982, CNN had only Derwin Johnson. Derwin had been in Beirut for months. Lebanon had been bombed and rebombed. Anything the Muslims hadn't destroyed, the Christians had, and the Israelis were bombing the rubble.

Johnson was performing heroically. He was a one-man band, competing with the network orchestras, matching them and sometimes beating them. But he was alone. Bill Zimmerman, with all his Beirut connections, was kept in Atlanta. Dan Schorr, who had been a fixture in Israeli circles for twenty years, stayed in Washington. CNN had no clue as to what was about to happen—or if they did, they didn't know what to do about it.

On June 5 the Israelis rolled. Derwin drove south through the Israeli lines, shooting footage as he went. He spent the night in a Shiite village and was warned that the Israelis were all around, there were no front lines. His Muslim crew figured it was time to head back to the hills. Derwin found an American student playing hooky from American University. The student drove, Johnson shot tape.

By the time they got to Israel, Derwin had a half-dozen great cassettes, which were fed to Atlanta. The only way for Derwin to get back to Lebanon was via Cyprus, Rome, Damascus, and then by car to Beirut. It took him six days.

No preparations had been made in Atlanta. No one had been sent to Beirut to back up Johnson. In the middle of a major Mideast War, CNN had one twenty-four-year-old kid shooting, producing, and reporting, and he was out of position.

For six days CNN had to rely on WTN's agency tape, the same tape that was available to all the networks and local stations that WTN serviced. CNN had the same pictures as everyone else. CNN had no reporters on the scene. It was the first time CNN was beaten on a major story.

In the second week of the conflict, CNN sent in Dick Blystone and Peter Arnett and cameramen and editors, but by then it was too late. Once the news audience discovers who is strongest and who is weakest on a major story, they will stay with the strongest network until that story's over. Burt Reinhardt taught me, "You could never spend too much money on the first day of a story, and you could never spend enough on the second day." Reinhardt had not followed his own advice. CNN was playing catch-up.

Consequently, CNN's ratings slumped. From June 1 to December 31, 1982, they averaged a .8 rating. It was a 20 percent drop, but I don't think anyone noticed besides Ted. Ted was a smart guy, he knew what he didn't know. He urged me to come back as president. I stalled.

A year later in his infamous 1983 interview with *Playboy* magazine, Ted admitted his ignorance about news. He said, "In many ways, I don't know how the company works. I watch it; I like it."

The interviewer was Peter Ross Range, who so infuriated Ted that their conversation ended on a flight to Las Vegas with Ted destroying Range's tape recorder, grabbing two of his audio tapes, and dumping them in the galley garbage bag. Range managed to salvage one tape. *Playboy* printed the interview almost verbatim. Ted later denied the incident, but in the cab from the airport, he bragged to the other passengers, "I really beat his ass."

To be fair, CNN was doing some brilliant things. Peter Arnett, who had been awkward, almost tongue-tied at first, developed very quickly. His stories out of Guatemala on the military massacres of the Indians proved his courage and his growing command of television skills. CNN excelled.

In January 1986, CNN was the only network that carried the explosion of the space shuttle *Challenger*. All the networks carried the launch and stayed with the shuttle for about a minute. Then, ABC, CBS, and NBC broke for a commercial. CNN stayed with the shuttle as it erupted in a ball of flame in midair. The networks, to their shame, were more interested in revenue than in news.

But, for the most part, CNN stood still. Over the years, it lost Zimmerman and Schorr, Hart and Walker, Farmer and Curle. Sullivan was long gone, and Freeman finally left when her contract was up in 1985. Burt Reinhardt found Larry King to succeed her.

The show never became the "advance the news one cycle" program that I had hoped for, but if CNN was going to do celebrity interviews, King was a whole lot better than Freeman.

There were the minor lapses in CNN's "journalistic standards." CNN ran a puff piece on Morocco, paid for by the Moroccan government, as hard news. The producer and the anchor were old friends of Ed Turner's, but Ed said he was not aware that it was a PR release when he ran it on the air.

CNN also carried a half hour of business news from Japan for which MITI (the trade organization of Japan, Inc.) paid the freight by getting CNN advertising from major Japanese corporations. The reporting was accurate, there was no bias, but the stories were always positive.

Then there was Ted Turner's baby, the international news half hour—a collection of stories from foreign broadcasters presented to an American audience exactly as the foreign broadcaster had made them. Sounds good, but it meant that Iraqi broadcasting presented Saddam Hussein's messages into millions of U.S. homes. All the world's dictators had their chance to preen before a worldwide audience.

It's difficult for an audience to recognize slanted reports provided by some of the world's most vicious dictators when they are mixed in with CNN's objective news. A half hour of propaganda gets a lot better reception when it's tucked into twenty-three-and-a-half hours of credibility.

CNN's Iraq arrangement paid off big in 1991. Iraqi television fed Peter Arnett's reports to the world for the first couple of days before it was put out of action by U.S. rockets. After that, Arnett used the WTN dish and maintained CNN's exclusive position, the only American broadcaster reporting live from behind enemy lines. Of course, he only reported what the censors permitted, but Peter tried to sneak things through, and close listeners sometimes got a grain of truth.

From 1982 to 1990, CNN ran at pretty much the same pace, kept the same schedule, and hung around a .7 rating. Then came the moment of glory: first quarter, 1991, the Gulf War. During the first two weeks of the conflict, CNN averaged 4 rating points. During the first quarter, January through March, CNN averaged 1,637,000 viewers every fifteen minutes. Maybe the best quarter any cable network ever had.

"CNN believes it will add more regular viewers" wrote the *New York Times,* "because the channel was seen by many people who had never watched it before." Didn't happen. When the war ended, CNN lost 80 percent of its audience. Over the last three quarters it averaged a .6. Still, over the full year it averaged a 1.2 rating, its best year ever.

Since then, it's been downhill, except for O.J. Simpson. CNN dropped from a .7 to a .6 to a .5, and in 2000, it's praying for a .4. O.J. made 1992 a good year, with a .88 rating, but O.J. doesn't have anymore wives to kill, and CNN is still waiting for an encore.

For a long time, the people who ran CNN thought CNN was good enough. When I was there Bill Bevins, the money guy, thought it was too good. He thought we could spend less money on it, and it would still be good enough. "Good enough" doesn't win in the news business. You've got to do something special or the audience moves on.

By the way, I did not go back to work for Ted Turner. At our last meeting on the subject, when Ted was at his most insistent, I asked him, "Who will Sandi Freeman report to, me or you?" He said, "She'll report to me." I said, "No, thanks."

Round 75: **You Don't Know What You're Talking About**

For eight years, Burt Reinhardt acted as the manager of CNN under Ted Turner, and Ed Turner was Burt's assistant. Burt was capable but cautious, didn't make any waves, and CNN didn't get into any serious trouble. In 1990, at the age of seventy, Burt became vice chairman of the network. Ted Turner went outside the organization and the television business to find Tom Johnson.

Before becoming CNN president, Johnson had been an assistant press secretary under Lyndon Johnson, worked for the Johnson family and then for Otis Chandler, the owner/chairman of Times Mirror. Johnson's experience was largely on the PR and business side of journalism. At the *L.A. Times* Johnson was a cheerleader, not a quarterback. He was well liked and had excellent contacts. When things were going great, he was great. If things needed fixing, he was impossible. He had not been much involved in the news side of the *Times,* but at CNN he acted as a hands-on journalist. Where Reinhardt had been as careful with news as he was with money, Johnson plunged headlong into waters far too deep for him.

First came the Noriega case. In 1971, the *New York Times* and the *Washington Post* won a Supreme Court decision that allowed them to publish the *Pentagon Papers* despite Nixon administration fears that publication jeopardized national security. The Supreme Court said, "Any system of prior restraints of expression comes to this court bearing a heavy presumption against its constitutional validity." CNN's actions in the Noriega case were so egregious that despite the heavy presumption in their favor, they managed to blow a hole in the rule against "prior restraint" that the American press had relied on for thirty years.

In November, 1990, General Manuel Noriega, the deposed president of Panama, was being tried on drug charges in Miami. His jailers were taping his phone calls, even the ones between him and his lawyers. CNN managed to get hold of the tapes and, for some unfathomable reason, decided to tell General Noriega's lawyer about them. The lawyer, not being the dumbest man in the world, claimed attorney-client privilege and immediately went to a judge, asking for an injunction to prevent the playing of the tapes by CNN. The judge granted it. CNN appealed.

Before the appeal was decided, CNN played the tapes. Bernie Shaw, that most careful of journalists, read (from a promo that he had not written): "Just a little bit later on *The World Today,* John Camp of our special assignment team, with those very tapes CNN has been ordered not to broadcast." CNN was parading the size of its journalistic phallus. The next day it got chopped off. The court of appeals upheld the lower court injunction.

CNN went to the Supreme Court. The Court would not hear the case. The district court's ruling stood. Anthony Lewis of the *New York Times* called it "CNN's Folly." He wrote, "the Cable News Network has inexplicably made the threat [of prior restraint] worse by provocative and lawless behavior." Maybe it's not inexplicable. Tom Johnson had been on the job for less than a year, and he didn't know the rules. It was strictly Amateursville.

William Hoeveler, the district court judge, had the pleasure of the last laugh. He had cited CNN for criminal contempt, and CNN's lawyers pleaded confusion, claiming they hadn't known the judge meant they couldn't play *those* tapes. After Hoeveler played the tape of Bernie Shaw proclaiming CNN's defiance, CNN's lawyers insisted that Bernie Shaw and the news guys had gotten it wrong. Judge Hoeveler commented, "It is ironic that CNN argues that its own reporting of the story should be ignored and disregarded as inaccurate. To the contrary, the court has the utmost respect for CNN's journalistic ability."

Hoeveler was defending CNN's journalistic integrity against CNN's own attorneys, who it seems would say anything to whine their way out of a contempt citation.

Ultimately, the judge offered CNN the choice of paying a huge fine or paying a lesser one and apologizing on the air. It was his way of saying, "Which matters more, your money or your honor?"

CNN had to think about it. Johnson withdrew with his lawyers for half an hour. I don't know whether or not he spoke to Ted, but I hope not, because when he came back, he said, he'd save the money and apologize. I never thought Captain Courageous would take the cheap way out.

In December of 1994, CNN scrolled a 177-word apology across its screen approximately twenty times over a two-day period.

During its appeal to the Supreme Court, CNN had been joined by the *New York Times,* the *Washington Post,* the AP, Cox, and Gannett newspapers as *amici curiae.* When CNN lost, the press lost its seemingly absolute freedom from prior restraint, and prisoners lost a large part of the lawyer-client confidentiality privilege. Noriega's lawyers had argued that the case against him should be dismissed because his jailers had taped his private legal conversations. In order to keep the case alive, the Court ruled that jailers had a right to tape lawyer-client conversations unless the client previously told them he was calling his lawyer. CNN, in its stupidity and arrogance, had compromised two of the ten amendments in the Bill of Rights. And there was more to come.

In 1998, CNN took on the Pentagon. It produced *Valley of Death,* a prime-time documentary on "Operation Tailwind," accusing the U.S. military of using sarin, a poison gas, in Laos to immobilize or kill GIs who had been captured by or defected to the Vietcong. The report had been specially prepared for the premiere of a new CNN/Time Magazine series called *NewsStand* and had been hyped to the heights.

Before I sound too holy, I'll say this: Had I been running CNN, we would not have produced "Tailwind." History should be left to historians. Stories thirty, fifty years old require years of researching, hundreds of pages of writing, reams of footnotes, and full disclosure of both sides of the argument. Twelve-minute television pieces do not permit that. Twelve minutes does not meet the demands of historical scholarship.

Furthermore, what would the story accomplish? It was thirty years old. It wasn't going to change anything. All it would do was give every dictator building a poison gas arsenal the right to tell the president of the United States, "You did it, why shouldn't I?" Nevertheless, as a journalist, if you tell your people it's okay to do a story, run it on your air and then don't back them, you're gutless and nutless.

The story had been prepared by April Oliver, a young reporter-producer who had done good work for CNN, and before that, PBS. Jack Smith, a veteran Chicago newspaperman, and a former senior producer at CBS, worked side by side with her. They had, and still have, no doubts about their story. Peter Arnett did a few interviews and presented the piece.

They relied heavily on information supplied by Admiral Thomas Moorer, the chairman of the Joint Chiefs of Staff when the raids took place. According to Oliver, Moorer admitted his knowledge of Tailwind and sarin gas, but Oliver's problem was that Moorer had given some of his key statements off camera. Oliver had only her handwritten notes to back them up. Nevertheless, CNN's lawyer, David Kohler, approved the piece.

About a week before airing, Tom Johnson took a look at the program and, despite his lawyer's assurances, decided to run the story past both CNN's Pentagon reporter and its military consultant, Perry Smith, a former major general. They advised Johnson not to run the story. Tom ran it anyway. Then lightning struck.

Johnson told the *American Journalism Review* that when "hundreds of critical comments came pouring into CNN from military groups and the Pentagon, I was alarmed, very concerned. I knew we had a big problem." Tom's big problem was that he had acted as managing editor, investigated, and approved the story. The question was would he now, under pressure, support the people whose work he had approved?

What did he do? He ducked.

Johnson called in First Amendment lawyer Floyd Abrams and asked him to decide whether or not CNN should've run the story. A lawyer, an outsider, was to determine whether Tom Johnson's reporters had done a good job on Tailwind. Abrams, along with David Kohler, CNN's in-house lawyer who had previously approved the piece, reviewed the evidence, interviewed Oliver and Smith, and then reported, "CNN's broadcast was not fair."

Tom Johnson had an excuse to back away from the story, and he did. Oliver and Smith were fired. Arnett was reprimanded and left the network six months later. Two executive producers resigned. CNN dropped money on Admiral Moorer. They paid him $109,000 in damages. Tom Johnson and Ted Turner personally called Moorer to apologize and said they had "ultimate respect for the military."

General John Singlaub—who had been head of the Special Operations Group (SOG) in Vietnam, and had also been cited as a source by April Oliver—denied he'd ever spoken with her about Tailwind. CNN dropped money on him, too.

Oliver had shown Abrams the handwritten notes of her interviews with Moorer and Singlaub. April had asked Abrams if she should sue Singlaub and use her notes to refute his statements. Abrams said, "In Great Britain, maybe. In the U.S., we do not sue our sources." April thought he was acting as her lawyer. She says that it was only after their second meeting that she was informed by CNN that Abrams was investigating her.

Despite Oliver's notes, despite her continuing belief in the story, despite Smith's affirmation, despite Abrams finding that the program had "some merit," CNN had cut and run.

Abrams, after doing on the one hand and on the other, finally determined that "a decision was made by CNN to broadcast accusations of the gravest sort . . . in the face of substantial persuasive information to the contrary." None of the people fired, none of the people disciplined made that decision. It had been Tom Johnson's call. Now, the CNN brass just wanted Tailwind to go away.

The story did not go away. When CNN paid off Moorer, others lawsuits followed. Oliver and Smith did not go gently. They defended the accuracy of their piece, both inside CNN and in the press. CNN was sued by people who had been interviewed for the program, appeared on the program, or were members of the unit that had participated in Operation Tailwind.

Other participants, claiming defamation, filed lawsuits. The plaintiffs included General Singlaub, who named April Oliver as a defendant along with CNN. Oliver, unable to find work as a journalist and attending law school, was looking for a chance to clear her name. When Singlaub sued, she countersued and cross-complained against CNN. She had found a way to have her day in court.

On January 17, 2000, Oliver, Moorer, Singlaub, and their lawyers and associates met to take Admiral Moorer's deposition. Throughout the morning, lawyers for the plaintiffs lobbed easy questions at him, suggesting that Oliver had been harassing him and had misrepresented his answers in the documentary. Then it was Roger Simmons's turn.

Oliver had hired Simmons, a gentlemanly country lawyer devoted to history and the Constitution, out of Frederick, Maryland. She had spent her Christmas break with him, reviewing documents. Immediately, after the interviews with Moorer, she'd entered her notes into a computer and kept the handwritten originals.

Simmons knew that Admiral Moorer had great respect for history and was a man of honor. He opened by asking Moorer if he had said, "The difference between a democratic and communist government is that in a democratic government we advertise and discuss our faults and that in the communistic government they cover them up." Moorer agreed that he had. Then Simmons talked Moorer through a brief history of the Vietnam War, and discussed Moorer's distinguished military career.

Finally, Simmons presented Moorer with a computer printout of April Oliver's handwritten notes from their interviews. Question by question, Simmons asked the Admiral if the notes fairly reflected Moorer's recollections of his conversations with Ms. Oliver. Time after time, the Admiral agreed that the notes were accurate. His answers indicated that Oliver had quoted him correctly about Operation Tailwind. Moorer admitted that sometimes defectors were killed and that he had been told by Singlaub that killing defectors was a priority. When asked about the use of sarin, the poison gas, Moorer said, "If the weapon [sarin] could save American lives, I would never hesitate to use it."

Moorer seemed to have confirmed the two basic points of Operation Tailwind. One, that some American defectors in Laos had been killed, and two, that sarin had been used to rescue American pilots. After Moorer's deposition, it was apparent that CNN's retraction was premature, cowardly, and dead wrong.

CNN's lawyers were delighted. It was obvious that April Oliver had information from Moorer that supported the accusations made in *Valley of Death*. At 5:15, as the group broke for recess, General Singlaub's lawyer said to Simmons, "You've just gutted everyone's case."

Following the deposition, Judge Joan Zeldon sent the parties to mediation. Roger Simmons's heart intervened: he underwent triple bypass surgery, and the mediator granted an adjournment. Finally, on May 26 and 27, April Oliver and Roger Simmons met with the Time Warner in-house lawyers, and with Nicole Seligman and Kevin Baine of Williams & Connelly, the powerhouse Washington law firm. Seligman had represented President Clinton during his impeachment. *Time,* or its insurance company, was using the best lawyers in town. No one from CNN was present. No one from *Time* magazine was present. There was only one journalist in the room, April Oliver, and she walked away with the money. I think of it as a triumph for the news side.

Under the terms of the settlement, neither Oliver nor Simmons can give an exact figure, but Oliver had sued CNN for $5 million. She pretty much proved her case, and, incidentally, she may have saved CNN and *Time* a lot of money in damages that, thanks to the Moorer deposition, they may not have to pay to the other plaintiffs.

As they sat down for their final negotiations, Oliver and Simmons had the gun. Good lawyers know how to negotiate when they have the edge, and I'm sure April took home a basketful of dollars. I don't think Roger Simmons is the kind of lawyer who leaves money on the table. April also got some satisfaction. She's told the Associated Press that she wants, "The public record restored . . . so I'm not buried under a sea of character assassination and a sea of disinformation."

Time Warner had played their cards cleverly. The settlement was announced late on a Friday afternoon. Few papers picked it up, and those that did gave it just a couple of paragraphs. Oliver deserves better treatment. I still don't know whether the story was right or wrong, but I do know that Oliver was diligent in her efforts and had evidence that her story was true. It was up to Tom Johnson to decide whether she had enough evidence and to decide that before, not after, he put the story on the air.

I suppose that, even with Moorer's deposition, some people will claim that *Valley of Death* was totally wrong. Still, if I had put that piece on the air, I would have taken the rap right alongside CNN journalists and CNN journalism. I would have been in that deposition room, helping to defend April Oliver, enjoying Roger Simmons's success, the discomfiture of CNN's enemies, and the joy of putting the videotape of Admiral Moorer's testimony on CNN air. I would have run Operation Tailwind again and said, "Come and get me now, Pentagon." I'll bet Ted Turner would have done the same thing if somebody had told him who April Oliver was, who Jack Smith was, and why he should fight for them. With fitting irony, Oliver got her big check within days of CNN's twentieth anniversary celebration.

Peter Arnett's departure leaves me bemused. I had hired him, and for fifteen years he toured the world's battlegrounds for CNN. His work in Guatemala and Iraq had earned him a lifetime job. All he had done on *Valley of Death* was follow orders. The producers requested his on-camera presence; CNN executives consented, but gave him a very short leave from his other duties.

Arnett interviewed a few participants, and read a script that others had prepared for him, but it was his face on the program. The Pentagon, which has had a hard-on for Arnett since his reporting days in Vietnam, went after his scalp. So did some CNN journalists who said that Peter's participation had disgraced them all. In the end, CNN let him go. There is only one management theory I know that justifies his departure. In Hollywood it is known as the Samuel Goldwyn System of Business Administration. It goes like this:

> How come you did
> What I told you to do
> When you know
> I don't know
> What I'm talking about?

Round 76: Bevins Dies Twice, but Only Once for Turner

The summer of 1982 was the summer of CNN's indebtedness. I was gone. Bill Bevins was the most important man at the company; he was raising the money. He got funding from Citicorp. He got the hot dog vendors and the cable customers to pay Ted in advance. CNN kept meeting its payroll, barely. Burt Reinhardt was slashing expenses. Bevins was grasping at straws.

On July 1, Satellite News Channel went on the air. Its structure was awkward. It was locked into the inflexible Westinghouse radio wheel: "You give us twenty-two minutes and we'll give you the world." I did not regard SNC as a serious contender, but the banks do. They would not lend Ted money. They were afraid of SNC's deep pockets. As long as SNC existed, CNN would be unable to raise its price to cable operators and would have competition in the advertising marketplace. If ABC and Westinghouse were prepared to absorb enormous losses, maybe they could put Ted out of business.

Ted had one thing going for him. He had the loyalty of the cable community. After all, he was "cable before cable was cool." The cable guys would stick with him as long as they could, but they would not subsidize CNN.

If worse came to worse, Ted had an alternative. In 1982 CBS had offered $300 million for CNN. NBC would top that. If Ted decided to sell, he could hold an auction; but for Ted, selling was out of the question. Ted loved CNN. Ted would resist a partner until one minute before the very end.

In the meantime, Ted would do just about anything to survive. Once, when Ted reported at a shareholders' meeting, he fiddled with the numbers. Bevins was there. As a wire service reporter raced for the phones, Bevins stopped him in the hall, grabbed him by the lapels, and said, "You can't write this, you can't write this, you can't report this!" "Why not?" asked the reporter? "It's not true," said Bevins. It went over the wire anyway.

Bevins and Ted had a difference of opinion. Bevins wanted his numbers to be right on. Ted didn't care too much. One morning, there was a director's meeting. Bill had prepared some numbers. Ted improved on them. Ted insisted Bill deliver the improved numbers to the board. Bevins didn't enjoy public presentations, particularly when the numbers had been improved. Nevertheless, he delivered the report.

When Bevins got back to his office, he walked over to his couch, and lay down. Bevins's secretary told Paul Beckham, Bill's number two, that Bill was not feeling well. Beckham walked in. There was Bevins, pale, sweating, and stretched out on the couch. "How do you feel?" asked Beckham. "Not well, pain in the chest," said Bevins.

Beckham called the fire department. The emergency truck arrived complete with hook and ladder. They wheeled in a gurney, pushed it over to the couch, and started to lift Bevins. Ted rushed in and yells, "What the hell, Billy! God damn! What the hell!" The fireman holding Bevins's feet looked around and saw it was Ted Turner. He reached out to shake Ted's hand and dropped Billy's feet. Bevins slipped to the ground. As they were wheeling Bevins down the hall, Ted turned to Terry McGuirk and said, "Terry, Billy's gonna die. Now there's only two of us."

Bevins surprised Ted—he lived. He had suffered a massive heart attack, but the doctors brought him back. He continued to work for Ted. He still spent all his time raising money. At one point, Ted, Bevins, and McGuirk visited TCI boss John Malone in Denver. TCI was trying to reduce payments to CNN. Bevins and Turner had worked out a plan. They wanted to talk about an overall deal with TCI that would provide long-term guarantees of subscriber numbers and subscriber fees.

In the middle of the discussion, Ted suddenly got up, walked around the table, and began performing. "You guys are our friends," he said. "I am doing everything I can for you, short of going out of business." Then, out of nowhere, he offered 5 percent of the company to Malone. Bevins turned white and popped a pill in his mouth. Malone and his people excused themselves to discuss the offer. They came back and said they'd have to think about it. Bevins heaved a sigh of deep relief.

When they got back to Atlanta, Bevins told Ted that the deal was too complicated right then. Three or four days later, Malone called and said they were not interested, right then. The stockholders saved 5 percent of the company.

While CNN was bleeding money, SNC was hemorrhaging. They were making no progress, even against Headline News. Towards the end, ABC asked me to consider running SNC. I declined. I thought their format and business plan were hopeless. ABC and Group W were locked in an unpleasant partnership. Dick Wald, Roone Arledge's number two at ABC, suggested that I could make SNC work. I told Wald that that would be like teaching an elephant to dance. "You've done that before," said Wald. I said, "Not when the elephant insists on leading."

After little more than a year on the air, SNC cut its losses. ABC/ Group W sold out to Ted for $25 million and agreed not to compete. Ted left them with a cruel memory. He told them that he was just about to go broke. If they had lasted another month they would have had him. People who worked at SNC still tell me that story with the sound of "if only" in their voice. It would never have happened. Ted could always have taken a partner. He didn't call his boat *Tenacious* for nothing.

A few years later Bevins quit. According to Gerry Hogan, Bill Bevins had asked Ted about his becoming president of TBS. Ted said not a chance, Bill left. He opened his own shop as a deal maker, but before he got very far, Ron Perelman, an extremely successful buyer and seller of businesses, signed him up. Bevins finally made the fortune he deserved, but once again he almost had to die for it. This time it was in L.A., working for Perelman, but once again it was a heart attack, and again the doctors brought him back to life. He quit the business.

He is now retired, happily married, living quietly in Atlanta, and laughing at the rest of us. Three years ago, he was shown Rick Kaplan's budget for new sets for the network. He said, "That's more money than Schonfeld spent to build the network and run it for seven months." Bevins never changes.

Round 77: **News 12: The Virtues of Virginity**

While CNN's been surviving, what have I been doing? I spent a year with Cox and signed a letter of intent to bring the BBC to the U.S. The Rockefeller Fund said they had the rights through their defunct Arts Channel. BBC was afraid of a lawsuit and sent a letter withdrawing their letter of intent with us.

I wanted to fight, but Garner Anthony, the CEO of Cox, and very much a gentlemen, said, "Reese, if they don't want us, we don't want them." Boy did I miss Ted Turner.

I moved back to New York and went to work for Chuck Dolan at Cablevision, where we launched News 12, the first local cable news service. Cablevision brought me back to my Newark roots. It was a politically connected company run by guys who had been brought up in big cities. Their leader was Charles (Chuck) Dolan.

Dolan is the only guy I know who started two great cable empires. He had founded Manhattan Cable and launched HBO; then he ran out of money. Time Inc. became his partner, but Chuck couldn't meet capital calls and he lost control of his company. Chuck decided to start over.

In those days, it was believed that cable succeeded only in areas where you couldn't get good reception of broadcast television. That was why Chuck had started in Manhattan. The skyscrapers got in the way of good pictures.

There were franchises available on Long Island, but Long Island is flat as a pancake. Television reception is good. The only reason to buy cable there would be for additional programming. There wasn't much. Chuck had launched HBO, Ted had put up TBS, and ESPN had sports. CNN was still a gleam in Ted's eye. Chuck took the chance anyway.

Even at Manhattan Cable, Chuck had believed in local news for local cable. In Long Island, he'd started with *Newsday,* Long Island's biggest newspaper. *Newsday* got tired of losing money and dropped out. Chuck called me. After Ted, Chuck was a pleasure. He actually had the money to do what we said we were going to do.

We started out modestly, six hours of news a day, three hours in the morning and three hours in prime time. Personnel was easy to find. CNN was an unhappy place. I hired away their best show producer, John Hillis, and News 12 became his thing. Bill Zimmerman was available, because CNN never recognized how good he was.

Long Island is more than a hundred miles long, and the eastern end was closer to Rhode Island than it was to New York City. I had to find a defining issue, a theme around which to build our news coverage. Was there an issue everybody cared about? Yes. The Shoreham Nuclear Plant. Should it open?

Newsday was cautious on the subject. They only printed a few stories about it, and their editorial policy was mildly supportive. Mostly, they wanted to ignore it. The plant had been built in the seventies and there were lots of problems, slipshod construction, poor maintenance. By

1984 it seemed as if the problems had been cured. But 1984 was after Three Mile Island, and nobody wanted a nuclear plant in his backyard.

I knew that the mere mention of Shoreham would bring viewers. I also knew that nuclear fears were so high that any kind of coverage, no matter how objective, would work against its chances of opening. There were day-by-day developments. Consumer groups and environmentalists would accuse, Shoreham would defend. We would cover every development in our news shows. *Newsday* would most often tuck it away in a few paragraphs on an inside page.

Once a week we carried a debate between proponents and opponents. After a few debates, LILCO, the utility company that owned Shoreham, refused to provide a spokesman. They knew they couldn't win. We made a deal. We gave them one hour, one week in four, to present their side of the case. The other three weeks went to the opponents. LILCO didn't want to debate anymore.

They decided to launch a PR offensive. The antinuclear groups claimed that since Long Island was an island, if there was an explosion, there wouldn't be a chance to evacuate. Where would the injured go? LILCO decided to do a simulation. They mocked up an explosion, sent in ambulances and EMTs, provided mock victims with ketchup-stained bandages, and demonstrated how well they would handle the situation. We carried it live. It didn't matter how well they handled it, bloody bandages are what the audience remembered.

We got our best ratings early in the morning, traffic time. "Telephone coincidentals" showed we had five times as many viewers as CNN between 6 and 9 a.m. Chuck came up with the idea of putting remote cameras on the highways. News 12 used the pictures. We didn't need traffic helicopters.

Dolan had started out as a news writer. When there was an editorial problem, he sided with the news guys. Local cable and local politics were inextricably intertwined. Cable systems got their licenses from the politicians. One of our reporters asked some tough questions of a town supervisor, the supervisor called the general manager of our cable system: "I worked hard for you guys, I got you your licenses, I'm fighting for new licenses for you, and your guy attacks me!" The GM called the news department, screamed and yelled at them. It was Bill Zimmerman he was yelling at. The newsroom went into shock.

Next day, I talked to Dolan. He was driving back from New York. I told him our problem. In the car coming back, he wrote in longhand a memo to all concerned. By the time Zimmerman, Hillis, and I walked into his office, he had copies ready. It should be the bible for every newsroom in the world. In part it goes like this:

> The purpose of this note is to emphasize a point about news coverage by Cablevision.
>
> In pursuing news as a Cablevision service, we have always recognized that the foundation of a successful news department is its independence. Editorial decisions must be made objectively. They cannot be influenced by the business and political environment in which cable television finds itself anymore than print and broadcast editors can permit their judgment to be influenced by considerations particular to their media. . . . Accordingly we want to make it clear to all inside and outside the company that the Cablevision news departments have only one function and that is to do their professional best to report the news as they see it. If this policy is misunderstood by anyone and you find yourself contacted in an effort to change what you have already planned for any newscast, we trust that you will refuse.

Then, using his street smarts, Dolan told the GM: "Supervisor X will get over this. He's not really unhappy, but if we let supervisor Z do it, and then we don't let him, we're in real trouble." It's like being a virgin. If you don't put out for anybody, it's okay. But if you put out for the first guy and not the next one, you've made an enemy.

Through Chuck Dolan I had met a Puerto Rican electrical contractor named Luis whose company, Luis Electric, was doing some work for Cablevision in the Bronx. He was a pleasant man who told me that he lived on Sutton Place in Manhattan. We talked at some length and got to know each other.

Later Chuck invited me to watch the Hearns-Hagler fight from his box at the Nassau Coliseum. Luis was also there. Hagler knocked out Hearns in three rounds. As I was leaving, a senior Cablevision executive put his arm around me and asked if I could drive Luis home? I take the Fifty-ninth Street Bridge, Sutton Place was right on my way.

As we started driving Luis said don't take the Fifty-ninth Street Bridge, take the Whitestone. The Whitestone went into the Bronx. He was living in the Bronx? Why, I ask? He mumbled something about his mother. I didn't get it, but he directed me somewhere with no street-lights and rows of white houses under construction. "Here," he says. I dropped him off. I didn't understand why I had been chosen to take him home.

Two years later, I read in the tabloids that a Jewish gangster, Irwin "Fat Man" Schiff, had been "hit" in a midtown restaurant. He was so big, so fat, that they had to take the door out of the frame to get his body out of the restaurant. He was reported to be a Genovese associate, in the electrical contracting business. His partner was my Puerto Rican friend Luis, the guy I had dropped off in the wilds of the Bronx.

Now I got it. These were the days of "minority contracting." The Mob had a Puerto Rican out in front. The Puerto Rican was laying cable in the Bronx for Cablevision. Okay, that's the way you have to do business in New York. I accepted that. But did they have to ask me to drive him home?

It took me back to growing up in Newark, New Jersey. When my neighbor, Al Borok, had this black guy turn his car on every morning and drive it over to his house so that he didn't have to worry about a bomb. Obviously, someone at Cablevision did not think I was indispensable. But by the time "the Fat Man" made the newspapers, I had left Cablevision.

News 12 became the first successful twenty-four-hour local news service anywhere. It proved that local news could be a cable business. I spent the next year as the Johnny Appleseed of local cable news. I tried to convince ABC New York to launch local news channels throughout the country. Their affiliates objected, their owned and operated stations objected; ABC was not ready to do battle with them.

I visited Gannett in Washington; they were not interested. I flew to Chicago and talked to Jim Dowdle at the Tribune company. A year later, he launched Chicagoland. Then I went to Washington and talked to Joe Allbriton, the owner of WJLA. He loved the idea and launched News 8 with my protégé John Hillis running the show. It was the second successful local cable news channel in the world.

Round 78: **Ted Wants to Own a Network**

While I was still at Cablevision, the word got out: Ted wanted to own a network. He always had. Now he was going to do something about it. My friends in Atlanta called, they said Ted was going to buy CBS or NBC or ABC.

I laughed. Ted may have been serious, but nobody else would be. Nobody in his right mind would sell a network to Ted Turner. He's off the wall. The establishment, the suits, the white shoe bankers who really run the world, they were not going to give Ted money to buy a network. He must be smoking something.

Ted and I had talked about a network, a fourth network, in 1981 and 1982. In 1977 I'd worked out a plan with Arthur Taylor, former president of CBS, and Ray Beindorf, former executive VP of CBS stations. The concept entailed creating a prime-time network using Metromedia stations, the nation's largest independent group, as its base. In those days, prime time was "Death Valley" for the Indys. We planned to give them three hours a night of network quality programming—entertainment, news, and sports—on weekdays, plus six hours on weekends. The independent stations were interested, but advertisers would give no commitments, and Taylor, a cautious man, dropped out. The venture died.

Now it was the early eighties. Ted was not a cautious man. He wanted a network—I presented him with the "build a fourth network" business plan. I was sure he could succeed where Taylor had failed, but Ted wasn't interested. He wanted to buy a "real network."

In 1985, I was still a doubter. I thought Ted's wildly eccentric behavior would give pause to investors or lenders whom I took to be serious men. But these were the eighties, the days of Drexel Burnham and junk bonds. Serious men were prepared to lend money to almost anybody if the interest rates were high enough and the deal fees were large enough.

Demon dealers would dance with the devil himself if they could make a profit, and the old guard was vulnerable to hostile takeovers. Turner had disposed of the Satellite News Channel. Now it was time to make his move, and with the new Wall Street guys, not so establishment, not so white shoe, maybe Ted had a chance.

All three networks were run by old Jewish men—men who had built the broadcast industry, who had grown up in radio, created television, invented the financial systems and programming strategies that had served the networks for decades, but none of these men had cultivated a strong successor.

With Ted on the prowl, RCA, NBC's owner, recognizing its weakness, sold itself lock, stock, and NBC to General Electric. Ted was furious, or so the word went in Atlanta.

He turned to ABC. Leonard Goldenson, the chairman of the network was over seventy, and the network had no clear line of succession. It was in better financial shape than NBC, and it had the youngest audience of the three networks. The Wall Street of the eighties might be prepared to back an energetic and ambitious young man with a record of success regardless of character.

Then an ABC vice president was discovered filching company financial documents, perhaps to feed them to an interested outside party. Goldenson, fearing ABC was ripe for plucking, chose his own buyer, Capital Cities, an ABC affiliate group.

Cap Cities was run by Tom Murphy and Dan Burke, both highly regarded broadcast executives. Goldenson approached Murphy and asked if Cap Cities would be interested in acquiring ABC. Absolutely, but they had to find funding. Warren Buffet, at the time the richest man in America, rode to the rescue and put up the money. Goldenson made the deal. Now ABC was off the table. For Ted, it was two strikes against him. Only CBS was left.

Early on, Ted had a secret plan—sell TBS to one of the networks. When the dust settled, and Ted was the largest shareholder in the network, he'd convince the other board members that he should run the company. He said that they would think they were buying him, but he would really be buying them. The mouse would swallow the elephant. He tried that strategy on CBS in 1981. They declined.

In 1985, he moved more aggressively. He would buy them. He lined up Lehman Brothers to do his financing. Lehman Brothers insisted he take a partner. He refused, they withdrew. E. F. Hutton moved in and proposed a highly creative, no-cash deal: Ted offered CBS stockholders stock in TBS, bonds, and other high-interest notes.

He would buy 67 percent of the company and agree to buy the rest of it at the same terms later. According to Paul Beckham, Bevins's number two, TBS was trying to arrange a $3 billion deal, even though it had never had more than a $200 million line of credit. TBS computers weren't big enough to print out a number that ended in as many zeros as a billion.

On April 23, 1985, the CBS board unanimously rejected Ted's offer. His frustration was complete. There were no more networks to buy. He looked for a consolation prize. In the elevator leaving CBS, he turned to his aides and said loudly, "Now, we've *got* to buy MGM."

Bevins, Beckham, and Turner went to Hollywood. MGM was owned by Kirk Kerkorian, a notoriously able negotiator who never got the worst end of a deal. He had bought, sold, and bought back MGM. On this occasion Mike Milken was representing both Turner and Kerkorian. MGM and TBS had waived "conflict of interest." Milken would try to raise the money for Ted at whatever price Ted decided to pay.

Turner and company negotiated with Kerkorian. Kerkorian came up with a number, the Turner group retired to consider it. Bevins told Ted he could bring the price down some more, but Ted really wants MGM. He told Bill, "We've negotiated enough, it's a fair price, let's take it." Will Sanders had said that Ted is a lazy negotiator. And I've said Ted would pay anything for something he thought he needed. Both Will and I were right.

Now, no one could protect Ted from himself except maybe Michael Milken. When he tried to raise the money, Milken came up a couple hundred million short. He told Kerkorian that it was the best he could do. Kerkorian accepted, and the deal was completed. Ted paid $1.5 billion. The price was much too high.

Ted discovered that a few years later, when it cost him control of his company.

Round 79: "I Should Have Killed Him"

Ted needed money to pay for MGM. So, after SNC folded and Turner had a news monopoly, he raised the price of CNN per subscriber from fifteen cents a month to twenty-five cents a month, a 67 percent increase. I knew that cable systems had a ninety-day right to cancel their contracts with CNN if Turner raised the price. I saw my opportunity and I took it. The time was ripe to launch a competitive news service.

I was still at Cablevision so first I talked to Chuck Dolan. Would he participate? He said he couldn't, but he wouldn't stand in my way. Would he subscribe to a news service at fifteen cents a month if it got off the ground? Chuck smiled and said, "Come back to me when you're ready."

I went to see Larry Grossman, head of NBC News. Although NBC was the right network, Grossman was not the right man. He talked too much. He had been a PR man and had gone on to help run PBS. I told Grossman that there was a ninety-day window to take on CNN and launch a competitive service. Our advantage would be price. The cable industry recognized that it was at Turner's mercy; CNN was so good that the cable audience would not permit the industry to drop it, unless there was a comparable service. Turner could charge whatever he wanted, unless we stepped into the breach.

By now, CNN had 40 million subscribers. We needed 13 million subscribers to get ratings from Nielsen so that we could sell advertising. I told Grossman that if the cable industry would give us the 13 million homes, we could launch a successful competitor to CNN. We would charge fifteen cents per subscriber, ten cents less than CNN's new rate.

Grossman said yes, providing that NBC affiliates agreed. I told him I would go to Denver and present the plan to John Malone of TCI, the most powerful man in cable. Even before I left, Bill Schwartz, the CEO of Cox Enterprises, called me. Cox had over a million cable homes when Turner hiked the prices, and Bill Schwartz did not want to be at Ted's mercy. He asked if I would work with Cox to develop a competitor. I told him about NBC. He wanted in.

When I got to TCI, the top brass, John Malone, John Sie, and John Sparkman, came to the meeting. I laid out the plan. I've never had an easier sell. Malone said TCI would put $2 or $3 million into the venture. They would take one or two seats on the board. Thirty minutes into the conversation, we were talking deal. It was my greatest high since CNN, but I had one more stop to make.

Bill Daniels, "the godfather of cable," was based in Denver. Daniels was a smart and tough rancher. He rode motorcycles and boxed. Boxing had left him with a flattened nose; one look told you not to mess around with Bill. In the late forties, he began to build microwave and cable systems to bring television to homes in remote areas. He launched system after system, built it up, and then sold it off to newcomers who wanted to get into "cable." He also created an investment bank and brokerage company that dominated cable financing in cable's early years.

Daniels had been an early supporter of CNN. I told him what I wanted to do. He was courteous but cool. His first question was, "You're not doing this just to get even with Ted, are you Reese?" I said no. I explained the value of a competitive service, a second supplier of news to the cable industry.

A smile spread across Daniels's face. "I get it, Reese," he said. "You want to be Showtime!" (Showtime is the competitor of HBO that gives the cable industry some leverage over HBO prices, but it is not nearly as successful as HBO.) "You want to be Showtime? We'll let you be Showtime. But there's one thing you have to do. You've got to call it the KTHN Network." "What's the KTHN Network?" asked I. "The Keep Ted Honest Network," said Daniels.

I called Grossman, walking on air. I told him of "our" success. He did not sound as pleased as I had hoped. He told me that he had mentioned our plan to the NBC affiliates, and that it had gone well. What he didn't tell me was that someone had leaked the story to Bill Abrams of the *Wall Street Journal,* and that I'd see it in the paper the next day.

In the *Journal* Grossman says, "CNN does a very good job, but competition is always healthy." He added that we would be charging ten to fifteen cents a subscriber and said that we needed 13 million cable homes. Talk about giving away your game plan. Once a PR man, always a PR man.

I was going full steam ahead when I got a call from John Sie. Sie said he's heard that NBC was talking to Ted Turner. I didn't know anything about it. I called Grossman, who didn't deny it. I called Sie back and told him. Sie said, "Our deal is off, Reese. It's every man for himself."

The best explanation I ever got was that, following the *Wall Street Journal* article, Ted had called Grant Tinker, the CEO of NBC. From what I heard, the conversation went something like this: Gee, Grant, you want to get into cable news, why didn't you talk to me? You know, if you get into the business and I stay in the business, we'll be out there killing each other. You'll cut prices, I'll cut prices, nobody makes money. The only guys who come out ahead on this are those cable bastards. Grant told Ted to talk to Grossman. Grossman was much taken by the offer. He did not know that Ted was just flashing a bit of thigh, and would never get into bed with him.

The seduction went on: NBC people and CNN people began to talk about how they would work together. The talks went slowly. In the meantime, Ted met with the major MSOs for face-to-face price negotiation. He opened the meeting with, "I should never have fired Schonfeld, I should have killed him." Then he made his deals. The MSOs would pay less than twenty-five cents per month; how much less I still do not know, but the MSOs agreed to stick with CNN.

Now Ted got back to NBC. Tom Wolzien, the guy I had tried to recruit from NBC six years earlier, was Grossman's point man on the CNN deal. According to him, NBC/RCA offered $225 million for a half interest in the company. Bill Bevins reached into his pocket and said here's what we think the company is worth. The number on his paper was $500 million, half was 250. They were $25 million apart, but RCA would not raise its offer. There was some question about editorial control, but Wolzien says that could've been worked out if the money was right. So over a difference of 25 million bucks, Wolzien thinks NBC/RCA walked away from one of the bargains of the century.

I never believed that Ted would sell CNN, but maybe by this time, 1986, his debt to Kerkorian was coming due, and he needed the money. Of course, there's another theory. When Ted was trying to raise money for CNN in 1981, he had put his billboard company up for sale. He got a firm offer; he took the offer to the bank and got a loan based on the value of the billboard company as established by the offer. In 1986 a former financial officer at TBS suggested that Ted may have solicited the NBC offer for the same purpose. We all thought that Ted was trying to build mass, not sell assets.

For whatever reason, there was no NBC deal. NBC went to one more cable show and learned the facts of cable life: Cable systems would not subscribe to NBC since Ted has dropped his price. NBC dropped out of the race.

Round 80: **Ted Loses Control**

By the end of 1986, Ted learned that Bevins was right about the MGM deal. Ted had told Bill not to negotiate further, that he thought Kirk Kerkorian's price was fair. Maybe it wasn't so fair. His obligations to Kerkorian were coming due, and he couldn't meet them. Kerkorian was in position to convert his holdings into common stock and take control of TBS. Turner would be a minority shareholder in his own company. He looked for a white knight: Rupert Murdoch and News Corp., Jack Welch and GE, or a cable consortium led by Time Warner and TCI, the two largest cable companies in America.

Murdoch flew to Atlanta with Barry Diller, then head of FOX. Turner was accompanied by Bob Wussler, his executive vice president. Wussler and Diller sniped at each other throughout the preliminaries. Murdoch and Turner were quiet, cordial, and noncommittal. Murdoch definitely wanted to buy. Turner definitely wanted to sell, but not, if he could help it, to Murdoch. Murdoch would not need Ted's help in running a news network. No deal emerged.

The GE negotiations went further. Welch offered fifteen dollars a share. Turner wanted nineteen. Neither would budge. Ted had one last alternative, the cable system consortium, which wanted no part of Kirk Kerkorian. They thought Kerkorian was too tough, too good a negotiator, and in the end might cost the cable industry a lot of money.

So the cable owners put up $550 million to pay down Turner's debt. In return, they would own 35 percent of TBS and have five seats on an eleven-member board. Ted would still own 51 percent. He appointed the majority of the board, but a "super majority" of the board must approve matters out of the "ordinary course of business." It developed that any expenditure over $3 million was "out of the ordinary course of business."

In 1989, Financial News Network was put up for sale, and Turner wanted to buy it. This deal was definitely not in the "ordinary course of business." Turner needed a "super majority." Run by Earl Bryant, FNN had dominated the financial news sector for years and was profitable, but Bryant had bought UPI, and the UPI losses were draining his company. Meanwhile, NBC had rolled out CNBC, a business network, a direct competitor with FNN. Bryant couldn't take on CNBC without a partner. First he went to ABC. A contract was about to be signed when Turner called Bryant and offered him a better deal. Bryant dropped ABC.

Turner had told Bryant that TBS would buy FNN. What Ted forgot to mention and what Bryant didn't realize was that Ted didn't run TBS anymore. He needed board approval.

In order to launch CNBC, NBC had bought a failing 10 million home PR network from TCI. It was believed that TCI had promised NBC it would not launch a competing business channel. Now, TBS, of which TCI as a member of the cable consortium owns a large chunk, wants to compete with CNBC. John Malone, TCI's boss, was on Turner's board. Whether because of a possible noncompete promise to CNBC or for some other reason, Malone adamantly opposed the acquisition.

Through the afternoon of March 23, 1989, the Turner board met in Techwood. Malone and his allies in one room, Turner and his supporters in another. Emissaries walked up and down the hallway carrying messages, politicking for support. Time Warner went with Ted, but Malone was the most powerful man in cable. He got the other votes. Ted needed a super majority; without Malone, he couldn't get it.

Bryant, on the edge of bankruptcy, went back to ABC. Once jilted, twice shy, ABC was not interested. FNN failed. The *Wall Street Journal* and NBC bid for the bones. NBC won. CNBC picked up 30 million homes and a financial news monopoly. Thirteen years later, CNBC had more viewers than CNN.

Ted had lost control of his company. He could still run the CNN meetings and harass his managers, but he couldn't spend money without the approval of his cable-owner partners.

Round 81: **Glory**

In January 1991, CNN caught lightning in a bottle. It was the Gulf War and everything was breaking right. Bernie Shaw, John Holliman, and Peter Arnett were in Baghdad, Holliman and Arnett by default. Richard Roth and Richard Blystone had declined the assignment. That left Shaw for gravitas, Holliman as the all-American boy, and Peter as the best war reporter of his generation. All of them in the right place at the right time.

Ted Turner's partnership with Baghdad television paid off. CNN had access that other broadcasters were denied. Days before the war started, CNN had sent in an INMARSAT telephone, which could transmit slow scan video reports via satellite directly to Atlanta. INMARSAT gear included a fair-sized umbrella antenna. Customs officials questioned the need for an umbrella in Baghdad. The CNN tech opened the umbrella, paraded around the airport, and said CNN was using it to avoid sunlight when shooting tape. The customs officials bought it and let CNN through. But when the gear was unpacked, there was one piece missing. The INMARSAT was nonfunctional.

CNN had brought in a backup, a "four wire," an open audio line that connected CNN Baghdad to CNN Amman to CNN Atlanta, twenty-four hours a day. The four wire was supposed to be routed through the Baghdad P.T.T., the Iraqi telephone company. No other network had brought in a four wire, and by the time they requested permission, the Iraqis denied it.

On the evening of January 15, Bernie Shaw interviewed a "highly placed Iraqi official." Baghdad was facing a United Nations ultimatum: Get out of Kuwait on your own or we will push you out. The deadline was the sixteenth. The "highly placed official" told Shaw that Iraq would reject the UN's demand. Shaw hurried back to the CNN bureau and, using the four wire, reported the news, live on the air. I was in Moscow, sitting in my hotel room, watching CNN, listening to Bernie Shaw telling the world that war would break out the next day.

Bernie, as careful as ever, emphasized that he was reading directly from notes, notes he had taken on a yellow, lined legal pad during the interview. In measured tones, with exact quotes, he reported that Iraq was adamant. There would be no pullout, no compromise. Bernie offered no comments. From the tone of his voice, the world understood that war was inevitable.

Within minutes, Bernie was called back to the phone. "Do you know what you just said?" asked Lou Dobbs. "The market's dropped forty, fifty points." You could hear Bernie's annoyance. "I told you, I was reading from my notes. I am sure." "Could you check again, Bernie?" Bernie repeats the reading from his notes. Lou has the good sense to shut up. He says thank you and goodbye. The market recovers. Bernie has scored a coup. Iraq had chosen Bernard Shaw and CNN to declare war on the United Nations.

The next day, I fly to Paris. I am consulting to Time Warner, so naturally I stay where they stay, the Bristol Hotel. The Bristol is Paris's premiere business dormitory. I walk into the room, turn on the television, find CNN, and discover that the war has begun. Shaw, Holliman, and Arnett report from their hotel room that Baghdad is under fire. We can hear the sound of bombs hitting and antiaircraft fire. The world has a front-row seat. CBS and ABC had also been talking live to their reporters in Baghdad. Suddenly, their phone lines went dead. U.S. missiles had taken out the Iraqi telephone center. CNN's four wire continued to operate. It was costing CNN $14,000 a day, but it was the best investment CNN ever made. Only on CNN can the world hear what is going on. We are hearing it from American reporters with no censor between us and the facts. I stay awake all night.

The next morning I go down to breakfast before my Time Warner partners. As I sit down, I hear, in every language from every part of the room,

"CNN, CNN, CNN." I look around. I want to stand up and shout, "I started CNN. CNN is my thing." Dan Brewster, who was then at Time Warner, joins me. The State Department has ordered all American journalists out of Iraq. He asks me what I would do if I were still running CNN. "I'd pull 'em out," I say. "How would you cover it?" he asks. "I'd send in Swedes," I say. "That's why God invented them." I go on to London.

On Sunday, I return to the United States. Since this is Time Warner, I'm flying the Concorde. In the lounge, I find Shaw and Holliman. It redefines bittersweet. I talk to them for a few minutes. Then Bernie excuses himself to make a phone call. John tells me Bernie is calling General Colin Powell. CNN has left Arnett in Baghdad. Bernie is asking General Powell not to send any missiles into the hotel where Peter is staying.

John and I get on the Concorde to New York. Bernie is flying directly to Washington. There are only fifteen, twenty people on our whole plane. It is war and people don't like to fly. On the plane, John is the celebrity. Everybody saw him three nights ago. The pilot comes out and takes him into the cockpit. He wants to take a picture with John. John tells me war stories. I love them. It makes me part of it, a little bit.

When the story broke, Jack Welch, the chairman of General Electric, was in Europe on a Department of Commerce tour with the CEOs of other major companies. He has watched CNN. So have all the other CEOs. He has not seen any GE commercials. He calls headquarters and wants to know why.

For years, Kay Delaney, the head of sales for CNN International has been trying to get GE to buy. They have laughed at her. On Friday, she gets a call from the GE ad buyer. He wants GE spots on CNN International, he wants them now, and he does not care what he pays. Jack Welch must see them before he leaves Europe. CNN had done the perfect thing and it is being rewarded.

CNN averages almost 3 rating points for the first quarter. For the next three quarters, CNN's ratings dropped by 80 percent, averaging a .6, their lowest ratings up to that time. Nevertheless, for the entire year, CNN averaged a 1.17, their best ratings ever. CNN caught lightning in a bottle, but they didn't know how to keep the lid on it.

Round 82: **Food, Food, Glorious Food**

In September of 1992, I was sitting at a back table in the Grand Ballroom of the Hilton, a guest of the *Providence Journal,* at a dinner for the Walter Kaitz Foundation. The foundation promotes minority employment in the cable industry. Everybody in cable was there. It's the typical rubber chicken dinner, but the cause is so good and the scholarship winners so worthy, it makes the food palatable.

The *Journal* and I had been working "together" for a year to develop a twenty-four-hour cable channel devoted to food. "Together" means that I got no money, but that I would own a piece of the network if it ever launched.

I was at a corner table way in the back when two *Providence Journal* executives rushed over to me, anxious to do a deal there and then. They would give me 5 percent of the channel, we would be partners in all future *Providence Journal* cable ventures, we would go fifty-fifty and share control of the management company that we'd create to manage them. It sounded fine. We shook hands.

Ten minutes later Ted Turner appeared, telling me he'd been looking for me all over the room. He asked me to come back and run CNN for him. It had been ten years since I'd left. CNN was going no place. After the brief glory of Baghdad, its ratings had sunk to an all-time low, Noriega was a disgrace, and Ted wanted me back. I love the news business. I wanted to talk about a deal, but I had just shaken hands with the *Providence Journal* on the Food Network. I live by my handshake. I said no.

Within two months, the *Journal* was weaseling on its handshake. They would have two votes in the management company. I would only have one. They would not necessarily include me in their new cable ventures. Instead, they gave me the right to do my own ventures and spend up to fifty days a year working on them.

Now I wanted to talk to Ted. I called him but couldn't get past Dee Woods, his valued secretary, whose enmity I'd incurred when CNN pushed her boyfriend out of our Affiliate Sales Department. I took the *Journal* deal, and the Food Network was born.

I had started work on Food in 1991. Between leaving Cablevision and starting Food, I'd produced *People Magazine on Television* for CBS and

Crime Watch Tonight for Orion Television. I'd signed a contract with TASS to transform it into a for-profit news agency. (When Gorbachev was deposed, the deal died.) But I'd spent most of my time working with Time Warner, under the aegis of Nick Nicholas, the delegated successor to Steve Ross as CEO of Time Warner.

We were developing, one step ahead of "globalization," an international business channel called the IBC. The idea was we'd be live with business news around the globe from the time the markets opened in Tokyo till they closed in New York. We'd planned on partners in Japan, Hong Kong, Moscow, Germany, England, and maybe France. The basic service would be in English, but our partners could preempt as many hours as they wished and broadcast in their national language. We would split the international advertising revenues from the basic channel fifty-fifty with our partners. Once they began their own programming, they'd split their local revenues fifty-fifty with us. Potential foreign partners were lining up. I was in Europe setting up a round of meetings for me, Nicholas, and Bob Miller who was heading up the Time Warner team.

In 1992, I was in TASS headquarters in Moscow, watching CNN on the newsroom monitor, we saw a split frame, Gerry Levin on one side, Nick Nicholas on the other. We turned the sound up. Nicholas was out. Levin would succeed Ross. I explained it to TASS. "No need," they said, "We know a coup when we see one." With Nick's departure, the project died, and I turned to Food.

The chief operating officer of the *Providence Journal* was Tryg Myrhen, whom I knew from CNN days. Tryg was another cable pioneer with a dream. He wanted to launch a cable channel that could be supported entirely by advertising. He asked me if I could do that with Food; after doing the calculations, I said we could. Tryg and I thought of it as a joint gift to the cable industry. We were finally giving them a network service that their subscribers would not have to pay for. We were a free "add-on."

We sought partners, other cable companies who would get a piece of our business in return for carrying our free service on their systems. We also offered them the opportunity to invest in the project. The *Journal* owned about 1 million cable homes itself and was part of a group of nine cable systems that owned another 5 million. We met with them. Some were interested, some were not.

Looking back, the most intelligent response we got came from Bob Miron, head of Newhouse cable systems. He liked the concept, he might carry it, but why should he invest in a service that was free, that was leaving money on the table? He said we should be charging for the service, and if we didn't, he wouldn't invest in it. I only wish that Tryg and I had listened to him.

For me, the Food Network was carpentry. To do CNN, I had built a news factory, for Food I would build a food factory. I enjoyed it, but I didn't love it. It wasn't news. It reflected competence, not inspiration.

I did the hard things: producing business plan after business plan, making sales calls on advertisers and potential cable affiliates. I did the easy things: working with Joe Langhan of the *Journal*, we put together schedules, we looked at outside programs, we considered talent.

Despite the free service, despite the efficiency of the food factory, despite the low cost of food programming, despite the number and dollars of potential advertisers, we weren't finding enough partners to launch.

Then, early in 1994, Congress passed a new cable law. One provision gave broadcast stations the right to demand payment from cable systems if the cable system included the station in its program lineup. That is, if a cable system wanted to carry a FOX station, it had to get the station's consent. Most people thought that meant the cable system would pay the station money.

TCI's John Malone had a better way, at least from cable's point of view. Malone offered Rupert Murdoch's Fox stations a cable channel for a new Fox cable network and said he would agree to pay Fox a subscriber fee for the additional service. Fox created FX. Malone gave it carriage and paid and if he was going by the rate card by the second year was paying about twenty cents per subscriber for it. Malone was paying Fox about $20 million a year, and Fox had the additional upside: It could sell advertising and build a billion dollar property. It was a good deal for both sides.

If TCI had paid Fox $20 million a year for the right to carry the Fox stations, it would not have had the opportunity to charge its cable customer more. Why should the customer pay extra to get a service he was already receiving? If TCI added a new network to its basic service, it could turn around and raise the customer's bill, because the new service was added value. TCI did that, added a small markup and were making more money than before. Fox got a new network and a steady stream of income. Everybody's bottom line improved, and the cable customer was stuck with the bill.

The plan was so good that ABC adopted it and launched ESPN2. NBC adopted it and launched *America's Talking,* which later became MSNBC. CBS, the company that had lobbied, fought for, and won the "retransmission consent" provision in the law, didn't know how to make money from it. They won their battle, but they launched nothing new and continued to get nothing for their programming.

The *Chicago Tribune* stations were also a candidate to benefit from "retransmission consent." Their stations were valuable. In New York, they carried the Yankees. In Chicago, they carried the Cubs and Bulls. In Denver, they had the Rockies and in L.A. they had the Angels. That gave them leverage, particularly with men.

I flew out to Chicago, laid out a deal, and offered the *Tribune* 20 percent of Food in return for their retransmission rights to at least 10 million homes. They also invested $9 million for an additional 12 percent, and we were in business. Our other partners contributed 6 million more homes; we were able to launch Food with 16 million cable homes under contract.

Like everything else in business, you spend eighteen months making a deal and leave yourself with three months to make a product. My wife, Pat O'Gorman, built an entire studio, control room, editing rooms, and office space in eighty-three days on the thirty-first floor of an elegant, New York skyscraper. We put up a plaque that read "The Pat O'Gorman Studio." She deserved it. Irv Rosner, who engineered CNN, engineered the Food Network. Fran Heaney, assistant art director at CNN, became the art director at the Food Network. Everybody brought everything in on schedule. It was easy working with people who had done it before.

We did our talent search CNN style. I went looking for a Food Network version of Dan Schorr, and I came up with Robin Leach. CNN had introduced Robin to television back in 1980. Now he was a star, somewhat fading, but still a big name, and a great performer when he wanted to be. He would host a nightly 10 p.m. celebrity/food talk show. He brought legitimacy and press with him.

Next thing I needed was credibility in the food world. David Rosengarten was a food journalist whose stuff got into the best food magazines. He knew wine, and he knew restaurants. In earlier years he tried acting and had done an unsuccessful pilot for PBS. The failed pilot got him his job with us. He showed more ease on camera than the other foodies.

We got lucky. Donna Hanover, one of the better news anchors in New York City, couldn't find work, because she was married to Mayor Rudy Giuliani and the local stations feared conflict of interest. Donna was a mother of two, a lovely presence on air, and the perfect person to talk about food news. Our schedule included a one-hour food news program with a hard edge. We had a crew in Washington covering the FDA and the Agriculture Department. We reported product recalls and the food economy. Donna and Rosengarten were a balanced ticket; Donna knew news, David knew food. Donna's hiring got us more press.

We did a health show. Dr. Lou Aronne, one of New York's leading nutrition doctors (his patients included Sarah Ferguson, Duchess of York) came on board to do a health call-in show with Gayle Gardner, an ESPN original and still a cable star. He was smart and easy to talk to. I thought he'd make it big. He didn't.

Then there were the chef shows. We introduced Emeril Lagasse and brought him to New York to do *Essence of Emeril.* I just told him to be himself, and for once it worked. We found Mario Batali in a small restaurant in the Village and inaugurated *Molto Mario.* It was like CNN. We got tapes from everybody. Bobby Flay in New York looked too good to be a real chef, but he could cook, and we teamed him with Jack McDavid from Philadelphia. The testosterone levels almost blew the cameras out. Five years later, the Food Network is still running *Chillin' and Grillin'.*

Mary Sue Milliken and Susan Feniger from the Border Grill restaurant delivered Mexican from Los Angeles. They were *Too Hot Tamales.* We went traditional and got Marion Cunningham and John Ash, both great chefs of the generation before. They were the favorites of the food purists.

We tried to schedule a chef for every taste. Pat invented *Chef Du Jour,* the perfect screen test for a new network. We brought in chefs from everywhere. They did five shows in two days. We watched their progress, either they improved during the two days or they didn't. We ran all the shows anyway, but some we really liked. Mario Batali did his first show there, so did Flay and McDavid, as did Ming Tsai.

We did *How to Feed Your Family on a Hundred Dollars a Week.* Michelle Urvater and her staff researched, wrote, and presented the show, based on USDA average prices and information from Peapod, the internet food delivery company. We took our role in the food world very seriously. Each year we did a telethon raising money to feed the homeless and the aging. Mrs. Gerry Levin was our chairperson. It couldn't hurt, and she did a terrific job.

I could do a whole book on the Food Network, but this isn't that book. There are good stories about everybody involved, but there are only two stories that I want to tell.

The first has less to do with food than with the way PBS does business. We wanted to buy the Julia Child shows and use her as our star. The *Journal* authorized me to offer up to $1 million for the rights, which were owned by WGBH, the PBS station in Boston. Henry Beckton, Jr., was the president and general manager of WGBH. Beckton sat on the board of the Providence Journal Company. He had to recuse himself from the negotiations, because he couldn't sit on both sides of the table.

Beckton turned the deal over to an assistant whose name will not be revealed here. We offered her the million dollars. She had a boyfriend who was a chef. He told her that Julia Child was worth more than $1 million. So we launched the Food Network without Julia. Three months later, we heard from Julia, wondering why her programs weren't on our air. Our need for them had decreased. We bought the lot for $500,000. Julia was a fifty-fifty partner in her series. Some anonymous boyfriend/chef cost her a quarter of a million dollars.

Once we owned the shows, Julia worked with us and became part of the Food Network family. She contributed a column to *Food News.* Sometimes foodie David Rosengarten interviewed her. Sometimes nonfoodie Donna Hanover did. No matter who it was, Julia always said the right thing in a simple and funny way. After I left, the Food Network managed to lose her. It was like CNN losing Dan Schorr.

When Food started, we were paying Emeril $300 a program. He did sixty-five *Essence of Emeril* in ten days for $20,000. Emeril thought he was worth more money. He talked to his agent, Shep Gordon, who said, "Just do it. Reese will teach you television."

According to a New York talent agent who didn't get to represent Emeril, his new contract with the Food Network pays him over $3 million a year for five years, and he could've gotten him more. But that's what agents who don't get the guy always say.

Shep Gordon, the very smart agent who helped Emeril get started, didn't get the big money either. When it came time to do the new deal, the commission went to my friend from CNN days, Kathleen Sullivan's agent Jimmy Griffin at William Morris.

I suppose Emeril's record of sixty-five shows in ten days also deserves an explanation. They were all half-hour shows, and they were produced under our "food factory" system. At the end of each show, the next recipe was ready, the graphics were loaded, the set was the same; it was a ten-minute break, ready, and shoot. The only problem with the factory is finding talent who's willing to work on an assembly line. But chefs have their own restaurants. They don't like to be away from the kitchen or the cash register. Emeril wanted to do eight shows in a ten-hour day. We thought he wore down after seven.

The other Food Network problems were the usuals: getting more homes and getting more advertising. We thought we'd have no trouble getting homes, because we were giving the service away. But there's one deal better than free: I'll pay *you* to carry it. Suddenly, our competition was offering cash for carriage. They'd also give their service away but only for a year or two. Then, they'd get ten or fifteen cents a month from the cable operator. We were giving our service away for ten years. We were giving them a better deal. Why wouldn't they take it?

After Fox's FX proved a hit, Rupert Murdoch turned to his first love, news, and planned a twenty-four-hour news channel to compete with CNN and MSNBC. But Fox had already given away "retransmission consent," how would it get cable operators to carry a third news service that most of them perceived as triplicative? Fox offered them money, a lot of money. He put ten, eleven dollars per subscriber on the table, he would give the operators one year free and then charge them twenty cents a month for ten years. Food Network was giving itself away for ten years. No question in my mind, Food Network was a better deal.

Shortly before he joined TCI, I talked with Leo Hindery who at the time owned cable systems with about a million cable subscribers. Fox wanted Hindery to carry Fox News and would pay him about $10 million. I suggested to Leo that if he took the Food Network for nothing and borrowed the $10 million from a bank, it would cost him less than taking $10 million from Rupert Murdoch and paying him a total of $24 million over ten years. Leo laughed. He told me that I didn't get it; he would be getting the $10 million from Rupert Murdoch, and the phone company to which he sold his cable system would be paying Murdoch twenty cents a month for the next ten years.

Leo has since sold his cable systems to AT&T, but, better than that, he was able to get about twelve dollars a subscriber from Rupert Murdoch. There's no way to keep a good cable man down.

A few years after I left it, the Food Network began to pay cable systems for carriage. It slowed its profitability, but it was the only way we'd get carried. What saved us was advertising revenue. It was better than predicted. George Babick, the former CNN salesman, did it again. The Food Network will gross more than $100 million in advertising this year. It will show its first profit. It will be a healthy one.

While I was building the Food Network, I was working with the BBC to develop a twenty-four-hour news channel in the U.S. Under my contract, I had fifty days a year to do my own projects, and I was spending them with the BBC. In 1994, it came to a head, and we announced that BBC News was coming to America and that I would be its chairman. The *Providence Journal* had never told our other Food Network partners about my right to do projects outside of the Food Network. They were dismayed.

"How can our CEO be the chairman of another company?" they asked. They demanded that I guarantee them my full-time services. The *Providence Journal* would not return to our original deal in which I was supposed to be a partner in all their cable programming ventures. It looked to me as if I had nothing to lose by leaving. My contract with and ownership in the Food Network were guaranteed. If they forced me out, I had a chance to spend more time on the BBC or other ventures and still sit on the Food Network partnership board and watch my investment grow.

I left at the end of 1995, but my BBC dream was already dead. The Hilliard brothers, sponsors of the project, did not come through with the money. It had been their idea, but when it became real, they did not have the courage of their convictions. They were not Ted Turner.

I didn't reckon on how fond I'd become of the Food Network. I was succeeded by an interim president and then by a disastrous president. Ratings dropped. It took four years and two more presidents before Food got it right. By then Scripps Howard had acquired the company and now seems to have solved its problems. Food's ratings are better than when I left. Sometimes they're better than CNN's.

Round 83: **A Smart Jewish Guy**

I can think of three different reasons why Ted merged with Time Warner. For five years he had been telling the people close to him that TBS was too small to survive on its own. He'd been looking to buy other companies, and it wasn't happening. So he decided if he couldn't buy, he might as well sell.

Two, there's the frustration; the board sat on top of him. John Malone praised his creativity and energy but killed his deals. Maybe he'd have better luck working for just one boss, Gerry Levin.

Three, there's Ted's old CBS plan: Let them buy him, be the biggest stockholder, and take over the company. The Trojan horse, the mouse swallows the elephant plan.

Gerry Levin had his own reasons for buying Turner: Disney had just taken over ABC, Westinghouse Electric had just bought CBS. Gerry saw that in order to survive media companies would have to grow larger. He saw TBS as his best opportunity and offered $7.5 billion for the company. The whole deal took only five weeks.

Levin flew out to Montana to meet with Ted. According to the *Washington Post,* he was picked up by Jane Fonda, who said, "I hope you're not going to make Ted upset." Levin said, "No, I think he's going to love this." Levin told the *Post*, "By the time dessert was served that night, Turner agreed to the outlines of the merger."

Levin always believed in merger. First, he believed that Time Life was too small to survive independently and brought in Warner Brothers. When the Disney/ABC merger created a $16.4 billion titan, Levin merged with Turner, which made him a $19.8 billion monster. Gerry wanted to make sure that his was the biggest.

Turner had negotiated well and assured himself of a vice-chairmanship and control of all cable networks including HBO, two seats on Time Warner's board, and $2.6 billion.

At first Ted was feisty. Shortly after their companies merged, Ted Turner, Gerry Levin, and Dick Parsons flew down to Atlanta to see a Braves game. On the flight, Ted turned to Levin and said, "Gerry, you're Jewish aren't you?" Gerry said, "Yes, Ted. Do you have a problem with that?" Ted said, "No. I always wanted a smart Jew to manage my money."

Then Ted turned to Dick Parsons, the COO of Time Warner, who is black, and said, "Now Dick, I don't even have to ask what you are, all I can say is you must be one talented son of a bitch to get where you've gotten."

Turner was marking his territory. He was telling Levin and Parsons, who were his bosses on paper, that he could say anything he wanted to them, and there was nothing they could do about it, he was the largest shareholder.

Whether or not Ted was trying his 1982 strategy—let them buy me, but I'll outmuscle them with the board and I'll take control of the company—he never was able to move up to the number one spot. He had not reckoned on Levin's staying power.

Gerry has done three mergers over the past dozen years. First he merged with the past, (Warner Brothers), then with the present (Ted Turner and TBS), and now he's planning to merge with the future (AOL). In that time period, he's also promoted himself to CEO of the combined empire. No matter who owns how much stock, Gerry's always emerged as CEO. Whenever the stock flagged, Gerry went out and merged with somebody else, the stock soared, and he kept his job.

Gerry indulged Ted Turner. When Ted wanted to continue the Goodwill Games after the merger, even though they lost millions, Gerry said okay. When Gerry wanted to sell Court TV, and Ted didn't, Gerry said okay. (Ted found new management and sextupled Court's ratings.) Gerry has let Ted be rude to him, he has adjusted to Ted's more outrageous exploits, but he's kept on running the company, and nobody on Wall Street is saying, "Gee, maybe Time Warner would do better under Turner."

Many people on Wall Street continue to have respect for Ted. They think Ted's presence at Time has helped drain some of the waste from Time Warner's formerly lavish lifestyle, but they do not feel that Ted Turner could run Time Warner.

After Gerry arranged his merger with AOL, he had even less reason to be concerned about Ted. In public, he deferred to him; Ted kept his seat on the dais at all the press conferences, but in reality his power was gone. Even before the merger, Gerry Levin and Time Warner were taking a hand in CNN. When Rick Kaplan couldn't get approval to spend $24 million on new sets, he went up to Time Warner and got his money. When Kaplan and Lou Dobbs battled because Kaplan broke into *Moneyline* to carry a Clinton speech live, Time Warner backed Kaplan and let Dobbs resign. After Dobbs left, Gerry actively tried to recruit John Huey, the editor of *Fortune,* to take over CNN/FN, but Huey stayed at *Fortune.*

Ted had been "marginalized." He had agreed to vote his stock for the AOL merger without assuring himself of any position in the new company. His careless negotiating style had cost him whatever leverage he might have had. The patient Gerry had outwitted and outwaited the impulsive Ted. When Levin and Steve Case, the chairman of AOL, announced a new table of organization for the merged company, Ted no longer had an operating role. He had not been consulted.

Afterwards the *L.A. Times* interviewed Terry McGuirk, now chairman of TBS, who said, "Did Ted want an operating role with the new company? Yes. Was he unhappy that he didn't get one? Yes. Is he on board with the new structure and embracing the new merger? Yes." But Ted continued to voice his gripes privately to reporters and to power brokers in the cable world.

At CNN's twentieth anniversary party, Levin and Case assured Ted that he would have a "much bigger canvas, he's going to be involved in every aspect of this whole company." Case said that Ted Turner has been his hero for twenty-five years. Everyone made nice. Ted knows what soft-soaping is and knows when he is being "handled."

The question is what will Ted do about it? He is tough enough and outrageous enough and probably self-destructive enough, to try to wreck the merger before it's done, but does he have the will to do it, to come back from the dead one more time? Maybe he doesn't even want to do it. Why should he want to run an Internet, magazine, music, movie company when he's always wanted to run a network; NBC may be available. When the AOL deal is completed, Ted may have the money to make a serious bid for it. And if he does it will be Gerry Levin who's made it possible. The AOL deal has made Ted a much richer man.

Round 84: I Can't Go Home Again

In the winter of 1997 after the merger, I tried to go home to CNN. I'd been gone from the Food Network for a year and a half. It had been sold to Belo Broadcasting; I still owned 5 percent. Time Warner stock was going up; my financial future was secure. I decided it was time to have some fun.

I had two options: I'd had an idea about putting the twenty-four-hour, local news channels into a national network. We would offer them national and international news, and special features, paying them some money (network compensation) and taking from them four minutes of commercial time every hour to sell nationally. Rupert Murdoch had proved that the idea worked with local sports networks. I thought news would work as well, but I would have to find partners, partners to provide money and news. I would then have to convince the local cable networks that the deal was good for them, too. That was a lot of work.

My other option was simpler: I could just go to work for somebody else. An old man sitting on the news desk, helping to break in the young and eagers; a savvy producer sitting in the editing room, putting together hard news stories; maybe even a wise field producer making sure good packages got into the network on time.

Either of those ideas would've been fun, but I went for simple. I called Ted and told him I'd like to go back to work for CNN. He told me that he was now satisfied with Tom Johnson. I told him I didn't want Johnson's job, I just wanted to get back in the news business. He told me to call Tom, he would set it up.

I made two trips to Atlanta. The first occurred just days after the Heaven's Gate cult mass suicide. MSNBC had just launched, and I compared its coverage with CNN. CNN was late and weak. MSNBC, helped by a strong San Diego affiliate, beat the hell out of CNN. By the end of the story, there was no reason for anyone, certainly not for me, to watch anybody but MSNBC. When I got down to Atlanta, I asked one of my hosts, not Johnson, why CNN was so late with the story.

It seemed that Ted Turner had lately laid down an edict: less coverage of "crime stories." CNN's overcoverage of the JonBenet Ramsey murder had troubled him, as it should've. But an edict from the boss scares the guts out of everybody. Would Ted think that Heaven's Gate was just another crime story? If CNN went live with it, would somebody get fired?

The desk thought it best to call Tom Johnson before making the decision. Tom pondered. By the time a collective leadership made up its mind, MSNBC had walked off with the audience. It was not a heartening omen for my return to the news business.

Following that revelation, I visited with Johnson, Gail Evans, whom I had hired as Sandi Freeman's booker and who had risen to be CNN's executive vice president, and Steve Korn who had been one of our lawyers when we sued to get into the pool. He was now CNN's COO, the old-timers called him the Burt Reinhardt of the future.

I thought I let the three of them know my goals. I did not want to run CNN, I did not want to participate in management. I wanted to be a grunt who could laugh at the suits. I was tired of trying to run things, I didn't want bottom-line responsibility.

Of course, I was kidding myself. Within hours of my arrival, I couldn't resist telling Tom Johnson how to run his business. I pointed out to him that his real competitors were not MSNBC and the still nascent Fox News but the twenty-four-hour local news channels: Long Island's Channel 12 and Washington's Channel 8 both had better twenty-four-hour ratings than CNN. Time Warner's New York 1 had five times more viewers in New York City than CNN did. There were new twenty-four-hour local channels opening up all over the country. Johnson did not want to hear about it. He referred me to Lynn Gutstadt, then head of CNN research, who hadn't paid much attention to the effect of local news channels on CNN viewing. She promised to do a study and send me the results.

Johnson felt much more comfortable comparing CNN's ratings with MSNBC's. For most of the day in 1997, MSNBC had only hash marks for ratings; Nielsen could detect no discernible viewing. Johnson didn't take into account that MSNBC was just getting started. When I pointed it out to him, he was not amused.

I had resolved not to mention my local news network idea in Atlanta, but I blurted it out anyway; I told Johnson that, based on the twenty-four-hour local news ratings, I was preparing a business plan for a network that would insert national news into local news networks. Since the local networks had good ratings and good clearance in their markets, there would immediately be sizable advertising revenue.

I figured that CNN, ABC, or CBS could prepare the inserts at little cost, pay a fee to the local cable affiliates, get time in return, and make a lot of money. Tom Johnson asked if I wanted a consultancy to explore the project for CNN. Aware how many ideas are smothered by consultancy, I declined. When I suggested the idea to Steve Korn, his only comment was, "Sounds like a good idea to me, how can we convince Ted it's his?" The more things change. . . .

On March 19, I was back in Atlanta, meeting with Gutstadt. She presented me with her numbers. They showed CNN doing quite well against local news networks. Her numbers matched none that I had seen from the local station in Washington. As it turned out, she was measuring her numbers against the CNN universe, which was larger than Channel 8's universe. That's like comparing grapefruits and oranges. Even taking that into account, the numbers didn't match. I thought CNN was living in a dream world.

I met with Mark Carter, CNN's director of strategic planning. He was exhibiting great frustration. CNN had an opportunity to hire ABC anchor Aaron Brown. Carter thought Brown was intelligent, articulate, and a strong broadcaster. By then, "news consultants" were studying CNN, analyzing its content, programming, and talent. Carter said that the "consultants" had run Brown's name and tapes past focus groups, and the groups concluded that Brown was no better than several anchors already at CNN. Mark wasn't just talking about Bernie Shaw or Lou Dobbs, he also included ordinary no-name CNN presenters.

I was stunned. It seemed as if the "news consultants," companies like Magid and ARD, were determining who CNN was going to put on the air. I asked Mark, "How come?" He shrugged. It was clear to me that, in going after Aaron Brown, Carter had been trying to upgrade CNN's on-camera talent, to bring in more intelligence, more substance. But the consultants said, in effect, "Intelligence and substance won't get you any more viewers. Aaron Brown is not worth the money." A director of strategic planning who gets his orders from news consultants has a very limited strategic planning role to play.

I've always felt that "news consultants" belonged at local television stations where general managers, who often knew nothing about news, need guidance so they can tell their news directors what stories to run, how many to run, and what anchors and reporters to hire.

Consultants may also excuse failure. If the news programs get low ratings, the bosses can say, "That's what the consultants told us to do." Then they hire new consultants, which gives them six more months to get the ratings up. Local news is a ruthless business.

Network news, that's different. Network newsmen are supposed to be journalists. They are to be left alone to run their own business. CNN is a network. Why was it relying on consultants and focus groups? Had it lost all confidence in its own news judgment? Furthermore, the consultants' recommendations were sent directly to Ted Turner. Did Ted need news consultants to tell him how to run CNN?

I have no doubt that if CNN had relied on news consultants in 1980, we would never have done live news. Researchers would have presented the concept to an audience; the audience, not knowing what live news was, would have shrugged it off. Live news is a concept. It's impossible to like live news as a generality. Yes, I want to see Tiananmen Square live, yes, I want to see Baghdad bombed live, yes, I want to see the *Challenger* missile launch live, but do I want to see news live? It all depends what's playing.

Live was CNN's audience accumulation method from conception. No one wants to miss Tiananmen Square, or Baghdad, or the *Challenger*. In order not to, the viewer may have to put up with many hours of "nothing very much happened." If the editor is smart enough, and the network is live enough, the audience will stay around and stay around and stay around, because they're afraid of missing a once-in-a-lifetime event. It's Zappa's "randomonium."

No researcher, no matter how many focus groups, can prove or disprove that theory. Focus groups cannot comment on what they've never seen.

The original CNN schedule was based on news flow: I believed then that the best reason for an audience to turn to CNN was because it was the best source of news on television. I believed that the flow of news on CNN would be strong enough to carry viewers with it for hours. The 1982 CNN rating book speaks for itself.

In 1997, CNN and its researchers were developing a different theory. It's called "appointment viewing." Appointment viewing means programming so compelling that viewers will make mental appointments to turn to it at specific times. In a world of a hundred channels and a choice of 35,000 programs that's asking a hell of a lot.

Gail Evans had developed *Burden of Proof* as a half-hour follow-up to the O.J. trial. It worked. After the trial ended, people continued to watch it in the afternoon. It became appointment viewing. Now Evans and the researchers were moving it into prime time, to try to boost CNN ratings, which it failed to do. The early success of *Burden of Proof* encouraged Gail to try to develop programs like it. Her strategy matched that proposed by the consultants. Gail liked consultants.

As reported frequently throughout this book, CNN's rating in the late nineties had dropped precipitously. Even before competition arrived, CNN was occasionally down to a .4. Tom Johnson went to consultants to find out what to do about it. He was also searching for a new head of news. Tom had been making a run at ABC's Rick Kaplan for several years. Kaplan was coy. He wanted to make sure, before he said yes, that he had a limited future at ABC and that he would get the title "president of CNN"; Tom did not wish to give it up. All this I learned in two days at CNN.

Johnson had set up a round table meeting for me with Chris Cramer, the head of CNN International, John Lane who worked for the documentary unit, and assorted other journalists and executive producers. I gave them my standard "There is much more news than you recognize" talk. It was a pleasant colloquy. I'm sure they felt the meeting was as much of a waste of time as I did. Then I went into a meeting with Johnson and Evans.

Johnson said, "Ted Turner tells me he 'couldn't control you.' Will I be able to control you?" I said, "Sure." I didn't tell him that one of the reasons I wanted to work there is to see how somebody else managed Ted Turner. I did tell him I wanted to work as a producer or on the assignment desk. I had no ambitions to head a news company. Years later someone asked me, "Who were you kidding? It's like Bill Clinton going back to Arkansas and saying all he wants to do is become attorney general." I had thought it was more like John Quincy Adams going into the House of Representatives and spending the last years of his life there happily. Looking back, I think the other guy was right, the only person I was kidding was myself.

For some reason, Johnson had opened up to me. He said that Ted controlled the network. He, Johnson, had been responsible for the Christie Brinkley morning show on CNN, which had been cancelled after a few months on Ted Turner's orders. I thought the show had been awful. I had covered Christie Brinkley for one of my *People* magazine shows, and I knew Christie was no expert on world events. I wasn't aware of her expertise in any other field either. Johnson said, and his eyes were tearing: "We were just beginning to get it right when Ted killed it."

As I walked out, I thought that Ted had achieved his dream. He had gotten a president of CNN who knew less about news than he did. I knew I could not go home again. If I wanted to get back into news, I would have to do it the hard way.

Round 85: **The Times, They Ain't A-Changin'**

I took my twenty-four-hour local/national news network plan to ABC. I told them that it would do for news what Rupert Murdoch had done for sports. Fox showed home-team games in dozens of cities across the country. These games ordinarily got anywhere from 4 to 8 rating points. The competition, ESPN, which is owned by ABC, offered only one baseball game all across the country. ESPN usually got a 2 rating. On its network Fox sold advertising time nationally and inserted the commercials into home-team games. National advertisers on Fox might reach twice as many people as national advertisers on ESPN.

The twenty-four-hour local news networks had ratings ranging from a 1.6 in New York to a .3 or .4 in Florida or Orange County, but overall they averaged better than a .5. There was CNN limping along with a .4, and even less in markets where it competed head-to-head with local news channels.

We could use the same advertising sales pitch that Fox did with sports. We would say, "People are more interested in hometown news than national news. The ratings prove it." Fox did well with advertisers, and I was sure we would too.

Even in 1997, it seemed easy to compete with CNN. The CNN audience wasn't getting any younger; its median age was around sixty. Local news had a median age around forty-three. Our salesmen could say, "Advertiser, you have to replace the younger news viewers who no longer watch CNN. The place to find that audience is our network."

I thought that ABC would readily understand the proposal. They owned ESPN, they knew that local sports was successful, and they were battling Fox for advertising dollars. My old ABC friends Herb Granath and Tom Cerio were very encouraging. Cerio even emailed Bob Iger, ABC's CEO, about the project. In the end though, it was not Iger or Granath or Cerio who counted.

The news division's executive vice president, Dick Wald, had been reasonably receptive; he didn't have the power to say yes, but he didn't say no. He said talk to Gerry Leybourne, head of ABC Cable. Leybourne liked the idea. She told me she'd tried to get ABC to launch a cable news network of its own aimed at younger viewers a couple of years before, but had been shot down. An audience with a median age in the forties pleased her, but she couldn't say yes either.

The critical question was, how much would the news project offend ABC's local stations? When ABC's owned and operated stations objected strongly, the network didn't even bother to take it to its other affiliates.

ABC was trying to start a soap opera channel on cable. The affiliates were objecting. They did not want ABC programming available on cable to compete with them. That could hurt the affiliate two ways: First, people who ordinarily watch soap operas on the stations might decide to watch it on cable. That would hurt the stations' afternoon ratings. Second, if the soap operas were shown in prime time, some viewers might desert the ABC prime-time schedule to watch the soaps. That would hurt the stations' ratings in prime time. The powers that were at ABC wanted a soap opera channel more than a news channel; they passed on the idea.

Eighteen months later, an ABC news executive told me that the national/local news channel had represented ABC News's last best chance to compete with NBC or CNN, both of which have more than one way of distributing news and, thus, laying off costs.

I went to lunch with Jimmy Griffin, by 1997 a member of the board of directors at William Morris. He represents Regis Philbin, Geraldo Rivera and Emeril Lagasse, among others. I told Griffin about my idea. He told me to wait a month because he was about to sign a contract with a very important news company who might be interested. The company was the *New York Times*. I thought it was worth waiting for.

The *Times* has had a bad record about television. It hadn't applied for a TV license when they were available. In 1975, when I started ITNA, some of my former colleagues at TVN had gone to the *Times* to propose that they start a news service for independent stations. The *Times* said no. I went to the *Daily News* station. The *Daily News* said yes.

In the sixties, the *Times* had bought a group of small- and medium-market television stations, but only because, it was said, the *Times* "family" owners had been left short of cash when the newspaper unions went on strike. The income from the stations would provide walking-around money for the family next time.

The only good sign for the project was that the *Times* had hired the William Morris Agency to look into television, so maybe they really were getting serious. When Jimmy said the *Times* was interested in our deal, I became very interested.

It developed that the *Times*'s interest was provisional. They'd been badly burned in a couple of other cable attempts. The *Times*'s president had been fired, and now everybody was gun-shy. William Morris had been brought in to give them some cover, but they wanted more. They wanted us, Griffin or me, to bring in a cable or broadcast partner. I tried Belo and Cablevision and got nowhere. Jimmy Griffin tried Liberty Media. Liberty, a TCI sister company, and William Morris were associated in *MacNeil/Lehrer*; Liberty agreed. Thus reassured, the *Times* said yes.

The *Times* offered its name, its content, and its funding to the partnership. Liberty would throw in funding and cable expertise. Our contribution would be producing the *Times* television stories and selling advertising time. I could do the production, and John Barbera, who had been head of sales for Turner Broadcasting, would handle the advertisers. Aside from Ted Turner, he's the best advertising salesman I ever knew. He became my partner.

Barbera left TBS in 1992 when the company went white shoe, and hired Booz Allen to restructure corporate management. The study determined that TBS was too entrepreneurial, and Barbera was "restructured" right out of his job. Terry McGuirk and Bill Shaw, TBS human relations head, flew up to Barbera's home one Sunday night and fired him. Steve Heyer, who had been a lead consultant for Booz Allen on the Turner report, wound up with Barbera's job. Another business maxim: Beware the "consultant," the job he wants may be your own.

When I first approached Barbera, he had his doubts. He'd grown up an Italian kid in Boston, where the people he knew said, "The *Times* is written in Moscow, edited in Tel Aviv, and published in New York." He thought we'd have a hard time selling it across the country, but once we were partnering, he began to read the *Times* with different eyes and found it a good paper. And, as it turned out, never once when we went on the road did any of our prospects suggest that the *Times* was too liberal for their markets. All thought the *Times* name would help them.

The *Times* and Liberty gave us development money, and we proceeded through the usual steps: We made a six-minute presentation reel. We developed a power point proposal. We did a five-year business plan, and a book. The *Times* decided it needed a ten-year business plan.

Only the *Times* would expect a meaningful ten-year business plan in an atmosphere as volatile as the current media scene. A five-year plan represents an informed hope, a fervent wish, and a deep prayer. A ten-year business plan is pure fantasy. Still, after eight months, we produced one that was satisfactory, but we had lost a lot of time.

As we went on the road in 1997, the *Times* backed off a step. When the *Times* accepted the business plan, they'd promised a definite go if we reached 10 million subscribers. This is a typical TV syndication approach, a firm go when a carriage goal is reached. All your customers understand that deal, and they accept it readily. It is a firm contract. If you reach 10 million homes, you have to go forward. The *Times* was not ready for that. Now, Barbera and I were not going out to negotiate, we were merely going out to explore.

Early in 1997, when we brought out our first business plan, most of the local news channels had lots of advertising time unsold. The channels were new, the market was weak, and advertisers were slow to sign up. We were asking them to give us four minutes of advertising time per hour. They wanted to give us less, but they were open to negotiation. We were guaranteeing them compensation that in many cases would have brought them to breakeven.

By late 1997, the market had changed. Local systems were selling more of their own time, but they still seemed willing to give us three minutes per hour. They needed our compensation money. On the up side, twenty-four-hour local news channels had been founded in Florida, Las Vegas, Dallas, and Houston, among other places. The market was widening. Our business plan still worked. Barbera and I returned to the *Times* with a favorable report.

Disaster struck. Liberty decided to pull out of the deal. They had $12 billion to invest. They had no time for $15 million ventures. I grant you, they were gentlemen about it. They would help us, they would arrange meetings, they might sit in, but no more money. The *Times* would have to go it alone. The *Times*, of course, would never go it alone. I should've backed out then, but by then I had fallen in love with the new version of the *Times* that its editor, Joe Lelyveld, had created.

It seemed to me that Lelyveld recognized that television, especially cable television, showed people the news. They no longer relied on a newspaper to tell them the news. So he turned the *New York Times* into a paper about the news. His hard news stories covered aspects of the news that television ignored. He added section after section of niche news, news about subjects rarely and superficially covered by television. He added first-class writers, he developed superb graphics, and introduced color. Since local television news was all crime and grime,

Lelyveld beefed up his metro section, and in the process, he turned the *New York Times* from a great daily newspaper into the greatest daily news magazine the world has ever seen.

The *New York Times* under Lelyveld has become a surprising newspaper. Only in the new *Times* can you learn about a species of birds in which the females mate with each other on the North Sea dikes, complete with pictures on the front page of the Science section. In the back pages of the Science section you could learn that Mississippi has banned the sale of vibrators. The old gray lady is pulling up her skirt, letting down her hair, and not telling anybody about it. I knew that if I produced television stories as compelling and unique as this, and they were shown on local news stations, the *Times* would add tens of thousands of subscribers.

Meanwhile, Jimmy Griffin tried to find other partners, as did I. All the prospective partners said, "What does the *New York Times* bring to the party? If we want to do this, why do we need them? We want to establish our own brand, not theirs." But as a television producer, I wanted the opportunity to turn the *Times* into television, so I continued to struggle against all the odds. If we got the cable channels to carry the service, we would all make a lot of money. But as each month passed, the cable systems themselves began to make money. Some of them didn't need us anymore. Still the *Times* diddled and dawdled.

Arthur Sulzberger, Jr., had just taken over as head of the New York Times Company, and deciding whether or not to go with us was his first major call; it seemed to me that most of the people around him were pushing him not to do it. The *Times* promised us an answer before Christmas of 1998; the executives were going on a retreat and would let us know when they got back.

It was no surprise, but a great disappointment when the *Times* declined. They would not go into the venture on their own, and they had decided instead to join with *MacNeil/Lehrer*, to try to start a half-hour news talk show on PBS. I suppose it was a fitting end. If they succeeded, it would be a conventional, dull, television show on a non-commercial network, and no one would hear about it again. As of this writing, they have not succeeded.

Whenever I see the *Times,* I think what wonderful television it might make. And without the *Times*'s consent, it often does. The networks and the local stations read the paper. They grab what they want from its pages, turn the stories into okay television, and the *Times* gets no credit.

If you're giving it away, why should anyone pay for it? The *Times* they ain't a-changin'.

Round 86: **CNN, It Ain't A–Succeeding! Why?**

During the past twenty years, CNN has become more established than the establishment, more traditional than the networks. During the past eighteen years, CNN's ratings have declined by 70 percent. In May 2000 the ratings were at a .28, the lowest of any month in CNN's history. In prime time, more people under fifty-five watched the Food Network than CNN. These numbers might curse the news business forever.

Some hope that the aging demographics of the American population will help CNN. "If there are more people over fifty-five, won't that help grow CNN's audience?" a senior CNN executive once asked me. "Not a chance," I told him. "People don't suddenly discover news when they turn fifty-five. People over fifty-five remember the Depression, remember the war, they grew up with news. For them, it's a habit." "Thank you," the CNN guy said. "That's what I've been telling them." Tom Johnson is still grasping at straws. CNN has got to change before it will get new viewers.

If broadcast executives and Wall Street funders come to believe that twenty-four-hour news networks produce only a .3 rating with two-thirds of the viewers over fifty-five, they will never start or fund another one. When they discover that in the spring of 2000, the Time Warner twenty-four-hour local news channel, New York 1, had five times as many viewers in the city of New York as CNN did, they'll start putting their money into local news.

Here are the Time Warner Five Borough New York City ratings numbers, average quarter hour, full day:

New York 1	1.6	26,000	viewers
CNBC	.6	10,000	viewers
CNN	.3	5,000	viewers
MSNBC	.1	1,250	viewers
Fox	.1	1,250	viewers
Headline		No discernible audience	

At this moment, with these ratings CNN seems a failure. When another generation of journalists studies CNN, I want them to understand it was not the news that failed CNN, it was CNN that failed the news.

Somewhere along the way, CNN became what it had been created to demolish. CNN has the same morning meetings as the networks, it chases the same stories, schedules them the same way, reports them the same way, maintains the same strangling bureaucracy, and looks like a lesser copy of its rivals. It is no longer original, no longer different.

It didn't have to be that way. In 1981/82, CNN presented a continuing stream of interesting stories: a missile site explosion in Damascus, Arkansas; a brain cancer "epidemic" in Houston, Texas; a Frank Sinatra hearing in Las Vegas; a G.I. carrying the wrong gun in El Salvador; the onset of the AIDS outbreak in San Francisco; David Stockman admitting live that his budget had been fudged. If you didn't see them on CNN, you didn't see them. To know the news, to see it happen, you had to watch CNN. The numbers bore that out.

In 2000, CNN's low ratings have become an advertising salesman's nightmare. Turner Broadcasting's Bob Sieber—the great genius of cable research, the man who along with Ted had been able to convince advertisers that a .7 rating was worth buying, who had for years been able to control the flow of information about CNN's ratings and demographics—began to talk instead about the reach and numbers of the CNN website; how many visitors it had, and how often they returned to the site.

Sieber is very good. In the old days, Sieber's advice to CNN salesmen was: When you don't have ratings, talk demographics; when you don't have demographics, talk ratings. Now Sieber seems to have added a third alternative: When you don't have either one, talk website.

I am alone with the ideal of the "pure CNN." The CNN of June 1, 1980. I want it to survive. I have seen the May ratings and the May demographics, and for the first time I doubt that CNN will prevail. I wonder if Ted Turner still thinks that CNN will be on the air when the world ends. Now that Ted is gone, will he take his tape of "Nearer My God To Thee" with him?

With its tiny ratings and aging demos, the only question left may be, will CNN die before its audience, or will its audience die before CNN?

By permission of Mike Luckovich and Creators Syndicate, Inc.

Round 87: **Opportunity Lost**

"**F**ucking HMO bastards, pieces of shit." That's what Helen Hunt says in *As Good As It Gets,* her 1997 movie. When I saw the movie, the audience stood up and cheered. I called around; audiences in Washington, L.A., and King Ferry, New York, did the same. Americans hate their HMOs, and by and large, the HMOs deserve it.

I am of the school of Horace Greeley, Joseph Pulitzer, and Henry Luce. The school that says there are no bad stories, only bad reporters. I think there are no dull news years, only dull news bosses. Here's the HMO story: greedy, inefficient insurance companies providing tardy, inferior medical services employ a slovenly bureaucracy that invariably screws up the billing, particularly repayment. That's the general perception and that's not a bad story. It's also a great way for a twenty-four-hour news service to establish its identity. That's the kind of story Greeley, Pulitzer, and Luce used when they were building their brands and emerging as "tribunes of the people."

I pitched a one-hour, prime-time daily talk show that would have launched an "HMO crusade" to MSNBC. They turned it down. In their news judgment, the story wouldn't last six months. They were wrong, so why hasn't anybody else picked up the story? Mass media have given up crusades; they're considered déclassé. What the media forget is if you'll speak for the people, they'll watch you or read you or listen to you. It's one of those rare opportunities to do good and do well at the same time.

Greeley, Pulitzer, and Luce had one great advantage. They were owner/editors. For three years I acted as if I were the owner/editor of CNN. In 1982 Ted corrected me. After that CNN just covered the same stories everybody else did.

CNN could have made a full hour every night out of HMOs. Each hour begins with a report from the field: a story of an American family caught in the grips of an HMO foul-up or, more surprisingly, a family expressing satisfaction with their HMO. It's not all old people. One day a week is pediatrics; another day, ob-gyn; another, doctors and nurses airing their complaints. In the studio there is a moderator. Consumers have their advocates, HMOs have their defenders. There are live phone calls. It is great television, it affects people's lives. I've never been able to get it on the air.

When I left CNN in 1982, I had a story that I thought could affect the news and differentiate CNN. Premier Leonid Brezhnev was dying, and so was the Soviet Union. I sent Stuart Loory to cover the death throes. Loory had covered Moscow for the *Herald Tribune*. He knew the territory, but Ed Turner brought him back immediately. Brezhnev hung on for a few months, the Soviet Union for a few years. Leaving Loory there during that key period might have made the fall of the "Evil Empire" our story. We would not have been surprised when Gorbachev surrendered to Reagan in Reykjavik.

In 1989–1990, CNN was represented by Steve Hurst, who was competent enough but not Stuart Loory. Hurst reported a rumor that Mikhail Gorbachev was quitting as general secretary of the Communist Party and would try to govern the U.S.S.R. simply as its president. Hurst said it couldn't happen. If Gorbachev was out as general secretary, he'd lose his job as president as well.

I thought Hurst had gotten it wrong. I thought Gorby was launching a trial balloon. If the West had supported him, particularly financially, he was prepared to leave the party. After Hurst and the rest of the Western press scoffed at the idea, Gorbachev denied the rumor, and the story died.

Later, when I was dealing with TASS, the Soviet news agency, I asked some friends what they knew about it. They told me that it had been a trial balloon, that Gorbachev *was* prepared to leave the party if the West would support him. They even pointed out to me the guy who had leaked the story, a close associate of Gorby's, who drank a lot. He was the perfect leaker, close enough to be believed, drunk enough to be denied.

Round 88: **Is Ted Going Wacko?**

When smart people say dumb things, be careful.

Ted has been telling the world he wants to buy NBC. In March 2000, he came right out and announced to CNN bureau managers that when the Time Warner sale to AOL is complete, he'll sell his stock and buy NBC, but the world is laughing.

NBC is worth $35 billion, according to GE, its owner. Ted's only got about $10 billion. "Where's he going to get the money?" Neil Cavuto, the Fox News business anchor, asks me. "It's wacko. What about Ted's anticompete clause?" Neil is too young to remember that Ted Turner made his fortune being called wacko by wiser men than Cavuto. Is Neil unaware that Wall Street might lend Ted the money? Cavuto asks me if Ted has a noncompete clause with Time Warner. I do not know; neither does Neil.

I called Time Warner—there is a noncompete clause. Ted cannot own more than 3 percent of a competitive company, nor can he serve on its board of directors. Does Time Warner regard ownership of a broadcast network such as NBC competitive? "Yes." How long does Ted's noncompete run? I'm still waiting for Time Warner to get back to me on that one. I called NBC's chairman, Bob Wright, and told his secretary I wanted to ask Bob if Ted had contacted NBC. Bob hasn't returned my call. There are an awful lot of balls in play, and I've got a deadline.

It's always tough to figure what Ted will do. All I've got is questions. Will he make a major fuss about AOL in order to get Time to release him from his noncompete? I can't believe he'll sit on the sidelines and sulk. The old Ted Turner, if he had painted himself into a corner, would have broken down walls to get out. Does Ted still have that much energy? Lou Dobbs says Ted may be too tired. I don't think so. (Keep in touch with MeandTed.com.)

At the moment, Time Warner's single concern is not so much that Ted plans to buy NBC, it's that he may use his AOL stock as collateral. If, after the merger, Ted decides to sell his shares it may drive the combined company's price way down. Information from this chapter has already appeared in the press. CNN executives searched for the source.

They called around to people who might have talked to me. They have not asked, "Did you tell Reese about Ted's plans to buy NBC?" They want to know, "Did you tell Reese Ted was going to sell his stock to do it?" The point is that Ted cannot keep his mouth shut. People within and outside the company have said that Ted will use, sell, barter, or do whatever to his Time Warner interests to acquire NBC. That is, of course, if he can beat the noncompete clause and raise the rest of the money.

Neil Cavuto was on to something. Ted is sounding "wacko." He sounds like the Ted I knew in 1980, panicked, uncertain about the future. At CNN's twentieth anniversary party, a journalist addressed

Ted as "Mr. Turner." Turner said, "It's Ted, don't give me this Mister shit. Mister, my ass. I'll be unemployed in six months." In 1980 he didn't know if CNN would work, in 2000 he doesn't know if he will work at CNN.

The great broadcasters of the twentieth century, Paley and Sarnoff, ran CBS and NBC for over fifty years. Turner ran TBS for seventeen years. After that, he had a board of cable owners controlling him and, finally, Gerry Levin sitting on top of him at Time Warner. His best ideas, his most brilliant forays were cut off by his bosses.

He's so concerned about his loss of power now that he told a London *Times* reporter that he's thinking about buying a nuclear weapon, "I'm a news power. Why shouldn't I be a nuclear power. We have a right to bear arms in this country."

At this moment, and I don't think it will last, I see Ted as a sad, almost tragic figure. He is King Lear after Lear's daughters have finished with him.

How did it all happen? It started when he paid much too much for MGM. Then he had to take money from the major cable system owners, and they took seats on his board of directors. He couldn't spend more than $3 million without their consent. No longer could he make major strategic decisions.

In 1992 the board, dominated by cable owners, thought the company had outgrown itself and requested that Turner bring in an outside consulting company and restructure TBS. Ted made a mistake. He pledged to the board that he would abide by the consultants' recommendations regardless of the outcome. (One insider says that Ted originally resisted the pledge but acceded at McGuirk's urging.)

Turner, McGuirk, and Gerry Hogan interviewed Booz Allen, selected them, and the rest is history. Hogan, who had been acting as TBS president and COO ex officio, couldn't get the title despite Ted's repeated promises, and left the company. Turner himself was in Montana with Jane Fonda for much of this period, and Terry was left to manage Booz Allen on a day to day basis. He saw his opportunities, and he took them.

On several occasions, the lead Booz Allen guys, Michael Wolfe and Steve Heyer, flew out to Montana for sessions with Ted to justify their recommendations. He acceded. For the most part, the study was supervised by McGuirk and within two years all of Terry's rivals were gone from the company.

With Hogan gone, Ted turned more and more to Terry. He loved and trusted Terry. The group around Ted, always circling each other, had long regarded Terry as the least able of the bunch. He did not sell advertising. He could not sign up affiliates. He had little head for numbers and no programming skills. What he had was Ted's absolute trust and the affection of many of those who had grown up with him in the cable industry. No small assets in the monarchical atmosphere of the early TBS before Booz Allen.

Two years after the study, during the New Year's weekend of 1994, Terry dispatched his last two rivals, John Barbera and Paul Beckham. The week before at a Christmas party, Barbera, with a few drinks under his belt, had told the assembled what he thought of McGuirk. The next Sunday night McGuirk and Bill Shaw made their move. They thanked him for the sixteen years he had spent building the company, told him not to come in the next day, and said they would send his personal things out to him by messenger. No settlement. Later, with a lawyer's help and a meeting with Ted Turner, Barbera managed to get a year and a half in severance. As he was walking out of Ted's office, Ted said, "Don't feel too bad, John. Some day it'll happen to me, and I'll just close the door and turn the lights out."

The Booz Allen table of organization made McGuirk the most important man in the company. Scott Sassa, then head of Turner Productions, was ordered to report to Terry. He left the company and joined Bill Bevins at Perelman. The CFO, Randy Booth, would report to both Ted Turner and Terry McGuirk. Steve Heyer, one of the Booz Allen consultants, came on board, absorbing the role of COO. On a day-to-day basis, McGuirk functioned as the CEO, with one exception. CNN would continue to report directly to Turner.

Ted usually came to Atlanta for a few days a month to conduct two meetings. At the TBS meeting, Terry McGuirk reported to him about the doings of his business. At the separate CNN meetings, Tom Johnson would fill Ted in about the news business. The TBS meetings were attended by advertising sales and affiliate sales and production and finance. CNN meetings were attended by news staff. It's a rare company that lets news staff meet face-to-face with the chairman.

I think even before Ted sold out to Time Warner, managing the company had stopped being fun for him. The board was always looking over his shoulder. At some point he decided that if he couldn't run it his way, he didn't want to run it at all. So he let Booz Allen, McGuirk, and Heyer do it their way. But he still enjoyed CNN. The board didn't bother him; Tom Johnson did what Ted told him to do. Ted looked at research and made the programming decisions.

In 1996, Ted sold TBS to Time Warner. Everybody got rich, but Ted was no longer even the titular boss. When he made a lot of noise, he was able to get his way about most things, but his new masters took a real interest in CNN. Gerry Levin sat in at the monthly CNN meetings. When Rick Kaplan, CNN's new president, needed more money, he went to Levin. Time Warner got involved in CNN personnel decisions. In 2000, Terry McGuirk's name began to appear on CNN memos. Ted was bowing out.

Ted was Gulliver, pinned down by the Lilliputians. First, Kirk Kerkorian had caught him in the net with the MGM deal. Then the board tied his hands when they wouldn't let him spend more than $3 million without its approval. Booz Allen, Heyer, and McGuirk shackled one leg when they eased him out of day-to-day control. Finally, Time Warner, its board, and Gerry Levin diluted his authority over CNN and left him cuffed and hobbled. He was vice chairman of Time Warner, the richest man in the world who worked for somebody else.

Maybe he is where I was eighteen years ago. No longer can he lead. He's got to follow or get out of the way. Ted has never been a follower, and it's easy for him to get out of the way now. The sheen has worn off CNN. Everybody knows its ratings have gone to hell. Everybody knows about Tailwind. Ted can blame that all on Time Warner and retire with honor. Then he makes his comeback. Whether he makes it with NBC or something else, I think he'll make it.

Ted's been saying a lot of dumb things lately. I go on alert when smart people say dumb things.

Round 89: **It's Their Party, but I Can Cry If I Want To**

Pat and I arrived in Atlanta on May 31. Checking into the hotel, I ran into Don Carney, CNN's original sports reporter, and Frank Beatty, an affiliate relations salesman. There was no getting away now. I was part of the twentieth anniversary. They hadn't even invited me to the tenth. . . .

I told myself I'm just down here as a writer looking for a last chapter for the book. I've picked my role, "bastard at the wedding." So far, it was playing out. The hotel was a place where low-budget salesmen stayed when they made sales calls in downtown Atlanta. It was a five-minute walk across a highway to the official site, which is a much better hotel. There was no room for us there.

Two of Pat's VJs, now married with children, were also staying at the hotel. When they saw me, they rushed over, "Is Pat here?" One of them had been editing CBS *Sunday Morning* from Kurault through Osborne. The other was a production editor. Both of them were blonde and pretty, and seemed more than satisfied with their lives and more than grateful to Pat. It was the beginning of Pat's triumphant march through the children of CNN.

Breakfast was scheduled for 8:30 at CNN Center in the other hotel, the one where the big shots stayed, worked, and played. First we got credentials. I picked up the official books, the badges, the pins, and the T-shirts. The name on my badge was Reese Schoenfeld. It was spelled wrong.

Ten years ago, Porter Bibb wrote in his biography of Turner, "Schonfeld, who did it all—conceived the network, hired the people, designed it from the ground up, and ran it for two years—really is the father of CNN and you wouldn't know it." Bibb says of Turner, "If you leave his team, he erases the tape on you."

It is twenty-one years since Ted and I put this thing together. Eighteen years since he fired me, eighteen years since Ted began his exercise in historical revision. This chapter is about spending two days in a world from which I had been excised. For twenty years, I had shaken my head from side to side, shrugged my shoulders and accepted the situation as, "This is who Ted is, you knew what you were getting into, and this is the way the world works when you're playing with the giants."

At some point, when the midgets of CNN, the hangers-on and the toadies try to take upon themselves the task of writing history, you've got to fight back and take charge of your own history, of your own life. And that's what this book is for, to get things straight. This is my version of reality.

As we walked into breakfast, Ted was coming down the stairs. He yelled, "Reese, how you doing?" I said, "Terrific partner, how are you?" "Can't wait to read that book," said Ted.

I opened the "Eleventh Annual CNN World Report Conference," a 120-page opus from the Turner PR department. Brief biographies of the participants were provided. Ed Turner, who had departed CNN three years before, was a panelist. He was credited with the hiring of Peter Arnett. I hired Peter Arnett. Ed was off recuperating at the time.

As Pat and I passed Ed Turner's table, I asked him, "How much did you pay Peter Arnett when you hired him, Ed?"

"I didn't hire Peter Arnett," said Ed.

"It's in the book," I said.

"Oh, you know how they are," said Ed.

That was my problem. I did know how they were, and I knew they'd rewrite history, and I knew that fifty years from now, anyone digging in the CNN archives would learn that Ed Turner hired Peter Arnett. Ed was also credited with assigning and managing "the Reagan assassination attempt." Ed was in Atlanta at the time, about four slots down the chain of command, trying to figure out what the bureaus were doing. But, "you know how they are."

Our table was forty yards from the podium. This morning we were to hear from Jimmy Carter, the same man who gave us an hour interview on June 1, 1980. The institutional memory is so weak that no one remembered that. Instead, Carter spoke about the "CNN Effect," the power of CNN to bring peace to the world. He proved it mostly by telling us the different ways he'd used CNN in his efforts at world peacemaking.

He thanked CNN for delivering his peacekeeping messages; from Panama, from Haiti, from Uzbekistan, from Korea, it was as if CNN had become his messenger boy. As I listened to Jimmy Carter and thought of CNN's sunken ratings, I constructed a graphic . . . a naked emperor racing down the street, messages in hand, genitals in jockstrap, and on his head a Western Union cap. The messages were other people's.

Tom Johnson took to the podium just after breakfast, opened with welcoming remarks, then shocked the hell out of me. He said, first, we should acknowledge the founding president of CNN, Reese Schonfeld, who is here with us today. Of course, he pronounced my name "Schonfield." First they couldn't spell it, now they can't pronounce it.

Forty yards from the podium, way in the back of the room, I stood up to a round of applause. I yelled, "Thank you, Tom, for throwing this party for me." I'm sure he didn't hear me. Richard Blystone up in front yelled, "Bring him back!" I didn't hear him, but he told me the folks around him did.

After Carter, we adjourned to Kofi Annan. I never got there. As I strolled over, I encountered a parade of the people who appear in this book. I couldn't pass up the opportunity to learn more about what they did back then. Mike Boettcher told me about Argentina and his hundred-dollar dubs. Ron Dean told me about Poland and the tape in his pants. I was taking copious notes.

As I talked to Dean, Tom Johnson saw me with my pen and notepad. He strode over. Ordinarily the most courteous of men, now he was angry. He wanted me to call him so that he could tell me his side of the story. He said *Me and Ted* is all wrong. I asked him, "How do you know what's in the book?"

He said, "I know." I told him the book was still in progress. "Editing hasn't begun," I said. "How do *you* know what's in the book?"

He said, "I know." He reiterated that I was not getting it right, I had not considered the competition.

Tom walked away before I could tell him that I *had* considered the competition. Nickelodeon's ratings have doubled since 1983 despite competition from Fox Kids, Disney, and the Cartoon Network. ESPN's ratings have stayed constant since 1985, despite a serious challenge from Fox Sports. Only CNN had collapsed.

As I went in to lunch, Ted Turner was coming down the steps. We looked at each other, I waved, he stuck his tongue out and waved it. At lunch I sat next to Liz Wickersham, Ted's former girlfriend. Liz told me that when Ted sticks his tongue out, it means he loves you.

Liz and I had a good time over old times. We talked briefly about the book, and I told her she comes off fine. She asked me how I was treating Ted. I said okay. She said she was glad. Twenty-one years ago she made nice between me and Ted in Vegas. Now, she was doing her best to make nice between me and Ted in the book. Liz was class and brass, from start to finish.

Next stop was, "Reflections of the First Twenty Years," a flashy, highly produced special, overseen personally by CNN's then president, Rick Kaplan. It featured Christiane Amanpour, Bernie Shaw, Lou Waters, Ed Turner, and Gail Evans, hosted by Larry King. It opened with a blooper reel of CNN's first six months. Then, a burst of self-congratulatory statements with two significant moments. In the midst of the panel, Bernard Shaw asked for a minute of silence in memory of John Holliman, the CNN original who died in a car accident in 1998. Just as the audience hushed, Larry King asked a question. Old radio hosts cannot abide silence.

Larry King asked Christiane Amanpour if she did her work on the world's battlefield because she enjoyed "fear." Amanpour hesitated for fifteen seconds, then asked, "Do you mean do I enjoy danger?" King acknowledged he'd used the wrong word; he said he used the word "fear" because he's Jewish.

On the way out, we saw Jane Maxwell. In 1974, when I walked into TVN, the Coors Beer News Company, Jane Maxwell was at the reception desk. Jane worked with me at ITNA; I brought her down to CNN, I watched her grow. She was now senior vice president of CNN for Special Events; that's the conventions, the political campaigns, the major presidential trips. I've always felt that no matter who runs CNN, Jane belongs to me. As we walked down the steps, Gerry Levin saw Jane Maxwell. Jane saw Gerry Levin. They shouted each other's names. She ran over to him, Gerry hugged her; I was jealous as hell.

Then came the cocktail party. My best moment was a reunion with Burt Reinhardt. Burt and I had known each other for the past forty-five years. Several people had told me that Burt wondered why I didn't interview him for the book. I told them that I was sure that Burt would not want to speak out. At the party, we found each other, and we sat and talked. For the first time since I left CNN, we felt like friends.

At about 6:45 p.m., Ted Turner arrived. He got up on a chair and made a little speech. He mentioned in passing that he might be buying another network. He asked Burt to join him and announced that Burt, now eighty, had asked to retire. Ted said he'd convinced him to stay on three days a week and that Burt still had an office and a secretary. Every-one applauded. He made Burt speak publicly, which Burt does not like to do. Burt thanked Ted, adequately but not effusively, and then thanked all the CNN originals for what they had done to make the com-pany work.

As Ted left, he called out to me, "Reese! Am I gonna like your book?" I said, "You will if you read it yourself, Ted. If you let your friends tell you about it, you'll hate it." He said, "Are you gonna be mean to me?" And I said, "Just read all of it, Ted." Ted said, "If you write a mean book about me, I'm gonna write a mean book about you."

Before Ted left the room, I called him over and whispered to him, "Don't leave CNN, Ted. You're the best one left." Julia Sprunt, on behalf of Gerry Levin, grabbed Ted's arm and led him away. Gerry and Ted marched out together. As they walked off, I turned to Pat and said, "That's damning with faint praise."

Thursday evening's reception for CNN and 15,000 of its closest friends featured Diana Ross and the Supremes. We had tickets, Pat and I, but no one realized that Pat O'Gorman and Reese Schonfeld were a pair. Our tickets were singles, far apart. I'm sure we could've worked it out, but we didn't want to. We just wanted to get home and go to sleep. It had been a hard day.

At about 4:30 a.m., June 2, 2000, I woke up. I was in Atlanta at a second-rate hotel, where the third-string guests of the CNN twentieth anniversary had been lodged, paying for my own room. CNN's ratings are at an all-time low, and I fear Ted Turner is abandoning our baby. Who its new father will be, I do not know. As for me, I am writing this book and developing a new version of CNN. I have reason to hope it will create another revolution, but I realize what I have lost at CNN.

It is eighteen years since Ted fired me. I never cried about it. On June 2, I did.

Round 90: **The Savior**

In 1997 I am visiting Atlanta. Everywhere I turn I hear the name Kaplan, Rick Kaplan. While I am looking for a job as an assignment editor, Tom Johnson is looking for a CNN leader and he wants Kaplan. Johnson has been running CNN hands-on. He has two deputies, Ed Turner, who brings in the news, and Bob Furnad, who puts it on the air. Turner and Furnad do not get along. The division of power does not work and CNN's ratings hover around .4. Johnson is looking for a savior.

If CNN has a prototype, Kaplan is its antitype. A longtime, high-level network producer with a big-spender reputation, Kaplan had briefly produced Cronkite at CBS. At ABC he produced Jennings and *Nightline.* In 1980, just before CNN launched, he had told the *L.A. Times* that Ted Turner would have to learn to spend money if he wanted to build a first-class network. Kaplan is prepared to teach him, but only if his terms are met.

In '97 Kaplan is not going anyplace at ABC, so he listens to Johnson's offers. He wants a big salary, the title of "President," and a commitment that CNN will spend more money on its product. Johnson dickers, then agrees to everything but the title. Kaplan won't come without it. Johnson consults Ted Turner, who finds the solution. "Make Kaplan president, I'll name you chairman." Given the title, Kaplan signs on.

In the meantime, Johnson ups Lou Dobbs to president of CNN Financial, Jim Walton to president of CNN Sports, names Bob Furnad president of Headline News, and Eason Jordan president of CNN International and news gathering. Kaplan had been flummoxed. The other presidents will report to Tom Johnson, not to him. Ed Turner does not receive a presidency. He had recently been named in two cases of sexual misconduct and been banished to Washington as a sort of ambassador without portfolio. CNN settled the cases. Shortly thereafter, he was gone.

Ted Turner did not choose Kaplan. He left that to Tom Johnson. Ted is not even at the news conference where Kaplan's appointment is announced. Gerry Levin is there, and he promises Kaplan that Time Warner will give CNN the financial resources Rick needs to do the job.

Kaplan is clearly Johnson's guy, and when Johnson introduces him to Turner, Ted looks over at Rick and says, "I didn't know they grew Jews that tall." Rick is six foot-seven, and Ted is just giving him a friendly shot. Aside from that, Kaplan says, he didn't see very much of Turner. Occasionally Ted would make story suggestions or complain about too much crime news on television, including CNN. Kaplan regarded Ted's remarks as harmless musings.

Kaplan knows what his job is. He's got to lift the ratings. At the press conference he says, "There's a much larger news audience than CNN has tapped." Now he's got to find it. He starts from a base point of .39, 60 percent down from 1982.

In Atlanta he found a news network in turmoil. For a couple of years the CNN news consultants had been sending long memos to Turner and Johnson, and they were taken seriously. The consultants did not like foreign news. Kaplan says that Bob Furnad had ordered that no foreign news be carried on CNN-America unless it involved Americans. Ted Turner had set up thirty-five foreign news bureaus and, according to Kaplan, Furnad wouldn't let their pictures on his air unless they had an American angle.

Another Furnad dictate forbade CNN anchors from changing a word of copy that had been presented them. Telling Bernie Shaw and Judy Woodruff that they couldn't change a word of the script written by some twenty-four year old with a year and a half in the news business was as insulting as it was unproductive. When Kaplan arrived he asked Woodruff how she handled Furnad's dictate. She told him that she and Bernie just ignored it.

By Kaplan's network standards, CNN program production was totally disorganized. News programs had coordinating producers, line producers, but no executive producers. When Kaplan talked to line producers they said the coordinating producers were responsible for the show. Coordinating producers said that line producers made the programs. Rick changed that.

Kaplan installed the typical network system by bringing in executive producers. CNN produced ten different news hours daily. Each hour was clearly defined. Each executive producer would run one program hour per day. I had conceived of news as one long, continuous stream. Kaplan thought of it as a series of different programs. He made his programs brick by brick, and he tried to make each brick perfect. Again

Kaplan's philosophy contradicted what I saw as CNN's basic principle: News is a river, it is not bricks and mortar.

Kaplan amended another CNN tenet when he recommended that his executive producers be cautious before taking live feeds from local stations. Seventeen years before I had told the *New York Times* that CNN would risk going live with one-alarm fires because they might turn into conflagrations. I was preaching uncertainty, randomonium. Kaplan looked for certainty. He says MSNBC and Fox were picking up too many live stories that meant nothing to anybody, and he wanted to differentiate CNN by avoiding "car chases."

Randomonium dictates "Take this story and take your chances." If it's a simple "car chase" or a "no one injured," apologize and move on to the next story. I want to let the audience gamble with me. Let the viewer discover, at the same moment as CNN, whether the live coverage is banner headlines or two paragraphs on the back page. Trust your producers to use discretion, but don't demand certainty before taking a story live. No one wants a "car-chase" network, but no one should take all the randomonium out of it, either.

On Thursday, July 29, 1999, Mark Barton, a disillusioned day-trader, killed nine people in two stock-trading offices in Atlanta. The executive producer waited to see the story develop. CNN was ten minutes behind the other networks. Rick Kaplan was not in his office that day. He didn't see WSB, a CNN Atlanta affiliate, put the story on its air almost a half hour before his executive producer pushed the button. Fox News, MSNBC, and many local broadcast stations took the story much sooner. CNN can't afford to be beaten on a big story in its hometown.

Rick made his executive producers work harder. Before he arrived, CNN fed the same news over and over again. Rick changed that. His executive producers watched the shows before theirs. Rick told them that the B and C section stories in the previous shows (that is, secondary news and feature material) could not be repeated in the next hour. If a B or C story were a "must" story, it should be reedited, rescripted, and revoiced. "Tell" stories, that is, stories told on camera by anchors should be rewritten entirely. It was more work for the staff, but CNN looked the better for it. The problem was, nobody noticed. There was no promotion. Kaplan's ratings did not improve. When he arrived, CNN had a

.39 rating. By June of 2000, CNN's ratings had declined 10 percent, and Rick was spending a lot more money.

Steve Korn, CNN's chief operating officer, had been given the job of keeping CNN's costs in line. Kaplan wanted $24 million to build and upgrade CNN sets. Korn said no. Ted Turner was no longer on hand to mediate the dispute. Kaplan went over Korn's head to Time Warner and got the money. That's when Bevins said that "Kaplan was spending as much money on sets as Schonfeld had spent to build the network and run the whole network for all of 1980."

Kaplan hired many new people, expensive people. He brought in Jeff Greenfield and Willow Bay. He brought in proven producers for the CNN/*Time* magazine series. He brought in the new executive producers. Some of the new people came from ABC, some did not. No matter where they came from, the CNN old guard called them the "ABC Mafia." Johnson and Kaplan were reported to be feuding. Lou Dobbs was quarreling with both of them. CNN was splitting into factions and Ted was not around enough to keep the peace.

In the midst of all this, Lou Dobbs reared his handsome head. Kaplan extended the *Moneyline* franchise with its valuable commercial inventory to a full hour. The Dobbs show would be able to bring in twice as much money. Lou always thought of *Moneyline* as the Lou Dobbs show, not as a CNN show. He had run his half hour *Moneyline* pretty much on his own terms. Now he wanted to run the full hour the same way.

On May 20, 1999, President Clinton went to Littleton, Colorado, to speak to Columbine High students. Kaplan inserted sections of the speech live into *Moneyline.* Dobbs objected on air. He said into the mike "CNN President Rick Kaplan wants us to return to Littleton." Dobbs was declaring war. The issue was: Who will run *Moneyline*'s airtime, Kaplan or Dobbs? Contradictory press releases emerged. For a minute it seemed as if Dobbs had won. Then Dobbs got into a fight with somebody bigger than Rick Kaplan: Time Warner.

Lou, backed by Rockefeller money, had decided to launch a new website, Space.com. He would be its chairman and take an active role. Apart from the obvious journalistic conflict—a website chairman commenting on the financial results and prospects of other websites—Time Warner could not tolerate one of its full-time employees spending hours a day on another venture. Dobbs had to choose between Time and Space, and he chose Space. The difficulties with Kaplan gave the story a special sizzle, but there was no way Dobbs could keep both jobs. I learned at the Food Network that no matter what my contract said, the CEO of Food Network could not be the chairman of BBC News America. (I hope Dobbs has more luck with Space than I had with the BBC.)

After Dobbs's departure, CNN ad revenues dropped precipitously. *Moneyline* lost one-third of its ratings, although Kaplan says its demographics are much improved. CNN has been left with a large audience deficit. It owes its advertisers many thirty-second spots. Kaplan says that CNN, which was on the road to a profit of $400 million this year, will have to settle for something well over $300 million. Dobbs says his departure has cost CNN more than $50 million.

In May, Ted Turner got back into the picture. Relying on his long friendship with Dobbs, he tried to make peace and bring Dobbs and *Moneyline*'s advertising revenue back to CNN. By then, the AOL/Time Warner deal had been announced, and Turner's disinterest in things CNN had become apparent. Nevertheless, Ted talked to Dobbs personally. Dobbs wanted to come back. It made financial sense, but the story got in the tabloids, and all of a sudden, the deal was dead. The *Daily News* headlined, "Ted's Told to Stuff It. Levin sent word to his vice chairman that he should knock it off. And Turner did." The story ends with Time Warner officials denying "there was any rift between Levin and Turner." If there is no rift, it's because Turner knows that his power is gone. CNN, according to Dobbs, is losing tens of millions of dollars in prime-time revenue. Even with $50 million on his side, Ted cannot win in a showdown with Gerry Levin.

Over the years, Ted's monthly CNN meetings had continued, but now Gerry Levin was sitting in at most of them. According to Kaplan there were no more outbursts from Ted, no more mockery of Tom Johnson or any of the CNN people. The meetings were polite, informational, and valuable. Kaplan welcomed the opportunity to tell Levin and Turner about the condition of the news division. Kaplan and the other news people heard directly from the top about corporate goals and about what the corporation expected from them.

In January 2000, Time Warner had a new corporate goal. It wanted to complete its deal with AOL as soon as possible. On January 10, Levin announced that AOL was acquiring Time Warner with CNN included.

Wall Street embraced the deal. Time Warner's stock soared, but in June, the press was no longer focusing on the deal. It was CNN's twentieth anniversary, and papers all over the world were reporting on CNN's weak ratings. Wall Street read about it, and for the first time, CNN was perceived as a loser. AOL, CNN's prospective owner, does not enjoy losers. The value of one of its important future assets was declining day by day.

Bob Pittman, the chief operating officer of AOL, created MTV. He knows how to make good television. He is sure that he can do a better job with CNN than its current management. With Ted on the sidelines, the management of CNN was Terry McGuirk and Steve Heyer.

In the new AOL/Time Warner structure, McGuirk and Heyer will report to Pittman. Word in Atlanta is that McGuirk wants desperately to retain control of CNN. Word in Atlanta is that Steve Heyer wants desperately to be in position to succeed Steve Case, the CEO of AOL and the soon-to-be chairman of AOL/Time Warner. McGuirk and Heyer are caught in the interregnum. They do not yet report to Pittman, but they will, and they've got to show him that they're taking action. In August, when Steve Case and Pittman talked to Gerry Levin, they suggested to him that it was time to do something about CNN. By "something" they seem to mean a bigger role for Pittman, but Gerry said, "Let's give Terry a chance." Terry knows he has to do something fast, and the thing he does is fire Rick Kaplan.

Round 91: Is It Good for the News?

On August 29, 2000, Terry McGuirk fired Rick Kaplan. He died for the sins of a generation of CNN leaders, under whom CNN's ratings had declined by 70 percent. Of them all, Kaplan was the least culpable, but he was in the wrong place at the wrong time. The barbarians were at the gate. AOL wanted CNN fixed. The skids were greased for somebody, and McGuirk and Heyer wanted to make sure it wasn't them.

McGuirk knows little about news, so he did what bureaucrats usually do; he ordered a study, which he called an "evaluation." He was leading it, along with Steve Heyer. The evaluating group consisted of a dozen or so CNN news executives, some researchers, and some PR people. They were tasked with figuring out a strategy for CNN 2000. Their real job is finding a fall guy and Kaplan is the likely candidate.

Content magazine calls me. They have heard that Kaplan has been excluded from the meetings. Do I know anything about it? I check it out. It is not true. Kaplan is not only at the meetings, he is behaving badly. McGuirk and Heyer have pulled an old bureaucratic trick. They've developed a ratings chart. Instead of comparing CNN's current ratings with the ratings before Kaplan arrived (.4), they compare CNN's current ratings with its ratings in January '99, the Clinton impeachment. CNN had a .6 then. They tell Kaplan that CNN's ratings have declined by 50 percent over the last eighteen months. The figures are right, but the conclusion is false. They're loading the dice. Kaplan explodes.

He blames the poor ratings on them. He has made changes at CNN but nobody knows about them because Heyer and McGuirk haven't spent any money promoting them. That may be true, but Kaplan has committed a major strategic error. He has blamed the failure of the product on his bosses. Never do that. The bosses are not going to fire themselves. The bosses brush off everything Kaplan says as alibiing. He's cooked. September 15 is the day he will go. Only he doesn't know it, yet.

On August 29, I get a call from the *New York Times.* "What do you know about Kaplan? Is he out?" I'm asked. I ask the *Times* reporter if he knows about McGuirk's "evaluation" and Kaplan's reaction. He does not. I fill him in. I tell him the research story. I tell him it looks like they're setting Kaplan up. I ask him what he has heard. He says that rumors abound but he has not been able to nail them down. I ask him if he has called Kaplan. He says that he does not get along with Kaplan. He asks if so-and-so is likely to be on the evaluation team. Absolutely, I say. He says he'll call her.

Next morning I see the story on the front page of the *Times* business section. It has Tom Johnson's fingerprints all over it but the most startling thing about it is that the *Times* mentions Ted Turner only twice, both times in an historical context. Ted is no longer relevant to what happens at CNN. Instead of an outspoken Turner statement, we are getting leaks from "executives close to the situation," who are obviously Tom Johnson and friends. Over twenty years CNN has changed from an up-front company, where Ted Turner spoke too openly and put his name on every word he said, to a typical broadcast network where inside politicians pick their favorite reporters and plant stories or angles in their reports.

The *Times* piece blamed Kaplan for all of CNN's troubles. It said that Kaplan instituted the idea of appointment programming to CNN as a remedy for low ratings in dull news periods. CNN was trying appointment programming long before Kaplan arrived. In 1997 Gail Evans, Johnson's executive VP, proudly claimed credit for introducing appointment programming and pointed to *Burden of Proof,* the CNN legal talk show, as a successful example. Later Tom and Gail scheduled *Burden of Proof* in prime time to push appointment viewing. It failed before Kaplan got there.

The *Times* also blamed Kaplan for *CNN NewsStand,* but *CNN NewsStand* was just a new name for *Impact,* a Time/CNN venture that Johnson had launched. The *Times* also mentioned the Tailwind fiasco. It says Kaplan "was absolved of the final responsibility for the broadcast [Tailwind] by Mr. Johnson." Why not? Tailwind was prepared before Kaplan joined the company and it was Johnson who decided to air the segment after vetting it personally. Johnson is heaping his sins upon Kaplan before McGuirk runs him out of town.

Johnson himself and his protégé Eason Jordan have lost power in McGuirk's reorganization, but you'd never know it from the *Times* story. It says Johnson will keep his job. Eason Jordan will take over as chief news executive. In reality, Johnson has lost his authority over CNN's budget and Jordan has lost control of CNN International. Johnson was doing his best to save face. The *Times* went along with him.

The next day the press got it right. The *Washington Post* does a who's up/who's down analysis. It reports that Phil Kent, formerly the president of TBS International, is way up. He is named CNN's chief operating officer. He will have day-to-day responsibility for the network. Kent will report to Heyer on business and operating issues. He will report to Johnson only on editorial matters. The *Post* says, "Some industry watchers saw [it] as a slap to Johnson." You bet.

The *Post* says that Eason Jordan has also been hit. Jordan is going to report to Kent on operating issues. The *Post* gives Jordan a double slap. Two CNN guys move up. Jim Walton, one of our old video journalists, and a protégé of Bill MacPhail, becomes president of all fifteen U.S. news networks and websites. Chris Cramer, a BBC alumnus, will take charge of CNN's international networks and websites. Walton and Cramer will report directly to Kent.

I get a call from a friend, a former *Time* magazine editor, who has just heard about Kaplan. He reminds me that after Joe Lieberman was nominated, people were asking, "Is it good for the Jews?" Now he has read about CNN. He asks, "Is it good for the news?"

No! For twenty years, CNN answered only to Ted Turner. Now, for the first time in its history, CNN will report to corporate. As erratic as Ted was, as unconventional as his news judgment may have been, he had a passion for CNN. He thought of it as his supreme achievement, and he did not treat it as just another business. At the recent executive committee meeting, it was Ted Turner who stood up against the advertising departments' increasing influence over news programming. Advertising salesmen were demanding special segments. "Brought to you by," so that they could bring in more sponsors. Ted said, "No," even if it meant some revenue loss. He wanted editors and producers to choose what segments went on the air, not advertisers.

Ted never worried about job security—his "name was over the door." The guys who are running CNN now are careerists, looking to hold onto their jobs or to move up the corporate ladder.

For fifty years Time-Life was run by Henry Luce. He was Ted Turner and then some. Everybody reported to him. He insisted on absolute separation of Church and State. That was easy for him, because he was both pope and king. Church was the editorial part of the business, State brought in the money. Luce did not let business considerations interfere with good journalism. I observed Luce's rules when we started CNN. After I left, Ted mixed money and news somewhat, but by and large, the news guys were left alone by everybody but Ted himself.

CNN's new bosses are neither Ted Turner nor Henry Luce. They do not make television. McGuirk's chief strength was his loyalty to Ted. Heyer's strengths are managerial and organizational. Phil Kent, the new player, comes out of Hollywood, where he was a consultant, later an agent. His record at TBS is good. He took over Turner International and cleaned up an organizational and political mess, but he did not make television. He just made it easier for other people to make television.

Time itself has compromised its standards. The magazine division's editor-in-chief, Norman Pearlstine, now reports to Don Logan, the division's CEO, on budgetary and editorial matters. At *Time,* Pearlstine can appeal a Logan decision to Gerry Levin, and Gerry Levin is a man who has been around journalism for a long time. There's no Gerry Levin at CNN.

The new CNN setup is similar to *Time* magazine's. Tom Johnson has become Norman Pearlstine, a guy with a title but limited authority. Johnson's role is even smaller. Walton and Cramer, the bosses of his two largest divisions, report directly to Phil Kent, who has no news experience. If Kent's underlings want to appeal his decisions, to whom do they go? McGuirk? Heyer? They don't know any more about news than Kent does.

McGuirk, Heyer, and Kent will run the CNN budget, and they who run the budget run the company. Three guys with no news experience are using CNN for on-the-job training. So, "Is it good for the news?" I don't think so.

Kaplan's firing was handled in typical McGuirk fashion. McGuirk is the man who called John Barbera, the head of sales for TBS, at home Christmas week and told him not to come to work the next Monday. On August 29, McGuirk and Heyer arrived at Kaplan's office and showed him the new executive flowchart. Kaplan told the *Washington Post,* "I realized my name was not on the list, that there was no place for me. . . . It's kind of like your girlfriend saying she doesn't like you anymore. There's no sense in asking why or saying, 'Yes, you do.' That decision has been made." It's because McGuirk is running scared that the news broke when it did. The September 15 date had been moved up two weeks so that Terry could show Levin and Pittman that he was doing "something."

The next day's CNN press release did not mention Rick Kaplan. It announced an "executive realignment." The *Post* said Kaplan had been "airbrushed right out of existence." Kaplan took it like a gentleman. He has only nice things to say about CNN and about Tom Johnson. He seems to be genuinely sorry for Johnson, who he says is in "over his head." He takes Johnson off the hook when he tells the *Post,* "What I was doing was not succeeding by itself. No one would argue about what the problem is now—the ratings are not going up."

Ted Turner never fired anyone for low ratings. Burt Reinhardt and Ed Turner were not fired when CNN's ratings dipped from a 1 to a .7. Tom Johnson was not fired when CNN's ratings slipped from a .7 to a .4. Rick Kaplan got fired when his ratings dropped from a .4 to a .3. AOL was waiting in the wings.

A week later, at a memorial service for Judd Rose, a CNN reporter who Kaplan had brought over from ABC, Johnson and Kaplan hugged warmly. They showed no grudge. Before delivering Rose's eulogy, Kaplan said that if he'd known so many industry leaders were going to be there, he'd have brought along his resume. Kaplan has seventeen more months on his contract and several job offers. He doesn't seem worried.

I saved my best CNN story for a *Variety* reporter. When she called, I told her about the August talks between Steve Case, Bob Pittman, and Gerry Levin. I told her that Gerry had said, "Let's give Terry a chance." Kaplan's firing is Terry's chance. McGuirk is betting on Heyer; Heyer is betting on Kent. They hope they can hold Pittman off until the ratings go up. If that day ever comes.

Round 92: **Can This Network Be Saved?**

For five years CNN was at war—first to launch itself, then to hold off Satellite News Channel. For the next twelve years, CNN was a monopoly. It acted like one. It got fat, sloppy, its ratings slipped, but nobody noticed. CNN basked in Baghdad's glow. Plaudits came easy, success was assumed, and mistakes forgiven. All the time, rot was creeping through the ranks. When ratings sank, the bosses excused themselves, saying "It's a slow news period." When CNN developed no stars, the bosses excused themselves, saying, "We don't want stars. News is our star."

All that ended when MSNBC and Fox challenged CNN. The press started looking at the numbers. Johnson got scared and brought in Kaplan. Then AOL bought Time Warner. McGuirk got scared and fired Kaplan because the ratings were so low. Even after his dismissal, Kaplan is still scratching his head, trying to figure out what went wrong.

Rick thinks that CNN has a crucial decision to make. It can try to change its editorial approach, its programming, and raise its ratings, or it can accept its .3 ratings, cut costs, and in the short term make a lot of money. Ted Turner would have gone for broke, but he's not making the decisions. McGuirk's attitude is yet to be determined, but I'm sure if it's left up to Pittman, he'll make a run at fixing CNN.

It's going to be an uphill battle. CNN currently enjoys a number of vanishing advantages. It's in 79 million homes, MSNBC is in 58 million, and Fox is in 54 million. Within a couple of years, MSNBC and Fox will match CNN's cable universe. When those networks are in 80 million homes, it is inevitable that CNN ratings will decline further.

Then there are the twenty-four-hour local news networks. Time Warner's NY1 has five times the audience in New York City that CNN does. The Headline News audience is so small, Nielsen can't find it. In Washington, D.C., News 12 beats CNN .6 to .5 month in, month out, and News 12 on Long Island has been beating CNN for fifteen years. Thirty million American homes now get a local news channel. In three years it will be 50 million. More competition, still lower CNN ratings.

CNN is also demographically challenged. Its median age hovers around sixty. In the past nine months, MSNBC has reduced its median age from fifty-four to forty-seven, a miracle of modern television. Most local news channel viewers are under forty-five. Younger is better. Advertisers don't pay for anybody over fifty-four. CNN spots are over-priced in relation to MSNBC, CNBC, and local news channels. They are bound to drop. For CNN, there is no comfort in the numbers.

I think CNN can only find comfort in attitude. That is not as hard as it sounds. Fox is conservative: a few hours of hard news, occasional news bulletins, a welter of conservative news talk commentary. MSNBC is young: five hours of news shows, occasional bulletins, a welter of highly produced news magazine segments, mostly reruns from NBC.

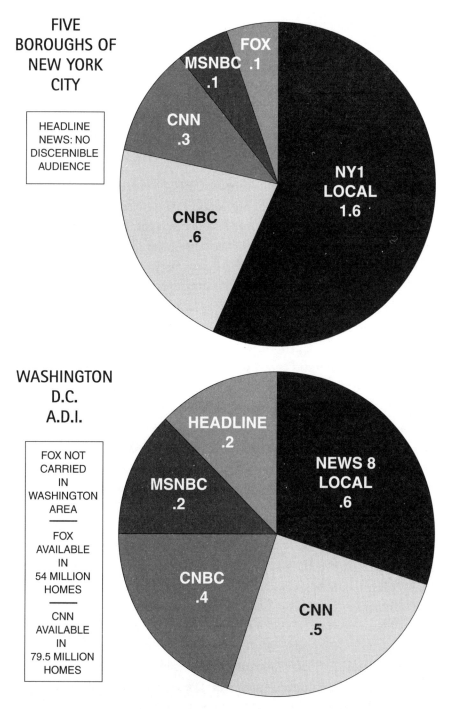

FIVE BOROUGHS OF NEW YORK CITY

HEADLINE NEWS: NO DISCERNIBLE AUDIENCE

FOX .1
MSNBC .1
CNN .3
CNBC .6
NY1 LOCAL 1.6

WASHINGTON D.C. A.D.I.

FOX NOT CARRIED IN WASHINGTON AREA

FOX AVAILABLE IN 54 MILLION HOMES

CNN AVAILABLE IN 79.5 MILLION HOMES

HEADLINE .2
MSNBC .2
NEWS 8 LOCAL .6
CNBC .4
CNN .5

Both MSNBC and Fox have program strategies that work. Dedicated conservatives watch Fox; most other viewers do not. Less than twenty percent of potential viewers watch Fox once a week. Those who watch, watch for a long time. MSNBC's younger viewers would rather watch well-produced, ten-minute stories than ordinary news programs. Meanwhile, CNN sticks to its bland, middle-of-the-road schedule. About thirty percent of potential viewers watch CNN every week, but they don't watch it for long.

While CNN was analyzing its shortcomings, MTV, the parent company of Nickelodeon, was trying to figure out how Nickelodeon had doubled its ratings while CNN's ratings dipped seventy percent. Betsy Frank, MTV's executive vice president and one of the best of the cable researchers, concluded that Nickelodeon's kids programs reflect creativity and imagination, but that CNN is stuck with poor ratings because "news is news."

Maybe it's Gerry Leybourne, Nickelodeon's longtime president, who made the difference. She established a soft, whimsical, but purposeful programming style. Leybourne had been a teacher of children, who knew how to amuse and educate at the same time. Gerry's attitude continues to differentiate Nickelodeon from its competitors: Disney, Fox Kids, and the Cartoon Network. Nickelodeon's ratings have stayed up.

Nickelodeon is not right about one thing. News is not just news. Roger Ailes's Fox News has anchors who sneer on camera. Fox's copy is sharper and more colorful than its competitors'. That's how they get ratings. MSNBC is not just news. It's mostly mini-documentaries. That's how it gets demographics.

Between 1980 and 1982, CNN got demographics and ratings. CNN chased chaos, tracked it, attempted to define it, but reveled in the knowledge that it could never impose order upon it. Newspapers with their columns, inches, and rigid deadlines cannot portray chaos. Neither can networks with their thirty-minute run downs and rigid schedules. They are both limited by time or space. Their stories have to end. CNN just rolled on and on and on.

Heraclitus said, "You cannot step twice into the same river." Neither can you step twice into the same news. The world changes every minute, CNN watches the world, you'd better watch CNN. If that sounds like a news promo, it is. That was CNN's promise in 1980, and we delivered on it. CNN would find a story, dive into it, tell a piece of the story, drop it, pick it up when something new happened, then drop it again, dipping in and out as the story demanded. That's why our audience stayed with us.

Bulletins would break in on live news, whole programs would be ripped apart on the air when important things happened elsewhere—that was "randomonium" (as Frank Zappa called it) and that was why we got ratings.

Obviously, I am no fan of neat and tidy news. My greatest challenge at CNN was to get producers and anchors and news desks to learn the "CNN way." Many of them still hoped to produce perfect, little TV gems; I wanted raw edges center screen. I needed programs to break apart as hot news blasted its way through "run-downs." So I strode down to the newsroom or sat in my third floor office and ordered live feeds and told the producers to put them on the air, sometimes with ten minutes' notice and sometimes with no notice at all, and I made the world stop and watch CNN, at least for a minute or two.

In 2000 CNN has a "neat and tidy" look, but backstage it is chaos. Kaplan has been fired, no one is sure who's in charge: there's McGuirk, there's Heyer, there's Johnson, there's Kent, and in the wings there's Pittman. In Hollywood vernacular, "nobody knows whose ass to kiss." I wanted chaos on the air, order in the management. CNN 2000 has it backwards.

Round 93: **Courage**

When we started CNN, it was me and Ted against the world. We were going to war, and he was a warrior. He had courage and tenacity, and for a battle he was the best ally anyone could have.

Unlike the Hilliards, who backed out on our deal with the BBC, Ted put his money where his mouth was. Unlike the *New York Times*, Ted did not govern by committee. Unlike Time Warner, Ted permitted no political coups. Unlike *Time* magazine, Ted was not mandarin, dictating journalistic form. Unlike the Ted of 1997, he did not rely on research; he went with his gut, which led him to me and allowed him to leave me on my own for almost three years. If I were going to go to war against the world once more, I'd still pick Ted for a partner. His courage outweighs his faults.

In May of 1980, in Las Vegas, I said, "My life was on the line for CNN." It was true. I had lived for that moment and the three years that followed. My first twenty-five years in the news business had been prelude. The years later, so far at least, have been postscript. Ted gave me my shot, I did my best, and if I were lying, I'd say, "No regrets."

Ted used to call CNN "my baby." My complaint is that he didn't bring "our baby" up all that well. With every word I write, I sniff for the aroma of sour grapes. I have reported CNN's ratings failures. I have recounted CNN's more notorious embarrassments. I don't think that's sour grapes. I'm just saying Ted Turner should've taken better care of our baby.

Ted was a creator of CNN. He paid for it, and for three years he alone was our entire promotion plan. Ted cleared the cable systems for CNN because he was cable before cable was cool. Ted sold the advertising for CNN because he had created the art of selling cable advertising. In 1979, Ted knew where cable was going. He was a cable professional.

I am the creator of CNN as it appears on the air. I designed CNN's content, format, and schedule. I recognized the promise of live news. I hired the executives who ran CNN for a generation. I hired the anchors and reporters. I originated the "CNN look." I selected the technical equipment. I designed and purchased our video and transportation network. I developed and purchased our computerized newsroom. I selected and leased the sites of the CNN bureaus. I established the "video journalist" system. I leased the CNN live truck, and I devised a so far union-proof employment system. In 1979, I knew where news was going. I was a news professional.

It sounds like the perfect partnership: a cable professional, a news professional, the Cable News Network. We both had our faults. My attitude was not entirely professional. I had an ego. I loved CNN, and I couldn't let Ted mess with it.

Ted's problem was his ego. A lot of men would've been happy with our partnership. They would've taken all the credit, and I would've pretty much run the place. Ted's ego was too honest. If he was going to take all the credit, he wanted to run the place.

Both of us wanted CNN to be worthy of respect. Neither of us wanted CNN to be "Chicken Noodle News." When Ted wanted to do on-air interviews with Fidel Castro, when Ted wanted to do on-air editorials, when Ted Turner wanted to put his cronies or his girlfriends on the air, or when Ted said he would make CNN the mouthpiece of the cable industry, I had to say no. Ted must've known that all of the above would've scarred CNN's reputation. Nevertheless, his ego demanded it, or maybe he was just testing to see how long I had the guts to say no.

Ted was George Steinbrenner redux. Bill Bevins saw the Turner/Steinbrenner analogy. When Ted asked me to come back, and I said no, Bevins said, "You could've been Billy Martin." Martin managed the Yankees for Steinbrenner five different times. He spent the last ten years of his life fighting with and being bullied by George. He died in 1989, after a day of hard drinking, when his truck went off an icy country road into the bottom of a ravine. I did not want to be Billy Martin.

Ted kept Tom Johnson around a long time, even with a losing record. The difference is, in baseball, newspapers report the standings everyday. It took newspapers eighteen years to report accurately on CNN's ratings.

In 1990, Ted produced a CNN tenth anniversary book: paid the author, made a distribution deal with Little, Brown, and made sure he had the last word. That was the book in which he said he fired me because I was making all the decisions. *I'm proud of making all of the decisions.* That's was what I was paid to do, and I did it right.

In 1979, when I was considering potential news partners, I wondered whom I could trust with an idea as powerful as CNN. It wasn't Ted, but he was so determined, so certain, I chose him anyway. Looking back, it worked out okay. CNN may not have done much good, but it has certainly done no evil. CNN's fate is now in the hands of others. I wish them well. I know one thing for sure. With Ted gone, CNN won't be anybody's baby anymore.

Coda

Chaos is back in town. It's November 24, 2000. There's still a chance Ted Turner may be running CNN, and nobody knows who's going to be president.

The AOL/Time Warner deal has been delayed until 2001. The Federal Trade Commission demands more and more concessions. Time Warner and AOL are reported to be quarreling over strategy. Time's stock has plummeted. No one knows how it will end, but if the deal falls through, Turner will still be in charge of all Time Warner cable networks.

Meanwhile, as long as no one knows who's going to be president, more than a million people watch CNN everyday. This is the first time in a presidential election year that CNN has faced competition. It remains the news leader nevertheless. Over the last two weeks, CNN has averaged 1.2 rating points, Fox .9, and MSNBC .8. November 2000 is another defining moment. The election story will determine audience preferences for years to come, and each network is approaching it from a different angle.

Fox has stuck to its conservative credo, questioning Gore's moves and motives while cheering Bush on. On election night it was Fox who named Bush the Florida winner and thereby gave him the election. All the other networks followed. In one of its boldest moves, Fox, the most opinionated of networks, has adopted as its slogan "We report. You decide." On election night, though, their slogan seemed to be "We decide. You [the other networks] repeat." Fox has given its viewers the news they want to hear the way they want to hear it. Their audience has doubled.

MSNBC daytime has adopted a style that comes closer to my hopes for CNN than CNN itself has done. Their anchors wander through a vibrant newsroom, seemingly picking up fresh news at each stop they make. Occasionally, they are ahead of their producers. They call in field reporters via satellite, adapt their programs to the new information, and call on different sources to validate or deny what they have just heard. They are not afraid of error, but, at their best, they insist on immediate correction. With news arriving from many conflicting sources, with reporters in the field not hearing each other, with scripts written minutes ago, outdated before they get into the presenter's hands, the anchor acts as managing editor. There are no hour-to-hour breaks; the news gathering just rolls on until Oliver North, Andrea Mitchell, and Chris Matthews arrive and stop doing news and start talking about it.

North and his colleague, Paul Begalla, do a poor man's version of *Crossfire* as they tap-dance around the election results. Mitchell and Matthews follow a Fox line. They play *Hardball* with Democrats and softball with Republicans. Neither of them seems to have the background knowledge to challenge their guests on even the most outrageous statements. Matthews's style is to make outrageous statements of his own and trample a guest if the guest dares contradict him. MSNBC has another weakness. It continues to play its ordinary news magazine programs whenever the news cools.

CNN remains CNN. It waffles its way down the middle of the road, letting each side say what it wants to say, invariably polite as it passes on from one designated spokesperson to the next. As I write this it is 3:05 p.m. Pete Williams, MSNBC's man at the Supreme Court, reports that the Court has just agreed to hear presidential candidate George W. Bush's appeal on the recount of votes in Florida. Minutes later, Fox flashes a bulletin to the same effect across the bottom of the screen. A few minutes later, CNN quotes AP on the story, then turns to in-studio "legal experts." It is ten minutes before CNN has a reporter of its own on-line. CNN seems soft and slow.

CNN has missed the chance to own the election story. It has failed to find an angle that will force viewers to come to it for information. I think back to Gorbachev's trial balloon about leaving the Communist Party and to Ed Meese's surprise confession of the Reagan Administration's wrongdoings in Nicaragua. Both times, CNN traveled the mainstream, playing the stories just like everybody else.

Suppose CNN's attitude was, "Come on guys, you know what this is all about. The Democrats are asking for three weeks to figure out if those Bush brothers stole the election." In Newark when I was growing up, we knew that no election was final until Longie Zwillman sent in the votes from the third ward. Longie could do wonders with those numbers. In this election, the results won't be final until Governor Jeb Bush sends in the votes from Florida. You've got to take a hard look at what the guy in Florida is doing; after all, he's the candidate's brother.

First, there are the butterfly ballots. They're suspicious, but, hell, the Democrats approved them. If you're going to steal the election that's the fair and square way to do it. Nobody has a right to complain, that's just bellyaching. Then the *New Yorker* discovers that the Bush brothers' cousin, John Ellis, has been sitting at the election desk at Fox news, feeding information to Jeb and George. That breaks all the rules. CNN can point the finger at the election results and its Fox competition at the same time. It's a double whammy. What's more, it could have launched an old-fashioned news war. CNN vs. Fox. The kind of war that builds ratings for both networks.

When Ellis called the Bushes, he put Fox in the middle of an ugly mess. The raw data that Ellis got is so confidential that no more than four people at CNN had access to it. The raw data started coming in at 1 p.m. By then, Ellis knew which districts were voting heavily for which candidate. Nobody at Fox can tell me when Ellis first started making calls, because Fox didn't know he was making the calls at all. But by midafternoon, voters in Palm Beach County were complaining of long delays and misleading assistance in casting their ballots. Black voters in districts that were going Democratic said they were harassed by state police demanding voter I.D. and checking for felony convictions. Sounds like Longie to me.

If I were at CNN, I would have sued Ellis and Fox. They made unauthorized use of confidential Voter News Service information worth millions and millions of dollars. CNN had put up 15 percent of that money. CNN is entitled to damages. We could depose Ellis, we could depose Roger Ailes, Fox's president, we could depose Jeb Bush, and, most fun of all, under the Supreme Court rules, we could depose George W. Bush. We could ask all sorts of questions. Had Jeb talked to the state police after he got Ellis's news? Did he talk to Republican campaign headquarters? What actions did they take? What did W. say, and to whom? Hell, we could have had a field day.

Any time a presidential election is won by five hundred votes and the candidate's brother controls the vote count, the media has a duty to be skeptical. If it had been a Latin American country, and the results had been determined by El Presidente's brother, reporters and anchors would have been snickering up their sleeves. This election deserved the same treatment, but for the most part the media have quoted Bush spokespersons as if they were preaching gospel.

When the Bush campaign asked Gore to do the "honorable thing," stop the protests, and let George W. Bush become president, that's what Richard Nixon did. CNN should have been out there correcting the Nixon recollections. In the Kennedy-Nixon election, the Republican Party challenged the results in eleven states, demanded recounts in two of them, and didn't give up until the day the electoral votes were cast. Everybody in the news business has let the Bush team get away with the Nixon story. If CNN had contradicted it in bold headlines, it would have shown that it had the smarts to fight the spin. The other networks might be suckers, but CNN gets it right.

CNN's got to be fair to both sides. On November 15, Al Gore goes on camera. He says six Florida counties added hand counts to their votes. The next day the *Orlando Sentinel* checks it out. Only two counties turned in hand counts, and one of them doesn't even have voting machines. The Great Exaggerator strikes again. But the one county that handed in the votes got its votes accepted and added one hundred votes to Bush's total. It set the precedent Gore needed. Why did he have to say six? More important, why didn't CNN call him on it?

For the most part, the Gore people seem to have taken the high road. They have trusted to lawyers instead of James Carville, and it has cost them dearly. The spinners go unchallenged, the lawyers sound like weasels. CNN should have been more resistant to the Bush party line.

I am not suggesting that CNN should have joined the Gore cause, but in an election decided by five hundred votes out of six million, CNN should have stood for accuracy over speed and voter inclusion over voter exclusion. Specific attitude and superior knowledge give the audience specific reasons to watch CNN. If Gore wins the election, so be it. If George Bush doesn't know how to steal an election, he doesn't deserve to be president.

On November 10, Bernie Shaw, one of the heroes of this book, resigned as anchor at CNN. CNN has no one waiting in the wings to succeed him. CNN has its largest audience in years—if ever there was a moment for Bernie Shaw to give the new anchor his blessing and the chance to strut his or her stuff before an audience of more than a million people it's now. But CNN has no one ready. It's the same old faces.

MSNBC, on the other hand, has found a new star, Lester Holt, who handles breaking news as if he were born to it. He is the best on-the-fly newsman I've seen since Bill Zimmerman. All three of the news networks have more than doubled their ratings since Election Day. The question is, where will the new audience go when this is finally over and done with?

I have made a decision. This book will have one more chapter: it will be published on MeandTed.com simultaneously with the release of this book. By then, we should know who won the election and where the news audience has found a home. There are other things we should know by then, such as Does AOL own Time Warner? If so, Ted Turner may be out for good, and Bob Pittman will be making the calls at CNN.

Jim Rutenberg calls me from the *New York Times*. (These calls are not uncommon. When newsmen are working on the same story and not competing directly, they often exchange notes. That's part of the reason so many stories sound alike.) Jim has heard that AOL is in Atlanta to slash costs and cut bodies. Do I know anything about it? I do not. It does not happen. Rutenberg has excellent sources in the current CNN administration. What I learn from this is that the CNN guys are still scared stiff of AOL. They are also setting Rutenberg up to believe that budget downsizing, if it occurs, will be AOL's fault. I'm not so sure; Steve Heyer is pretty good at cutting budgets, too.

There are other reports from CNN. Now it's program changes. Following in the footsteps of Fox and MSNBC, CNN is looking at more commentary and fewer newscasts, especially, in primetime. The *Atlanta Constitution* reports that Sid Bedingfield, the executive vice president of CNN/US, says he wants "provocative opinions delivered with energy and passion." But he adds, "It doesn't mean were going to an all talk format."

CNN may be killing its 8 p.m. news program in favor of a Wolf Blitzer interview show and a Greta Van Sustern talk show. It is the end of counterprogramming. CNN is playing copycat. They're going to do just what the opposition is doing, only they hope to do it better. If Bedingfield thinks Blitzer can beat Chris Matthews's *Hardball*, good luck to him. CNN has finally decided that there isn't enough news to fill a twenty-four-hour day.

Time Warner stock has fallen 40 percent from its high, attained the day the AOL deal was announced. Wall Street seems unsure the deal will go through. I'm betting it will. I've said up front that I'm a gambler. I still own stock in Time Warner, stock that I got from Ted for launching CNN. I'm holding onto it. I need a lot of money to fund my new venture in the news business, more than the Time Warner stock is worth now. I'm betting that it goes way up.

Ted owns billions of dollars' worth of Time Warner stock. I don't know what he plans to do with it. Maybe he's still counting on it to help him buy NBC if NBC doesn't sell itself to somebody else first. Maybe he'll use it to keep his influence on the Time Warner board. He's still got some interest in CNN; he attends the CNN monthly meetings, but his friends say he seems awfully tired, and maybe he'll just rake in his marbles and go home. I'd hate to see Ted left with a pile of money and nothing else. In 1999, Ted said he didn't care about money. It was only the way the world keeps score. The score doesn't count until the game is over, and Ted shouldn't give up the game.

Index